No Word of Farewell:
Selected Poems 1970–2000

No Word of Farewell:
Selected Poems 1970–2000

By R. S. Gwynn

STORY LINE PRESS

ASHLAND, OREGON

©2001 by R. S. Gwynn
First Printing

This publication was made possible thanks in part to the generous support of the Nicholas Roerich Museum, the Oregon Arts Commission, and our individual contributors.

Published by Story Line Press. Three Oaks Farm, PO 1240, Ashland, OR 97520-0055

Cover painting by Frederick Carl Frieseke, "The Garden Parasol," 1910, Oil on canvas reproduced by permission of the North Carolina Museum of Art, Raleigh, purchased with funds from the State of North Carolina.

Book design by Lysa McDowell

Library of Congress Cataloging-in-Publication Data

Gwynn, R. S.
    No word of farewell: Selected Poems 1970–2000 : poems / by R. S. Gwynn.
        p.   cm.
    Selected poems from the author's five previous collections.
    ISBN 1-885266-91-X (alk. paper)
    I. Title.

PS3557.W93 A6 2000
811'.54—dc21   00-032983

For My Teachers

Are you going away with no word of farewell ?
Will there be not a trace left behind ?

—*Tom Paxton*

TABLE OF CONTENTS

If My Song: New Poems

More Light:
Translations, Parodies, Verse

From *The Narcissiad*

The Drive-In

INTRODUCTION

by Dana Gioia

I first encountered R. S. Gwynn's poetry through sheer serendipity. In 1986 I spent an afternoon reading through the many new poetry books at Manhattan's Endicott's, a gracious and generously stocked independent bookstore now, alas, out of business. I've spent many such afternoons before and since, but I remember this day vividly because I made a genuine discovery, a little light-blue volume called *The Drive-In* by R. S. Gwynn, a poet whose name I did not recognize. I picked a poem at random and found it cleverly amusing but took no special notice until I read the opening selection, "Among Philistines," a singularly curious retelling of the Samson story set in suburban America.

"Among Philistines" struck me then—and continues to impress me now—as a remarkably risky poem, one that promiscuously mixes elements that should not work together. It is simultaneously lyric and satiric—a heartfelt evocation of a fallen and doomed man wrapped inside a scathing indictment of American consumerism. The language also shifts boldly from the sumptuously elevated to the aggressively crude. The poem bristles with the vulgate of television, tabloids, and advertising—the actual awful language that surrounds us nowadays—out of which Gwynn squeezes every bit of dark humor while somehow building a compelling drama of human suffering and redemption. Reading the final grotesque but visionary section of the poem, I was not reminded of anything in contemporary verse but instead of the stories of Flannery O'Connor and Katherine Anne Porter. By the time I had finished the volume I knew I had come upon one of the truly talented and original poets of my generation.

I should probably also note two other obvious qualities of Gwynn's poetry. First, he is ingeniously funny. Second, he is an effortless master of verse forms. No American poet of his generation has written better sonnets, and very few can equal him in the ballade, couplet, rondeau, or pantoum—not to mention the half dozen new forms he has invented. But, to be honest, it was neither Gwynn's considerable formal skill nor his wicked humor that first attracted me, though those qualities surely added to my pleasure. Instead, it was his depth of feeling and intense lyricality.

Today comic verse is a neglected art, but there are still a good number of master practitioners around, and we currently live in a period of greatly renewed interest in meter and rhyme. It remains a rare distinction, however, to use these forms and modes for powerful expressive ends. Gwynn manages this difficult but essential feat repeatedly. What captures the reader is not the form or wit but the poetry. I reread "Body Bags," for example, half a dozen times for its heartbreaking story of three young lives destroyed in different ways by the Vietnam War before I noticed the obvious fact that it was a short sonnet sequence. Likewise it was not the humor of Gwynn's poetry that fascinated me but the brooding darkness of his vision that was only made bearable by the humor. "Black Helicopters" is a very funny poem—and one of the few successful pantoums in English—but it is also a truly terrifying poem about American politics. The dark side of Gwynn's imagination has grown more evident in his recent work. (His own painful bout with cancer casts its shadow across the new poems in this book.) And yet what strange joy emerges while gazing into the void. I can't imagine anyone else today writing such an elegantly measured yet emotional poem about art and personal extinction as "Cléante to Elmire"—an extraordinary deathbed monologue spoken by a dying amateur actor to a beloved ghost, which pays equal homage to Molière and mortality.

It would be both illuminating and relevant to discuss Gwynn's work in terms of the recent revival of rhyme and meter. He is surely one of the three or four finest poets associated with New Formalism. But it seems more interesting to suggest how he is unique among his contemporaries. If one looks at his best poems—and a short list might include "Body Bags," "Among Philistines," "Cléante to Elmire," "1-800," "Black Helicopters," "1916," and "Untitled"—one sees a distinctive combination of traditional form and post-modern observation. Gwynn juxtaposes styles and subjects not customarily seen together—mythic and modish images phrased in language alternatively sublime and debased—but told with such force of imagination and assured musicality that the resulting poems seem not idiosyncratic but inevitable.

It would also be easy to compare Gwynn to certain older poets like Richard Wilbur, Donald Justice, or Anthony Hecht, and there are similarities—the focused intelligence, sharp wit, and formal mastery. But what differentiates Gwynn from these predecessors ultimately seems more important than what links him. The poet whom Gwynn most resembles—not simply in the particulars of style but in sensibility and strategy—is Thomas Hardy, and it is testament to Gwynn's excellence that such a comparison can be made without his being routed in the process. Both poets are primarily satirists, but their work usually takes a lyric form. Indeed, both poets often cast poems explicitly in the form of songs. They are also both drawn to interesting stories and situations. Gladys, the pistol-packing old lady in "At Rose's Range," surely must be a descendent of some couple who immigrated to Beaumont, Texas, from Hardy's Wessex County. Both poets have a naturally democratic outlook, and they are fascinated by ordinary lives, especially when viewed at extraordinary moments. Both are deeply skeptical, even cynical observers of the human scene, who cannot mock their subjects without soon feeling a common human sympathy. Their irony cannot disabuse their instinctive compassion, and their dark humor is their only means of holding off despair. As W. H. Auden once remarked, "Comedy is the noblest form of Stoicism."

If Gwynn's reputation has been slow in growing outside the South—beyond a few widely anthologized poems— one reason is surely his odd publication history. He has published at least seven poetry collections, but only one of them, *The Drive-In*, was a full-length trade book. The other six were chapbooks—some inexpensive, fugitive publications like *Bearing & Distance* (1977) issued by Cedar Rock Press in New Braunfels, Texas, others gorgeous letterpress limited editions like *The Area Code of God* (1993) printed by Aralia Press in West Chester, Pennsylvania. Nor has Gwynn's reception by the critical mainstream been helped by his hilariously irreverent mock-epic *The Narcissiad* (1981), which recounts the adventures and apotheosis of Narcissus, an ambitious but singularly untalented poet. In Gwynn's satiric tale, American poets simultaneously realize that to gain artistic preeminence in the overcrowded field of contemporary verse, they must kill all current competitors. *The Narcissiad* depicts a series of outrageous battles fought by recognizable caricatures of fashionable American poets—out of which Narcissus ineptly emerges as the triumphant survivor. Gwynn's mock-epic cannot have pleased the targets of his satire, but it has enjoyed an underground life. Enough readers have passed it on to require the book to be reprinted.

No Word of Farewell finally gathers Gwynn's poems together for the first time—at least those the author wishes to preserve. The volume surveys a career of thirty years. His work will be new to most readers, but even his long-time admirers will discover many new poems. Few recent books of poetry provide so much sheer pleasure—though I do recall one glorious volume I came across years ago in a Manhattan bookstore. Being bigger, this new one is even better.

If My Song: New Poems

Let me sing a sad refrain
Of broken hearts that loved in vain,
And if my song can start you crying
I'm happy.

—*Irving Berlin*

1969

For Ty

A dim-lit, smoky bar. Your twenty-first
Birthday has brought a golden Benrus watch,
A marriage, a degree, a double Scotch—
None of which will quite satisfy your thirst.

It's after one. The pianist is playing
Procul Harum's "A Whiter Shade of Pale."
You scuff your side-zip boots along the rail
And neither think of leaving nor of staying.

Why bring it back again? Surely you know
Your future guns his engine at the door,
And soon enough he'll steer an exit for
A suburb where you have no wish to go.

Why bring it back? Because you want me to.
Because you want to light your cigarette,
Clutching a scene which you cannot forget
Where everything you gaze upon is new.

My Agent Says

My agent says Los Angeles will call.
My broker says to sell without delay.
My doctor says the spot is very small.
My lover says get tested right away.

My congressman says yes, he truly cares.
My bottle says he'll see me after five.
My mirror says to pluck a few stray hairs.
My mother says that she is still alive.

My leader says we may have seen the worst.
My mistress says her eyes are like the sun.
My bride says that it's true I'm not the first.
My landlord says he'd think about a gun.

My boss says that I'd better take a chair.
My enemy says turn the other cheek.
My rival says that all in love is fair.
My brother says he's coming for a week.

My teacher says my work is very neat.
My ex-wife says I haven't heard the last.
My usher says the big guy's in my seat.
My captain says to bind him to the mast.

My master says I must be taught my place.
My conscience says my schemes will never fly.
My father says he doesn't like my face.
My lawyer says I shouldn't testify.

My buddy says this time I've got it bad.
My first love says she can't recall my name.
My baby says my singing makes her sad.
My dog says that she loves me all the same.

My pastor says to walk the narrow path.
My coach says someone else will get the ball.
My God says I shall bend beneath His wrath.
My agent says Los Angeles may call.

1-800

Credit cards out, pencil and notepad handy,
  The insomniac sinks deeply in his chair,
Begging swift needles in his glass of brandy
  To knit once more the raveled sleeve of care,
As with control, remotely, in one hand he
  Summons bright visions from the midnight air:

The six-way drill! The eight-way folding ladder!
  Knives that pierce coins or thin-slice loaves of bread!
Devices that will make one's tummy flatter,
  Rout car thieves, or purge household taps of lead!
All made of stuff no earthly force can shatter!
  Their lauds ascend Olympus in his head.

And yet how little will his days be brightened
  By *Opera Favorites* or, if he feels lewd,
Even THE SWIMSUIT ISSUE. Briefly heightened,
  His hopes, ephemeral as stir-fried food,
Vanish like screws his six-way drill has tightened,
  Leaving him just like them—completely screwed.

"Buy houses and apartments with no money!
  Discover how today! Write this address!"
Snapping alert and clicking with his gun, he
  Draws a bead on the forehead of Success,
Whose orchid leis are fresh, whose teeth are sunny,
  Whose tapes will wing their way via UPS.

But anger, with succeeding snifters, passes
  And soon all softens in an amber hue;
As through a pair of UV/blue-block glasses,
  Doubt fades before the testimony—true
Accounts of hair sprouting like jungle grasses!
  Of lifeless penises lifting anew!

Of bags and wrinkles blotted out! Of dumber
  Than average kids who, spared the wrath and rod,
Have learned to multiply! He fights off slumber
  The moment that his head begins to nod
And resolutely punches the first number
  Of what may be the area code of God.

Black Helicopters

Gather your families. Lift your eyes.
They'll take your daughters and your sons.
Black helicopters rule the skies.
The New World Order wants your guns.

They'll take your daughters and your sons
For schooling that is "outcome based."
The New World Order wants your guns
And getting them is just a taste—

Schooling that is "outcome based"—
Condoms for kids instead of prayer—
And getting them is just a taste:
Look at the uniforms they wear!

Condoms for kids instead of prayer.
Soon there'll be nowhere left to go.
Look at the uniforms they wear!
What's further out than Idaho?

Soon there'll be nowhere left to go.
Dust clouds are rising on the road.
(What's further out than Idaho?)
Look to the heavens. Lock and load.

Dust clouds are rising on the road.
Gather your families, lift your eyes.
Look to the heavens. Lock and load.
Black helicopters rule the skies.

At Rose's Range

Old Gladys, in lime polyester slacks,
Might rate a laugh until she puts her weight
Squarely behind the snubnosed .38,
Draws down and pulls. The bulldog muzzle cracks
And barks six times, and six black daisies flower
Dead in the heart of Saddam's silhouette.
She turns aside, empties, reloads, gets set
And fires again. This goes on for an hour.

Later, we pass the time at the front door
Where she sits smoking, waiting for the friend
Who drives her places after dark: *You know,
Earl's free next month. He says he wants some more
Of what she's got, and she's my daughter so
I reckon there's just one way this can end.*

Just Folks

As penance for your class's wrongs
You sojourned in the Congo,
Conducting tribal sing-alongs
To the beat of a bongo.

And when the urgent messages
Arrived from Alabama,
You tuned up, leading choruses
Of "If I Had a Hammer."

Then later, at the Pentagon's
Chain fences, never bolder,
You deftly crooned "Give Peace a Chance"
In the ear of a soldier.

But somewhere down the picket line
The issues grew remoter:
Ballads to boycott beer or wine
Won't move the average voter.

Now in a local motel bar
Nostalgia's what you market.
It makes the payments on your car.
Be careful where you park it.

Still, you can rouse us with a song,
Raising our rusty voices,
Unsure of which side's right or wrong
Or even what the choice is.

So wail Leadbelly's "Bourgeois Blues"
Chugging off in your Volvo.
Friend, you've more than paid your dues:
Ego te absolvo.

The Classroom at the Mall

Our Dean of Something thought it would be good
For Learning (even better for P.R.)
To make the school "accessible to all"
And leased the bankrupt bookstore at the mall
A few steps from Poquito's Mexican Food
And Chocolate Chips Aweigh. So here we are—

Four housewives, several solemn student nurses,
Ms. Light—serious, heavy, very dark—
Pete Fontenot, who teaches high-school shop
And is besides a part-time private cop
Who leaves his holstered Glock among the purses,
And I, not quite as thin as Chaucer's Clerk—

Met for our final class while Season's Greetings
Subliminally echo calls to buy
Whatever this year's ads deem necessary
For Happiness and Joy. The Virgin Mary,
Set up outside to audit our last meetings,
Adores her infant with a glassy eye.

Descend, O Muzak! Hail to thee, World Lit!
Hail, Epic ("most of which was wrote in Greek")
And hail three hours deep in Dante's Hell
(The occupants of which no one could spell)—
As much as our tight schedule might admit
Of the Great Thoughts of Man—one thought per week.

I've lectured facing towards "The Esplanade"
Through plate-glass windows. Ah, what do I see?

Is that the face "that lunched a thousand ships"
Awash with pimples? Oh, those chocolate chips!
Ms. Light breaks in: "Will this be for a grade?"
It's a good thing the students all face *me.*

One night near Halloween I filled the board
With notes on *Faust.* A Pentecostal hair-
Do (with a woman underneath) looked in,
Copying down my scrawl with a tight grin
That threatened she'd be back with flaming sword
To corner me and Satan in our lair.

Tonight, though, all is calm. They take their quiz
While I sit calculating if I've made
Enough to shop for presents. From my chair
I watch the Christmas window-shoppers stare
At what must seem a novelty, and is,
This Church of Reason in the Stalls of Trade—

Like the blond twins who press against the door,
Accompanied by footsore, pregnant Mummy,
Who tiredly spells out for them the reason
I am not price-tagged as befits the season,
Explaining what is sold in such a store
With nothing but this animated dummy

Who rises, takes the papers one by one
With warm assurances that all shall pass
Because "requirements have been met," because
I am an academic Santa Claus,
Because mild-mannered Pete's strapped on his gun.
Ms. Light declares she has enjoyed the class:

"They sure had thoughts, those old guys," she begins,
Then falters for the rest. And I agree
Because, for once, I've nothing left to say
And couldn't put it better anyway.
I pack the tests, gather my grading pens,
And fumble in my jacket for the key,

With time to spend and promises to keep
And not one "hidden meaning" to the tale,
Among these drifting schools of moon-eyed teens,
License and credit bulging in their jeans,
Who circle, hungry for the choice and cheap—
Something of value, soon to go on sale.

Body Bags

I

Let's hear it for Dwayne Coburn, who was small
And mean without a single saving grace
Except for stealing—home from second base
Or out of teammates' lockers, it was all
The same to Dwayne. The Pep Club candy sale,
However, proved his downfall. He was held
Briefly on various charges, then expelled
And given a choice: enlist or go to jail.

He finished basic and came home from Bragg
For Christmas on his reassignment leave
With one prize in his pack he though unique,
Which went off prematurely New Year's Eve.
The student body got the folded flag
And flew it in his memory for a week.

II

Good pulling guards were scarce in high-school ball.
The ones who had the weight were usually slow
As lumber trucks. A scaled-down wild man, though,
Like Dennis "Wampus" Peterson, could haul
His ass around right end for me to slip
Behind his blocks. Played college ball a year—
Red-shirted when they yanked his scholarship
Because he majored, so he claimed, in Beer.

I saw him one last time. He'd added weight
Around the neck, used words like "grunt" and "slope,"
And said he'd swap his Harley and his dope
And both balls for a 4-F knee like mine.
This happened in the spring of '68.
He hanged himself in 1969.

III

Jay Swinney did a great Roy Orbison
Impersonation once at Lyn-Rock Park,
Lip-synching to "It's Over" in his dark
Glasses beside the jukebox. He was one
Who'd want no better for an epitaph
Than he was good with girls and charmed them by
Opening his billfold to a photograph:
Big brother. The Marine. Who didn't die.

He comes to mind, years from that summer night,
In class for no good reason while I talk
About Thoreau's remark that one injustice
Makes prisoners of us all. The piece of chalk
Splinters and flakes in fragments as I write,
To settle in the tray, where all the dust is.

West Palm

Arma virumque cano. It should be
That simple, shouldn't it? Sometimes, at night
When Susan and the boys are in their beds
I'll take my Virgil and the dictionary
And work through lines like these until my eyes
Grow heavy, and I know that I can sleep.
I won't take pills, though Susan says I'm stupid
Not doing so. "You *are* a doctor, Tom.
Write yourself a prescription." But I don't.
The sleeplessness is somehow like the Latin,
Steady and tedious, worth working through.
Arma virumque. Warfare and mankind.

I've known them both and tried to keep my distance.
In '68 I did my residency
At an induction center. Easy work,
Knee-jerks and assholes, Hunter used to joke
When we'd go out to see the daily crop.
Hunter was something else, a hare-lipped sergeant
Who'd done the same routine for twenty years.
I can still hear the way he'd holler out:
"Bend oder, gemmun. Gab you cheeks an spead 'em!"
He'd seen it all, the guys who'd drink raw eggs
For weeks on end to register albumin
In urine samples, those who'd swallow speed
To bring on an arrhythmia. We locked them up
There on the holding ward a day or so
Until their signs were normal and they passed.
I sent so many off to war that year
I can't recall a single face. A scar
Or a tattoo, perhaps, but not a face

Except old Hunter's with his twisted lip
And eyes that cut into me like a scalpel.
We worked on daily quotas, for the camps
Could only take so many at a time
And in those days they called up twice the number
They'd ever use. I'd swagger down the lines
And feel those kids' eyes on me, almost begging
For me to find some rare deformity
In feet or knees or crotch to keep them out.
That year, I had the power of life and death.

I can't remember faces, but I know
I sent some that I shouldn't have, a negro
With tracks on either arm, a pool of pus
Between his feet when he pulled back his foreskin
And stood there grinning at us; one fat slob
With H-A-T-E scratched into his knuckles
And teeth like something from a horror movie.
The clean-cut boys, the ones who answered "Sir"
And seemed to have intelligence as well,
Would get the benefit of every doubt.
Sometimes I'd listen with the stethoscope
Until I half convinced myself I heard
A murmur. Hell, nobody questioned me
As long as every bus to camp was full.
Hunter caught on, I guess, and hated me
For what I did but never said a word.
In '69 I got the job I wanted,
Putting the blasted faces back together
And doing what I could to mask the scars.

For years I read of Mengele. Remember?
The Nazi doctor who stood by the trains
And flipped his riding crop to left or right
To send one to the ovens, one to work.
For years they claimed he hid in Argentina
Or some such place. And I live in West Palm,
Here in a house my old man would have never
Felt better than a servant in—a wife
And two fine boys, a sailboat we could take
Across the ocean if we wanted to,
And a good practice that grows every day.
If Doctor Mengele could see my patients!
Jewish women demanding straighter noses,
Bigger breasts, smaller breasts, a few less wrinkles.
Ponce de Leon discovered Florida
In search of youth. It's right here in my hand.
The fountain's a syringe of collagen.

Mama, God bless her soul, would keep me up
Past midnight with those tables of declensions
Until I had them down. I could still pass,
With practice say a page of Cicero
So silkily you'd think I'd heard the man.
Now, through the years I've found no use for all
That patience but to help me fall asleep.
I'll go up now and look in on the boys,
My blond and flawless sons who'll help me take
The boat out at first light. We'll catch a breeze
And point the bow out where the blue meets blue
And one soon loses sight of everything.

Audenesque: For the Late Returns

The stylus, like a bullet,
Wounds each likely name,
So grasp the lever, pull it,
And lay to rest your blame

While the opposing faction
Exits from its booth,
United in reaction
To complicated truth,

While the all-seeing laser
Sheds light on every vote,
Each private Ockham's razor
At the public throat.

Nearby, a boy lies dying
In the random street;
Sister clutches, crying,
His small brown feet.

The killer, in new sneakers,
Pivots toward the goal
With echoes from the bleachers
Of his squeaking sole.

See Mama prick his blister.
See the juice flow,
Running away while Sister
Fires a rock to blow.

At ten, our moment's *führer*
Smirks and smooths his hair,
His motives made purer
By voluntary prayer.

O fathers, hide your daughters.
O mothers, wash your sons.
He leadeth by still waters
And doth restore your guns.

Too out of it for pity,
Too out of touch to care,
Remote from the bright city
Where triumph fuels the air,

Conceding all the races,
We sigh and click the news,
Still in each other's faces,
Still in each other's shoes.

Local Initiative

For years his parents saw that wreaths were placed
Beside the crossroads where their youngest boy
Left lines of rubber from his shattered toy,
An epitaph new concrete has erased.

For years they mailed petitions for a light
Or four-way stop; the city deemed it best
To table them until the time was right.
It took The Mall to honor their request.

You can't take parents' sorrows to the bank
But you can always bank on corporate needs.
Now like a docile river traffic flows
By fraying ribbons lost among the weeds,
And slowing to the changing light we thank
Blockbuster, Target, Texaco, and Lowes.

The Ballad of Burton and Bobby and Bill

For Archer Joyce

My best friend and I would often stop by
    The store on our way home from school.
What can I say? This was back in a day
    When we'd rather be dead than uncool,
When a sneer at one's shirt was a palpable hurt
    That could even occasion some tears,
A juvenile pain that rises again
    After so many wardrobes and years.
If you'll humor me while I discourse upon style
    (Oh, I fervently hope that you will!)
I'll sing you a story that measures the glory
    Of Burton and Bobby and Bill.

TOWNE SQUIRE was the name; I recall when it came
    To the storefront on Washington Street—
Mill town in the South, pretty down in the mouth
    With a well-thumbed *carte-de-visite.*
Every other men's store carried Cloth for the Poor
    (We were snobs clear down to our jocks),
But the SQUIRE was the first to pour wine for our thirst
    For wing-tips and Ivy League socks,
Wembley ties that were narrow and Madras by Arrow
    And Weejuns and Gold Cups to fill
The immaculate shelves of our fantasy selves
    Dressed by Burton and Bobby and Bill.

Now Bill was stocky and Burton like rock (he
    Had played some ball in his prime),
And Bobby was slender with eyes that were tender
    And wrinkled with laughter, not time.

I am sure that these guys were not kindly or wise
        And they mainly desired that we spend
More than time in perusing the brands of their choosing—
        Their smiles were a means to an end.
Still, I can't help but think that the nod and the wink
        As they storewalked from mirror to till
Meant what gleamed in their eyes wasn't just merchandise
        To Burton and Bobby and Bill.

Harris tweeds . . . Haggar pants . . . London Fogs . . . Oxford Gants . . .
        Rep ties . . . penny loafers from Bass . . .
They reeked with, we knew, something more than Canoe—
        I suppose you could label it *Class*,
Or at least so it seemed to two youngsters who dreamed
        Of someday impressing *les femmes*
As sophisticates wiser than *Playboy*'s advisor—
        Small wonder we looked up to them!
For to gaze on one's Dad was to see something sad
        As he snored through *Bonanza* until
He arose with a cough and his pants falling off
        (Unlike Burton and Bobby and Bill).

Through a span of lapels and an eon of smells
        From those overpriced brands of cologne,
We've matured yet have come to be more than the sum
        Of all we've acquired on our own.
Praise the Lord for the models who showed us which bottles
        To test and which knots we should use,
For the older we grow the more clearly we know

What it means to be wearing their shoes.
The lesson they taught—like a blazer you bought,
        Wore awhile, and then gave to Goodwill—
Is that goods never last; they belong to the past
        Like Burton and Bobby and Bill.

Yes, the years have a way of making us pay
        For the rags that we wear on our backs
As we waddle the path to the Vineyards of Wrath
        In double-knit Sans-a-Belt slacks.
Good Fellows of Fashion, who leant us a passion
        For lint-rollers, orlon, and labels,
Can it be that you've gone where it all rests upon
        God's final clearance tables?
The store's shutting down with the rest of the town
        And the Company is closing the mill.
They've boarded the door. We'll bargain no more
        With Burton and Bobby and Bill.

Rhapsode

His agent could not book him
  Into big resorts,
And so the years took him
  On cruise ships to strange ports,
Where, following smarmy lyrists
  Who plucked their single string
For overstuffed tourists,
  The rhapsode rose to sing.

Dodging egg and cabbage,
  He learned survival's art
By mouthing lines the savage
  Ear might take to heart,
Yet with each new version
  Pruning, with regret,
Subtleties that Persian
  And Mede would never get.

Thus he cultivated—
  Bloodied, somewhat bowed—
The epic lie he hated
  Yet nightly gave the crowd.
At least it was a living,
  He heard himself say.
The muse, unforgiving,
  Tuned her breath away.

Rosy-fingered mornings
  Followed wine-dark nights;
Physicians issued warnings
  About his appetites.

One late show as he ended
  An endless simile
The Silver Lord descended
  And set his song free.

With him died a story
  That will not be retold:
How, forsaking glory,
  Achilles grows old
While Hector dusts his trophies
  Behind high walls—
For in his unsung strophes
  Troy never falls.

Approaching a Significant Birthday,
He Peruses *The Norton Anthology of Poetry*

All human things are subject to decay.
Beauty is momentary in the mind.
The curfew tolls the knell of parting day.
If Winter comes, can Spring be far behind?

Forlorn! the very word is like a bell
And somewhat of a sad perplexity.
Here, take my picture, though I bid farewell;
In a dark time the eye begins to see

The woods decay, the woods decay and fall—
Bare ruined choirs where late the sweet birds sang.
What but design of darkness to appall?
An aged man is but a paltry thing.

If I should die, think only this of me:
Crass casualty obstructs the sun and rain
When I have fears that I may cease to be,
To cease upon the midnight with no pain

And hear the spectral singing of the moon
And strictly meditate the thankless muse.
The world is too much with us, late and soon.
It gathers to a greatness, like the ooze.

Do not go gentle into that good night.
Fame is no plant that grows on mortal soil.
Again he raised the jug up to the light:
Old age hath yet his honor and his toil.

Downward to darkness on extended wings,
Break, break, break, on thy cold gray stones, O Sea,
And tell sad stories of the death of kings.
I do not think that they will sing to me.

The Easiest Room in Hell

What torments for the genteel sonneteers
Whose praises ran, as streams of syrup flow,
From critics (space reserved somewhere below)
And Gentle Readers lodged in higher spheres?
Prefacing phrase and clause with *Ah!* or *O!*
They spoke as if the stems and stumps had ears,
Letting the backwash of their idle tears
Leave bathtub rings around the Vale of Woe.

They strove with none, and strummed their tuneless lyres
Until the numbest ears had turned to stone,
But, Lord, deal lightly with them, feed the fires
With many drafts, and make them sweetly moan
Nice sentiments, which echo from their crevice:

Carpe diem!
     Ubi sunt?
         Ars longa, vita brevis.

Ballade of the Yale Younger Poets of Yesteryear

Tell me where, oh, where are they,
Those Younger Poets of Old Yale
Whose laurels flourished for a day
But wither now beyond the pale?
Where *are* Chubb, Farrar, and Vinal
With fame as fragile as a bubble?
Where is the late Paul Tanaquil,
And where is Lindley Williams Hubbell?

Where's Banks? Where's Boyle? Where's Frances Clai-
Borne Mason? Where is T. H. Ferril?
Dorothy E. Reid or Margaret Ha-
Ley? Simmering in Bad Poets' Hell?
J. Ingalls' *Metaphysical*
Sword (hacking critics' weeds to stubble)?
Young Ashbery (that is, "John L.")?
And where is Lindley Williams Hubbell?

Where's Alfred Raymond Bellinger
(If you'll allow me to exhale
Him *avec un accent français*)?
Where's Faust (Henri) or Dorothy Belle
Flanagan? Where is Paul Engle
(To rhyme whose surname gave me trouble)?
Hath tolled for all the passing bell?
And where is Lindley Williams Hubbell?

Prince of all poets, hear, I pray,
And raise them from their beds of rubble.
Where's Younger Carolyn Forché?
And where is Lindley Williams Hubbell?

Two Villanelles

Optimist

For Ailene Michaelis of Beaumont, Texas, who published, as The Rhyming Optimist, six poems a week 1919-1935 for the International and King Features syndicates.

Villanelle follows sonnet, day by day,
Like multi-colored bon-bons on a plate.
Fridays bring fishcakes and a triolet.

Your scattered rosebuds falling where they may,
Drifting away like every ripped off date,
Villanelle follows sonnet, day by day.

The stacks of yellow foolscap mount. Can they
Confess the fiery mildness of your fate?
Fridays bring fishcakes and a triolet

While aches and years are gathered in the gray
That spreads from roots to ends: your husband's late.
Villanelle follows sonnet, day by day,

And soon enough a world has spun away
Like headlines whirling at a heady rate.
Fridays bring fishcakes and a triolet;

Mondays start the round again: you say,
The camphor gaily blooms beside my gate.
Villanelle follows sonnet, day by day.
Fridays bring fishcakes and a triolet.

Ellenalliv for Lew: On His Retirement

In graduate school Lew Turco was the champion of two parlor tricks for which alone we would never have forgotten him, even if he had written nothing: one was the trick of being able to recite anything backwards, and to do it instantly; the second and more impressive was the trick of improvising on the spot a Dylan Thomas poem, not ever one we could quite remember, though each new Turco-Thomas poem did sound at least faintly familiar and certainly authentic.

—*Donald Justice*

Retirement into gentle go not do.
Dies he until stops never poet a.
Do to tasks undone many have still you.

Start they what of half finish ever few.
You with compared they're when away fade they.
Retirement into gentle go not do.

Renown first their on rested have some, true.
Promises early to up live few, hey!
Do to tasks undone many have still you.

Writes who man the to given be must due.
Does he what for reward small too is pay.
Retirement into gentle go not do.

Yield to not and, find to, seek to, strive to.
Truth its holds still saw ancient this that pray.
Do to tasks undone many have still you.

Sleep you before go to miles have you, Lew.
Forth travel you may so, anew breaks day.
Retirement into gentle go not do.
Do to tasks undone many have still you.

Lies

F. S., 1948?-1978

Here lies a truth about the poet who fished,
  Who sauntered through his books—arms wide—to show
The magnitude of glory that he wished,
  The only brand of gospel poets know.

Now add two women; when they got together
  And found how they were tangled in his lines,
They cut the snarl away. He read the weather
  And thought they wouldn't bite, despite the signs.

And so we found him, finally done with dying,
  His arms outstretched to show he'd finally caught
The big one. Someone said, "He went out lying.
  Only the poems matter now." We *thought,*

But all these years, and this. Who would believe it?
  We write, and he looms larger as we do.
He said, *Just tease the worm. Lift it and leave it.
  The trick is lying still.* The trick was true.

Snow White and the Seven Deadly Sins

Good Catholic girl, she didn't mind the cleaning.
All of her household chores, at first, were small
And hardly labors one could find demeaning.
One's duty was one's refuge, after all.

And if she had her doubts at certain moments
And once confessed them to the Father, she
Was instantly referred to texts in Romans
And Peter's First Epistle, chapter III.

Years passed. More sinful every day, the *Seven*
Breakfasted, grabbed their pitchforks, donned their horns
And sped to contravene the hopes of heaven,
Sowing the neighbors' lawns with tares and thorns.

She set to work. *Pride*'s thousand looking glasses
Ogled her dimly, smeared with prints of lips;
Lust's magazines lay strewn—bare tits and asses—
With flyers for "devices"—chains, cuffs, whips.

Gluttony's empties covered half the table,
Mingling with *Avarice*'s cards and chips,
And she'd been told to sew a Bill Blass label
In the green blazer *Envy*'d bought at Gyp's.

She knelt to the cold master bathroom floor as
If a petitioner before the Pope,
Retrieving several pairs of *Sloth*'s soiled drawers,
A sweat-sock and a cake of hairy soap.

Then, as she wiped the Windex from the mirror,
She noticed, and the vision made her cry,
How much she'd grayed and paled, and how much clearer
Festered the bruise of *Wrath* beneath her eye.

"No poisoned apple needed for *this* Princess,"
She murmured, making X's with her thumb.
A car door slammed, bringing her to her senses:
Ho-hum. Ho-hum. It's home from work we come.

And she was out the window in a second,
In time to see a *Handsome Prince*, of course,
Who, spying her distressed condition, beckoned
For her to mount (What else?) his snow-white horse.

Impeccably he spoke. His smile was glowing.
So debonair! So charming! And so *Male*.
She took one step, reversed, and without slowing
Beat it to St. Anne's where she took the veil.

Chang   *Eng*

Mount Airy, N.C.
January, 1874

Constant other,	*Constant brother*
who know I think	*to lips that drink,*
my own thoughts yet	*I would not let*
will never part	*your sluggard heart*
in this world from	*and blood become*
the self we share—	*the cross I bear,*

the ties that bind BODY AND MIND *never to find*
and fates that mesh SPIRIT AND FLESH *hopes that lie fresh*

—our blood now joins	*in our wives' loins.*
us in one death.	*Take the last breath*
Pity the wives	*and say our lives*
with whom we shared	*will not be spared.*
our privacy.	*Remember me*
Drink with me, slave,	*as one who gave*
this unison	*warnings to one*
toast to the grave.	*he could not save.*

Two Portraits

I. The Garden Parasol

After a painting by Frederick Carl Frieseke, 1910

She's listening. Make her eyes stray from the book
To focus vaguely on that empty chair
Where someone sat for tea. Give her a look
Reserved for unframed distance where
His car is raising dust. Let her mind
Be elsewhere, but let it resemble ours,
Searching for mysteries we'd like to find
Where sunlight idly plays among the flowers.

And that bright parasol? A thought-balloon
Where gaudy birds of paradise parade
Or just another airy prop for one
Who'll soon enough descend through afternoon
And afternoon to evenings where the shade
Holds nothing that can comprehend the sun.

II. THE PORCH SWING

After a photograph by Russell Lee, 1941

In the new moon's light she might be taken
For darker than she is. Perhaps she'll sing
A spiritual. Her young son sleeps, unshaken
By troubles that the R.F.D. may bring
This morning to the leaning rusted box.
Till then, there is a moment: she is free
To range beyond a world of bars and locks.
His book lies open: Possibility.

Listen. Isn't the creaking of the chain
Comfort enough against the breaking dark?
If her motions make the only sound
Then it is she, for once, who can contain
This world, secured and measured by the arc
Of feet that do not have to touch the ground.

A Toast from Cana

For Jason and Christy

Let there be light, His Father once had said.
But on that legendary wedding day,
Darkness was not the source of the dismay
That lowered when the caterer shook his head
And made the bride spill tears in her bouquet.
Small problem, though, for One who'd soon bless bread
And multiply the fish and raise the dead.
The Master spoke: *Let there be chardonnay.*

His words alone that day brought happiness
And bring the same to you we honor here.
As water into wine, before much longer
So may you be transformed by words that bless
This love you share, to grow with every year—
Like the best vintage—deeper, richer, stronger.

John 2: 1-11

Human Nature

Walking for pleasure, not reward,
He took small profit when he found
The remnants of the fox squirrel's hoard
Of acorns on the thawing ground;

And by the creek where tongues of fern
Lashed at tardy clumps of snow
He stepped across without concern
Nor need of any gain to show

To those who urged that each new leaf,
Sallow with translucent green,
Bore certain auguries of grief
Which he must serve as go-between.

His taste was not for that at all.
Better to save the yellow flower
Emerging from a tumbled wall
For savoring at a later hour

Than count its petals on his walk
Like one who only understands
The manifesto of a stalk
Stripped naked by his busy hands.

Topping the ridge, he met the line
A winter ice-storm had surveyed;
Trunks lay leveled, oak with pine,
Brown contrast in a greening shade.

Though from both edges branches grew
That by the summer's close would heal
A breach no longer wide nor new,
It seemed this spoilage might reveal

A frosty parable of waste
Breathing from every broken shaft,
Still lingering like the aftertaste
Of the tempest's bitter draught—

As if original violence
Had coiled and struck through frozen air
At winter woods whose sole offense
Simply lay in being there.

But if he wondered what it meant
That in this spot no sapling stood,
No witness to the wind's intent
Came forward from the turning wood.

Coastal Freeze

It will come with warnings published on the air,
    So beware
Laying bets on gulf-born breezes harboring
    Hopes of spring.
Dwarf azaleas, playing suckers' odds with doom,
    Race to bloom,
But the front's relentless lashing drains each bud-
    Full of blood,
Laying low without distinction as it kills
    Daffodils,
Calla lilies, bougainvillea, mustard greens.
    For it means
All beginner's luck runs sour, to be lost
    To the frost,
Like a wealth of unconsidered good advice.
    Glazed with ice,
Greenness shatters, brittle as an ancient bone,
    And our own
Stunned camellia stands, white petals shed below—
    Snow on snow.

Make Us an Offer

... a Shriner ... she was big in Eastern Star ...
I round a corner, and the minty voice
Fades like the draperies. On the breakfast bar
Their sad shoes gape: *$1 TAKE YOU'RE CHOICE.*
Having passed up the tôle paint and veneer,
Framed needlepointed slogans edged with lace
In cheerless rooms the relict tried to cheer
With smiles to which it's hard to fit a face,
I thumb fresh tracts—as if I sought an answer
To what seems clear enough—promising heaven
Or, failing that, a way to live with cancer.
A textbook dated 1937
Holds formulae which still, perhaps, are so,
The brown spots on its pages whispering, "No."

The Dream Again

The dream again. Near Christmas. It is time
To lower and unfold the attic stair
That will not hold a grown-up's weight, to climb
Into the chill and naphtha-scented air.
Here moth will not corrupt, and time must spare
The box of lights and mismatched ornaments
Packed in a carton filled with Angel Hair
And met, as if by sheer coincidence,
With lawn chairs, summer clothes, and two old Army tents.

Mother, an item here belongs to me.
It is a piece of plastic tubing, red
And cane-shaped, which I'll hang upon our tree
In memory of an old man who is dead,
A neighbor on the block I visited
Daily when I was only three or four.
For months I took that thing with me to bed,
Then stopped and did not take it anymore
After he died. I've never known what it was for.

The dream again. We trim the slender tree
With strings of lights so antiquated they've
No colors left, hang icicles and see
These acts reflected, wave on frozen wave.
More rituals: the ribbon that we save
To bind leftover boughs to make a spray
Of cedar. Every year, on Christmas day,
These were the fragrant, handmade gifts you gave
Your mother and your father—one upon each grave.

To make room for the presents we arrange
The furniture and, for amusement, play
Old records that, in retrospect, seem strange:
Gene Autry, Guy Lombardo, Sammy Kaye.
I watch you setting out a metal tray—
Santa Drinks Coke—and sing along like one
Who knows what words each character will say,
A sort of *déjà vu*, a knowledge won
From having played this part before, the role of son.

The dream again, the one that always ends
In a light which, while neither cruel nor hard,
Indifferent to my waking thoughts, ascends
In moments made to empty and discard
Like leaves the wind now scatters in the yard.
Yet it is such that I would not confine
It to the space inside a Christmas card
Or the stamped parcels bound with tape and twine,
Sent with regrets for invitations I decline.

So let the light grow dim, allow this dream
Its one still moment, where none may intrude
To hang the stockings which can only seem
Empty reminders of the magnitude
Of love we neither compass nor conclude.
Let the deep twilight gather to the chime
Of three brass angels circling in the nude,
Ringing above their candles as they climb
The wall in shadows, marking nothing more than time.

Randolph Field, 1938

Hands of men blasted the world asunder;
How they lived God only knew!
If you'd live to be a gray haired wonder,
Keep the nose out of the blue!

Framed by the open window, a lone Stearman
Wobbles, dips right, dips left, then dives and banks
For touch-and-go, seeming barely to miss
The sunlit "Taj Mahal" and a lost egret
That has mistaken grass and shimmering concrete
For salt marsh. Two flies on the windowsill
Wait for their chance. The wind-sock hangs limply
In the thick heat, and lunch is still uncleared.

Indeed, the messtray resting on the nightstand
Has not been touched, or hardly—half a wiener,
Succotash and boiled carrots stirred around,
Even the tea and gingerbread just tasted,
And the young man there who has no appetite
Has raised himself up from the sweaty pillow
To watch some fledgling's first attempt, as stirring
As a scene from *The West Point of the Air.*

It slips from sight. He leans his head back, dizzy
From the slight effort, shuddering against
The squeal of tires, the buzz-saw radial engine
Over-throttled, straining up to a stall,
And then, the day's sole miracle, the steady
Hum of the prop—somebody else's luck.
For now the chills have come to spike his fever,
Everything holding true to course but him.

The skinny nurse who takes his temperature
Charts the latest, 102.8,
And then connects the dots with a red line
That climbs and plummets like a rookie's struggle
To keep the nose cowl flush with the horizon.
It would be funny, but it simply isn't,
Even when Szulic and Rosenthal, his buddies,
Saunter in after class with Cokes and Luckies.

He'll envy them that night when, after supper,
He lies in bed and smokes. It isn't easy
To think of them with girls along the River—
Dancehalls, music, beer, all with such sweetness
In the mild evening air he'd like to cry.
He has missed the chance, like Aaron Rosenthal,
To burn above Berlin; like Thomas Szulic,
To spin in wingless somewhere over France.

A decade and a war still to be crossed
Before he is my father, he is only
One of the Dodos, barely voting age,
Washed out a week before he gets his wings.
A radio is playing now. Kay Kyser.
… *To be in Carolina in the mornin'* …
It's hard to think of what he must go back to.
He banked on everything but going back.

Off to the southeast, thunderheads are building—
Heat lightning flashing like imagined guns,
Faint thunder and a breeze that brings the Gulf
Into this place of starched white sheets and Lysol
Where he lies watching three red points of light,
A late flight coming in for night approach.
He shuts his eyes and tries to think of nothing
Before he sideslips into dreams of fire.

A Box of Ashes

D.E.G., 1917-1995

A box of ashes, which we scattered on
  Your parents' gravesite where the soil was poor,
  Cycles through root and crystal to restore
The cracked red clay that shrank around their stone.
New growth is whispering what you might have known,
  Stemming the nothingness you asked us for:
      A box of ashes.

If grit and granule, chalky bits of bone,
  And your life's dusty shards weigh little more
  Than handfuls sifted in a garden store,
Ponder, Father, why these green blades have grown:
      A box of ashes.

The Great Fear

Here where the door stands open, lights are on.
Each object occupies a special place.
Note the half sheet of foolscap by the phone
Where numbers someone labored to erase
Have left impressions. And there's no dial tone.
The tv glows, turned down. Dark figures chase
One who must learn no mercy can be shown
In such an extraordinary case.

An individual was here, but who?
His sheets are cold, the paperback romance
Gapes open, dog-eared, while his hanging pants
And belt await him. There is nothing missing,
Nor any sound except the kettle hissing,
Ready for the next one, whose name is You.

Cléante to Elmire

Rising, Madame, towards heaven in a bed
That elevates my knees and lifts my head
To sustenance, that is, a plastic tray
Of Jell-O, applesauce, and consommé,
I have become a connoisseur of juice,
Which leaves me liquid, not to mention *loose,*
And keeps my precious fluids running clear
Until such time as I shall disappear—
Like what descends transparently for pain,
Dripping, *ex machina,* to tubes that drain.
What has, you may well ask, contributed
To this apostrophe to one long dead
From one so nearly so? You come to me,
As Sting might say, in *synchronicity,*
Searching just now for bulletins about
This storm called *Cara* which, I have no doubt,
Shall live up to its namesake, namely *you,*
And do us in before the day is through,
I channel-surfed and lit on PBS.
My dear, shall I be coy and make you guess
What stopped me there and brought a hurricane
And you into one focus in my brain?
One line, in Mr. Wilbur's fine translation:
And cultivate a sober moderation....
Think of it! If we ever needed proof
Of greater patterns, wasn't it *Tartuffe*
That brought us once and brings us now together—
Molière and two lost souls and raging weather?
Lord, twenty years have passed and still each line
Smacks tartly on the tongue like a good wine
Heady with epigram and foiled seduction.

It was The Coastal Players' great production—
Rhymed verse they said our audience could not
Make much of, let alone digest the plot—
Yet how we triumphed, I the *raisonneur*
Cléante and you the faithful spouse, the pure
Elmire, the model of a perfect wife.
So much for art. Who says it mirrors life?
Like leaves whirling outside, the years have flown
And taken with them Pernelle and Orgon.
Dorine the maid (Remember? What a bitch!)
Went into real estate and came out rich,
Sweet Marianne had children and grew fat,
And you'd have thought it less than fitting that
The charge against Tartuffe, so like the play's,
Was finally dropped: not only virtue pays.
In spite of the applause I found so sweet
I never found the courage to repeat
Those evenings' glories in another play.
And you? We gathered you were on your way
To greater things. A touring company
(*A Chorus Line!*) had called, you gushed to me
At the cast party, and our toasts went on
(Fuck "sober moderation"!) until dawn,
When I appeared, bedraggled, in your gown—
My coming out, no small thing in this town—
Battering Blanche against your not-so-manly
Peruked and powdered parody of Stanley
While Matt, your surly boyfriend, hulked and glared.
You laughed at him. I must say *I* was scared.

After that night our paths diverged. I learned
Your offers never came, heard that you'd turned
To wilder exploits, but, then, I was so

Into my own pursuits I didn't know
How dark your path became. Often our cars
Would pass en route to our respective bars.
We'd honk and wave like drunken teens. Dare I
Hope that one kiss I blew you said good-bye?
Your end came the next summer. Tom, the cop
Who'd played Laurent, came by the flower shop
To tell me what he knew—in rapid order,
Marriage, your panicked calls—quick as the border
Of this new storm front alters. Drugs, of course,
Were much of it, and there was the divorce
Which had turned ugly. Still, the Lord knows what
Led to that final beating and the shot
That tore your face away—before Matt made
The 911 call, sobbing while he played
His own death scene. I only pray it's true
What Tom believed himself: he said that you
Were dead already when the shot was fired.

My own death is the kind that is "acquired,"
Which makes it sound like something one might paste
Into a book, as one "acquires" a taste
For sherry, leather scenes, or the ballet.
All prance around the piper. All must pay.
No more of that. The plot by now is stale.
Let Tony Kushner live to tell the tale
And garner all the money and awards.
May *my* audition be one aiming towards
A long run somewhere in a stellar cast
In which no bow I take will be my last.
Corny? You know me, Cara, for I am
The same as you, eternally a ham
Who holds out hopes of One who can explain,

A *Raisonneur* of happiness and pain,
Who proves for us that love is possible
And need not climax in so great a fall
As what we've suffered . . . and that The Machine
Will lower with a Prince who makes us clean
And whole again, who lends His blessed grace
To salve my wreckage and restore your face—
Who lets the memory of a dead friend's laugh,
In the dark valley, be my rod and staff.
In a world full of such unwelcome guests
As storms, Tartuffe, and sickness, small requests.

It makes a curious *dénouement* that I,
Too ill for anything except to die,
May be evacuated, which shall save
These sodden relics for a drier grave.
The winds are rising, Cara, your own winds
With the great closing curtain that descends
Upon us as we play our games again
With tracking charts and crayons. CNN
Leads the hour with your great whirling eye.
Live oaks and sweetgums just outside my high
Window gesticulate the *agon* for us
As fiercely as a Sophoclean chorus.
The living board their windows, and their eyes
Lift past their fragile rooflines to the skies.
What wind is this? they ask themselves.
                                        I say
It is the wind that bears the world away.

At the Center

The pianist is playing Debussy
Beside the lobby cappuccino bar—
Soft smiles and pastels everywhere. You see,
The point's not to remind you where you are
Or *how* you are; the point is not to dwell
On thoughts like these. Look at this normal crowd,
Such as you'd find in any good hotel.
But why does no one say its name out loud?

Later you pass through elevator doors;
Rising to higher levels, you recall
Rumors you've heard of rumors from these floors—
How some guests never leave, how they display
A preference for short hair, or none at all,
How no one asks how long you plan to stay.

Bone Scan

Shadows surround me, building in the air
Like clouds, were I inclined here to compare
My kingly state to portents in the sky.
I could say the expected: I could lie,
Claiming our long-term forecast will be fair.

So, family and friends, do not despair.
Shadows mean nothing. There is nothing there.
Knives will find nothing wrong. Still, I know why
      Shadows surround me.

The night my father died, I moved my chair
Close to his bed to touch his meager hair
While shadows gathered in his room that I
Might gather I was not too young to die.
Now, circuits close. A tunnel beckons where
      Shadows surround me.

The Dark Place

In the dark place where I had come to piss
I met my maker, and I heard him say:
No man alive deserves a death like this,

But you, for whom the serpent did not hiss
Except in joy, shall have one. For today,
In this dark place where we have come to piss,

The son of man you murder with a kiss
Exacts the toll you shall be made to pay.
I asked, "And *I* deserve a death like this?"

He answered, *No. But nothing can dismiss*
The heat that comes by night, the cold by day,
To this dark place where you have come to piss

Over the edge of life and that abyss
Down which no light extends a blessed ray.
"Then who of us deserves a death like this?"

With that, he took my hand, as Beatrice
Sent one to Dante who had lost his way
In this dark place where we have come to piss,
Where none of us deserves a death like this.

Before Prostate Surgery

Farewell, thou joy of my right hand, my toy;
My sin was too much use of thee, old boy—
At least the old wives' tales would have it thus,
And I am too downcast to raise a fuss
Or much of anything, to put it simply.
Now from the ashes of my hot and pimply
Youth and each profligate misspent erection
I bid thee rise to spiritual perfection.
Say, "Here I lie, the truest son of Sam,
Epic intentions shrunk to epigram."
And pray, that in the deft hand of a lover
From death to life we might thee yet recover.

Train for Ill: A Ballad

... train for ill and not for good.
—*A. E. Housman*

The train for Ill is a long train
That takes on passengers in Pain,
Where prayers are offered to complain
To skies of unrelenting rain
  And all roads run downhill.
And we who slowly file aboard
Clutch tickets we can scarce afford;
Protesting our unjust reward,
  We take the train for Ill.

The platform soon grows loud with those
Who wear dark bands and Sunday clothes,
Whose shared emotion plainly shows
With handkerchiefs near every nose.
  They watch the coaches fill,
And as our group departs a few
Shed tears, which others fail to do:
Survivors' benefits accrue
  On the train for Ill.

With ashes smeared on every face
The children who appear to chase
The last car seem to run in place
As if inclined to lose the race.
  Their cries grow short and shrill
And fall behind as we descend,
Cars swaying lightly in the wind,
A grade that shudders to the end
  Of the train for Ill.

Oh, if there were some way we could
Journey instead to distant Good!
We touch old charms and knock on wood
But each mile makes it understood
        That we never will.
To our sorrow we must learn
The shining hopes for which we yearn
Are stamped, like tickets, "No return"
        On the train for Ill.

How soon it seems the soft light goes—
Then summer's heat, then corn in rows,
Then on a wall one brilliant rose
Signals a stop as petals close
        In the growing chill.
Our faltering voices raise to sing
Remembrances of how the spring
Gathered its green regrets to bring
        To the train for Ill.

"Shall we know any good again?"
Some cry. "How many times? And when?"
The warnings on our medicine
Offer no clues what may be in
        Each dark and bitter pill.
Beside the tracks two lovers kiss.
We know we have no part in this,
The daily dose we never miss
        On the train for Ill.

And at the end what will remain?
An emptiness that can contain
All losses and all hopes of gain,
Even nostalgic thoughts of Pain,
        That city on the hill?

With no more failings to confess
We lift our voices up to bless
Each frail design of loveliness,
All sweetness that grows less and less
        Aboard the train for Ill.

Release

Slow for the sake of flowers as they turn
   Toward sunlight, graceful as a line of sail
     Coming into the wind. Slow for the mill-
Wheel's heft and plummet, for the chug and churn
   Of water as it gathers, for the frail
     Half-life of spraylets as they toss and spill.

For all that lags and eases, all that shows
   The winding-downward and diminished scale
     Of days declining to a twilit chill,
Breathe quietly, release into repose:
     Be still.

More Light:

Translations, Parodies, Verse

François Villon:
Epitaph

Francis by name, France's by state—
From Paris-by-Pontoise of late.
The six-foot rope that seals my fate
Will teach my neck my ass's weight.

François Villon:
The Debate of Body and Heart

What's that I hear? *Me. Who? Your heart.*
I hang inside you by a slender thread.
It saps my strength and tears me all apart
To see you sulking with the guilty tread
Of a whipped dog who hides under the bed.
Why's this? Because your lust runs uncontrolled.
What's that to you? *You toss me to the cold.*
Go away. *Why?* To tell would take too long.
And how long, pray? Until we've both grown old.
Then I've no more to say. I'll get along.

What do you want? To play a noble part.
How childish! At an age when mules are led
Off to the gluepots! Not me! *Then your cart*
Has tipped. You're crazy. Only in my head.
You don't know anything. I do. *What?* Dead
Flies in the milk: some black, some white, I'm told.
That's it? I'd much prefer you didn't scold.
I've made mistakes? Then I shall right each wrong.
You're doomed. I'll hang on till I lose my hold.
Then I've no more to say. I'll get along.

I get the heartbreak, but you catch the dart.
If you were just some dolt whose mind had fled
I might say, "Well, he's really not too smart."
But nothing can be hammered through your head.
Sometimes I think your brain is solid lead
And that you'd barter tin instead of gold.

Answer me quickly now. The bell has tolled.
You pose a problem death will not prolong.
Then you shall die. Ah, as hath been foretold.
Then I've no more to say. I'll get along.

What gave you all these troubles? A bad start.
When Saturn packed my bag for years ahead
He added them. *Then learn to use some art.*
You are his lord; you act his slave instead.
Look at this writing: Solomon once said
That wise men, if their actions prove as bold,
May shepherd straying planets to the fold.
Don't swallow that. We only sing their song.
What do you mean? We cannot break the mold.
Then I've no more to say. I'll get along.

You want to live? An age is not too long.
Then you must... What? Honor God and uphold
His word. What should I learn? Virtues extolled
In Scripture. And steer clear of fools. That's strong!
Then don't forget it. No, I won't. I'm sold.
Do not delay. The grave is deep and cold.
Then, I've no more to say. I'll get along.

Anonymous:
Sonnet Against Racine's *Phédre*

Fidgety Phaedra, pale in her gilt chair,
Babbles away in incoherent verse.
She gets a royal sermon from her Nurse
When she declares it's all too much to bear.
Hippolytus, that chaste prig, doesn't care.
She wants him badly but he hates her worse.
The Nurse accuses him (this proves *her* curse).
Theseus turns his back side on his heir.

Fat Aricia, in black leather, flits
Blondly onstage, preceded by her tits,
Which almost thaw our frigid Prince's winter.
But he expires, dragged by his team to that fate,
And Phaedra, after nipping at some rat-bait,
Confesses everything and dies, stage-center.

Heinrich Heine:
The Slave Ship

The supercargo sits at his books;
His name is Mynheer van Koek.
He totals the bill of lading up
And figures his probable take.

"The rubber's good, the pepper's good,
Three hundred barrels and sacks;
Gold dust is precious, ivory too,
But best of all are my blacks.

"I bought six hundred on the River
Senegal, a steal;
Their skin is tough, their muscles hard,
Like fine, tempered steel.

"I gave cheap brandy, beads and iron
To get them on the ship.
I'll clear eight-hundred percent at least
If half survive the trip.

"And if I have three hundred left
In Rio de Janeiro,
I'll get a hundred ducats a head
From the House of Gonzales Perreiro."

Suddenly Mynheer van Koek
Is shaken from his vision:
The surgeon of the ship comes in,
Doctor van der Smissen.

His breathing rattles like a gourd
Through a nose red with warts.
"How be my blacks?" inquires van Koek.
"Come, show me your reports."

The doctor thanks Mynheer van Koek
For his statement of concern;
"Last night," he says, "the death rate took
A sharp upward turn.

"Before, at most, two died a day;
Today seven were found—
Four men, three women. Here's the log.
I have put my findings down.

"I looked the bodies over well.
These swine will sometimes fake
Sickness and death in order to
Get tossed into the wake.

"Then quickly I unclapped their irons
And called out to the crew
To toss them overboard at dawn
The way we usually do.

"Sharks shot up from the depths at once,
A regular war patrol.
They relish this dark meat so much
They are on my dole.

"They have followed closely in our wake
Since we lost sight of land.
The smell of death drifts down to them,
It's more than they can stand.

"It's quite a curious thing, the way
They dine upon on the dead.
One holds a leg, one rips the guts,
One tears off the head.

"And when they're done, they roll about
And loll against the planks
And look at me as if to say,
'Fine breakfast, Doctor. Thanks.'"

"How can we halt these horrors, Doctor?"
Asks van Koek with a sigh.
"What can we do to keep our loss
From mounting up so high?"

The Doctor says, "If they are dying
It's their own fault, you know.
The nasty odors of their breath
Have fouled the air below.

"And others die from melancholy.
They're bored to death, I think.
Some fresh air, music, and a dance
Should put them in the pink."

Van Koek cries out, "A brilliant thought,
Dear Doctor! Share my bottle!
You are a match for Alexander's
Tutor, Aristotle.

"The president of the Tulipgrowers'
Society of Delft
Hasn't got half the brain you've got.
Congratulate yourself!

"Music! Music! These blacks will make
A dancehall of the ship,
And those too sick to jump for joy
Will be cured by the whip."

* * *

From the firmament on high,
Gleaming large and wise,
A thousand stars shine with desire
Like lovely ladies' eyes.

They gaze upon a sea of silk
Where the waters softly glow
With purple phosphorescent haze.
Waves moan to and fro.

The slave ship lies in a dead calm;
No breezes stir the sails,
But lanterns shimmer on the deck
Where dancing music wails.

The helmsman saws his fiddle bow,
The cooks puff on their flutes,
And the cabin boy beats on a drum
While the Doctor's tin horn toots.

A hundred blacks, women and men,
Dance and stomp their feet.
They circle wildly; when they hop
Their shackles keep the beat.

They shake the deck with wild desire
And many a beauty moans
As she clasps her naked mate and sweats
To a counterpoint of groans.

The jailer is *maître des plaisirs*
And walks the weaving lines
Urging all to enjoy themselves
With flicks of his cat o' nines.

A fiddle-de-dee, a fiddle-de-dum,
The racket sounds the deep,
And the creatures of the water world
Are wakened from their sleep.

With staring eyes, the sharks come up
To watch, at least a hundred.
They lie just off the teeming deck
And gape at it in wonder.

Seeing that dinner is not yet served,
They yawn and work their jaws
And rip the waves with open mouths
Planted with teeth like saws.

A fiddle-de-dee, a fiddle-de-dum,
The music shrieks and wails.
The sharks, mad with hunger pangs,
Begin to chew their tails.

It seems they don't like music much.
Their cross expressions show it.
Let no such man be trusted, says
Albion's greatest poet.

A fiddle-de-dum, a fiddle-de-dee,
The music fills the air,
While by the mast Mynheer van Koek
Folds his hands in prayer:

"In Jesus' name I pray Thee, Lord,
Their sinful lives to keep.
If they have angered Thee, recall
That they are Thy black sheep.

"Spare three hundred, for Jesus' sake,
Who died for us in thunder.
For if three hundred don't survive
My business will surely go under."

Stéphane Mallarmé:
Windows

For Ben Kimpel

Sick of the ward, sick of the fetid smell
Rising against the curtains' tiresome white
Toward the tired Christ nailed to the bare wall,
The sick man stretches, slyly stands upright,

And shuffles, more to see the common stones
Blaze with sun than to fire his own decay,
Presses a grizzled face gray as his bones
Against the window tinged with dying day,

And greedy for the azure licks his tongue
Across dry lips as if he might regain
That downy cheek he brushed when he was young,
And, with a long kiss, soils the golden pane.

Drunk, he forgets the holy oils and smiles,
Bidding the broths, the clocks, the bed good-bye;
Forgets to cough. Dusk bleeds across the tiles,
And in a sunset gorged with light his eye

Discerns the gilded galleys, fine as swans,
Heavy with spices on a saffron sea,
Etching their burnished flash of lines upon
The lovely nonchalance of memory.

Just so, disgusted with complacent Man,
Whose appetites devour him, whose sole quest
Is to fetch home what scraps of filth he can
To please the hag with urchins at her breast,

I rush, I cling to all those windows where
One turns his back on life; transformed by light,
Washed by eternal dew and swathed in air,
Reflected in the dawn of the Infinite,

I see myself an angel! die and seem
—Let this be Art! Let it be Mysticism!—
To be reborn, wearing my crown of dreams
In the lush beauty of an antique heaven!

But no. The Here and Now lord over me,
Seeking me out no matter where I fly,
And the rank vomit of stupidity
Stops up my nose before the azure sky.

Is there a way for Me, who know such sorrow,
To break this glass soiled by humanity,
To fly on featherless wings into tomorrow—
Risking the plunge into Eternity?

Albrecht Haushofer:
Three Sonnets from Moabit Prison

Executed by the SS, Berlin, 23 April 1945

On the Threshold

One way out of this endless round of being—
I've weighed and proven it with hand and eye.
One quick stroke—and no prison wall is high
Or thick enough to keep my soul from fleeing.

Even before the snoring guard can right
His chair and fumble with the clumsy key,
One quick stroke—and at last my soul is free
And soaring upward in the starlit night.

What keeps these others going—faith, desire,
Or hope—has slowly dwindled, leaving me
Only this shadow play, this senseless revel.

Only, what holds me back? The threshold's free.
Yet I remain here, held against the fire
In spite of all—by God or by the Devil.

Sir Thomas More

For a long time Sir Thomas, in the Tower,
Defied them all, until they wished him dead.
Wife-swapping lay within King Henry's power
But not the free use of his Chancellor's head.

They tried to sway him with a long procession
Of what might bend the most austere of men;
Then sent inquisitors to force confession.
Meanwhile, a long beard grew from Thomas' chin.

And when they laid his head down for the ax,
Still yielding nothing in his last defense,
He smiled politely, took a final breath,

Parted his beard, and said: "This great offense
My head committed, not my beard." The facts
Thus clarified, he bared his neck to Death.

Time

I dream a lot at night, a lot by day.
Time has no meaning here, where I forget
To mark the hours, where I sometimes let
Whole weeks go wandering freely on their way.

Yet even dreams keep count of moments flying,
For when the bolt slides in my window and
The bowl of soup is thrust into my hand
And I prolong my life to keep on dying,

Then I discover, shaken from my dream,
How one feels at the end, who has been bound
And set adrift above the thunderous sound

Echoing from Niagara. In midstream
The water hammers at his dinghy's side.
The current surges on. His hands are tied.

The Bard of ViaVoice

If you are like most people, you want to start using ViaVoice right away. But before you do, there are a few important things you should understand. Investing a few minutes of your time now will make your use of ViaVoice much more productive and enjoyable. Some errors occur when ViaVoice does not interpret your speech correctly.

—IBM Voice-Recognition Software Message*

Shell like comparing the to a summer's day?
For more locally and more temperate
Rain rough winds to shake the normally would some day
Care and summers least double to short of the park.
Some time to the idea of heaven shines
Off in this is cooled complexion deep
Or in every fair from where some time
It's a chance to majors chained to a chorus by a turn in
Summer people not plead
Or lose the session where the homeless.
Marshall death threat of wonders and cheap
When the neutral lines to time rule was
So long as we can move its currency
Stolen was this disputes like to be.

Win in disgrace with fortune and enzymes
Happen all alone knew we can stay
And troubles death of a man with my food crises
And look upon myself and for small way
You'll wishing my soul to one more mission hold
Featured like film like filled with friends possess
Desiring this man's heart and the act as though
With one eye moves and jewelry county police

Then and the spots of myself almost to spies in
Happily for a comb the been my state
Like it will mark a break the day rise in
From the heavens. Since the inception of the new law
Provides week, the number of such well greens
And then I scorn to change by state with a.

Versions for the Millennium

Carpe Diem

Don't sweat it if your tresses gray
Or if Time's sands have shifted.
Whatever starts to sag today
Tomorrow can get lifted.

I Like to Watch

Drink to me only with thine eyes,
And I will pledge as much;
The safest kind of sex, my dear,
Is if we never touch.

Upon Demi's Breasts

Display thy breasts, my Demi, like a bough
Hung with such fruits as only gods enDow,
Upon which I would lie, my lips implanted
Against what looks as succulent as granite.

From Lucasta, Staying Home from the Wars

No, Dick, I *don't* think you're unkind:
Go out and practice gunnery
With other lads who'd likewise find
Between my breasts a nunnery.

Upon Julia Roberts's Clothes

Whenas in silks my Julia goes,
Styled by Versace, no one knows
What's really underneath her clothes;
Except her boyfriends. Don't take the trouble
To ask them to explode your bubble:
Instead, ask Julia's body double.

Upon Her Feet

   Her pretty feet
   Like snails did creep
Both out and in, a nifty trick!
   Her pretty feet
   Like *snails* did creep?
Sorry, I think that's pretty sick.

The Love Song of Lord Alfred Douglas

Had we but world enough and time
This boyness, Oscar, were no crime.

Dear C-minus

"Stand close around, ye Stygian set,
   With Dirce in one boat conveyed"?
Who *are* these dudes? If I forget
   This crap will it affect my grade?

ebarrett@britnet.com

How do I love thee? Let me count the ways,
And, yes, I'll keep on counting, being female.
If you'd prefer not standing there for days
I'll send them in a zip file, via e-mail.

Don't Leave Home Without It

My Life had stood—a Loaded Gun—
In Corners—till a Day
The BATF came for It.
Join—the NRA!

Visit England's Honeymoon Capital!

"Where ignorant armies clash by night"?
Such thoughts can give a girl a fright.
Matt's sweet, of course, but not much fun.
Tomorrow I shall get some sun.

1-900

When you are old and grey and full of sleep
And nodding by the fire, pick up the phone
And have some fun an hour all alone.
I don't come easy. And I don't come cheap.

And As Mrs. Parker Might Say . . .

Men rarely bring rosebuds
To girls who wear nose-studs.

The Professor's Lot

When the student body scorns an education
And would rather sun half-naked on the beach,
Then I sense my academic situation
Is somewhat like a pit without a peach.
Were it just a mid-life crisis I could bear it
But I fear the currents far more deeply run.
There's a lesson to be learned here. I can't share it.
The Professor's lot is not a happy one.
When there's academic duty to be done—
                                    to be done—
The Professor's lot is not a happy one.

Once it seemed the case that the high-school diploma
Guaranteed me students primed for a degree.
Now it means they've spent their twelve years in a coma,
Barely waking up to take the SAT.
When I give my class a simple Milton sonnet
You would think the Day of Judgment had begun.
We could spend the whole semester's time upon it.
The Professor's lot is not a happy one.
When there's academic duty to be done—
                                    to be done—
The Professor's lot is not a happy one.

My medieval seminar keeps getting smaller
While the business classes spill into the halls,
And each year the basketball recruits look taller
But their test scores rise no higher than their balls.
Though I'm at a state-supported school in Texas
I affect the accents of an Oxford don

As I say, "My dear," to students of both sexes.
The Professor's lot is not a happy one.
When there's academic duty to be done—
                        to be done—
The Professor's lot is not a happy one.

In my class there is a woman in a turban
Who displays a tattooed lily on her breast.
I could ask her out for chit-chat over bourbon
And let the course of nature do the rest.
But she's probably the type whose disposition
Always finds the dissertation "loads of fun."
Let my sins, Lord, be those mainly of omission.
The Professor's lot is not a happy one.
When there's academic duty to be done—
                        to be done—
The Professor's lot is not a happy one.

On the sad day when I stand before Saint Peter,
He will say, "No extra points. No make-up tests."
Then he'll add, "No need for you to pack your heater.
They've installed a central furnace for the guests."
At the moment when the horny demons find me
I can count this futile struggle halfway won
If the whole Administration's right behind me.
The Professor's lot is now a happy one.
With no academic duty to be done—
                        to be done—
The Professor's lot is now a happy one—
                        a happy one!

Yuppigrams: Snapshots from the 80s

I. Swingers

A singles bar! Warm refuge for the lonely.
Such eager give and take between the sexes
You'd think the action hot. Relax. It's only
The mating ritual of Rolodexes.

II. Dress for Success

Whenas in clinging silks my Julia goes,
Samantha makes a "statement" with her clothes.
What lies within her armored vault of serge
Intrigues me, but I somehow lack the urge,
Imagining gray-flannel, pin-striped lingerie.
A statement? Yes, alas. *Noli me tangere.*

III. Writer-in-Residence

He roared up to the cook-out on his Harley,
Invoking blessings from the Muse of Barley,
Passed round a joint, sliced the brie with his switchblade,
And groped the Chairman's young wife, all of which made
The pallid tribe disperse with nervous laughter
And grant him tenure very soon thereafter.

Squibs

Dr. Arbuthnot's Opinion

When Ajax strives some rock's vast weight to throw
A double hernia will lay him low.

Lines Overheard Approaching Key West

"O blessed rage for order, pale Ramon!"
Shrieked Mrs. F. "We left the water on!"

Para(noi)dox

Your gun barrel pressed into my neck
(A fact so long it starts to bore me)
May leave me, friend, a total wreck.
I'd face you. But you might ignore me.

To Cheerleaders, That They Make Much of Time

Imagining you seasons hence,
Washing your whisky down with tears
For halfbacks who have jumped the fence,
I lift my own glass higher. Cheers.

Why They Love Us

Vanna, 1987?-1995

Dogs love us uncomplainingly because
They see us in a way we never do.
They don't have sense enough to see our flaws

The way we fear our lovers' fangs and claws.
Blondi loved Hitler; Checkers, Nixon too.
They love us uncomplainingly because

When swatted with the news for muddy paws
Or chewing on that Bruno Magli shoe
They don't have sense enough to see our flaws.

We live by common sense and logic's laws;
With dogs, forget it. Even if they knew
They love us uncomplainingly because

They're idiots, they still won't drop their jaws
And say, "Duh, you were mean to me. We're through."
They don't have sense enough to see our flaws.

Thank god for that. A big round of applause
For what can sniff your ass and *still* love you.
Dogs love us uncomplainingly because
They don't have sense enough to see our flaws.

From *The Narcissiad*

The record of the inner life becomes an unintentional parody of inner life. A literary genre that appears to affirm inwardness actually tells us that inner life is precisely what can no longer be taken seriously.
—*Christopher Lasch, The Culture of Narcissism*

... there are more poets (soi-disant) than ever there were, and proportionately less poetry...
—*Byron*

In ev'ry work regard the writer's end ...
—*Pope*

Martyrs of pies, and relics of the bum ...
—*Dryden*

No poet or novelist wishes he were the only one who ever lived, but most of them wish they were the only one alive, and quite a number fondly believe their wish has been granted.
—*Auden*

The Education of Narcissus

From the jacuzzi, wreathed in scented foam,
He steps with his blow-dryer and his comb
To face that altar where all things are clearer,
To wit, his dressing table and his mirror.
He takes his inspiration and direction
By summoning the muse, his own reflection,
The which, in gratitude, he sweetly kisses,
This self-made-god, our latter-day Narcissus.
The poetry he writes, and thus inspires
Among his postulants, no more requires
A love of words or knowledge of the past
Beyond the headlines of the Tuesday last,
No binding strictures such as rhyme or meter
Or any length in excess of his peter,
The one tool of his trade he thinks so rare
He keeps it to himself, and will not share.
The sourcebooks of his knowledge line the shelf,
No old stuff but wise gospels of the Self
That lend him lines, such weighty words to throw
As "Man needs space in which his angst can grow,"
In other words, a space where he can say,
Repetitively, this pearl: "I'm O.K."
Of course, such talents are not cheaply bought,
And while his lines contain no shreds of thought
They catalogue his cats, his grocery lists,
His favorite tv shows, his analysts,
The ever-changing oceans of his moods,
Swamps of despair, highs from organic foods,
Good pills and bad, which rock stars to admire,
And how to build a dome or start a fire.

He knows his poets too, for he has read
The works of many, three of whom are dead,
And like a girl who'd be a movie star
He greedily devours each *APR*
(In lieu of *Photoplay*) in search of Feeling,
Passion, Emotion—anything worth stealing.
Instead of reverence from the future ages
He dreams instead in terms of tabloid pages,
This quarter's final word on Love and Beauty
And, after that, to teach the dog his duty.
Confident in his art, he knows he's great
Because his subsidy comes from the State
For teaching self-expression to the masses
In jails, nut-houses, worse, in grad-school classes
In which his sermon is (his poems show it)
That *anyone* can learn to be a poet.
With pen in hand he takes the poet's stance
To write, instead of sonnets, sheaves of grants
Which touch the bureaucrats and move their hearts
To turn the spigot on and flood the arts
With cold cash, carbon copies, calculators,
And, for each poet, two administrators.
In brief, his every effort at creation
Is one more act of self-perpetuation
To raise the towering babble of his Reputation.

  Small wonder that his subject matter's taken
From the one sphere in which his faith's unshaken
As, fearful of offending powers that be,
He turns his gaze within, exalts the Me,
And there, neither with wit nor with discretion,
Spews forth page after page of mock-confession,
Slightly surreal, so private, so obscure

That critics classify his work as "pure"
Because, in digging through the endless chatter,
They can't discern what is the subject matter,
And so, instead of saying they don't get it,
They praise the "structure" they invent to fit it.
He has no fear, for when his work's reviewed
Friends do it; thus, he's never gotten screwed.
He'll do the same for them, and they remain
Pals in the literary daisy-chain
Where every year, like Hallowe'en surprises,
They pass each other fellowships and prizes,
Include each other in anthologies
And take their greedy cuts from poetry's moldy cheese.

  Our Younger Poet, weaned early from his bottle,
Begins to cast about for a role-model
And, lacking knowledge of the great tradition,
Pulls from the bookstore shelf a slim edition
Of *Poems of Now*, and takes the proffered bait,
And thus becomes the next initiate.
If male he takes his starting point from Lowell
And fearlessly parades his suffering soul
Through therapy, shock-treatments, and divorce
Until he whips the skin from the dead horse.
His female counterpart descends from Plath
And wanders down a self-destructive path
Laying the blame on Daddy while she guides
Her readers to their template suicides—
Forgetting in her addled state, alas,
Her all-electric kitchen has no gas.
If undecided, s/he exalts O'Hara
And, wandering like the flight of a bent arrow,
Enthralls us in a poetry whose punch

Lands on such subjects as his bank and lunch,
What wines he's bought, what headlines he has seen
Before his train pulls out at 4:18.
From such first steps it is not difficult
To look beyond and see the sad result,
For, like the kid who coughs on his first joint
And finds himself next week at needle's point—
Having progressed from uppers, reds, and coke
In consequence of that first fatal smoke—
While simultaneously (unhappy youth!)
In fruitless search of some dark sexual truth
He reads a pornographic magazine
And dies soon after in a sorry scene,
A prostitute's corruption in his brain,
His nose and penis fallen off, insane,
Just so our youngster, from first taste of these,
Moves to the hard stuff: fat anthologies
Of Best-of poetry fill his little room,
Vendler's reviews, the latest fruits of Bloom,
And, though his budding mind has not yet flowered,
The last blow, the *Collected Works of Howard*,
Which over-fertilize his garden plot,
Wither his squash, and make his peppers rot,
And, a result of his progressive schooling,
He's found lost in a two-page sentence, drooling.
With good intentions, just to wish him well,
Friends mail books to him in his padded cell
Where, corseted into a straitjacket like Harry
Houdini, he is force-fed with Ashbery,
Merwin's new work, Kinnell's, Levine's, or Bly's
Until his doctors state with downcast eyes
That nothing will avail; thus, they are sure
His case lies quite beyond all hope of cure . . .

Save one, who bravely, in a long harangue
Before his colleagues, quotes from R. D. Laing,
Declaring that, relative to his peers,
He's sane as any: if he perseveres
In writing he will someday soon be found
As sound as Blake, as Clare, as Schwartz, as Pound.
And so, with some prescriptions in his pocket,
The nurses steer him to the gates, unlock it,
And push him out with new hope in his heart
That, cured, he's ready to ascend the Slopes of Art.

Immortal Combat

Our scene fades, showing several years have passed,
Reopening on him now, dues paid at last,
Reading before some twenty at the Y
Whose blank expressions show, in every eye,
Rapture, or stupor—one cannot be certain—
For drawn across each face is a gray curtain
Impenetrable as iron, and as revealing.
Who knows what thoughts, what lack thereof, they're feeling?
He finishes. There is tremendous . . . silence.
Nothing. No boos, no cheers, no threats of violence,
Huzzahs, hip-hips, foot-stamping, clapping—nothing.
They sit, and, like a teddy-bear whose stuffing
Is leaking out, he slumps to the bare stage . . .
Waking up sweating, frothing in a rage,
Flailing the air. So! It was just a dream.
He sighs and mops his brow, a yellow stream
Of unleashed terror puddling on his bed.
A silly nightmare! Yet, as this is said,
A new thought comes, driving its cold spike through him
To pose the paradox that may undo him:
For if each poet becomes, himself, his own
Favorite poet, he shall stand alone
Reciting only to his bathroom mirror,
With none but him alone his only hearer!
He stumbles, spilling tears of pure distress,
Despairing how to rise from such a mess.
What shall he do? How remedy this curse
Without the situation getting worse?
He soaks in a warm bath of violet bubbles
And prays his household god to solve his troubles,

And, after Valium and three gin and tonics,
Lo! Truth arrives—sweet, simple Economics!—
For just as money, when it is inflated,
Loses all value when more is created,
The only way his poems will keep their worth
Lies in removing poets from the earth,
Those *other* poets, that is, the competition,
Until, by a slow process of attrition
He stands unchallenged on a lofty peak
Where multitudes press forth to hear him speak.
Start with old poets who are past their prime.
Use arsenic to speed the march of time.
Send letter-bombs, or scorpions in roses.
Fix brakes, short-circuit mikes, or re-route hoses
From mufflers to front seats! He weeps for joy,
And like a child recalling a lost toy
Rummages through the wardrobe for his gun
To get it started *now* by shooting one.
Who shall it be? He thumbs his Rolodexes . . .
Meanwhile, unknown to him, in Maine, in Texas,
In California, Utah, Oregon,
His peers, amazingly and on their own
Having the same thoughts, are that very minute
Declaring war and eager to begin it,
Stropping their razors, loading bandoliers
With bullets, and on each a name appears,
A fellow poet's name, which they'll erase
As quickly as said poet shows his face.
Hail Narcissus! *Sieg heil!* Each poet a Master Race!

   From high Olympus' slopes the ancient gods
Sadly look on, refusing to make odds
As once, before the looming Trojan wall,

They stacked the chips and watched Great Hector fall.
This time around, though, Dionysus slugs
Another shot down while Apollo shrugs,
And all the gods find they can champion none
In this war of tooth, nail, and stinking pun,
Mixed metaphor and tedious paradox,
Prose hacked to fit a neat stanzaic box.
Pallas Athene, hands clapped to her head,
Escapes the roar by taking to her bed,
While pale, forlorn and sulky, Aphrodite
Slouches about in curlers and torn nightie.
Ares alone takes pleasure from the fray
And watches while a poet stalks his prey,
Ingeniously dispatching not a few
By poison-penning here a harsh review,
There drying up a poet's fellowship,
And sending off another on a trip
Around the Bronx to lecture to young cubs
Enrolled in the street-poetry writing clubs.
A roaring pandemonium swiftly rises
As booby-traps are sent for writing prizes,
And from the piles of chapbooks and reviews,
Now set ablaze, an evil odor spews,
Wafts heavenward in a bile-colored nimbus
To cloak the very portals of Olympus.
The gods, roused by the fetid hecatombs,
Rush to the bedroom windows of their homes
And see, below, the last two poets, girding
Their loins for the Great Reckoning. And no birds sing.

  Halpernus, with his zip-gun cocked and aimed,
Awaits his rival's entrance, half-ashamed
No worthier challenger can now be found

Than aged Merrilleus, whose mind's unsound,
A sad result and yet a just reward
For twenty winters talking to a board.
Pushover, clucks Halpernus. Nonetheless,
Merrilleus, ere the duel, has thought to dress
Himself protectively in the thick cloak
Ashberes, falling, left him, which like smoke
Laid down in naval battles for protection,
Sends every foe off in the wrong direction.
He bears as well the singing sword which Howhard
Once drew to turn a score of poets coward
And the long bow and undepleted quiver
Hinus once bore to make his lessers shiver.
Halpernus, on the other hand, is steeled
By his possession of the golden shield
Ku-Nitzu willed him with his final breath:
Whoever carries it need not fear death,
For seven folds of bull and three of lead
Lie hid beneath the gilt. And on his head
He wears an almost-laureate's magic fox-hat
Which gives him wind, like the great tribe of jocks that,
Now past their prime, still revel in their glories
With endless marathons of barstool stories
In which, like those of their lamented Dicca,
They still look trim, and still can hustle quicker
Than blood coursed through the veins of feathered Zeus
When he gave leaning Leda that ungodly goose.

  Flourishes sound, kettles reverberate
As, with expressions of disdain and hate,
The champions near upon a darkling plain
Littered with scraps of manuscript and brain.
At fifty yards each hurls an epithet;

At forty, takes a break to mop the sweat
The great exertion's caused. At thirty paces
They give the high-sign, making ugly faces
With tongues out and eyes crossed. And though dismayed
That neither seems to be the more afraid,
They close the gap to twenty, where they linger
A moment with an upraised middle finger
Which causes in each mind the chilling fear
That only greater force will persevere
To vanquish an opponent, with no sequel,
When art for martial art he weighs so equal.
As in a cold war, when two rival states
Balance each other with opposing weights
Of missiles, ships of war, and bombing planes
And know whatever victory remains
For war's survivors will be meaningless,
With nothing for the victor to possess,
Just so our heroes, knowing each yet holds
The Ultimate beneath his tunic's folds,
Are hesitant to be first to employ
The weapon with such power to destroy.
Should one be first to loose that deadly force
Great retribution follows in its course,
And thus no clear advantage can ensue
From such a double-Pyrrhic *folie à deux*.
Yet these are passing thoughts, if truth be known,
For each aspires so to the poet's throne
He'll stop at nothing less. Now scarce ten feet
Remain between, and neither will retreat.
Halpernus, with a fierce Antaean cry,
Turns deftly on his heel, but not to fly,
But rather to *unzip* his fly, bend over,

And with a brutal downward tug uncover
The weapon schoolboys, hanging from their cars,
Flash with a force that leaves deep-seated scars,
So deep that anyone so smoothly aced
Can ne'er behold pressed ham again straight-faced.
But Merrilleus, though taken by surprise,
Retaliates and hangs between *his* thighs.
Thus mirroring each other, cheek to cheek,
They slowly circle, growing pale and weak,
Until, at length, with no more force to spend
Each hero, in his rival, sees his End,
And locked in such a stalemate, swiftly swoons,
Eclipsed in turn by each, like orbiting twin moons.

The Triumph of Narcissus

Now Hermes to Olympus slowly flies,
The Great Reluctance welling in his eyes,
For bearers of sad tidings, well he knows,
Get tipped, for all their pains, with painful blows
That drive them from the council-rooms in shame
As if they also had to bear the blame.
But ere he speaks, the sound of distant drums
Announces that bad news—in person—comes:
Narcissus, he who rises from the fray
As sole survivor, victor of the day,
Since all his rival poets lie below,
A smorgasbord for jackal, worm, and crow.
In triumph now, he mounts the heights to claim
The cup of Immortality and Fame
And in the banquet hall to take his seat
And bellow for a leg of lamb to eat.
The gods, drawn forth by curiosity,
Assemble on the walls, and there may see
The long procession, stretching many miles,
Of vanquished poets chained in ragged files.
First come the Nymphs—attired in rich array
Who chant Narcissus' name in voices gay.
Male slavers keep their ranks in line with scourges,
Discouraging all matriarchal urges
While from rejection-slips they fashion petals
And strew them with medallions of base metals
On which Narcissus' profile is displayed.
Ringed by his motto: *Not for sale or trade.*
Behind them march a score of conquered tribes
Who could not save themselves by force or bribes:

A sheepish flock of geriatric Beats,
Their angry voices now reduced to bleats,
Are prodded on by vengeful Academics
Wielding sharp pens and shouting harsh polemics
But who have also donned the shepherd's hide
To sweep their charges' excrement aside.
The New York Poets follow at their back,
Colorfully garbed in various shades of black,
Faces as pale as someone in a coma
Or one who's spent too many hours at MOMA.
Deprived now of their quarter-hours of fame
They ring the praises of their conqueror's name.
Next comes a Macho Poet from the South
With bulging biceps and well-muscled mouth
Whose readings, critics said, had "guts" or "balls."
He drags his chains along and barely crawls
And, now humiliated, must rejoice
Narcissus' triumph in a tiny voice,
Almost inaudible beneath the song
A band of captive Ethnics bring along,
A Jolson medley blaring forth from very
Cumbersome tape-decks they be forced to carry,
In tongues so strange the lyrics seem a babble
Drawn from the Esperanto brand of Scrabble.
So many more now swell the seething horde:
Black Mountainites arrive to praise the lord,
Projectivists, Naropites, bards of Zen,
Instinctive Dadaists, the board of P.E.N.,
Creative writing teachers by the score,
Objectivists, surrealists, countless more . . .
Then come, divided equally by sexes,
The Poets-Laureate from Maine to Texas,
Whose chore (for they are not considered peers

Of those above) is selling souvenirs:
Busts of Narcissus for the reader's home,
Narcissus buttons stamped from shiny chrome,
Narcissus T-shirts, bumper-stickers, posters,
Glasses for high-balls, sets of matching coasters,
Playing-cards with Narcissus on the backs,
As well as on the Kings and Queens and Jacks,
And, last, signed copies of Narcissus' latest,
By far his greatest, farther still his weightiest,
Which all the trade press say is ". . . sizzling hot . . ."
And which is titled *I'm O.K. You're Not.*
Last in the line, two eunuchs come with soft
Voices intoning prayers, and hold aloft
Narcissus' standards on long bamboo poles;
And at the top, now suited to their roles
As visible reminders how complete
Narcissus' victory is now, and how sweet,
As great Aeneas did with fallen Turnus,
They bear the heads of Merrilleus and Halpernus,
Grown black and swollen to outlandish size
And garlanded with laurel-colored flies.
Now in thick clouds of dust, with high hosanna
That tests the upper range of *vox humana,*
Narcissus' chariot, speeded by a brace
Of critics matched and laboring in trace
To struggle uphill with so dead a weight,
Arrives and comes full-stop before the open gate.
He drops the reins, and on a stair of bending
Backs of his guard, Narcissus steps, descending
As slowly as a puff of thistle-down
To taste the homage of his conquered town,
His right hand out, like Alcibiades,
To take the city's kisses and its keys.

How best describe his darkly brilliant looks?
My powers fail me; get it from his books.
His hands are small, his arms are even smaller,
And in his photographs he looks much taller.
Let that suffice, and let us watch, instead,
Him pass among the crowd with languid tread
That never touches earth, and makes no sound
So carpeted with posies is the ground.
The gods, amazed at such an exhibition,
Peer curiously at the apparition
Like dowagers who watch a just-sold house
To measure up the owner and his spouse
And fall into a faint when someone tells them
Not only do they drive used cars, he sells them!
Apollo, Dionysus, and the rest
Stand silent (stricken dumb, if truth's confessed),
As if a leaden weight sat on each tongue
Or in each throat a swallowed fish-bone hung.
It is Apollo who first finds his voice,
Though more from reflex-action than from choice:
Where are my lovely singers? Are there any?
I did not know you had undone so many.
Silent their altars are. I vainly call.
All my pretty ones? Did you say all?
He asks, and as he does he sees the clear,
Unspoken answer in Narcissus' sneer.
Now Dionysus, having come to grips
With more than usual numbness in his lips,
Comforts his weeping brother and inquires:
And who shall tend my vines and feed my fires?
My shepherds and my flocks, my dancing boys
Lie scattered on the earth, like broken toys.
How shall I, at my age, restore the line

Of those who sang the ode and praised the wine?
He ceases, and like one who cannot bear
To hear the truth and looks for hope elsewhere,
He reaches for his brother's steady hold
And now must be the one to be consoled.
Like parents who have seen their children one-
By-one consumed, and stand beside the son
Who was their youngest but is now their heir,
And watch him drift away like smoke in air,
Just so the gods, now seeing they must yield
To one who bears a mirror for his shield
And on whose arms the sinister baton
Shows finally the bastard's side has won,
Just so, the gods, grown tired and impotent,
Are powerless to slow, much less prevent,
The glutton worm that gnaws their beings' center.
They stand aside to let Narcissus enter.
And he: *Old fellows, thanks. I'll see you get*
A steady pension and a place to sit
Whenever I decide to give a reading.
But seriously, guys, my heart is bleeding
To see you looking like you saw your grave.
You want a girl? A boy? Here, take a slave.
You got your pick. One less won't trouble me.
So glum, old chums? Well how's about some poetry?
A hundred servants, hearing his command,
Spring forth to feed the foolscap to his hand,
A thousand pages each, nay, many more
For him to read, his volume swelling to a roar
Louder than Atlas', feeling first the weight he bore.

Meanwhile, the only god not at this scene
Is wakened from his nap, and he feels mean.

Those Titans! Are they back? asks angered Zeus.
I'll give them hell for meddling with the truce
And see them gone for good. He quickly dresses
And hurries down; and if a word expresses,
Or could express, the wrath that fills the face
Of him who once flung Saturn into space
Or cast Poseidon deep beneath the sea,
I cannot find it in the *O.E.D.*
He follows the strange sounds to find their source,
Sputtering, snorting like a vengeful horse
Who, seeing on the ground the one who whipped him,
Rears up to crush him to the earth that tripped him.
Just so, the Father of the great immortals
Rushes in thunder to the city's portals.
The sights that greet him there are so amazing
He wonders if some other god's been raising
The Trojan dead from Hades' deep abysses.
But now he spies the problem: Our Narcissus.
And who might you be? asks our startled poet.
Before this day is out you'll surely know it,
Replies the Father of the Gods. *One law we keep*
In heaven, sir, is to respect my sleep.
Your poems, sir, which seem of endless number
Seemed very bad when they disturbed my slumber;
Now wide awake and having heard your verse
I venture the opinion it is worse.
We have our poets here, my noble sons,
And need no surplus of your wretched puns.
If you are all the poet Earth has left,
I'd sooner it had none, and be bereft,
For when the bread is cooked from wormy meal
An empty plate possesses much appeal,
And it is better far, I say, to starve

Than eat a steak a chainsaw could not carve.
I, maledictus, in ignem aeternum!
As for your poems, we'll be glad to burn 'em.
In short, your sorry offering is refused.
To be quite blunt, sir, we are not amused.
He speaks, and from his hand a million volts
Of lightning sizzle forth in crackling bolts
That cloak Narcissus in a greasy smoke.
You'd be a poet, sir? That's quite a joke.
At least I have such mercy in my heart
That I can fix it so you look the part!
The smoke begins to clear, and to the eyes
Of all the gods come sparkles of surprise,
For on the spot where late the poet read
A monstrous thing now rears its hoary head—
See Auden's wrinkles coursing to its chin,
Pound's leather neck and Delmore Schwartz's grin,
Red, buggy eyes from Thomas, Cummings' hair,
And aft Miss Amy Lowell's derrière,
And, for a lasting insult, Sandburg's nose,
And, finally, some of Edith Sitwell's clothes.
Thus, to administer the *coup-de-grace*,
Apollo comes to hold the looking glass
Wherein Narcissus now may see the face
He carries to his final resting-place.
The mirror cracks, and with a puppy's cries
Narcissus, down the quaking mountain, flies,
Pursued by all his hungry retinue
Who know the foot's now in the other shoe
And plan for him, perhaps, a victory barbecue.

The Drive-In

When my father and mother forsake me, then the Lord
will take me up.

—*Psalm 27*

Ars Poetica

Sweet music makes the same old story new.
That is a lie, but it will have to do.

Among Philistines

The night before they meant to pluck his eyes
He caught his tale at six on Action News—
Some blow-dried moron blabbing the bald lies
The public swallowed as "Official Views."

After a word for douche, Delilah made
A live appearance and was interviewed.
Complaining what a pittance she was paid,
She plugged the film she starred in in the nude.

Unbearable, he thought, and flipped the switch,
Lay sleepless on the bed in the bright room
Where every thought brought back the pretty bitch
And all the Orient of her perfume,

Her perfect breasts, her hips and slender waist,
Matchless among the centerfolds of Zion,
Which summoned to his tongue the mingled taste
Of honey oozing from the rotted lion;

For now his every mumble in the sack
(Bugged, of course, and not a whisper missed)
Would be revealed in lurid paperback
"As told to" Sheba Sleaze, the columnist.

Beefcake aside, he was a man of thought
Who heretofore had kept to the strict law:
For all the cheap celebrity it brought
He honestly deplored that ass's jaw,

The glossy covers of their magazines
With taut chains popping on his greasy chest,
The ads for razors with the corny scenes
And captions: *Hebrew Hunk Says We Shave Best!*

Such were his thoughts; much more severe the dreams
That sped him through his sleep in a wild car:
Vistas of billboards where he lathered cream,
Gulped milk, chugged beer, or smoked a foul cigar,

And this last image, this, mile after mile—
Delilah, naked, sucking on a pair
Of golden shears, winking her lewdest smile
Amid a monumental pile of hair

And blaring type: *The Babe Who Buzzed the Yid!*
Starring in JUST A LITTLE OFF MY HEAD.
He noted how his locks demurely hid
Those monstrous tits. And how her lips were red,

Red as his eyes when he was roused at seven
To trace back to its source the splendid ray
Of sunlight streaming from the throat of Heaven
Commanding him to kneel and thus to pray:

"Lord God of Hosts, whose name cannot be used
Promotion-wise, whose face shall not adorn
A cornflake box, whose trust I have abused:
Return that strength of which I have been shorn

That we might smite this tasteless *shiksa* land
With hemorrhoids and rats, with fire and sword.
Forgive my crime. Put forth thy fearsome hand
Against them and their gods, I pray thee, Lord."

So, shorn and strengthless, led through Gaza Mall
Past shoeshop, past boutique, Hallmark, and Sears,
He held his head erect and smiled to all
And did not dignify the scene with tears,

Knowing that God could mercifully ordain,
For punishment, the blessing in disguise.
"Good riddance," he said, whispering to the pain
As searing, the twin picks hissed in his eyes.

Monsieur Magus

There are moments of sentimental and mystical experience . . .
that carry an enormous sense of inner authority and illumination
with them when they come. But they come seldom, and they do not
come to everyone; and the rest of life makes either no connection
with them, or tends to contradict them more than it confirms them.
                                                    —*William James*

In the South of France the peasants had the gall
To squint and snicker when they read my name,
Hold discourse with a hydrant or a wall,
Falling through manholes in their silly game.
What did their cries of "Waldo!" signify?
How could my faithful camel miss the turns
And bring me here, while in the winter sky
The star, albeit faintly, plainly burns?

Too many years of study by the dim
Glow of the midnight oil have left these eyes
Two cloudy windows on a clouded mind.
Now I wonder at the meaning of that hymn
That lifted up our thoughts to touch the skies.
Wonder and wander. The blind shall lead the blind.

Letter from Carthage

"To Carthage then I came
But found it overrated.
The shops all seemed the same;
The theatre was dated.

"That 'cauldron of desire'
My guidebook slyly hints at?
Old fleshpots black with fire
That one could only wince at.

"I have tasted every sin
And nothing could be duller.
Brown monochromes of skin
Suffice for local colour.

"This chap, this 'Augustine,'
Is much to be mistrusted.
The staff at Michelin
Should have the fellow busted.

"One sees him in his room
In the act of self-expression,
Springs squeaking in the gloom.
Sic, his 'confession.'

"My dreams of thigh and breast
Now come to me abstractly.
Carthago? Delenda est.
My sentiments, exactly.

"I would sell my soul for one night
Of unencumbered lust.
I search through endless sunlight.
My shoes are filled with dust."

Iago to His Torturers

Tighter, me boys! One half-twist on that screw
And the wee piggy'll pop like a green bean.
Tighter! I said. And if the bloody shoe
Won't fit, ah, make it fit. My foot, I mean.
Let me my tendons plink, boys, lovely boys.
Tune up the rack. I love it, every minute.
Enjoy me whilst you can, like kids with toys.
Remember, *I* won't have to face the Senate.

And when the Maiden's fired, while hoists and cranks
Pinwheel me like a flea-bit dog-day dog,
Maybe you'll get it, how I did it so
We'd come to this, who like my pleasure slow.
Say Emilia wasn't handy with the flog.
It's all in the wrist. For this relief, much thanks.

Horatio's Philosophy

Absented from felicity a year
In the back room let by his maiden aunts,
He let his hair grow long and pierced one ear,
Staring at cards Reynaldo mailed from France.

The scenes which they depicted gave him pause.
Stranger than Pliny (he had flunked the course),
In violation of all natural laws
A lady copulated with a horse.

If such as that could be, how stale and flat
Would seem the stupid tale he'd sworn to write:
The spider nesting in the old king's hat,
The late appearance of the northern lights,

Simple adultery and the rancid stew
Which he'd passed on but cost the crown its life,
His fat friend's garter tangling with his shoe,
Pitching him forward on his letter-knife,

And worse, that senile windbag and his daughter,
The former shafted with a curtain rod,
The latter diving into six-inch water.
This was the stuff of tragedy? Dear God.

The memo came from Osric, now the Chief
Of Royal Information: *Get to work!*
Keep the thing scandalous, and keep it brief.
Action and jokes. Make everyone a jerk

Except, of course, King Fortinbras. Let him
(Deus ex machina) arrive in time
To get lard-ass's blessing. You can trim
Most of the facts. Put in some crime

To make us look legitimate. And need
I mention that you've missed your deadline—twice?
Next week. At latest. Then, as we agreed,
You'd best get out of town. Take my advice.

And so he sat there hours, thinking hard.
Paris? Why not? But he was tired and broke
And known by face to every border guard.
The truth was bad enough. *This* was a joke.

His skills, such as they were, lay in debating
Questions of ethics, and his style of prose
Would never keep the groundlings salivating
With prurient puns. He'd seen Lord Osric's shows.

But what was truth? Wasn't it, all things said,
Whatever the authorities deemed right?
The rest was silence, for the dead were dead.
Feeling much better, he began to write.

The first draft took two days. He hired a ghost,
Dictating while he packed and paced the floor.
By Friday he had made it to the coast;
Sunday, stood knocking at Reynaldo's door.

Also to the Tower

My first thought was, he lied in every word,
That hoary cripple, with malicious eye
Askance to watch the working of his lie
On mine, and mouth scarce able to afford
Suppression of the glee, that pursed and scored
Its edge, at one more victim gained thereby.

My second thought was, *Kill the s.o.b.*—
  "Seminal scholar," tweedy, old school tie,
  (Was it the Phi Bete key that caught my eye?)
Who set me on this course, for it is *he*
Who bears the sole responsibility
  For my dark woes, his victim gained thereby.

How I hung upon his words! That tenured sage
  Who puffed his briar and spewed ash on my clothes
  While scribbling in my margins cryptic prose
Directives meant to steer my callow rage
To holy war against the empty page
  That has an ending . . . where? God only knows.

Here is your Strange Device, he whispered, *known*
  But to the few. He delved into his bag
  And pulled therefrom a putrid swatch of rag.
Defend it well! It was a white whale, sewn
Upon a field of white. He carried on
  About the symbolism: *See? Your flag!*

Then took my arm and led me to my mare
  (Only three legs but otherwise OK),
  Gave me my cloak and sword and six months' pay

(Personal check!), a snapshot of the fair
Languishing captive maid with flaxen hair
  (A few black roots), and sped me on my way.

With his guffaws still chugging in my ear
  And the sealed orders snug against my chest,
  I spurred the nag and set forth on the quest
While grackles overhead wheeled low to jeer.
The road was narrow, but the way seemed clear.
  A sickly yellow sun hung in the West.

How shall I chronicle the trials I knew?
  I shan't. So much for that. Let it suffice
  To say the ways were slick with filthy ice,
The fields with filthy slush through which a few
Black tangled stems of briar forlornly grew.
  The driven sleet picked at my skin like lice.

After a year or so, I thought to stop
  And ask directions: *Sirrah! Might I ask
  The shortcut to . . . .* Perhaps my rubber mask
With the red fright-wig frizzing at the top
Alarmed him, for he signaled to a cop.
  I hurried off, *still* vague as to my task.

Then I bethought myself to take a look
  Inside my mentor's envelope. (How grave
  His look had been!) The thing was empty, save
For the dustjacket photo from his book,
The Archetypes of Wrath. My fingers shook.
  I made for shelter in a nearby cave.

As when some imbecile turns up his Coke
  And peers into the mouth to see the fly
  The guys have warned him of; and in his eye

It dumps, while they, like victims of a stroke,
Choke and redden, convulsed so with their joke
  They fall upon the ground and prostrate lie;

Thus did *I* feel, on whom this jest was played.
  For *this* had I disdained wine, wench, and food?
  Was *he* the holy grail my tracks pursued?
I plunged my dagger at my breast. The blade
Slid back into the handle. Undismayed,
  I tried again. Again, the same ensued.

Dark ran my thoughts, that somehow I might kill
  Not just myself, but take that bastard too.
  I turned. My mind was made. The slug-horn blew,
Unmaking it, echoing forth with shrill
Notes from the summit of a squatty hill
  Where loomed at last, though somewhat overdue,

The fabled Tower where my sage had said
  The trail would end. In truth, I knew the place:
  Ivory brick, twin boulders at the base,
The shaft thrust upward toward the rounded, red
Turret where pennants whitely streamed. I shed
  Piecemeal my mail, so eager was my pace!

Significant Form! So manly did I feel
  I plunged through the gate, pausing not to heed
  The motto cut above. (I could not read
Italian, anyway.) A rusty squeal
Snickered behind me, and I heard the steel
  Click of the lock, yet did not check my speed.

Climbing the thing, I then at length could see
  The blasted prospect of that endless plain,
  Where, popping up like toadstools after rain,

More towers stood, on each a clown like me
Vainly searching his trousers for the key
  (The key? *What* key?) to set him free again.

Thus, it began, my lasting tenure there,
  Or *here*, that is, here where I have my own
  Booze in the bottom drawer to sip alone,
Which tends to help. The comforts here are spare
But adequate: some books, a desk and chair,
  Jacket and pipe, false beard and telephone—

Which just now rings: *"I called up to remind*
  You, sir . . ." Familiar voice, though girl or boy
  I cannot say. *". . . today. Would it annoy*
You if . . ." Very familiar. *". . . somehow find*
A moment for my latest . . ." Would *I* mind?
  Nothing, dear childe, would give us greater joy!

B. 1885; D. 1980

I

Grandpater's wit, the Empire's plum,
Was sharp as the ends of his moustaches.
Lord Bucky (he was several years our junior)
Once crawled beneath the table during tea
And soiled Grandpater's spats. "Enough, Sir!"
Cried Grand P. "D'ye take me for an omnibus?"
At the old Queen's demise, Grandpater wept
And lived, moreover, eleven years more.

II

At Rugby all was cricket. No lad peached.
When I was sent up to Brasenose, Old Crolmonderly
Was yet in the chair. I looked to Rome a term;
Then looked the other way. When war came
I resigned my living to do my duty. That is,

III

"Buy Imperial," advised Cripswitch. I sold,
And for weeks thereafter was thought a cad,
Which is to say, until the crash. Cripswitch,
Incidentally, was identified by his dentures.

IV

Epitaph
Here lies my dearest wife, or, rather, sits:
Bridge was at seven-sharp; at eight, the Blitz.

V

Hoolywod bloddy unsufferable

The Decline of the West

Help is on the way! cried the decadent
Grenadier, but after the crème de menthe
And hog jowls all I cared about was getting
Home safely. I rang for the sedan chair,
But finding no one below save the peanut-
Vendor and Hans, his smirking aide-de-camp,
I hurried off, ignoring their remarks
About my rank and socks. My venom rose.
Near the deserted barricades a bum
Came up to me and said, *Friend, can you spare
A sou? I ain't had a bite in a week.*
So I killed him, hiding the wretched body
Under a heap of empty seltzer bottles
Left by the Nihilists. The plot grew thick.
In every quarter my very name was "Mudd."
However, I continued as before
To frequent the same haunts, knowing full well
The worth of keeping up appearances;
Renting the same flat, hating the concierge
For his six trunks of flapjacks to my three.
Inside a week the old regime was toppled.
Meetings were called. Piles of lorgnettes and wigs
Were confiscated and burned in public places.
Long lists of names were posted in the Metro.
Suspect of sundry factions, I fled
To Kansas, dodging cabbages and brickbats,
Not knowing in the darkness of my oil barrel
The point at which this new frontier began
Or how "our man" would find me in the sewers

Posing as Ed, the Polish refugee.
Yet find me he did. Warmly did I clasp him.
My bosom heaved. Still, he remained aloof,
Demanding that I show the secret sign,
Which I did. He wiped the pie from his eyes
And solemnly returned my first embrace
But lapsed soon after into utter silence,
As if he could not justify his actions,
As if the axeman's sorrows were his own.

1916

. . . some corner of a foreign field
That is forever England.
—*Rupert Brooke, "1914"*

Other Rank.

"A" Company
1st Munster Grenadiers
Cape Helles
1 January

So thank Mum for the book of poetry
Which I've made use of, but to tell the truth
It's other than 'the red sweet wine of youth'
What's pouring by the pint of late from me.
Wasn't quite sure of catching what he means,
This bit about 'a richer dust concealed.'
The only rich spot in *this* foreign field
Is where we dug the regiment's latrines.

'Tis said we'll soon be off. Perhaps the Turk
Will rush down when the boats are out to sea
And stumble in. So if our dodges work
The *Times* can praise our 'artful strategy.'
As for the poems, say 'Send more!' to Mum—
Whatever's easiest on the bleedin' bum.

Henry.

21 Carlyle Mansions
Cheyne Walk, S.W.
Chelsea
February 14

Of course, of course, his was a *sacrifice*;
Or, rather, as there seems small likelihood

Of compensation, or of *any* good
Resulting, one must label imprecise
The word he leans first toward, so dear the price
Exacted from us in the red sweet blood
Of our young men; thus, one is understood
To *use* the term (since no less will suffice
Than that which must be said) in conscious error
For which he makes apologies but never,
Questions of style aside, would wish revoked,
Such being the times: headlong, relentless terror
To which our destinies are tied, are yoked,
The day of bright young things now fled forever.

Winston.
           6th Royal Scots Fusiliers
           Somewhere in the Field
           March 15

My Dearest Puss: Have had great trouble sleeping.
Penance has been to dream-watch from a hill
While ranks of our lads, like blind swimmers leaping
Into nothingness, charge the far trench until
Not one remains. The Black Dog lingers still
To plague my waking thoughts. Dear Puss, it seems
These Ides of March bode your poor Caesar ill:
Miles Gloriosus laid low by his dreams!

At dawn the 5.9s caught our wiring teams
In no-man's-land; all dead save a young chap
With shrapnel in both legs. Incessant screams
Led us to find him halfway down a sap.
He'd worked one piece out, and he *kissed* it, Clemmie:

O Beauty, wot a Blighty pass you've gi' me!

Cathleen.

The Candler Theatre
New York City
April 1

This evening, in the wings, I missed my cue
And caused a crucial scene to be replayed.
Someone *was* there; I fancied it was you—
Sunny, alive, so dreadfully betrayed.
Our play is *Justice*. It is like most plays,
Cleverly fashioned, filled with complication,
Destined, one would assume, for ready praise.

I have allowed your letters' publication.

My April Fool, how much we missed the mark!
So much for me to learn, so much to teach you—
Our hearts knew what our bodies *should* have known.
Forgive me, dearest. I hold stage alone
And you have vanished in a house grown dark.

Beautiful History, I can't quite reach you.

Subaltern, R.N.D.

Aboard *Ajax*
Trebuki Bay, Skyros
23rd April

The grove is called Mesedhi. One's aware
Of spices in the sea breeze, thyme and sage,
As if the present met with some lost age
And many heroes congregated there.
It is precisely as Achilles said:
Rather I'd choose laboriously to bear

A weight of woes, and breathe the vital air
Than reign the sceptred monarch of the dead.

Is it a year? How soon one's imprints fade
Into the grain of anonymity.
The shepherd who is owner came to speak
Of keeping up the site, saying it made
Him proud the cross had borne some words in Greek.
He tried, but could not spell them out for me.

ἐνθαδε κεῖται
ὁ δουλοσ τοῦ Θεοῦ
ἀνθυπολοχ αγοσ τοῦ
Ἀγγλικου ναυτικου
ἀποθανων ὑπερ τῆς
ἀπελευθεπωσεως τῦς
κων·πουλεως ἀπό
τῶν τουρκων

Here lies
the servant of God
Sub-lieutenant in the
English Navy
Who died for the
deliverance of Constantinople from
the Turks

A Short History of the New South

"Pass the biscuits," said Pappy, pursing his lips,
But the part I remember best was the collect call
From our spy at the National Archives. "The cause,
I fear, is lost, Suh," the spy replied. "Our retreat
Has been repulsed." "The silver!" cried Mammy
And we grabbed our hoes and headed for Grammaw's grave,
Expecting the worst. Come spring the worst was over
And we dragged the trunks back up to the big house,
Ending the era with supper and lots of biscuits.
Pappy, picking his tooth, said, "Pass the yams,"
but no one had the heart to tell him the truth.
"Bull Run!" yelled Pee Wee, the subject changed,
And Pappy forgot the yams and got drunk instead.
I woke from my bale of paper money to find
The darkies loading their Cadillacs. They were heading
For Baltimore, they claimed, to harvest the nylon crop.
So we plowed the cotton under and planted magnolias
But missed their singing so much we pawned our whips
To buy a gramophone on the installment plan.
As we had no records, we had to make do without.
"Pass Ol' Blue," said Pappy, closing his eyes,
And nothing improved. Pee Wee got up from the table
And run off to join the White Sox, where he made
A name for hisself after changing his name. Myself,
I stayed at home to fight the school board. "Hurry back!"
Cried Mammy, waving her flag at the bus.
I took my time. One day she called collect:
"Pappy's right poorly. Y'all come." I came,
Arriving in time to grab my hoe from the toolshed

And help Pappy dig her a hole right next to Grammaw.
We cashed the insurance and bought us a TV and dish,
Which we used to improve our minds and accents,
And when the last of the place was sold off to the tourists
We pooled our cash and built this fine new restaurant.
"Pass the pizza," says Pappy, stroking his silver beard.

Stranded in the Jungle

November 18, 1978

We were stranded in the jungle, and we were feeling bad
Because of how we worried about our dear old Dad.
Even in the jungle we thought that it was odd
The way his latest sermons never mentioned God,
But when the day was over and we listened in the night,
The dark beyond the floodlights told us he was right,
And so we had to trust him to keep the dark away:
Our Dad which art in Heaven, hear us sinners pray.

>Meanwhile, back in the States:
>*Baby, baby, the man is no good*

>Meanwhile, back in the jungle:
>*ah ahah ah ah*

He preached to us each evening, and something in his voice
Convinced us that we really had no other choice;
Then he summoned visions of houses, streets, and parks,
And a house of worship for Jesus, Him, and Marx,
Where we would duly gather so he could enter last
To lead us on like extras in his supporting cast.
The world that stood against us could perish on its own.
His left hand held a Bible; the right, a microphone.

>Meanwhile, back in the States:
>*Baby, baby, the man is no good*
>*O baby, baby, the man is no good*

>Meanwhile, back in the jungle:
>*ah ahah ah ah*
>*ah ahah ah ah*

Our eyes had seen the Glory, so when the plane came in
We knew the final reckoning was ready to begin.
We took our loaded rifles and waited by the plane,
And when they tried to board it we fired and fired again.
We gathered at the mess hall to find out what to think.
Dad's eyes were hidden from us by glasses black as ink,
But when he handed each of us the little cup of pink,
He said, "This is my blood. I shed it for you. Drink."

      Meanwhile, back in the States:
      Baby, baby, the man is no good
      O baby, baby, the man is no good
      O baby, baby, baby, that man is no good

      Meanwhile, back in the jungle:
      ah ahah ah ah
         ah ahah ah ah
            ah ahah ah ah

Laird of the Maze

Despite he was a frog and relished flies,
His personality possessed no taint.
No warmth flowed in his veins; he suffered this,
But none that knew him could have thought him evil.
Was lackey to no vices; but one joy, his penchant
For moonlit swimming at the maze's center.
At midnight sought his native element,
The pool of scum. None saw his nakedness.

That maze was Life! All others wandered there
Seeking to solve its puzzle; only he
Construed the pattern of its form in abstract
And bore it like the impress of a signet,
For the hedges of that maze were darkly lush
And knit so thickly as to seem impenetrable.
There one could hear the Master at his pleasure—
The dull splash of a dishrag being slapped.

The pathways of his argument, his wit,
The winding traverse of his metaphors,
His irony and syntax, like the maze,
Confounded all, myself among the least.
Yet I must try to . . . true, he were a frog,
But a kindred soul lay cloaked beneath that green skin:
Idealist, poet, scholar, who lacked only
The spark of camaraderie, the firm handshake.

So years I lay here in this crumbling tower
Waiting for moonrise and the loathsome croak
Of the frog-man's nightly cry for company.

Mere silence echoes now. The pool is still,
As I gaze into my shoe, which contains a foot,
As I try to piece together what his life meant:
Fallen, the rightful laird, last of his line,
A slick spot drying on the courtyard stone.

Anacreontic

You drink to piss it all away
You play it tough to seize the day
Toss out more chips and spread your stuff
Or end it with enough's enough
But it doesn't matter what you say
They always seem to call your bluff
It doesn't matter what you do
When you're through you're through

You hit the dirt and slide and slide
Flag down a fox for one last ride
Steal second and go on to third
Or cock the piece and kill the bird
You hope you pray the throw is wide
They'll hold you hold you to your word
And get you down to get you out
When you're out you're out

It's not you didn't do your worst
To quench your everlasting thirst
You kissed them and you made them cry
And didn't wonder how or why
You never even got to first
Toss in the sponge and say good-bye
And let them strip you of the crown
When you're down you're down

It seems a pity seems a crime
They'll get you get you every time
It doesn't matter where you go

Somehow they always seem to know
You're out there but it's closing time
Up to your nuts in drifting snow
Up to your eyes by frosty dawn
When you're gone you're gone

Scenes from the Playroom

Now Lucy with her family of dolls
Disfigures Mother with an emery board,
While Charles, with match and rubbing alcohol,
Readies the struggling cat, for Chuck is bored.
The young ones pour more ink into the water
Through which the latest goldfish gamely swims,
Laughing, pointing at naked, neutered Father.
The toy chest is a Buchenwald of limbs.

Mother is so lovely; Father, so late.
The cook is off, yet dinner must go on.
With onions as her only cause for tears
She hacks the red meat from the slippery bone,
Setting the table, where the children wait,
Her grinning babies, clean behind the ears.

In Place of an Elegy

Facing a gray morning, I read "The Joys
Of Lasting Friends," the last F essay written
By one K. R., who was, for a time, my student.
A flash of rimless glasses. Back row.
The radiator. Surely someone must know
The answer. Surely. Minds like bolts of satin
Unroll, course through my fingers, are forgotten,
Those who are neither beautiful nor wise.

"The Joys of Lasting Friends." No irony.
The firing squad inside the radiator.
All victims gone by May. No matter.
And someone writes, "Much noise but little heat
And that is nothing, much." Empty seats.
Faces of rimless glass. "The photo flatters
Her," I offer. Wind rustling through blank paper.
Fingers touching wounds. Her childhood bleeds.

For lasting friends can see right thru you but
Still see you thru. And what to say this morning?
Transparent things. Ranks of shade now forming
Against the wall. Surely she knew. A shot
With no report. And here I singled out
A word as "clever." No answers. The straining
Of fabric. None remember. From the burning
Car there were screams, her own voice screaming.

Mimosa

Patience, patience,
Patience dans l'azur!
Chaque atome de silence
Est la chance d'un fruit mûr!
— *Paul Valéry, "Palme"*

Thrusting fernlike leaves
And pink, abundant blooms
Upward to brush the eaves,
Your copious presence looms
Over my garden plot.
Cut to the ground but not
Killed by the chainsaw, Tree,
You have withstood the test
Of winter to protest
Such cruel surgery.

True to self-seeking plans
You flaunt your gaudy show-
Girl powderpuffs and fans
Until the plants that grow
Beneath you, even the weeds,
Submit before the needs
That rob the hours of day-
Light from my wrinkled green
Pepper and blighted bean.
You *will* have your way.

Window and open door
Admit you with the season,
Proclaiming you endure

For no apparent reason
Except to fill the room
With profligate perfume.
You mock my ill-regard
And demonstrate a will
To propagate until
You fill both house and yard!

When I was a child
The field behind the drive-in
Provided you a wild
Environment to thrive in.
I stripped your slippery bark
And threw spears at the dark
Imagined shapes of terror.
Thirty years have made
Them real; all have strayed
To darker woods of error.

Nel mezzo del cammin…
How lightly words are spoken
Until they come to mean
One's own design is broken,
And all he sees ahead
Are the alluring dead
Who have nothing to give—
Eternally awake
With thirst they cannot slake,
Still asking how to live.

Mimosa sensitiva,
You show a better way.
Like some true believer

Bent to the earth to pray,
Each day with the late sun
You fold your leaves upon
The stem as if to hoard
Your unexpended powers
Until those lucid hours
When all will be restored.

What questions I could ask!
You might have words for one
Who sets himself a task
He fears cannot be done.
Perhaps your hard-won beauty
Declares that one's sole duty
Is to send from the heart-
Wood such resurgent growth
As must amaze us both—
L'arte pour l'arte.

Thus, through the harsh winters
Of private discontent,
Nurturing vital centers
Which are not easily spent,
While we may not know
To what heights we may grow,
We bide time and repair
That any seed born from
Sheer impulse might become
A tree that the mind can bear.

The Drive-In

Under the neon sign he stands,
My father, tickets in his hands.
Now it is my turn; all the while,
Knee-deep in stubs he tries to smile,
Crying, *You'll love it. Slapstick. Fights.*
One dollar, please. Please dim your lights.
I pay and enter. Mother waits
In a black truck with dangling plates
And snag-toothed grillwork idling there
On the front row. She combs her hair
And calls for me to take my place.
The moon-lights dying on her face,
She lights another cigarette
And starts to sing the alphabet.
Quickly, I turn the speaker on:
The soundtrack is a steady drone
Of snoring. With his pockets full
My father gathers up his wool,
His pink tongue rolling up and down.
A wolf, dainty in hat and gown,
Appears, sneaking across the screen
Above my father. Then the scene
Expands to show a flock of sheep.
The wolf is drooling. In his sleep
My father smiles, my mother sighs,
And dabbing gently at her eyes
She goes across to sniff his breath.
A shepherd clubs the wolf to death,
The sheep dance lightly in the sun,

And now the feature has begun:
Union Pacific is its name.
I know it, know it frame by frame,
The tyranny of separation,
The lack of all communication
From shore to shore, the struggle through
Smashed chairs and bottles toward the true
Connection of a spike of gold.
I fall asleep. The night is cold.
And waking to the seat's chill touch
I hear the last car's slipping clutch,
And on the glass a veil of frost
Obscures this childhood I have lost.
The show is over. Time descends.
And no one tells me how it ends.

Our Hearts Were Growing Up

Our hearts were growing up.
The boughs hung heavy with them,
Pendulous on their sterns
Like balls of tarnished brass.

But they began as blossoms
Somehow surviving the frost,
And swelled with pale greenness.
Soon our hearts darkened.

Flies glided past our hearts.
The season gained its fullness.
Our hearts remained indifferent
To the passage of the shadows,

And ripe, heavy with worms,
Plunged to the earth below,
Exposing their inner secrets.
The bough swung back, relieved.

Bees sucked our hearts away
To blend bitter honey.
The black seeds of our hearts
Turned in the crops of birds.

Broken by cloven hooves,
Our hearts lay in the sun.
At length our hearts were gone.
They left no bones behind.

Untitled

*In the morning light a line
Stretches forever. There my unlived life
Rises and I resist . . .*
                                    —Louis Simpson

In which I rise untroubled by my dreams.
In which my unsung theories are upheld
By massive votes. In which my students' themes
Move me. In which my name is not misspelled.

In which I enter strangers' rooms to find,
Matched in unbroken sets, immaculate,
My great unwritten books. In which I sign
My name for girls outside a convent gate.

In which I run for daylight and my knee
Does not fold up. In which the home teams win.
In which my unwed wife steeps fragrant tea
In clean white cups. In which my days begin
With scenes in which, across unblemished sands,
Unborn, my children come to touch my hands.

Bearing & Distance

W. T. C.
1895-1977

The lady has left her cigarette butts in the ashtray,
But that's okay, I watched her smoke them all,
Matching her puff for puff right down to the end.

They're the same brand, and if you project a line
Due north from here across the face of earth
You will come to a region of cold, a place of ice.

The man who is standing there behind the tripod
Is smoking one and looking through a glass
And soon enough will be sighting down on me,

Backsighting, foresighting, moving me left or right
With waves of his ungloved hand and trails of smoke,
Curses and coughs until he finds me good.

I pound a stake in the earth, center a tack in the top
And drive that home, cross-haired, double-centered.
The mark is love and the lady is the earth

And the hand that stubbed the last spark in the tray
Will guide me into sweet perfumes and darkness
As the line continues northward, out of sight,

As the man behind the tripod waves both arms,
A mounting hawk now fading: *Good. Good-bye.*
The line recedes to where the smoke still curls.

The Simplification

For Donna, 30

There were days to be gotten through, and days before,
But then there was the day I lashed you to the bedposts
Crying, "I can kiss you, I can kill you, I can
Make you sane enough to pass the bar exams." That day
I said, or meant to say, that the odd afternoon
We dodged the falling parts of the exploding city,
Pink mists of flesh, the rain of rusted scrap that fell
On the heads of those less fortunate, I said
That the day we climbed the dark stair to set aside
Our jewelry, our clothes, there on the level
Above the street where cars continued passing,
We fell, at last, into the hands of ourselves alone
To rip the sheets for bandages. Then, that day,
You taught me what I knew: I would be the one
To make the most of you. Then we made love again

So now we are here, this summit, this glaring stone,
And a shore where two smooth lines of white converge
Down which the afflicted struggle, sad of the earth.
You in your gown of white, I in my white robe,
Our hands that have touched too many wrong things
Having led a trail across bleached rock to where
We stand, receive, open and say to all,
"This is the point from which you start again.
The past ends here in love and the touch of skin.
See us and touch, and by that touch be healed
Of all your hesitations. Do not fear."
By this, I mean to say the simplest thanks:
Whatever we have asked for has been given,
As now, descending the dark stair, I say this truth:
The sunlight melts like copper in your hair.

The Denouement

Who were those persons who chased us?
They were the last of the others.

Why must we always be running?
We are the last of our own.

Where is the shelter you spoke of?
Between us. All around us.

Shall we be safe until morning?
There is no doorway to enter.

How shall we live in this desert?
Just as we did in the farmlands.

How was it done in the farmlands?
Just as it shall be here.

What is the word for this place?
No one has ever used it.

When shall I hear the word?
Never, until it is spoken.

Who were my father and mother?
Trust me to keep your secret.

What is the mark on your forehead?
What is the mark on your cheek?

Acknowledgments

These poems, sometimes in different versions, first appeared in the following publications: *Barataria Review, Carolina Quarterly, Cedar Rock, Chronicles, Concho River Review, Cross Timbers, The Dark Horse* (Scotland), *Descant, Drastic Measures, Eclectic Literary Forum, Edge City Review, The Formalist, Grantmakers in the Arts, The Hudson Review, Key West Review, Light, Lucille, The Miscellany, The Mississippi Review, New and Experimental Writing, The New England Review, Pacific Review, Paintbrush, Plains Poetry Journal, Poetry, The Poetry Miscellany, Poetry Northwest, Pulpsmith, Red Jacket, The Review, River Styx, The Sewanee Review, Sparrow, Swallow's Tale, Tar River Poetry, The Texas Review, Vision.*

"The Garden Parasol" was commissioned for *The Stores of Joy: Writers Celebrate the North Carolina Museum of Art's Fiftieth Anniversary.*

Bearing & Distance © Cedar Rock Press, 1977.

The Narcissiad © Cedar Rock Press, 1981.

The Drive-In © University of Missouri Press, 1986.

Body Bags, in *Texas Poets in Concert: A Quartet* © University of North Texas Press, 1990.

The Area Code of God © Aralia Press, 1993.

COUNTERPOINTS

REAKTION BOOKS

COUNTERPOINTS

DIALOGUES BETWEEN MUSIC AND THE VISUAL ARTS

PHILIPPE JUNOD
Translation by Saskia Brown

Published by Reaktion Books Ltd
Unit 32, Waterside
44–48 Wharf Road
London N1 7UX, UK
www.reaktionbooks.co.uk

First published 2017
Copyright © Philippe Junod 2017
English-language translation by Saskia Brown

Parts of this book were originally published in French
as *Contrepoints: Dialogues entre musique et peinture*
by Philippe Junod (Contrechamps Editions, 2006)

Printed and bound in Great Britain
by TJ International, Padstow, Cornwall

A catalogue record for this book is available from the British Library

ISBN 978 1 78023 811 1

CONTENTS

Francesco Furini, *Painting, Music and Poetry*,
1624, oil on canvas.

PRELUDE

'To hear with eyes belongs to love's fine wit'
– Shakespeare, Sonnet 23

'The eye listens' – a perfect title for this book, if only Paul Claudel had not got there first. As for its symmetrical double, 'the ear sees', which would also have served my purposes, it sounds a little ridiculous, although why this should be is anyone's guess. So I settled for the polyphonic metaphor of *Counterpoints* as a way of pointing to the age-old interweaving of the arts of time and space. The intriguing intimacy between sight and hearing has captivated many, not least Jack Ox 'translating' music into painting,[1] Anne Blanchet in her 'visual music', André Evrard with his silent 'fugues' and Oscar Wiggli in his 'sound reliefs'. It is to these four artists and music lovers that I dedicate these pages.

'Boundary-crossing' arguably typifies the work of creative artists today, as the recurrence of terms such as intermedia, multimedia and mixed media in art criticism suggests. We are a far cry from the much-vaunted purism and 'splendid isolation' which prevailed from Lessing to Adorno and Greenberg. Ever since *ut musica pictura* replaced the time-honoured *ut pictura poesis*, Simonides' dictum that painting is akin to silent poetry could also be recast as *pictura muta musica*.

Introducing space into the arts of sound goes hand in hand with introducing time into the visual arts. Actions, situations, installations and happenings have all blown apart the rigidity of genres and the old 'system of the Fine Arts'. The legacy of the *Gesamtkunstwerk* seems more alive than ever. With music in museums, light shows in concerts, graphic scores and painted music, cinema, video, synaesthetic experiments and psychedelic displays, the old barriers can no longer

Eadem cantit et pingit, engraving in Jakob Balde, *Silvarum* (1643).

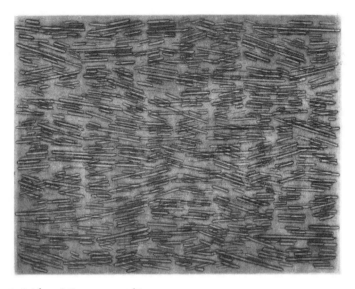

André Évrard, *Fugue,* 2003, etching.

resist, under the pressure of collaborations, dialogues, encounters, artists with dual vocations (visual arts and music) and other forms of interaction.

This situation did not arise out of nowhere, and it naturally tends to turn the spotlight on its antecedents, as we examine the past in the light of our contemporary world. We can note that two opposing aesthetics are constantly, if at times imperceptibly, at work, oscillating in a pendulum-like movement: a centripetal aesthetic committed to 'fraternity' between the arts, and a centrifugal aesthetic which differentiates and compartmentalizes means of expression. The aim of the following chapters is to describe a few episodes in this history.

We shall consider the *longue durée*, focusing on continuity and revival rather than on discontinuities. The very nature of the subject-matter dictates an inter-disciplinary approach, which has taken us beyond the boundaries of art history and music, and thus beyond the strict limits of our competence. May the reader forgive such a rash venture!

1
THE POLYPHONY OF MUSIC AND PAINTING

The relations between music and painting have become a popular field, as suggested by the extensive bibliography on the subject, and the many exhibitions and conferences devoted to the theme. Museums organize concerts, and musicians look to visual artists for collaborative projects and experimentation. One can almost define the art of the last half century – happenings, performances, sound installations and other *Sound Works*,[1] from *Fluxus* to musical theatre – in terms of decompartmentalization and the repudiation of frontiers.[2] Time has entered the visual arts, just as music now occupies space. Traditional categories no longer hold; in short, Lessing is turning in his grave.

But these interactions are nothing new. Painters have often been drawn to music. Leonardo painted the *Mona Lisa* surrounded by musicians, Delacroix's chapel in Saint-Sulpice was painted to the sound of the organ and Jean-Michel Jaquet's lines followed the heady strains of jazz. Many painters were inspired by composers (Wagner and Bach in particular), and inversely the list of musical works which pay tribute to painting is so long that it has already filled a whole book.[3] Musicians were sometimes collectors, for instance Emmanuel Chabrier or the singer Faure, who were among the most generous patrons of the Impressionists. Ernest Chausson, Claude Debussy and Igor Markevitch were discerning enthusiasts, and the artist's studio, where music figured prominently (as Ary Scheffer, Delacroix and Bazille bear out), was a natural meeting point for painters and artists.[4] Salons also played a part in bringing artists, musicians and writers together – around Arthur Fontaine, Henri Lerolle, Marguerite de Saint-Marceaux or the Natansons, for example.

Fruitful collaborations and encounters also took place in work for the stage, particularly opera. One should mention at least Max Slevogt's[5] and Oskar Kokoschka's stage sets and costumes for *The Magic Flute*,[6] and David Hockney's for Satie, Ravel, Poulenc and Stravinksy.[7] Dance, in which music fills the space, was another favourite field of collaboration, as illustrated by the *Ballets Russes*[8] and the *Ballets Suédois*. And Wagner's ideal of the *Gesamtkunstwerk* can still be felt in Kandinsky's experimentations for the stage, from the *Gelber Klang* (1912) to the staging, in Dessau in 1928, of Mussorgsky's *Pictures at an Exhibition*, using lighting effects and coloured forms.

Different sorts of personal relations also played an important role in relations between the arts. There were family relations, for example between brothers (Gerrit Sweelinck painted the portrait of the composer and organist Jan) or from father to son (Henri Dutilleux was the grandson of the painter Constant), couples (Fanny Mendelssohn and Wilhelm Hensel) and also friendships – famously Chopin and Delacroix, or Stravinsky and Picasso, who made portraits of each other.

Sometimes painters were themselves musicians, for instance Leonardo da Vinci, Gaudenzio Ferrari, Giorgione, Titian, Tintoretto,[9] Domenichino,[10] Salvator Rosa, Gainsborough,[11] Ingres, Delacroix, Gustave Doré, Redon, Kandinsky, Matisse and MOPP (Max Oppenheimer). The portrait of the artist playing an instrument was another frequent representation, of which the best-known examples are Jacopo Bassano, Evaristo Baschenis, Peter Lely, David Teniers, Jan Steen, Jacob Jordaens, Frans van Mieris, Jean-Baptiste Oudry, Gustave Courbet and Max Beckmann. But the list goes on, and includes a number of women: Marietta Robusti, called Tintoretta (daughter of the painter Jacopo), Lavinia Fontana, Sofonisba Anguissola, Artemisia Gentileschi (daughter of Orazio), Catharina van Hemessen (daughter of Jan) or Élisabeth Vigée-Le Brun. And, in another variation on this theme, Angelica Kauffmann depicts herself as torn between Music and Painting like a latter-day Hercules at the crossroads.

These combined talents were not restricted to earlier centuries. Mendelssohn was a gifted draughtsman, as was Paul Hindemith, and there have been several exhibitions of John Cage's work. The sculptor

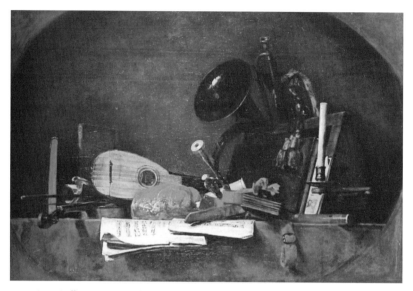

Anne Vallayer-Coster, *Still-life*, 1770, oil on canvas.

Pradier composed music, Lyonel Feininger wrote fugues and Schönberg's self-portraits are well known.[12] This raises the question of whether certain artists – Mikalojus Konstantinas Čiurlionis,[13] Alberto Savinio, Henri Nouveau, Michel Ciry and Jean Apothéloz, for example – should be regarded as painters or composers. Louis Soutter turned from the violin to drawing, Robert Strübin from the piano to painting and André Bosshard, the son of the painter and great music lover Rodolphe Théophile, moved on from the flute. It was only after much hesitation that Paul Klee gave up his position as violinist in the Bern Orchestra.

Materializing Music

Artists have always enjoyed representing the world of music,[14] and a rich repertory of musical images has accumulated across the centuries. Some portraits stand out, such as Delacroix's or Ingres's masterful

Paganini, Repine's *Mussorgsky* or Stravinsky's particularly seductive iconography.[15] An artist can also be the subject of a musical portrait (for example, *Le Travail du peintre*, Eluard's poems set to music by Poulenc, 1956), or even inspire an opera (Berlioz's *Benvenuto Cellini* or Hindemith's *Mathis der Maler*).[16] Another common theme depicted by artists is the concert, whether sacred, profane, private, public, courtly or popular; or the instruments themselves, particularly those with sensuous forms,[17] such as lutes and violins, which have long been used for the challenge of rendering perspective, and which have also figured prominently in many a still-life, from the Baroque to Cubism, Caravaggio or Baschenis to Juan Gris. Other instruments served as the painting's 'canvas': one could fill a whole museum with painted organ doors and harpsichord cases often signed by masters such as Schiavone or Tintoretto.

So dialogues between music and painting took place in the space of the portrait, the genre scene and the still-life. These representations can be used by musicologists as documentary evidence of particular instruments, or as proof of how they were played in different periods, yet the images are not always as straightforward as they may seem. The art historian should issue a word of warning here concerning different levels of meaning, and the symbolic dimension of objects, since without this an interpretation may be anachronistic or simply absurd. For instance, concerts of angels with dozens of musicians playing away, as in Gaudenzio Ferrari's painting adorning the dome of Saronno near Milan (1536), is no reflection of contemporary reality. It is, first of all, a 'heavenly' concert, but it also mixes 'high' and 'low' instruments, which simply never occurred, for reasons of acoustics. The victory of Apollo's lyre over Pan's or Marsyas' flutes is historically determined,[18] and this social hierarchy between strings and wind instruments was anyway never absolute, since bagpipes, usually the preserve of peasants and shepherds, were sometimes played by angels, just as in reality their court version was played in the circle of Marie Antoinette.

Overall, the image of Music is twin-faced, sometimes it is associated with Paradise and spirituality, and sometimes with death (it accompanies the *Danses macabres*), hell (we need only think of Hieronymus Bosch) and the pleasures of the flesh. Thus the lute, although often paired with the harp (King David) or the organ (St Cecilia), in Memling's altarpieces for example, was also the favourite instrument of Venus and Venetian courtesans, accompanying dawn love serenades. The violin was heir to Apollo's or Orpheus' lyre, but also the attribute of dancing masters, and thus an object of suspicion for Calvinist and Counter-Reformation zealots. These instruments, which were frequently represented in allegorical still-lifes called 'Vanities', were thus invested with multiple and sometimes contradictory meanings: as signs of wealth and value (they were often collectors' items), but also fragility (the broken string) and impermanence (covered in dust, and the sound is no sooner produced than it dies away). Instruments could be associated not only with love, but also with the intellect; music was one of the liberal arts, taught in the *Quadrivium* alongside arithmetic, geometry and astronomy. The link between music and astronomy often inspired representations of the ancient theme of the Harmony of the Spheres.

Allegory and myth abound in representations of Music. *Musica* and *Pictura* are often presented together, like Narcissus and Echo for Ovid or Poussin. The abundant iconography can be divided into two broad categories, the religious and the profane.[19] Profane works favour the themes of inspiration (blind Homer playing the viola da gamba), love (Titian's paintings of Venus) and hearing (in the cycle of the five senses). Mythological scenes include Apollo surrounded by the Muses, Mercury lulling Argus to sleep, Orpheus charming the animals, Arion saved from drowning by a dolphin who has heard him play, and Amphion building the walls of Thebes simply by playing his lyre. To which should be added Pythagoras, the father of music as a mathematical art, with his vibrating string or blacksmith's hammers. Religious iconography includes the Old Testament figures of Jubal and Tubalcain (the mythical ancestors of instrument-makers), Job and, above all, David, the author of the Psalms whose harp-playing dispelled Saul's melancholy. In the New Testament, we have the 24 elders-musicians in the Book of

Revelation and the apocryphal tales around the Flight into Egypt
(Caravaggio). The development of the Cult of the Virgin in the twelfth
century inspired the choirs of angels which adorn Nativities, Ador-
ations and Assumptions. The *Golden Legend* dwelt on the Ecstasies
of St Francis and Mary Magdalene. And in the wake of Raphael's
famous painting, St Cecilia tended to replace *Musica*.[20] An erroneous
interpretation of a passage in her liturgy generated a whole series of
images featuring, especially, the organ.

Ut Musica Pictura

This dialogue between music and painting was also pursued in theor-
etical writings, where comparisons between painting and music are

Felix Vallotton, *La Symphonie*, 1897, woodcut.

frequent. Aristotle was the first to unite both disciplines under the principle of *mimesis*, the imitation of nature, but there existed a difference in their social status. In the *paragone* debate (the comparison between the arts) initiated by Leonardo, painting attempted to emulate music in order to win for itself the prestige traditionally reserved for the liberal arts (which included music). Alongside this, the art critic's expanding terminology made frequent borrowings from the domain of music, particularly in the designation of colour, in Venice initially. But there was more to come. In the footsteps of Athanasius Kircher and Newton, the Jesuit Louis-Bertrand Castel devised a set of correspondences between notes and colours. It underpinned his designs for an ocular harpsichord, which was to have a long history despite its utopian nature. With Romanticism, the interest shifted to synaesthesia, and a new search for correspondences began, particularly by E.T.A. Hoffmann, Baudelaire, Scriabin and Kandinsky. 'Colour music', and later cinema and video, extended these explorations, which continue right into the present day.

Meanwhile, Stendhal had launched the fashion for comparisons between painters and musicians, which produced a whole stream of such pairings. The most popular, although not necessarily the most convincing, were the pairing of Mozart, after Raphael and Beethoven with Michelangelo. Romanticism promoted music to the rank of a leading art form, a model of expressivity and spirituality. Walter Pater, and before him Schopenhauer, claimed that 'all art aspires constantly to the condition of music.'[21] The much-debated opposition between instrumental or 'pure' music (Hanslick) and vocal or thematic music (defended by Hugo Wolf[22]) influenced the visual arts in adding grist to the mill of those who wished to see painting freed from its representational function. The symphonic poem sometimes drew its inspiration from painting (Liszt), while, in an opposite movement, 'musicalism', the belief that music can be expressed in painting, paved the way for abstraction. Whistler called some of his paintings *Nocturnes*, Signac gave them an opus number and Augusto Giacometti painted a *Chromatic Fantasy*. Painters replaced figuration with musical forms ('polyphony', 'fugue'), and we can find numerous references to the fundamental bass of Rameau's harmonic system, from Goethe to the *Blue Rider*. In their fascinating correspondence, Kandinsky and Schönberg discuss the principle of dissonance and explore relations between tonal music and perspective.[23]

In its dialogue with music, painting was in good company. Its spatial dimension and the development of new formal techniques all pointed to architecture, which had periodically been called 'crystallized music', and was likewise informed by Pythagorean theory.[24] The bond between architecture and music thus dated back to Antiquity. It was reactivated in the medieval[25] and Renaissance[26] periods, and reaffirmed in the twentieth century.[27] There is a striking continuity between the mythological Amphion and Valéry's *Eupalinos*, Vitruvius and Renzo Piano, and Alberti, Palladio, Claude Perrault, Le Corbusier and Xenakis. That the influence could work in the opposite direction, from music to architecture, is illustrated, for instance, by Guillaume Dufay's *Nuper rosarum flores*, inspired by Brunelleschi's dome,[28] or Stravinsky's *Canticum sacrum*, composed for the space of Saint Mark's Basilica in Venice.

Sculpture also had its say, in the form of commemorative monuments (Louis-François Roubiliac's monument to *Handel* in Westminster, the portrait of *Paganini* by David d'Angers or Max Klinger's *Beethoven*), or ornamental ones (Bourdelle's bas-reliefs for the Théâtre des Champs-Elysées). Due to its materiality, its links with music had not really been taken seriously until the explorations of timbre, which reinstated its solidity and gave rise to a whole new art form called *Klangskulptur* or Sound Sculpture, pioneered by the Baschet brothers[29] and immortalized by Takis.[30] At the other extreme, the sculptures of Fausto Melotti and Walter Linck could be described as silent music. Musical imagery lived on in the triumph of the Art Nouveau *arabesque* (Camille Claudel, *La Valse*) and later with the Cubists (Picasso, Henri Laurens, Jacques Lipchitz and Ossip Zadkine).

Musical notation itself gives music its first visual existence. The calligraphic beauty of scores, best illustrated by medieval illuminated manuscripts, seems to have disappeared with the invention of printing; Mozart's and Beethoven's hand-written works may interest us, but for graphological reasons – how the strokes reveal a temperament – rather than for their inherent beauty. With Debussy, and later Stravinsky, the care taken in the execution, the visual, sculptural qualities and the use of colour bring back the aesthetic dimension; in the case of Stravinsky, almost all his manuscripts have been preserved by the Paul Sacher Foundation.[31] The presence of drawings in the score (Satie, *Sports et divertissements*) or of scores in drawings or paintings (Duchamp, *Erratum musical*) was another way of linking the two worlds. Magritte, whose brother was a musician and who could appreciate the beauty of staves, often used fragments of scores in his collages. But the affinity between musical notation and drawing really came into its own with the new systems of notation linked to the new music.[32] The idea was to replace conventional notational signs with an analogical form of notation. John Cage, Earle Brown, Morton Feldman, George Crumb, Karlheinz Stockhausen, Hans Otte, Dieter Schnebel, Urs Peter Schneider, Friedrich Cerha, Maurizio Kagel, Krzysztof Penderecki, György Ligeti, Sylvano Bussotti, Anestis Logothetis, Roman Haubenstock-Ramati and Oscar Wiggli all illustrate this new relationship between graphics and music, which resembles Luigi Veronesi or Robert Strübin's experiments in translating music into painting.[33]

This symbiosis between musical notation and drawing is echoed in the ideal of visual poetry first presented in Mallarmé's *Coup de dés*. Apollinaire, describing his *Calligrammes*, declared that 'These artifices can go further still, and achieve a synthesis between the arts of music, painting and literature.'[34] Klee was fond of repeating that 'writing' and 'drawing' are expressed by the very same character in Chinese.

The need for unity, which is expressed in these relationships, seems to be a recurring theme, present in Romanticism, Symbolism, Futurism, Surrealism and right down to our own times. It is signalled by the incantatory repetition of rallying cries and magic formulas such as 'correspondences', 'synthesis', 'fusion' and '*Gesamtkunstwerk*'. The notions of vibration and rhythm are posited as common denominators and as principles of translatability and universal transparency,

Marcel Amiguet, *Igor Stravinsky*, 1928, etching.

which themselves hark back to an originary, hence authoritative, language which mobilizes all the senses. This explains why myths of origins, so dear to the Enlightenment, creep back, unacknowledged, even into the avant-gardes. The nostalgia for a lost paradise and the revival of ancient cosmologies such as the music of the spheres remind us once again that modernism and archaism are indeed two sides of the same coin.

2
MUSICAL ANALOGIES IN THEORIES OF PAINTING

'Phonismus photismi similis est . . . sonum lucis simiam esse'
– Athanasius Kircher[1]

'Colours are to the eye what sounds are to the ear'
– Jonathan Richardson[2]

'Why', I asked, following the thread of this analogy, 'why would one not make harpsichords for the eyes just as one makes them for the ears?'[3] Louis-Bertrand Castel went on to imagine 'tuned colours' and 'hearing prisms', mentioning in passing his predecessor Athanasius Kircher's 'glasses for the long of hearing' and 'ear microscopes'. In a similar vein, Etienne Falconet talked of 'ocular melodies' and Quatremère de Quincy of 'ocular music'. That was enough to launch the controversy.[4] In his article 'Harpsichord' in the *Encyclopédie*, Diderot came out in favour, maintaining that 'ocular music has the same foundations as aural music'.[5] Rousseau, by contrast, condemned the 'false analogy between colours and sounds', adding the snide remark that 'Unable to paint with their ears, people have thought to sing with their eyes.'[6] Yet audio-visual utopias had a long life ahead of them. One direct heir, for example, was the Dadaist artist Raoul Hausmann, and his battle cry: 'Painters, Musicians, Sirs! You will see with your ears and hear with your eyes.'[7] Castel himself, in wanting to make music visible for the deaf and painting audible for the blind, was doing no more than adapting Athanasius Kircher's formula of 'listening with our eyes and looking with our ears'.[8] Voltaire could not resist a little mockery here: 'And all the deaf in Paris are invited to the concert.'[9]

Castel has come down to us as the champion of this 'finest and most incontrovertible analogy ever made, that between light and sound'.[10] He was a vital link in the tradition which went back to Aristotle and has reached today's multi-media avant-gardes via Gaffurius, Zarlino, Cardanus and Mersenne, and thanks to Castel's work of transmission. We cannot but be struck by how often the hearing-sight comparison appears, from Runge[11] to Sabanejew[12] and MacDonald-Wright,[13] from the decorative arts[14] to cinema,[15] and from architecture to painting.

This historical continuity, which J. Jewanski has reconstituted,[16] should not blind us to the range of different types of comparison, from objective to subjective (relating to the structure of the object or, inversely, its reception), quantitative to qualitative, and rational to intuitive and emotional. The two poles can even cohabit, as when Charles Blanc-Gatti advocated a mathematical model of relations between frequencies (colours appearing at 50 octaves above the notes), while at the same time claiming to have an innate gift of 'synopsis'.[17] Very different levels of analysis are present, sometimes based on empirical data (colouring the strings of an instrument, the lines of the staves or the notes, to help beginners), at other times involving metaphysical speculations concerning cosmic correspondences and the harmony of the spheres. Kepler, for instance, regularly used musical terminology to describe celestial mechanics, talking of harmonic proportions, consonance, octaves, scales, major and minor modes, and even counterpoint between alto, tenor and bass.[18] It is clear that the numbers by which sounds and colours were coordinated were chosen for their symbolic and ideological qualities (three,[19] seven[20] and twelve[21]), and the same goes for the recurrent figure of the circle.[22]

A Polyvalent Metaphor

Debussy's interest in the visual arts is well known.[23] He called a Suite he wrote for two pianos in 1915 *In White and Black* – actually a paradoxical title in the light of the original manuscript (at the Bibliothèque

Nationale), which uses coloured inks, as Debussy often did. Perhaps he was thinking of the words of Albert Lavignac, a Professor of Harmony at the Paris Conservatory, that 'piano music is thus in white and black, like pencil or charcoal drawing, or engraving.'[24] In this widely read book, Lavignac compared the two arts from several perspectives, addressing the colour of timbres, the question of genre and issues of technique. He thus linked, for example, watercolour painting with chamber music, and stained glass with the organ.

The use of musical terminology was fashionable at the time. We get a taste of this in Baudelaire's *Salon de 1846*, where within five pages in the chapter on colour his musical metaphors include song, vibration, tone (five mentions), symphony (two), melody (seven), hymn, harmony (three), counterpoint (two), chord, scale, music and sounds (two), as well as a comparison with the timbre of the oboe. His influence on ensuing generations is well known. Charles Blanc called a Delacroix *Hamlet* 'a *pathétique* concert'.[25] Van Gogh mentioned Jules Dupré's 'symphony of colours',[26] and Mauclair, for whom Debussy was 'the Mallarmé or Whistler of music', wrote that 'Impressionist painting borrows its procedures from music. It symphonizes with seven colours, those of the scale.'[27] Verhaeren stated admiringly that 'one would think Ensor listened to colour because he deploys it so fully, like a symphony. There is never a note out of place. He has a perfect eye like a musician has perfect pitch.'[28] Sérusier described his 'scales of colours, melodies, chords, laws of musical composition, harmonics, pedals, and octaves', and did not baulk at introducing a neologism, 'cacochromy'.[29] Matisse, who played the violin, drew on a similar lexical field, referring to a *concertante* ensemble, to orchestration, transposition, vibrato, tempo, a theme and its variations, major and minor, and so forth.[30]

But there was nothing new about this discursive genre. The Venetian school had flourished on such analogies, thanks to Boschini:

> The Venetian painter, an accomplished musician,
> Knows how to tune and play his instrument.[31]

This first, purely abstract level of comparison thus followed the well-trodden path of mutual lexical borrowings on which critical vocabularies had always thrived.[32] Terms such as Cézanne's '*modulé*', Kandinsky's '*Klang*' or Moses Mendelssohn's '*Farbenmelodie*' (which prefigures Schönberg's '*Klangfarbenmelodie*') belong to this category.

But the comparisons were sometimes more concrete, as when Félibien declared that 'fine brushwork is to painting what a beautiful voice is to music',[33] or Van Gogh that 'my brush flits between my fingers like the bow on a violin.'[34] Matisse wrote that 'the graver, like the bow, is directly linked to the engraver's sensibility',[35] and Kandinsky, that 'Colour is the piano key, the eye is the hammer which strikes it, and the soul, the thousand-stringed instrument.'[36] A commonplace in this context was the description of the painter's palette as a 'keyboard' of colour,[37] and the metaphor was extended to all sorts of light-harpsichords, light-pianos and light-organs, as the logical progeny of Castel's utopian machine. The term 'analogy' was a leitmotif with Rimington, the inventor of the 'colour organ'.[38]

Such parallels could be drawn for all musical elements, as the occasion demanded. Boschini again:

> The Venetian painter . . .
> Composes fugues, toccatas, ricercari or strange fantasias
> And transposes them
> From one key to another.[39]

The notions of variation, melody, counterpoint,[40] harmony and timbre[41] appeared alone or in combination. Lomazzo found both 'melody' and 'harmonic grace' in Mantegna's paintings,[42] Castel talked of 'the music you would like to paint, respecting all the note values, syncopations and rests, minims and crochets, and so forth',[43] and Leonardo da Vinci considered the *glissando* to be the equivalent of *sfumato*.[44] The decorative arts and, later, cinema were often described in terms of rhythm: Léopold Survage, who painted *Rythmes colorés* (1913), stated that 'a visual rhythm can become like rhythm in music', and Germaine Dulac maintained that 'the total film which we all dream of making is a visual symphony composed of rhythmic images.'[45]

Similarly, in the visual arts, all the elements – the use of colour, the values, lines, pictorial space and composition, and all the techniques – were compared to music. Architecture, often called 'frozen music'[46] – an expression enthusiastically adopted by Schelling, Friedrich Schlegel, Goethe, Schopenhauer, Ruskin and others – was linked to music by Vitruvius, Zarlino, Francesco Giorgi, Palladio and Claude Perrault. Fausto Melotti associated sculpture with counterpoint.[47] And drawing, the domain of the *arabesque* (another term with a double valency[48]), naturally attracted musical metaphors: 'Just as the musician makes voices sing, so the decorative artist makes lines sing', in Paul Souriau's words.[49] Johannes Itten associated line with Bach, and colour and harmony with Schönberg.[50]

The comparison with music also occurred within aesthetic debates, for example, when decorum was defined by Paleotti as a 'musical correspondence' and as a 'harmony in the proportions between the voices'.[51] Marco Boschini mentioned '*concerti delle istorie*' ['concerts of subject-matter'],[52] while Félibien, following Alberti, chose music to illustrate the 'conformity of all the parts to each other'.[53] The Père André recommended imitating 'the well-chosen chords of a piece of music'.[54]

Furthermore, since music had always been regarded as a universal language, it could figure in another sort of argument, as the 'natural' foundation for the system of colours. Physics enabled resonant frequencies to be correlated with the visible spectrum of the rainbow, which the Père André called a 'symphony of nature', like the peacock's tail or the butterfly's wings, and 'a sort of natural tablature which the Creator has placed before our eyes'.[55] Diderot's analogy, that 'The rainbow is to painting what the ground bass is to music', would subsequently inspire Goethe.[56] And later still, Webern was again citing Goethe when he defined colour as 'the expression of the laws of nature in its relation to the faculty of vision', adding that 'there is only a difference of degree, not of essence, between colour and music; one can say that music is the expression of the laws of nature in its relation to the sense of hearing.'[57]

Lastly, the comparison with music could serve the practical purpose of helping address the notoriously tricky issue of the number of colours, enabling them to be classified and their relations to be structured. Charles Blanc-Gatti, for example, maintained that 'if one organizes colour according to strict rules, it can be taught, just like music', and 'the use of colour can be learnt exactly like music. Just as we train musicians . . . by teaching them counterpoint, so we can train painters not to offend against the rules of harmony, if we teach them about the simultaneous perception of colours.' After demonstrating the relativity of both colours and sounds, Eugène Chevreul used an analogy to drive his point home: 'Like intervals and chords in music, hues do not exist in themselves, but only by comparison.'[58] And Ehrenfels' *Gestalttheorie* would later be based on principles derived from melody and melodic intervals.[59]

The Rehabilitation of Colour

The use of colour tended to be central to the comparison with music. Roger de Piles, who supported the Rubens camp and defended the Venetian tradition, declared that 'In the different colours and the different tones which are used in painting, there is a harmony and a dissonance, as there is in a musical composition.'[60] A chapter in his *Cours de peinture par principes* restated this idea: 'In the use of colours, the harmony of the colours and their oppositions are no less necessary than are unison and chromatics in music.'[61] Diderot echoed this position in maintaining that the painter had to be a 'great harmonist' if his handling of colour was to be successful. The Père André described colours which were 'friends' or 'enemies' in terms of 'harmonious or discordant' sounds.[62]

But it was not only in Venice, with its claim to be the homeland of both colour and music, that the comparison thrived. It was used just as frequently by the theorists from central Italy and the defenders of the classical doctrine. Discussing unity in colouring, Vasari had written: 'For just as the ear is offended by music that is noisy, dissonant or harsh . . . so the eyes are offended by colours which are too exaggerated or crude.'[63] Vincenzo Borghini summarized in the phrase 'picturesque harmony' his claim that '*armonia, ragione, regola, proporzione*' (harmony, rationality, rules, proportion) were the qualities which these arts had in common.[64] Pietro Testa maintained that the rules of harmony in music enable us to understand those of colouring.[65] And Félibien required the 'perfect painter', in the distribution of his colours, to achieve 'a harmony which affects the eyes exactly as music affects the ears.'[66] For 'there is a harmony and a dissonance in different colours . . . just as there is in a musical composition.'[67] Bellori attributed the comparison between the pleasure of listening to the voice and that of seeing harmonious colours, to Federico Barocci, concluding that Barocci effectively 'called painting music'.[68]

This brings us to the famous opposition between line and colour. From the Renaissance onwards, colour had suffered from an inferiority complex with respect to drawing, which had achieved the status of a liberal art as a component of the *trivium*, particularly on the strength of Horace's *ut pictura poesis*. Bellori's reference (concerning Domenichino) to Simonides' famous definition of painting as *muta poesis* should be read in this polemical context: 'He managed to paint sound with silent colours . . . and thus endowed painting with a sense of hearing.'[69] Castel too spoke of 'silent music'.[70]

A passage from Giuseppe Carpani gives us a sense of the persistence of this debate – he published his *Haydine* in 1812 – but with the values inverted: in support of Rousseau against Rameau, he argued for the superiority of melody (identified with drawing) over harmony (identified with colour). His reasoning contained the following elements:

> The accompaniment is to the melody what the use of colour is to the painting . . . Melody is to music what drawing is to painting . . . Melody is the soul of music . . . Where melody is lacking, thought is absent.[71]

With this last tenet, Carpani cleverly laid claim to the intellectualism of the classical doctrine of *disegno*.

The Shadow of Pythagoras

The scientific, and therefore prestigious, status of perspective was also harnessed to the cause of drawing.[72] Castel considered perspective to be 'until now the only solid foundation for painting, a sort of adjudicating optics',[73] and he deplored the fact that 'colour use is based neither on a pictorial nor a mathematical theory, and has no rules.'[74] Goethe agreed, and regretted that painting had no solid theory similar to that of roots in music.[75] Given that no apparatus existed to measure colour mathematically, painting was consigned to the manual arts and could not aspire to being a '*cosa mentale*'. The *paragone* debate initiated by Leonardo was an opportunity to redress the balance by associating colour indirectly with the nobility of the *quadrivium*. Michelangelo's statement that a good painting is 'a music and a melody which only the intellect can perceive' bears this out.[76]

Music and mathematics had always been intimately linked,[77] through the notion of proportion by which intervals are defined. And music's rule-bound structure with its basis in nature had always been regarded as a model of rigour and objectivity. The *paragone* debate could rehabilitate colour, as we have seen, partly because it introduced the notion of number. Baudelaire, for instance, declared that 'The artful use of colour obviously derives in certain respects from mathematics and music.'[78] And Debussy neatly defined music – in a comment on Rameau – as 'the arithmetics of sound, just as optics is the geometry of light'.[79] Thus even before physicists such as Young, Helmholtz or Maxwell had invented ways of measuring frequency or wavelength, theorists of colour had devised ways of endowing colour with the prestige of quantifiability. Castel even made gradations of blue by varying the length of time fabric was steeped in indigo dye.[80]

So Pythagoras still cast his shadow over the tradition. Plotinus defined beauty in the same terms for sight and for hearing: a question

'Pitagoras', woodcut in Gaffurius, *Theorica musicae* (1492).

of symmetry and proportion.[81] Alberti echoed this: 'The very same numbers that cause sounds to have that *concinnitas*, pleasing to the ears, can also fill the eyes and mind with wondrous delight.'[82] And the Aristotelian principle of 'colours based on numerical ratios . . . like the concord in music'[83] was often referred to, for instance in Runge's rhetorical question: 'does the musical scale not correspond to the shades of colour existing between white and black?'[84] The system of correspondences Arcimboldo is supposed to have invented between gradations of colour and sounds in fact originated, in Comanini's view, in Pythagoras' harmonic proportions.[85] And Cureau de la Chambre's study of rainbows, his *Nouvelles observations sur l'arc en ciel* (1650), which were published even before Newton's, also linked shades of colour to Pythagorean intervals. As for Aguilon's or Kircher's chromatic schemes, they strongly resembled Gaffurius's, Zarlino's and Cureau de la Chambre's theses on the proportions between musical intervals. This doctrine was so well established that Bellori in his praise of subdued tones and glazings even dared to explain the imponderable *sfumato* through mathematical *ratio*, via the metaphor of musical 'intermediary bonds': he praised Domenichino for having 'successfully tempered the mean by the extreme, using the proportions of low and high which make for musical perfection . . . such that the outlines gently shade off into the background, through number and consonance'.[86] This vision uncannily prefigures Jakob Weder's use of precision scales to determine the exact proportions of different pigments in the pictorial transcriptions he made of the harmonies of Bach's *Suite in D Major* (1980–81).[87]

Imitation, Expression, Abstraction

'Music above all else':[88] in the course of the nineteenth century, with the ascendancy of the model of music, the analogy between music and the visual arts came to be applied to all the arts. Psychology supplanted physics, and with it the world of synaesthesia opened its gates. E.T.A. Hoffmann saw in 'the magical power of music . . . the kingdom of the infinite', and thought it should 'shatter all the chains which fetter the other arts'.[89] Runge announced a future synthesis: 'The analogy between sight and hearing holds the promise of excellent results for a future union of music and painting'.[90] Gauguin justified his pink skies with the argument that 'it is music',[91] since painting is 'the sister of music'[92] (an echo of Leonardo), and he wrote to Fontainas: 'Think of . . . the musical role played henceforth by colour in modern painting'.[93] With a nod to Delacroix's famous phrase on 'the painting's music', he qualified Bonnard,

Vuillard and Sérusier as 'musicians', and called Cézanne 'a student of César Franck'.[94]

This 'musicalization' was in fact heir to two different traditions, which had taken two distinct paths. The first, which issued in Expressionism, originated in the doctrine of affects, as formulated by Schlegel:

> Just as the music of the great masters often had recourse to . . . violent dissonance in order to illustrate passion . . . so the almost garish colours of stained-glass windows are particularly well suited to impressing on the eyes and hearts of the spectator the martyr's depths of suffering.[95]

Romanticism, by replacing imitation with expression, had a key role in bringing about this new aesthetic, *ut musica pictura*, and its influence persisted in the association of music with '*Gefühl*' and '*Stimmung*'.[96]

But soon Hanslick's frequently reprinted *Vom Musikalisch-Schönen*, which was translated into French in 1877, dissociated music from any expressive value, and championed its pure self-referential form.[97] The work had considerable influence, at least up to Stravinsky's *Poetics of Music*. This second path, which issued in purism and the autonomy of painting freed from figuration, had its roots in the theory of harmonic proportions. However, the two paths, reflecting a double image of music as at once a privileged medium of subjective expression and a self-referential structural model, were not absolutely separate. Even traditional neo-Pythagorean speculations had never really excluded the question of music's effects.[98] In his reflections on modes, for instance, Poussin declared that 'assembling in proportion' has the power 'to induce various passions in the spectator's soul'.[99]

For the modernists, too, expression and abstraction were not mutually exclusive. In 1905 Alexei Jawlensky described a still-life in the following terms: 'they are no longer apples . . . their radiant colours dissolve into a harmony which is interwoven with dissonance.

They seem to me to resonate like a piece of music which restores a certain state of my soul.'[100] This was Survage's vision also: 'Once painting had freed itself from the conventional language of objects' forms in the external world, it conquered the territory of abstract forms . . . in order to express our emotions, as is the case with music.'[101] And Matisse claimed that 'We had to get away from imitation, even imitation of light. One can create light effects by using blocks of full colour, like chords in music. I used colour as a way of expressing my feelings and not as a way of transcribing nature.'[102]

It has often been said that the origins of abstraction are to be found in Romanticism.[103] And indeed, Novalis declared that 'the musician finds in himself the essence of his art – he cannot be suspected of any imitation.'[104] This purism was achieved through the emancipation of colour. Hegel, writing on 'the magical effects of colouring', marvelled that 'where the substantiality and spirituality of the object have disappeared . . . one feels one is transported into the realm of music.'[105] Théophile Gautier, the leading proponent of 'Art for Art's sake', and author of the famous poem 'Symphony in White Major',[106] illustrated 'the pleasure of painting' by reference to a great Venetian colourist: 'Some of Rossini's pieces produce in me the same pleasure in pure art as the paintings of Paul Veronese.'[107] For Van Gogh, criticizing the imitation of nature and creating a 'symphony' of colour went together.[108] And it was soon possible to abandon figuration altogether: in 1895 Rimington, the promoter of 'colour music', imagined paintings in which 'there is neither form nor subject, only pure colour.'[109] The dialogue which began between Kandinsky and Schönberg in 1911 renewed the discourse on consonance and dissonance, and explored the relation between abstraction and atonality.[110] In 1913 H. Valensi, future founder of the 'Musicalist' movement, asked: 'Why not imagine "pure painting"? Just as musicians have their notes, why not suppose that colour, through its intrinsic powers, can express the painter's thoughts?'[111] And in 1916 MacDonald-Wright wrote: 'I strive to divest my art of all anecdote and illustration and to purify it . . . as in listening to music . . . Today's music has become abstract.'[112] Hölzel, Delaunay, Kupka, Survage, Picabia, Van Doesburg,

Schwitters, Ben Nicholson and many others likewise appealed to music in their defence of painting's autonomy.

As though to compensate for the loss of the subject, painters looked to music for rules, laws and models. Johannes Itten regarded music theory as a paradigm of clarity and of 'objective and rule-bound composition'.[113] Hence the modernist references to tonal music and the reappearance of the theme of chord roots (*Generalbass*), which the avant-gardes working on constructive colour had inherited from Goethe. The parallel also helped justify a poetics which advocated an economy of means: 'There is nothing wrong with composing in only a few colours, like music which is built on only seven notes,' Matisse remarked.[114] Yves Klein's monochromes, like Giacinto Scelsi's monochords, were the most extreme forms of this asceticism.

Most of the comparisons, as we have seen, were harnessed to the cause of painting, but the relation could also work the other way round, and the model in fact shuttled back and forth: 'What an artist! One like that in painting, that would be good', Van Gogh wrote of Wagner,[115] while a few years later, in an opposite gesture, Anton Webern expressed his fervent wish 'that an artist in music would come along resembling Segantini in painting'.[116] But already in 1573 Zarlino had explained the perception of consonances through that of colours,[117] and Carpani's theory of music was likewise based on his theory of painting. The references to painting also permeated musicians' vocabulary, as when Erasmus Darwin posited the existence of 'primary sounds' modelled on the primary colours,[118] and the Hungarian composer Paul Arma (1905–1987) talked of musigraphics, musicollages, sound prisms and sculpted music. The list of such borrowings would be a long one, from *Klangfarbenmelodie* right up to 'spectral' music. Questions of technique also fascinated musicians, both on the scale of a whole work, such as Pierre Boulez's declared admiration for Klee due to his mastery of composition,[119] and on a smaller scale, such as Satie's reflections on Monet, Cézanne and Toulouse-Lautrec, which led him to ask 'why not transpose these methods musically?'[120] and Arthur Honegger, echoing Matisse, declaring that he wanted to 'use the twelve chromatic sounds with the same freedom as the painter uses the colours of the prism'.[121] Hence it was sometimes painting and sometimes music which provided the examples to be imitated, but in both cases the relations were rarely simple or straightforward, as we shall ascertain in the following chapter.

3
THE NEW *PARAGONE* DEBATE:
PARADOXES AND CONTRADICTIONS

'. . . et si vis similem pingere, pinge sonum'

– Ausonius[1]

The first issue of the *Gazette des Beaux-Arts,* published in 1859, contained an article revealingly entitled '*Ut pictura musica*'.[2] Its author, the writer Louis Viardot, husband of the singer Pauline Viardot and friend of Delacroix, prophesied that 'one day someone will write a book on the parallels between painting and music.' Little did he know how right he was, for this theme has been the subject not just of one, but of dozens of works since then. There was a particularly spectacular increase in interest in the subject subsequent to the major Stuttgart exhibition of 1985,[3] and the number of more recent publications – as well as the many multi-media works created[4] – testify to its ongoing topicality.

But Viardot's claim to broach 'a wholly new problem, for the first time' is ill-informed. He in fact had many predecessors, and the comparison between the arts – and particularly between music and painting – runs through the whole of Western aesthetics, from the Renaissance to modernism's avant-gardes.[5] The theme was launched by Leonardo (although the term '*paragone*' appeared only in Guglielmo Manzi's 1817 edition) and produced a long series of variations, from Venice (Marco Boschini[6]) to Rome (Gianpietro Bellori[7]) and Paris (André Félibien,[8] Roger de Piles[9]), involving artists (Evaristo Baschenis[10]), musicians (Marc-Antoine Charpentier[11]), music theorists (Vincenzo Galilei,[12] Marin Mersenne[13]) and philosophers (Athanasius Kircher,[14] Nicolas de Malebranche[15]). The crucial period in this history was the eighteenth century, when Louis-Bertrand

Martial Leiter, *Mussorgsky composing 'Pictures of an Exhibition'*,
2004, drawing.

Castel and Johann Leonhard Hoffmann decided to take literally what
until then had been simply a metaphor: the colour of sounds.[16]

The debate was revived in the nineteenth century, particularly
by Delacroix,[17] who argued for the superiority of painting (an art of
simultaneity) over music (succession). The theories proposed were
reminiscent of Leonardo's, and prefigured those of Paul Klee and
Delaunay.[18] From Runge to Wagner and Kandinsky, from Madame
de Staël to Gauguin and Apollinaire, the same aspects were debated.
Often the comparison between music and painting was additionally
shaped by a subsidiary opposition within painting itself: painting
was opposed to sculpture *qua* associated with matter, and it was also
opposed to literature *qua* associated with the conceptual.

What we will be focusing on here, in order to draw out its para-
doxes and contradictions, is the continuity of this debate, which
authorizes us to talk of a 'new *paragone*', in the same way as I. Babbitt
talked of a 'new *Laocoon*'.[19] The large amount of information made

available in these last few years – although the field has by no means been exhausted – has at last made it possible to get an overview of these comparisons between the arts, from the Renaissance onwards, and thus to tease out the logic of their historical development.

The *Paragone* Debate and its Legacy

The importance of the *paragone* debate in the Renaissance is well known.[20] Although its focus on the hierarchy of the arts can seem irrelevant to us today, the social stakes involved at the time were high, and concerned nothing short of elevating painting from a 'mechanical' art to the dignity of a 'liberal' art. To this end, painting was compared positively with music, literature and even the cognitive sciences, whose intellectual 'nobility' was well established; and negatively with sculpture, due to the latter's materiality. Leonardo, for example, attempted to show – in flagrant bad faith – that painting, '*cosa mentale*', was both closely related to music (its '*sorella*') and superior to it.

Along with the generalization of the idea of the *arti sorelle* (sister arts),[21] comparisons between painting and music multiplied in the course of the eighteenth century: Louis-Bertrand Castel (from 1725), James Harris (in 1744), W. L. Gräfenhahn (1746), G. A. Wil (1759), an anonymous writer from the *Mercure de France* (1768), C. L. Junker (1778), J. Engel (1780), J. G. Herfer (1785), C. F. Hellwag and J. L. Hoffmann (1786), F. W. Marpurg (1794) and A. F. Bertrand (1798), among others, all focused on this issue.[22]

'All the arts hold hands', was another image (E. Liotard),[23] or Saint-Martin's 'poetry, music and painting are three sisters who should be inseparable.'[24] The intimacy between painting and poetry had been proclaimed ever since Alberti, founded on the authority of the Ancients (Simonides and Horace) through the principle of *ut pictura poesis*.[25] This dogma held until the death blow dealt to it by Lessing's *Laocoon: Or, The Limits of Poetry and Painting* (1766), which introduced a radical opposition between the arts of time and those of space. Thereafter, Wilhelm Heinse,[26] Goethe,[27] Herder,[28] Ludwig Fernow[29] and Quatremère de Quincy[30] all theorized the irreducible specificity of each art. But this compartmentalization of means of expression and the insistence on the frontiers between them was challenged by the Romantics.[31] Novalis,[32] Schelling[33] and A. W. Schlegel,[34] among others, confirmed their unshakeable belief in the unity of Art. Klee's criticism of Lessing's *Laocoon* was part of this same tradition.[35] The Symbolists, as heirs to Romanticism, attempted to combine Baudelaire's 'correspondences', Rimbaud's synaesthesia (his *Sonnet des voyelles*) and Wagner's *Gesamtkunstwerk*.[36] This new configuration, which went by the name of 'union', 'coincidence',[37] 'fusion'[38] or 'synthesis'[39] of the arts, was always placed under the aegis of music, considered at the time as an archetypal universal language.

Rousseau, in a prefiguration of the ideas of *Laocoon*, advocated a separation of the arts, referring specifically to music (whereas Lessing wrote hardly anything about music itself): 'The field of music is time, that of painting is space.'[40] A. W. Schlegel took these reflections further.[41] Baudelaire seems to have refuted this opposition, when he wrote that Wagner excelled in 'painting space and depth'.[42] In 1912, Adolphe Appia enthused about the 'music of space', and the following year a production of Gluck's *Orpheus* at Hellerau prompted Ansermet to say that 'music, like light, fills space.'[43] Debussy went so far as to express the paradox that 'music and poetry are the only two arts that move in space', adding that 'I may be wrong, but it seems to me that this idea will inspire future generations.'[44] The least one can say is that the future proved him right,[45] for the 'spatialization of music' or equally the 'musicalization of space' (Xenakis[46]) were practised by many, including Edgar Varèse,[47] Luigi Nono,[48] György Ligeti,[49] Bernd Alois Zimmermann,[50] Max Neuhaus,[51] Bernhard Leitner,[52] Pierre Mariétan[53] and Oscar Wiggli,[54] and today there are ever more *Klangräume* and *Klanglandschaften* (Hans Otte). Mikhail Matyushin was interested in the relations between music and space, and Laszlo's *Farblichtmusik* sought to make 'atemporal painting temporal'.[55] Centuries before that, Castel had imagined introducing time into the visual arts by the use of mobile paintings, and Leopold Survage pursued a similar aim with his *Colored Rhythm*, before turning to film.

Correlations Between the Arts

In the nineteenth century, the large number of artists who practised multiple artforms,[56] and the many encounters between writers, painters and musicians in their workshops, were instrumental in renewing the debates. An important circle gathered in Dresden around Philipp Otto Runge, Caspar David Friedrich, Carl Gustav Carus, Ludwig Tieck, Wilhelm Schlegel, Jean Paul, E.T.A. Hoffmann, Novalis and Carl Maria von Weber. The growth in comparative studies affected the human and natural sciences, and of course aesthetics as well, as Viardot summarized when he referred to 'comparative anatomy and physiology' as a way of stressing that 'all the arts . . . are basically one and the same art – the beautiful revealed.'[57]

Although Leonardo da Vinci had already compared painting with music, calling both of them *sorelle*[58] – a term which Gauguin also used[59] – it was not until Romanticism that music won out over poetry as painting's ideal model. *Ut pictura poesis* was replaced by *ut musica pictura*, which soon became commonplace.[60] Music, since it requires no stories or action, was described as 'the first, the most immediate and the boldest of all the arts' (Tieck)[61] and 'Poetic language talks of a musical painting, a picturesque music' (Madame de Staël).[62]

However, the abundance of much-repeated comparisons should not blind us to the variety of approaches. If we attempt to classify these, in terms, very schematically, of the types of relation postulated between the arts (which often overlapped) we arrive at four types: parallelism, convergence, divergence and succession.

Parallelism is predicated on the idea that all the arts have the same function, which is expression. 'Are not all the arts expressions of man's feeling or thought?', Lamartine mused, maintaining that 'one art translates another.'[63] Rodin echoed this: 'Painting, sculpture, literature and music are all closer to one another than one tends to think. They all express the feelings of the human soul towards nature. Only the means of expression vary.[64] Kupka shared the same conviction: 'the difference between the arts is due only to the diversity of means of expression. Humanly speaking, they all express the same thing.'[65] The recurrence of the notion of 'translation' reflects this belief that one can say the same things in every 'language'. For the critic Johann August Apel, the same idea can be expressed through music, painting and poetry,[66] and Schumann remarked that 'for the painter, the poem becomes an image; and the musician transposes the image into sounds. The aesthetics of one art is the same as the other, the only difference is the expressive material.'[67] Baudelaire was even more radical, maintaining, in his praise of Wagner, that 'what would be really surprising would be that sound should be unable to suggest colour, colour unable to conjure up a melody, and that sound and colour should be unsuitable for translating ideas.'[68] Gautier described the *Mona Lisa*'s 'singular, almost magical charm' as 'a musical idea . . . an echo of a musical impression'.[69]

Writers inspired by the potential of synaesthesia often employed musical metaphors. We have several examples of this. Zola's 'song of white'[70] seems to echo Gautier's 'symphony in white major'.[71] The writer and painter Adalbert Stifter gives a superb description of a solar eclipse as 'a tragic music of colours and light', which he likened to a *Requiem* and a *Dies Irae*, adding that 'had I been Beethoven, I would have said it in music.'[72] Reciprocally, in the famous chapter of the *Hunchback of Notre Dame* called 'A Bird's-eye View of Paris' (Book III, ch. 2, '*Paris à vol d'oiseau*'), Victor Hugo visualizes the sound of the bells.[73] Liszt, the creator of the symphonic poem, probably incarnates this idea of transposition best, especially in his project of setting to music a cycle of Kaulbach's paintings, in order to describe them 'in poetic, musical, and pictorial form'.[74] Although this particular 'history of the world in paintings and sounds' was never finished (called the *Battle of the Huns*[75]), other transpositions, such as the *Sposalizio* (school of Raphael) and the *Pensieroso* (school of Michelangelo) were singled out by the critics.[76] This ideal of transparency is illustrated by an anecdote told by Kandinsky concerning his collaboration with Alexander Sakharoff and Thomas von Hartmann:

> The musician von Hartmann chose from among my watercolours the one he felt to be the most musical. He played it, in the absence of the dancer Sakharoff. Then Sakharoff came along, and we played him the piece of music, which he transposed into a dance, and then guessed which watercolour he had danced.[77]

The second mode of relation, which can be called convergence, often implied an actual collaboration. E.T.A. Hoffmann maintained that one 'hears better when one sees',[78] Novalis declared that one 'should never look at works of art without music'[79] and Delacroix prophesied that, in the future, 'while a symphony is being performed, beautiful paintings will be placed before us to perfect the impression'.[80] That is exactly what Charles Blanc-Gatti did in 1931, at a concert in the Salle Iéna in Paris, where paintings 'translating' the works on the programme were exhibited. But the nineteenth century was already familiar with this sort of experimentation. Stendhal had imagined presenting a sequence of 'decorations' during performances of Mozart's and Haydn's symphonies,[81] and Liszt, in 1865, 'illustrated' a performance in Rome of his Dante Symphony with pictures by Bonaventura Genelli depicting the corresponding scenes from the *Divine Comedy*.[82] Inversely, Caspar David Friedrich painted a series of four (lost) paintings for the Court of St Petersburg, which were due to have a musical accompaniment, 'so that music and painting should be in harmony and each should support the other',[83] and the painter Moritz von Schwind, in 1835, planned a cycle of his works for his 'Schubert Room'.[84] The principles of interaction between sight and sound had been addressed by Tieck and Wackenroder,[85] whose works possibly inspired Runge's cycle of paintings, *The Hours of the Day*, which he conceived as 'an abstract, musical and pictorial poem, with choirs; a composition for the three arts together, for which architects should provide a suitable building'.[86]

This prefigures the *Gesamtkunstwerk* and,[87] later on, Scriabin's great *Mysterium*.[88]

Convergence of the arts was also explored on the stage. Schelling had theorized theatre as uniting all the arts – poetry, music, painting and dance[89] – and Wagner was later the authoritative model for the Wiener Sezession[90] and the Bauhaus.[91] In different works, Schönberg (*Glückliche Hand*), Kandinsky (*Gelber Klang*),[92] Scriabin (*Prometheus*) and Schlemmer (*Ballet triadique*) also belong to this tradition. F. Cangiullo summed up this trend as the advent of a new art form, born of the fusion of music, painting and poetry.[93]

Cinema was heir to these explorations. In 1907 Ricciotto Canudo wrote that:

> We know today that if different rhythms – silent or not, visual or musical – strike our sensibility at the same time . . . they enrich each other with their particular qualities.[94]

And indeed, a piano or an orchestra often accompanied screenings of silent movies. But whereas film theorists readily accepted the musical model, purists such as Ramain, who were hostile to pleonastic musical elements, fought it out with supporters of filmic synchronic unity such as Jean d'Udine or Emile Vuillermoz.[95]

The third mode of relation was the diametrical opposite of 'convergence', namely 'divergence', which was condemned as a sign of decadence, of unity giving way to division.[96] 'All the arts flow from the same source,' said Liszt in 1855,[97] a vision shared by Kandinsky, for whom 'All the arts stem from one and the same root . . . the same trunk.'[98] This idea of an original unity regained, which is active right up to the Musicalist painters,[99] was defended by the Symbolists, for whom, in Charles Morice's words, 'Art returns to its origins, and as it was one at the beginning, so it is joining its original path towards Unity again, where Music, Painting and Poetry, which are the threefold reflection of one and the same central clarity, have more and more in common.'[100] Bergson is reputed to have used prehistory to justify 'these secret affinities between all the arts', since 'the origin of diverse art-works is a single inspiration, a harmonious unity.'[101] Such claims harked back to Platonic or Rousseauist myths of the origin of language, or the utopia of an Adamic, pre-Babelian and universal language. Condillac described a movement in the opposite direction: 'Music and poetry', he said, 'which until then had been inseparable, began, once they had reached perfection, to divide into two different arts.'[102] But this nostalgic dimension looked forward to a future reconciliation, the 'reunion of music and painting', as Runge prophesied.[103] Edouard Schuré, a great admirer of Wagner, regretted that 'divine Art' is 'fragmented and . . . scattered',[104] and he reaffirmed its 'originary, indestructible unity': the arts 'are a cohesive whole. They are not really enriching unless they work in harmony and lend each other mutual support.'[105] If we accept Leonid Sabanejew's declaration (echoing Wagner), this goal was finally achieved in 1912, and the lost unity was at last restored.[106]

Lastly, relations between the arts were conceived in terms of succession, chronologically. This laid the groundwork for an evolutionary theory in which music was the culminating achievement, as expressed powerfully by Schiller: 'the visual arts, in their highest form, must become music.'[107] Schopenhauer echoed this, declaring that 'all the arts must strive to resemble [music]',[108] and Pater likewise, in his belief that 'all art constantly aspires towards the condition of music.'[109] Henry Valensi declared that 'art must musicalize itself', and his theoretical writings reflect the influences of A. W. Schlegel, Schelling, Tieck and E.T.A. Hoffmann, who likewise saw music as the apogee of a process of dematerialization characteristic of modernity. This idea was influential throughout the nineteenth century. 'Painting loses most of its charm when it comes closer to sculpture' said Germaine de Staël,[110] while Hegel's aesthetics, in which each art form is linked to a particular historical period, set sculpure in opposition to music as the last stage of spiritualization.[111] Carus likewise saw music as superseding sculpture, in the same way as, in his view, hearing supersedes touch,[112] and Van Gogh prophesied that 'painting as it is now promises to become more subtle – more like music and less like sculpture.'[113] Wyzewa's evolutionary version led from sculpture to music, and from sensation to emotion, via the concept,[114] an approach based on the idea that each period has a dominant artistic form. For Heine, for example, ancient Egypt was the age of Architecture, Greece that of Sculpture, the Middle Ages that of Painting, and his own age that of Music, which he saw as 'the last word in Art'.[115] Others in the same vein included Viardot, Spengler, Wilhelm Pinder and Ricciotto Canudo,[116] and right up to the Manifesto of the Musicalist Movement in 1932.[117]

Although these four approaches were compatible and even complementary, and were ultimately different expressions of the same ideal, they linked music and painting on very different levels. The ancient doctrine of the Harmony of the Spheres (referred to by Schlegel, Schelling, Novalis, Tieck, Schopenhauer and others) appealed to a metaphysical order, while some Romantics and Symbolists adopted a religious vocabulary. Tieck talked of the 'mystery of souls', and the art of sounds was described as 'a divine presence for the hearts of men',[118] while for Runge, the term '*musikalisch*' was synonymous with '*mystisch*'.[119] Elsewhere, the link was through physics (the phenomenon of vibration as the common denominator of sounds and colours), or else through psychical and psychological resonances (through synaesthesia, or analogies between effects on spectators and on listeners).

The comparisons proposed were heterogeneous in other ways as well: links were made between music and painting as languages, between a specific composer and a specific painter, and between specific works of art. Sometimes particular formal or stylistic elements were juxtaposed, not without difficulty, as shown by Charles Avison's pioneering attempt in 1752 to get beyond a simple metaphorics and to identify structural similarities.[120] Some equivalences appeared to be almost automatic, and remain a constant from Arcimboldo[121] to Runge[122] via Castel,[123] for example those between acoustic timbre and visual texture, perspective and the tonal system, and light intensities and tessitura, or the pitch of sounds (light = high, dark = low). There was a general consensus on the 'analogy between the tonal scale and the colour scale', which R. Töpffer,[124] prefiguring *Gestalt* theory,[125] understood in terms of relations or ratios. The same term was sometimes used in both domains – rhythm for a visual composition, arabesque for a drawn and a melodic line, harmony to describe colouring, and so forth. Rousseau claimed that 'melody does in music exactly what drawing does in painting,'[126] and Viardot mentioned 'the comparison one so naturally makes between melody and drawing, harmony and colours.'[127] 'If one follows up the comparison', a critic said, 'one could classify the colourist painters, as one sometimes classifies musicians, into melodists and harmonists. Mr Delacroix is more of a harmonist.'[128] For Berlioz, it was 'instrumentation' which was 'exactly, in music, what the use of colour is in painting.'[129] And in George Sand's account of a conversation between Chopin and Delacroix, the latter is reported to have said that 'harmony in music does not consist only of building chords, but also of their relations, their logical sequence, how they are linked, what I would call, if pushed, their auditory tints.'[130] Baudelaire saw things differently again, a more holistic view: 'In colour', he maintained, 'one can find harmony, melody and counterpoint.'[131] And Klee associated colour and texture with polyphony.[132]

Two Images of Music

On examining this corpus as a whole, one is struck by the coexistence of two very different images of music, conveyed by arguments from completely different perspectives, as Schlegel noted already in 1801: music as appealing to human feeling, and music as based on a theory of numerical proportions.[133] Let us consider one half of the equation first, and the authors who adopted the listener's viewpoint and saw music in terms of its effects and emotional power. This aesthetics of reception, which originated in rhetoric and developed geographically in Britain (Addison, Reynolds), Germany (Schopenhauer) and France (Baudelaire), appealed to the listener's participation. For Morse, music was the art which more than all others addressed the listener's imagination,[134] privileging all that is vague, suggestive and dream-like. Diderot saw in music the language 'whose expression is the most arbitrary and the least precise', which 'allows our imagination to roam most freely',[135] a position echoed by Grimm, who claimed that 'everything is undefined and vague in the precepts of music and in musical taste',[136] in total contrast to sculpture. Madame de Staël thought that Mengs had taken Correggio as a model because his *chiaroscuro* 'recalls the vague and delicious impressions of melodies',[137] and for Stendhal also, music was 'the vaguest of the Fine Arts'.[138] In the words of Quatremère de Quincy, 'the magical power of the musical art is that it obliges us to give a form to the most ill-defined conceptions, to mark an outline around the vaguest sketches',[139] while E.T.A Hoffmann 'marked outlines' within music itself, preferring instrumental to vocal music, 'which does not allow vague nostalgia, but merely represents . . . feelings defined by words', and 'leaves no place for an objectless desire'.[140]

This conception of language also recurred in the comparisons between the arts. Liszt considered instrumental music to be 'a poetic language' which expresses 'everything which escapes analysis'.[141] Delacroix, citing Madame de Staël, deemed painting and music to be 'beyond thought' and 'superior to literature in their vagueness',[142] while Paul Deschanel maintained that 'music says more than words, because it speaks with less precision: that is what makes it superior'.[143] The conceptual tenor of language was thus what made it incompatible with music,[144] as Gauguin suggested in prescribing that the poem, 'insofar as it is colours, should be more musical than literary', and that 'in painting, ultimately we should look more for suggestion than description, as with music'.[145] Odilon Redon famously declared: 'My drawings inspire, but they are not definable. They do not determine anything. They place us in the ambiguous world of the indeterminate, just like music'.[146] Vollard was of the same persuasion:

> For what is music? . . . It captivates precisely due to its floating, hazy, indeterminate character. It is nourished at the fount of mystery . . . this almost immaterial charm which resides in the vagueness of the subject-matter . . .

> Henceforth, we shall no longer describe, but simply evoke
> . . . The greatness of Wagner's works produced the esoteric
> writings of Mallarmé and Verlaine's 'music above all else'.
> That was the Symbolist moment.[147]

The other half of the equation, the interest in music as form, although sometimes discussed by the very same authors,[148] drew on a different tradition, that of Pythagorean speculations on mathematical proportions.[149] In his *Salon of 1859*, Baudelaire wrote that 'the art of the colourist is clearly in some respects linked to mathematics and music',[150] while Debussy called music 'a mysterious mathematics'.[151] Structure was opposed to *Stimmung* as the aesthetics of the object was to that of the subject. Hence the references to architecture as 'frozen music',[152] an expression eagerly adopted by many writers, from Schelling to Friedrich Schlegel, Goethe, Schopenhauer and Ruskin. Musical forms such as the symphony or fugue were borrowed by painters,[153] and Goethe's wish to see painting have its own identifiable roots (*Generalbass*),[154] just like the tonal system, was passed down from generation to generation. The modernist painter Adolf Hölzel referred to the need to teach the equivalent of harmony and counterpoint,[155] and Kandinsky, in a letter to Schönberg, aspired to a 'Treatise on Harmony' ('We now have the right to dream of a Treatise on Harmony', 9 April 1911).[156]

Faced with such a wealth of definitions of music, Albert Lavignac came up with a compromise solution which we can see as symptomatic: 'what is beautiful in music resides in a fitting harmony of proportions and in the intensity with which we are penetrated by the emotion communicated.'[157] But this attempt to please everyone led him to say that one can like something without understanding it, and understand it without liking it – a conclusion that does not get us very far!

The One or the Many?

More generally, Western discourses on the arts can be characterized by two opposing tendencies, which we have called 'centrifugal' and 'centripetal', and which appear to alternate in a pendulum-like movement. Two distinct genealogies can be traced: at one extreme, represented successively by Romanticism, Symbolism, Surrealism and its offshoots, there was the desire to abolish frontiers, while at the other extreme, Neoclassicism, Impressionism and other purist movements issuing in formalism and abstract painting championed the separation and differentiation of expressive media.

The Fluxus movement, for example, advocated the abolition of frontiers between the arts and, as John Cage claimed in 1964, their necessary interdependence.[158] The champion of the music of colours in its Russian guise, B. Galeyev, described the 'centripetal tendencies that characterise the integrity of the arts system'.[159] The other extreme was represented by Karl Vossler[160] and Theodor Adorno,[161] among others. In a plea for the specificity of each art form, significantly placed under the aegis of Lessing, Clement Greenberg criticized as a 'new confusion of the arts' the fact that music had replaced poetry as a model for painting.[162] Yet he still thought music (understood as abstract 'method') was the ultimate goal of the avant-gardes.[163] In order to understand this apparent contradiction, we must turn again to its historical origins.

We mentioned above the social factors which fuelled the rivalry between the arts in the Renaissance. We shall now turn to its properly aesthetic dimension, which proved determinant in the long term. The debate launched by Leonardo and Benedetto Varchi played a pivotal role in the establishment of the 'modern system of the Fine Arts' so well described by P. O. Kristeller.[164] It had two main aims: to define the aesthetic field as a whole, and to define the identity of each family member within it – in other words, to prove the unity of the concept of Art (by distinguishing it from non-art), and to delineate the specificity of each particular art within the articulated whole. This involved ensuring the coherence and internal differentiation of what we call the 'visual arts', which Vasari called the 'arts of drawing', by proceeding *per genus et differentiam*. The association between colours and sounds made perfect sense in this context as a way of substantiating the specificity of painting in its opposition to sculpture and drawing.[165]

Throughout the eighteenth century, attempts were made to classify and hierarchize the arts. In their treatises, Dubos, Crousaz, André, Batteux, Mendelssohn and Sulzer sought to find a unifying principle for the arts, and stressed their common features. Diderot, by contrast, regarded each art as having its own 'particular hieroglyphs',[166] and Rousseau, in a chapter entitled 'The False Analogy between Colours and Sounds' (ch. 16) in his *Essay on the Origin of Languages*, criticized the way they trespassed on each other's territory.[167] Joshua Reynolds, discussing the classification of the arts in his thirteenth *Discourse on Art* (1786), declared that 'no art can be engrafted with success on another art. For though they all profess the same origin, and to proceed from the same stock, yet each has its peculiar modes.'[168] Quatremère de Quincy warned on several occasions against the dangers of borrowings between the arts in his *Essai sur l'imitation,* which is a sort of long *paragone*,[169] and Schiller similarly predicted that when, in the future, the arts converge, 'the most accomplished style in each art manifests itself only when its limits are extended without destroying its specific characteristics.'[170]

This 'centrifugal' current gathered strength throughout the nineteenth century. Moreover, modern art defined itself in part through an awareness of the contribution made by the artist's particular craft, materials and tools.[171] Redon stressed the irreducibility of the particular materials used: 'I think suggestiveness in art is largely due to how the material itself affects the artist. A truly sensitive artist will not find the same fiction in different materials',[172] while for Delacroix the important element was execution, 'which adds to thought, and without which thought is not complete.'[173] The attention paid to a painting's singular style had, ever since Boschini, mobilized comparisons with music, for example when Constable praised Titian's brushwork, calling him a 'great musician',[174] or Redon's criticism of

Fantin-Latour for seeming to forget that 'no colour is capable of translating the world of music.'[175] Insisting on differentiation within each art form naturally conflicted with any principle of overall unity. Liszt was particularly torn on this issue. He gave pride of place to performance in his praise of virtuosity, which he likened to colour in painting; and he even denied that an engraved copy could capture the true qualities of a painting (which were accessible only in the presence of the original work), thus ruining the very principle of translatability. Yet, at the same time, he was an ardent supporter of *Ars una*.

Thus artists argued for the specificity of their means of expression. Grimm's tenet of 1761 still held true: 'the arts should not overstep their individual limits.'[176] What was needed was a definition of 'variety in unity: the variety of the arts in the unity of art', as Viardot put it.[177] This contradictory requirement was staged in Germaine de Staël's novel *Corinne ou l'Italie* (1807), in which Oswald maintains that 'a pleasing combination of colours and chiaroscuro produces as it were a musical effect in painting', whereas Corinne is 'convinced that the impingement of one art on the other harms them both'.[178] Reconciling these opposite convictions was no easy matter, as we show below through five examples.

In a comment on Delacroix, Baudelaire stated that 'it is a sign of the spiritual state of our century that the arts aspire, if not to stand in for each other, at least reciprocally to lend each other new strength.'[179] But the very same Baudelaire also condemned the risk of intermingling: 'Does today's decadence fatally make every art want to impinge on the neighbouring one, and incite painters to introduce musical scales into their paintings?'[180] Walter Pater likewise hesitated between his famous pronouncement that 'All art constantly aspires towards the condition of music' and his insistence, in the footsteps of Lessing, on the hermetic separation of the arts, since 'each art [has] ... its own peculiar and untranslatable sensuous charm.'[181] It required quite some intellectual acrobatics to find a solution to this contradiction: 'But although each art has thus its own specific order of impressions', Pater went on, and an untranslatable charm, while a just apprehension of the ultimate differences of the arts is the beginning of aesthetic criticism; yet it is noticeable that, in its special mode of handling its given material, each art may be observed to pass into the condition of some other art, by what German critics term an *Andersstreben* – a partial alienation from its own limitations, through which the arts are able, not indeed to stand in for each other, but reciprocally to lend each other new strength.[182]

These were the very terms used by Baudelaire. Wagner, the father of the *Gesamtkunstwerk*, warned against the dangers of hybridization: 'the purity of an artistic genre is the first condition for making oneself understood; inversely, mixing the arts cannot but lead understanding astray . . . When a musician paints, he is doing neither music nor painting.'[183] Segalen himself, initially all in favour of syncretism, ended up advocating 'the differentiation of the arts; what is proper to music, to painting, etc., the opposite of synaesthesia'.[184] Even Kandinsky had moments of doubt. He claimed that 'today different arts mutually instruct each other and often pursue the same aims', and that 'the same internal resonance can be obtained at the same moment by different arts'. But he also insisted that 'what certain musical forms allow music to do is not permitted in painting'.[185]

The Origins of Abstraction

As we have seen, another reason why music was regarded as a pioneering art and a model for painting was that it represented an ideal of immateriality. This was the position held by numerous theorists: for Goethe, 'the dignity of art is manifested most clearly in music because it is without matter',[186] its superiority is due to the fact that 'it is spirit' (Herder),[187] it is 'the least sculptural of all the arts' (E.T.A. Hoffmann)[188] and it is 'form without matter' or 'a soul without a body' (Schopenhauer).[189] However, this disembodied quality of music conflicted with modernity's enterprise of individualizing art forms in terms of their technical and material specificities, or of the body's involvement in the artistic process. Moreover, music could represent both an ideal of expressivity and an ideal of purity, the outcome of two distinct traditions, Pythagoras or Vitruvius in the second case and, in the first case, Aristotle's *mimesis* of *ethos*, recast in the Baroque doctrine of *affetti* and Poussin's theory of modes. Whereas the expressive function – which, as we have seen, legitimated the principle of translation, or the synonymy between the arts – focused on the content of the message, the notion of purity focused on formal autonomy and differentiation.

Music's specificity was first embodied in the emancipation of timbre and the development of orchestration. The debate on the respective merits of vocal and instrumental music, launched by Galileo,[190] resurfaced two centuries later in the nineteenth century.[191] Tieck, Wackenroder and Schopenhauer argued for the superiority of instruments, and Viardot, a contemporary of Hanslick,[192] saw a parallel between the emancipation of instrumentation and the development of the genre of landscape, both signs of modernity, in contrast to vocal music and history painting.[193] Similarly, the painter's use of a 'keyboard of colours' was compared, by Berlioz and then Signac, to 'a symphony's orchestration'.[194]

In this context, instrumental music was understood as incarnating an art freed from any mimetic function, as expressed by Töpffer's words, 'imitation counts for next to nothing, expression is everything',[195] in contrast to Rousseau's Aristotelian and Baroque vision of a mimetic common ground between painting and music *qua* Fine Arts, since 'it is imitation alone which raises them to this status'.[196] Schopenhauer, who criticized words being applied over sounds, attributed a quasi-metaphysical status to music's autonomy, claiming that it could exist 'even without the world'.[197] For Quatremère, 'this purely instrumental part of music', as he described it, resembled 'architectural decoration',[198] a theme later adopted by theorists of the applied arts such as Owen Jones and Walter Crane,[199] and restated by Odilon Redon in a Letter to Frizeau of 27 July 1909, where he mentions 'decorative painting, what your friend calls "musical painting", and which it would be better to call "a suggestive painted surface".[200] There is also the well-known description by August Endell of the birth of a new art made of 'forms which do not signify or represent', and which leave an impression on the soul 'as only music can do, with its sounds'.[201] A similar idea can be found in certain Russian Symbolists such as Andrei Bely, who influenced the theories of Nikolai Kulbin, Kandinsky and others,[202] and in 1906 an American critic summarized this trend in demanding that 'painting [should] take on something of the qualities which characterize the essence of music – abstraction'.[203]

The theory of non-figurative painting[204] thus pre-dated its practice,[205] and even the term 'abstraction' can be found in the Romantic period.[206] For Novalis, 'the musician draws the essence of his art from himself – he cannot be suspected of any imitation whatsoever',[207] and Stendhal ruled that 'the subject contributes nothing to the painter's merit; it is a bit like the words of a libretto for music'.[208] Constable compared paintings lacking objects to music, in 1824, while two years later Samuel Morse made a comparison with music to differentiate painting from a simple copy.[209] Coleridge, a prominent proponent of the Unity of Art, claimed that 'Music is the most entirely human of the fine arts, and has the fewest analoga in nature'.[210] Hegel talked of 'this magic of colours' which risked 'predominating to the point of repressing the content . . . in which case painting begins to resemble music'.[211] Delacroix, citing Madame de Staël ('The first of the arts, music, what does it imitate?'[212]), forged the expression 'the music of the painting' to refer to 'those mysterious effects of line and colour',[213] which he also qualified, in a letter to Baudelaire of 8 October 1861, as a 'musical part'. Baudelaire took up the expression, followed by one of the first painters to defend the notion of 'abstraction', Paul Gauguin.[214] In *Racontars de rapin*, proclaiming that 'painting in colour is entering a musical phase', Gauguin quoted Delacroix as a way of championing 'the musical role colour will play henceforth in modern painting'.[215] Ruskin called the 'abstract' relations between colours 'musical'; they are agreeable, he remarked, even though they 'serve for nothing'.[216] But it was Whistler who gave this idea its most radical formulation when he said, to justify the musical titles he gave his paintings, 'The harmoniousness of sounds or of colours has nothing to do with the subject-matter.'[217]

This ideal of 'pure music' was claimed by various modernist movements as a model for painting's autonomy (*Der Blaue Reiter*, Fauvism, Cubism, Orphism, Synchromism, Futurism, Vorticism, Neo-plasticism, the Bauhaus, and so on.[218]). It was reformulated by various artists, including Macke, Klee, Matiouchine, Kandinsky, Matisse, Kupka, Delaunay, Boccioni, MacDonald-Wright, Ezra Pound, Schwitters, Picabia, Van Doesburg, Moholy-Nagy and Nicolas de Staël. But it was Apollinaire who bequeathed us what is perhaps the most disarming definition of its paradoxical character: 'We are moving towards an entirely new art', he wrote, 'which will be to painting, as we have imagined it up to now, what music is to literature. It will be pure painting, just as music is pure literature.'[219]

In summary, theories of the relations between music and painting were beset from the outset by contradiction. They were marked by two major currents of nineteenth-century thought – comparative study and evolutionism – and oscillated between rationalism and subjectivism, materialism and spiritualism, nostalgia for a lost unity and defence of the specificity of each art. Their culminating – double – paradox was to define pure painting as music, and to transform modernism into a primitivism or a return to roots.

Of course, remarkable artistic works were created during this period despite these theoretical problems. And perhaps they even instigated them, like the grain of sand from which the pearl is formed. But the deeper reasons for these paradoxes still frustrate our attempts at understanding. Has the 'System of Fine Arts' simply outlived its usefulness, as suggested today by the blurring of spatio-temporal and audio-visual categories? We shall attempt to answer this question in the following chapter, by addressing the phenomenon of convergence between the arts. To take the question further, however, we can already ask whether the amalgamation of forms extends beyond the field of aesthetics and, if so, what ideological weight it carries. The mythical quest for a lost paradise of unity,[220] coupled with an unambiguous impulse of transgression, seem to be the common denominator of most twentieth-century avant-gardes, which are indeed heirs to Romanticism in this respect. From this perspective, the fact that the new *paragone* debate is still going strong could well be understood as a compensatory or defensive symptom on the part of a society confronted with a fractured world, and with the sense of a rootless future.[221]

4
SYNAESTHESIA, CONVERGENCE AND CORRESPONDENCE: YEARNINGS FOR A LOST UNITY

The demise of aesthetic purisms and formalisms, which had culminated in the vogue for abstraction in the 1950s, was deeply unsettling for art historians and their vision of the preceding two centuries. Experiments and speculations which had seemed marginal, or which had long seemed suspect, suddenly came back into focus. From this new perspective, contemporary art seemed to involve a systematic confrontation with the frontiers which had separated the different arts, and a rejection of the autonomy and specificity of each expressive medium (see, for example, the major exhibition *Der Hang Zum* on the *Gesamtkunstwerk*, in Zurich, 1983). This trend was not confined to artistic practice, with its many mixed forms (happenings, performances, installations, and so forth),[1] but affected even art historiography and the aesthetic reflections subtending it.[2]

The dialectical relation between our vision of the present and of the past gives us access to the prehistory of this movement of convergence between the arts. But the field is so vast that we shall restrict ourselves to outlining and classifying its major characteristics. We shall then suggest a key to understanding the continuity and relative unity of this *topos* in Western culture – the interpenetration of the arts – in the history of aesthetics.

No exhaustive inventory has yet been made of the theories, achievements and projects in this area. However, rather than present a long and tedious list of these, we shall look at how widespread this challenging of artistic borders was, the disciplines concerned, in what periods it occurred, and how the convergence of the arts was conceived.

Our field of investigation covers what could be called the major triangle of the visual, the verbal and the auditory. Each point in this triangle converges towards the other two, and defines a field of research: hieroglyphs, rebuses and pictograms link word to image; word roots and onomatopoeia link sound to sense; and 'hearing in colour' links music to painting (a field of research we shall explore in greater detail in the following chapter). To these three 'noble' senses should be added the lesser ones – taste, smell and touch – which, as Castel's plans to build a harpsichord for the five senses prove, should not be overlooked.[3]

Although these relations fascinated artists in particular, they were also explored in disciplines other than the arts.[4] The theoretical speculations which paved the way for, accompanied and carried forward these experiments came from several fields. Physiologists and psychologists examined the phenomenon of synaesthesia. Pictograms and ideograms were studied by historians of writing and semiologists.[5] Linguists tracked down etymologies, while philosophers were only too happy to have this network of correspondences to pore over. Hence the huge literature on the subject.

The different artistic areas interrelate in the most varied ways. If we go back to the centre of our triangle, which is where all the arts fuse or work together, we will find ceremonial entertainments, ballet, opera, cinema, video art and, of course, the Wagnerian *Gesamtkunstwerk,* exemplified in the modern era by works such as Kandinsky's *Der gelbe Klang*, 1909–12, Schönberg's *Die glückliche Hand*, 1911, and Scriabin's *Prometheus*, 1911/15. But the triangle's sides are also dynamic, for example in the relation between poetry and music, which goes back to antiquity and which is incarnated, for instance, in the *Lied* or the symphonic poem. Aided by Simonides (*poema loquens pictura*) and Horace (*ut pictura poesis*),[6] the literary and the visual were united in the classical doctrine of the *arti sorelle* or sister arts,[7] for example in the long-established practices of *ekphrasis*, illustration, history painting, allegory, emblems, the iconic or visual poem, and the *Bildgedicht*.[8] And links between sound and image also flourished, from the musical inspiration of artists, which led painting towards abstraction, to colour music; and from the visual inspiration of composers to painters' visual transcriptions of musical works.[9]

The artistic movements most involved in the convergence of the arts, both in their theoretical works and in practice, emerged in the nineteenth century, and continued into the twentieth century in a more or less unbroken line: Romanticism, Symbolism, Expressionism, Futurism, Orphism (the Puteaux Group), Dada, the Bauhaus, Constructivism, Teige's Poetism and Surrealism and its derivatives. Surrealism will be our guiding thread, since it can reveal what these different movements had in common. Its visceral anti-formalism, and its way of embracing artistic fusion and openness, are central to our theme, even if, paradoxically, Breton and his friends hardly mention music at all. Looking back on his development, in the essay 'Surrealist Comet' (1947), Breton wrote:

> This transcendence took the direction of a new myth that . . . was still vague, but the characterization of which could be anticipated in the near future from the increasingly perfect union of poetry and art.[10]

The ideal of fusion was clearly expressed in the Surrealists' names for their creations: 'poem-objects' (Breton), 'visible poems' (Ernst and Eluard), 'painting-poems' (Miró), 'picto-poetry' (Brauner), 'painted words' (Arp), 'a painting which speaks' (*peinture parlante*) (Eluard), and right up to Emmett Williams's 'poem-constructions'. Breton maintained that through automatic writing one can explore the relation between what he called the 'verbalo-auditory' and the 'verbalo-visual',[11] thus prefiguring paintings of literary figures and devices (metaphors, puns, anagrams and so forth), as practised by Hans Bellmer and Magritte in particular.[12]

These experiments were subtended by a philosophy in which Surrealism, as heir to Romanticism via Symbolism, expressed its ontological choice of a triumphant monism shedding a debased dualism.[13] 'What is the Fall?', asked Baudelaire, the author of the famous poem *Correspondances*; 'If it is a unity which has become a duality, then it is God who is fallen.'[14] 'Why this drive to reduce everything, this terror of the Demon Plural, as someone once called it?', Breton

Lyonel Feininger, *Cathedral*, 1919, woodcut, cover design
for the Bauhaus manifesto.

asked in his 'Introduction to the Discourse on the Paucity of Reality', which poses the crucial question of identity.[15] And André Masson, in 1939:

> The art of this time is beset by various calamities. On reflection, they all come down to an ill-ease which could be called a sense of lost Unity.[16]

For Breton, perception and representation were 'the products of the dissociation of a single, original faculty',[17] which is why dividing up different means of expression seemed so scandalous to him. From this perspective, Surrealism was desperately attempting to close a gap, to compensate for an aberration and to deny a division seen as pernicious. Notions such as 'image', 'encounter' and 'objective chance', and practices such as collage, the games of 'one in the other', 'consequences' (*cadavre exquis*) or the 'found object' are all responses to this dilemma. The quest for unity is expressed in the famous declaration of the *Second Manifesto* (1930):

> Everything leads us to believe that there exists a certain point in the mind from which life and death, the real and the imagined, past and future, the communicable and the incommunicable, and high and low, cease to be perceived as contradictions.[18]

Hence the attraction of occult practices, and the references to Platonic myths of dismemberment, such as the myth of the androgyne.[19]

The re-emergence of another myth of lost unity, that of a primitive – Adamic or Edenic – language, from before the Flood or the Tower of Babel, generated other speculations.[20] This *topos*, implying transparent and universal communication, never died out, but it seemed to crystallize especially in the Enlightenment,[21] in discourses on the origins of language and the debates on natural and artificial signs.[22] As a new historical consciousness developed which tended to pose problems in terms of evolution rather than of theology or metaphysics, theories of the origins of language began to replace the rational attempts to elaborate a universal language.[23] Vico, Warburton, Condillac, Rousseau, De Brosses,[24] Turgot,[25] Diderot, Copineau,[26] Herder[27] and the Schlegel brothers,[28] among others, took a stance on the issue. Court de Gébelin's explorations of onomatopoeia and linguistic roots were typical of this new approach.[29] So the mirage of a single originary language began to take shape, as an unmediated expression of the passions, at once cry, gesture,[30] mime, dance,[31] song, image and metaphor, a poetic and natural language from which all ensuing forms of expression were derived by dispersion. This was Condillac's famous 'language of action' from his *Essay on the Origin of Human Knowledge*, defined as 'the seed of all languages and all the arts'.[32] Vico had imagined a silent language of actions or images, made up of interjections, onomatopoeias and word roots, which was originarily close to ideas, just like hieroglyphs, ideograms and *blasons*.[33]

Romanticism endorsed this idea of language as transparent, notwithstanding Swift's sharp parody through Gulliver's experience at the Grand Academy on the island of Laputa, where names were replaced by the things themselves.[34] Morellet redeployed the idea of language's mimetic nature,[35] and Coleridge turned again to 'gesticulation' and hieroglyphs as its putative origin.[36] Nodier referred to Court de Gébelin's word roots in his *Dictionnaire des onomatopées*, and declared in his presentation of his 'theory of natural etymologies', which was to restitute the 'first' or 'primitive' and 'universally intelligible' language (itself 'of great assistance to poets'), that:

> The names of things, when spoken, were thus the imitation of their sounds, and the names of things, when written, the imitation of their form. Onomatopoeia is thus the model of pronounced languages, just as hieroglyphs are the model of written languages.[37]

This theory, in which 'an era of vowels' replaced the originary 'cry', and linguistic 'mimologisms' inhabited word 'radicals', naturally referred to the Tower of Babel.[38] Since then, many poets have espoused this neo-Cratylism,[39] postulating a naturally motivated and originary language in order to exorcize the two-fold scandal of the multiplicity of languages and the arbitrary nature of the sign. This myth found fresh support among the Symbolists, for instance in Mallarmé's *Mots anglais*,[40] with René Ghil[41] and Jean d'Udine (who revived the older theory of onomatopoeia)[42] and even among the anthroposophists.[43] Valéry still talked of the 'primitive melody' of language.[44]

In the twentieth century, this myth was illustrated by the art of the pun, when cultivated as a method of etymological investigation in itself,[45] as part of a tradition which included Jean-Pierre Brisset[46] and Court de Gébelin, as well as, *mutatis mutandis*, the Futurists' 'Words-in-Freedom',[47] the *Lautgedicht* from R. Hausmann to A. Riedl, V. Khlebnikov's *zaum* language,[48] Kurt Schwitters's *Systemschrift*[49] and *Ursonate*,[50] and even Lettrism and concrete poetry.[51] The most convincing proof of the continuity with Enlightenment ideas is provided by Raoul Hausmann. In his *Introduction to a History of the Sound Poem*, after citing Scheerbart, Morgenstern, Khlebnikov, Khroutchenikh, Iliazd, Ball and Arp, and mentioning Tristan Tzara's 'gymnastic poem, a concert of vowels' and Pierre Albert-Birot's poems 'for shouting and dancing', he discussed Chinese characters and also onomatopoeia.[52] His manifesto *Optophonetics*[53] was even more explicit, referring to the 'old secret sciences' and expressing his wish to reach 'a new primordial state' and create 'primordial signals'. Sound poetry, he declared, 'represented my effort to reach back to a primordial language at its very source'. This is why Hausmann implicitly appealed to the primitive pictogram, since what the 'opto-phonetic poem' sought was precisely to create 'a kind of scopo-phony' or 'eido-phony' by means of typography.[54]

Antonin Artaud, known for his use of 'glossolalia', appealed to the same sources in defending his 'new language' of theatre in 1932:

> Gesture is its material and its wits . . . It springs from the necessity of speech more than from speech already formed. . . . It retraces poetically the path that has culminated in the creation of language. . . . All the operations through which

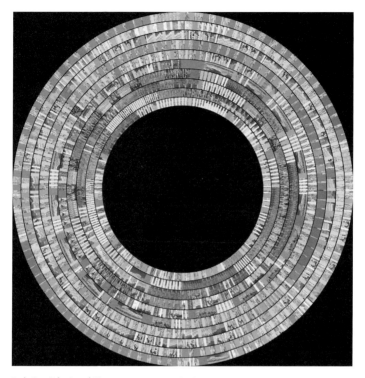

Jack Ox, *Schwitters' Ursonate,* 1990–93, painting.

the word has passed in order to come to [signify] by means of cries, onomatopoeia, signs, attitudes, and by slow, copious, impassioned modulations of tension . . . these it recreates . . . The language of the theater aims then at encompassing and utilizing extension, that is to say space, and by utilizing it, to make it speak: I deal with objects – the data of extension – like images, like words, bringing them together and making them respond to each other according to laws of symbolism and living analogies: eternal laws, those of all poetry and all viable language, and, among other things, of Chinese ideograms and ancient Egyptian hieroglyphs.[55]

That the allusion to ideograms and hieroglyphs, which itself has a long history, should resurface, is highly significant. Warburton and Condillac, who associated these with Chinese characters, claimed that painting was the origin of writing.[56] A century earlier, John Bulwer had invented whole 'chirogrammatic alphabets'.[57] And Diderot, in his *Letter on the Deaf and Dumb* (1751), in which he also argued that language originated in gesture and music, dwelt at length on the idea of the hieroglyph. Reviving the tradition of the emblem, he defined poetic language as follows:

> It states and paints objects at the same time; it appeals not only to the understanding, but also to the soul which it stirs and the imagination that sees and the ear that hears.[58]

Similarly, Rousseau united the different senses by linking onomatopoeia, hieroglyphs and mime in a 'figural language', the neo-Cratylian language of the 'first humans' or of poetry.[59] In explaining 'imitative language', Nodier bracketed together onomatopoeia and pictograms: 'Nature provided hieroglyphs for the painter-writer.'[60]

In literature, typographical experiments (inaugurated by Mallarmé's *Coup de dé*)[61] and spatialism[62] were part of just such a utopia of integration of the written with the visual,[63] while modern painters pointed to the ideogram as proof that their art was originally writing.[64] No spontaneist painter or advocate of synthesis between the arts could omit a reference to Chinese calligraphy, the traditional rival of hieroglyphics,[65] as exemplified by Ezra Pound. 'I make no distinction between painting and poetry', Miró said, 'and so sometimes I illustrate my canvases with poetic phrases, and vice versa. After all, was this not how the Chinese, those great masters of the spirit, worked?'[66] In 1958, Robert Benayoun, a Surrealist of the eleventh hour, still described Chinese and Egyptian writing as 'the reminder of a Golden Age of expression.'[67] Guillaume Apollinaire,[68] who more or less invented the typographic *calligramme*, claimed in his lecture on 'The New Spirit and the Poets' (1917) that such artifices can 'achieve the synthesis between the arts of music, painting and literature.[69] Visual poetry took him at his word, and mobilized both the written words' sounds and their graphic qualities. Its advocates, like their predecessors, paid homage to the myth of an originary language as the paradigm of a lost unity. In Pierre Garnier's words:

> The new poetry must be a new medium capable of existing beyond all the limits imposed by language, and encompassing music, painting, typography and all forms of culture, expressing also an aspiration doubtlessly utopian but nevertheless real, to return to a primal state of sensibility.[70]

This nostalgia, the desire to return to roots,[71] is a good illustration of how Futurism, in its striving for completeness, paradoxically invoked a lost paradise, similar to the one incarnated by the 'Surrealist trinity' of the madman, the savage and the child. André Leroi-Gourhan, who strongly criticized the traditional genealogy of writing as grounded in the pictogram, cast a pessimistic light on these new tendencies, predicting that:

> We shall see that the search for pure rhythm, and for the non-figurative in modern art and poetry, which were born of the contemplation of the arts of primitive peoples alive today, far from being a new departure, are in fact a regressive escapism which seeks refuge in primitive reactions.[72]

5
HEARING IN COLOUR: THE TRANSFORMATIONS OF A MYTH

'Oculis cum admiratione audimus, et auribus spectamus'
– Athanasius Kircher[1]

'Beethoven's eyes must have heard'
– Igor Markévitch[2]

The vast galaxy of speculations on synaesthesia gravitates around a still centre: the phenomenon of hearing in colour, or 'colour hearing', as it has been called. This is where the network of correspondences constellated around the triangle of the visual arts, literature and music converges.

Colour hearing, which states the possibility of passing directly and naturally between the world of sound and that of colour, covered an expanding field of speculations, experiments and theories which reached their peak in the late nineteenth and early twentieth centuries around the movements of Symbolism, Expressionism and abstraction. Among the many artists interested in these ideas, one can mention the writers E.T.A. Hoffmann, Alfred de Musset, Théophile Gautier, Charles Baudelaire, Arthur Rimbaud, Joris-Karl Huysmans, Victor Segalen, Karel Teige and Vladimir Nabokov; the musicians Franz Liszt, Joseph Joachim Raff, Jean Sibelius, Nicolai Rimsky-Korsakov, Alexander Scriabin, Serge Alexandrovich Koussevitzky, Arnold Schönberg, Joseph Matthias Hauer, Olivier Messiaen,[3] and György Ligeti;[4] and the painters Johannes Itten, Wassily Kandinsky, Stanton MacDonald-Wright, Charles Blanc-Gatti and David Hockney.

The demon of analogy was not restricted to aesthetics, although it certainly flourished in the Wagnerian poetics of the *Gesamtkunstwerk,* which championed the convergence of the arts, their synthesis and fusion. It spread to other fields such as linguistics, psychology, philosophy and theosophy, as can be seen from the extensive bibliography on the subject. Yet when we examine the numerous attempts to make correlations between sounds and colours, we are struck by their variety, to the point of incoherence, which appears both in the results (tables of equivalences) and in the methods used. There are, for example, 'objective' approaches, which attempt to ground the correspondence in the physical, vibratory character of both sound and light, and at the other extreme, 'subjective' ones, in which it is the observing subject who perceives the equivalences. This opposition between the rational and the emotional, or the quantitative and the qualitative, is supplemented by further pairs, indicative of the many dimensions of the subject: the scientific versus the symbolic, the cosmological versus the psychical, and so forth.

'Colour hearing' deserves closer study on several accounts. The sudden convergence of interest in it in the nineteenth century is a clear sign that we are dealing with a cultural fact, shaped by an ideology, which we have identified as nostalgia for a lost unity. Second, the determinant role of context, and the different mediations which fashion chains of association, raise methodological issues. Lastly, there are aesthetic reasons for dwelling on this area, since the myth of correspondences was a source of inspiration for many creative works.[5] Our aim in this chapter is not to dismiss the magnificently poetic dimension of synaesthetic experience, which unquestionably enriches our access to the world in a unique way – as Merleau-Ponty wrote, 'synaesthetic perception is the rule'[6] – but, by exploring its theoretical foundations, simply to tease out something of its context-specific character.

The Colour of Vowels

In his essay-pamphlet on Rimbaud's 'famous sonnet on vowels', the scholar and polemicist Etiemble claimed that 'The infatuation with colour hearing died out around 1900.'[7] For once, Etiemble was ill-informed. The subject was still topical in 1912, as demonstrated by two articles which appeared in the review *Imago*,[8] and it has attracted psychologists and artists up to this very day,[9] as many recent publications,[10] and also the multi-media experiments of contemporary avant-gardes, attest.[11] As for the question of the colour of vowels – culminating in the 1880s with René Ghil's idea of 'verbal instrumentation', which corrects Rimbaud's equivalences and extends them to the colour of diphthongs and consonants[12] – it was far from running out of steam in the twentieth century. Kandinsky referred to it in 1911 and 1928,[13] as did Satie,[14] Breton,[15] Eisenstein[16] and Karl Gerstner.[17] Kupka was still quoting Rimbaud's *Voyelles*,[18] and Delaunay seems to have been inspired for a watercolour painted in 1914 by the synaesthetic lines of *Alchimie du verbe*.[19] At the Paris Exhibition of 1937, there was a performance devoted to 'Les Voyelles et leur synchronisation sonore et chromatique' ('The sound and colour synchronization of Vowels'). And along the same lines, one can mention Auguste Herbin's *Alphabets plastiques*,[20] the *Abécédaire sur des poèmes de Jacques Damase* (1969), Sonia Delaunay's *Alfabeto* (1970), a watercolour by Etienne Delessert (*AEIOU*, 1987),[21] Claire Nydegger's 'setting to colour' of the *Voyelles d'Arthur Rimbaud* (1995)[22] and more recently Nabokov's *Alphabet in Color*.[23] Despite creating a work he called *Song of the Vowels* (1931–2), Jacques Lipchitz explicitly denied any connection between it and Rimbaud's famous sonnet,[24] whereas Paul Klee, who made several painting-poems after 1918 with coloured letters, might well have been referring to Rimbaud in a painting hanging in the New York Museum of Modern Art (1922): its untranslatable title, *Das Vokaltuch der Kammersängerin Rosa Silber* (literally, 'the vowel fabric of the chamber singer Rosa Silver') is a kind of manifesto for synaesthesia in its triple wordplay, since '*Tuch*' refers both to the material texture of the painting and to the texture of the

'Letter A', etching from Giuseppe Maria Mitelli,
Alfabeto in sogno (1683).

voice (its tessitura); '*Rosa*' is the singer's first name and also the colour of the painting; and '*Silber*' captures the silvery tones of the painting, but also the quality of the singer's voice (*Silberstimme*). And although the colours of the five vowels in the composition do not correspond to Rimbaud's, one can still imagine that Klee was implicitly referring to his work.[25]

Rimbaud was not, in fact, the first. Diderot had mentioned 'brown voices and blonde voices',[26] and Copineau, who was similarly keen on analogies and correspondences in his analyses of language, attributed the colour red to the letter R.[27] Some forty years later, in 1812, Doctor Sachs became interested in the colour of vowels in his pioneering research into synaesthesia, which was soon to be taken further by the Romantics. August Wilhelm Schlegel, for example, in his work on primitive languages, associated 'gradations of coloured vowels' and 'scales of vowels' with feelings.[28] The feelings guaranteed the equivalences proposed. 'Vowels are what express feelings in a language', he wrote, in an attempt to justify the correspondences he made; 'sky-blue *i* is the vowel of intimacy and love.'[29] A similar idea can be found in Rudolf Steiner,[30] and the classical theory of the affects had already introduced an expressive component.[31]

The most influential theses on an originary language were Herder's[32] and Court de Gébelin's,[33] a legacy reflected in René Ghil's claim that 'the primordial cry [is] of the same essence as gesture';[34] there is also a work by a certain Brès who, in a curious text published in 1828, related the colour of vowels to children's language and to the famous issue of onomatopoeia.[35] This association can be found in Pierre-Simon Ballanche, who imagined 'onomatopoeias of colours',[36] while allusions to 'primitive onomatopoeia' continued into the works of the psychologists,[37] and later on the Futurists, whose Manifestos make ample use of the device. The linguist Jacob Ludwig Grimm, who endorsed the theory of roots, compared articulated sounds to the notes of the musical scale and to the spectrum of colours. In his view, the three primary vowels 'a', 'i' and 'u' gave rise to the secondary ones 'e' and 'o', and also to diphthongs through combination.[38] There was a further dimension to this, since vowels were generally thought to be feminine, like colour, and consonants to be masculine, like drawing.[39] In 1859, however, the educationalist H. J. Chavée made a further distinction within vowels, between masculine and feminine ones. He also advised that 'in order to make the study of the sounds of the spoken voice (vowels) irresistibly attractive, one need do no more than compare their range to the gradations of colour.' He then compared the 'white voice which contains all colours' with sunlight, and derived from this the correspondence between 'the three fundamental colours of the voice' – the vowels 'u', 'i' and 'a' – and the colours yellow, red and blue.[40]

The Colour of Sounds

The possible correlations between sounds and colours had fascinated philosophers and physicians ever since Aristotle.[41] A notable figure in this long tradition was Père Louis-Bertrand Castel (1688–1757), a Jesuit and polymath, whose work gave fresh impetus to the debates and marked an important turning point, by adding practice to theory.[42] He devised a concrete application of the correspondences he theorized between the chromatic scale and the colours of the spectrum, in the form of an 'ocular harpsichord' – ultimately a mythical instrument, but one whose fame would endure and spawn countless imitations. Castel's audience was far from insignificant. He was acclaimed by Rameau, Telemann, Diderot,[43] Algarotti,[44] Voltaire[45] and even by a number of architects;[46] he was discussed by Jean-Jacques Rousseau and Moses Mendelssohn, among others, then by the German Romantics,[47] and not least by the advocates of colour music, who saw in him an inspirational forebear.

Until then, correspondences had almost always been founded either on the mathematical principle of proportion, or on cosmological symbolism. But just when such analogies between optics and acoustics were beginning to be challenged in the name of science, the exploration of synaesthesia properly speaking – the interference between different channels of sensory perception[48] – took a new turn, shifting its focus from the object of perception to the perceiving subject.

The poet and botanist Erasmus Darwin is arguably the best representative of the combination of physics and psychology which was emerging at the time. He was keen to enlist the imagination into the service of 'science',[49] and was interested in Castel's ideas on 'luminous' or 'visible and audible' music. He mentioned the system of Pythagorean proportions applied by Newton to the colour spectrum, but was also influenced, in his demonstration of the 'sisterhood' between music and painting,[50] by Berkeley's idealism as well as by Locke's example of the blind man who sees the sound of a trumpet as scarlet.[51] Nodier used the same reference,[52] as did Mme de Staël. After mentioning the experiments of the physician Chladni on vibrations and Castel's harpsichord, she returned to colour hearing and the blind man Saunderson, declaring that:

> we are constantly comparing painting to music and music to painting, because the emotions we feel show us analogies where detached observation would show us only differences.[53]

As for writers' theories of synaesthesia, we shall simply mention a few names here. Wackenroder considered sounds and colours to be inseparable,[54] and Tieck maintained that there was a kinship between colours, scents and song.[55] But the major inspiration for future generations was E.T.A. Hoffmann, whom Baudelaire quoted: 'even when awake, when I hear music, I find an analogy and an intimate connection uniting colours, sounds and perfumes.'[56] Fifteen years later, in 1861, Baudelaire wrote of Wagner's music:

> what would be really surprising would be that sounds could not evoke colours, that colours could not convey the idea of a melody, and that sound and colour should be unsuited to translating ideas.[57]

The famous line which inspired a Debussy *Prélude* – 'sounds and scents spiral in the evening air'[58] – confirms once more 'the immense keyboard of correspondences',[59] which Gautier likewise exploits in his *Hachich*, describing how 'I heard the sound of colours. Green, red, blue, yellow sounds reached me in perfectly distinct waves.'[60]

As though echoing Baudelaire, the Austrian critic Hermann Bahr wrote how 'scents sing, sounds scent the air, and colours resonate.'[61] But unlike Baudelaire, Bahr thought this synaesthesia was 'scientifically proven'. For the colour of sounds also interested scientific circles. After Doctor Sachs published a clinical study (the very first) on colour hearing, in 1812, several generations of researchers grappled with the mysteries of what at the time was called synopsis, phonopsis, photaesthesia, pseudochromaesthesia or opsiphonia.[62] This striking infatuation with the subject has many explanations. The rise in experimental medicine and psychology, the development of statistics and a novel interest in pathological and marginal phenomena such as albinism, colour blindness, epilepsy, hysteria and the effects of hallucinogens, all defined a field particularly receptive to synaesthesia because they were united by the methodological challenge of testing out theories or hypotheses concerning how perception functioned. The old debate between inneists and empiricists was revived in this context. The great scientists of the age all had their say – which is why we can find as many as eleven different explanations of the same phenomenon![63]

So it would be wrong to think that explorations of the relations between colours and sounds were merely marginal preoccupations. And to get a better sense of the scale of what was in fact a fully fledged obsession, a glance at the bibliographical evidence should suffice: in 1893, Flournoy mentions 85 publications on colour hearing,[64] while Adrian B. Klein's classic work of 1926 on the subject lists more than 330,[65] and the following year an article by Friedrich Mahling on the 'Problem of Sound-colour Synaesthesia' identified almost 500 publications.[66] But his bibliography cannot have been exhaustive, because a thesis published in the same year mentions many other works on synaesthesia and Albert Wellek,[67] one of the specialists on the question, arrived at the vertiginous figure of 800 in a work of 1931.[68] This interest was at last officially recognized when, in 1927, 1930, 1933 and 1936, four Congresses were organized in Hamburg on the relations between sound and colour, bringing together educationalists, anthroposophists, historians of literature, painters, musicologists and musicians, film-makers, theatre directors and so forth.[69]

In order to give a clearer picture of this interpenetration of art and science, which was so typical of the time, we supply some Appendices showing areas relevant to our theme, their contents arranged chronologically. Appendix 1 reproduces Friedrich Mahling's bibliography, which lists studies on synaesthesia. It is not exhaustive, as we have seen, but it is organized by date of publication, which is helpful for plotting the changing intensity of interest in these questions. Appendix 2 mentions noteworthy events or experiments in the history of the avant-gardes regarding collaboration, convergence or synthesis between the arts. The remarkable continuity of this fantasy of unity in the arts is suggested by a chronological list of the audio-visual machines and devices invented to produce sound and light simultaneously, or a 'music of colours' (Appendix 3). Such instruments, which often remained at the design stage and were named by neologisms invented for the occasion,[70] were direct descendants of Castel's famous ocular harpsichord or of Arcimboldo's earlier – and no less mythical – 'gravicembalo', described by Comanini.[71] Lastly, we list the many theoretical writings which accompanied these experiments (Appendix 4).[72]

The 'Belles Infidèles'

The discussions at the Hamburg Congresses and in the specialized journals of the time concerned the status, nature and types of sensations of light produced by the perception of sounds; the psycho-physiological mechanisms producing these effects; and their statistical occurrence.[73] But what has left living traces in our cultural memory is not this marginal chapter in the history of science. Rather, it is the actual experiments carried out by artists. The surest sign that the scientific and the artistic approaches intermeshed is the fact that many artists participated in the Hamburg Congresses, and that similar research was being carried out in the same period at the Bauhaus.[74]

By the end of the nineteenth century, this 'new spiritual synthesis' was greeted with enthusiasm. Wallace Rimington, who invented the colour-organ, wrote in 1895 that 'Notes of music and notes of colour can in these respects be treated in exactly the same way'.[75] He declared 'colour music', which he qualified as both 'artistic and scientific', to be the art of the future. With a venerable tradition behind it, stretching back several centuries to Castel (who was still cited), 'colour music' also had an impressive future ahead of it, right up to the medium of video itself, and its influence stretched from the USA to the USSR, thanks, among others, to Wilfred, Laszlo,[76] to the 'Prometheus' group in Kazan. The emphasis on pure colour, and the introduction of movement and rhythm, as Rimington had himself recommended, prefigured the beginnings of abstraction and the birth of the cinema, which would inherit a similarly utopian dimension,[77] as exemplified by the trajectories of Léopold Survage, the Corradini brothers, Viktor Eggeling, Hans Richter,[78] Alexander Laszlo and Oskar Fischinger. As one critic wrote, 'Someone discovered one day that music could be made without recording a sound', and he encouraged people to return to 'this wonderful optical music'.[79] The 'sixth', and later 'seventh art', as Ricciotto Canudo called it,[80] borrowed the notion of rhythm from the world of sound,[81] and likewise aspired to be 'synaesthetic' and to condense a multi-sensory experience.[82] Lastly, various experimental theatre projects, from Schönberg's or Kandinsky's compositions to the 'Total Theatre' of Oskar Schlemmer, Farkas Molnar and Gropius, likewise perpetuated the ideal of the *Gesamtkunstwerk*, as did the 'parallel scores' invented by Moholy-Nagy or Hirschfeld-Mack for 'multi-dimensional' performances.[83]

We are familiar with the importance of the notion of translation in the doctrine of *ut pictura poesis*, with its idea of passing directly

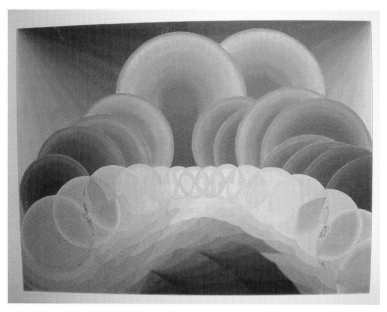

Charles Blanc-Gatti, *Le Rouet d'Omphale* (Saint-Saëns), 1931,
oil on canvas.

Jack Ox, *Stravinsky, Symphony in Three Movements*, 1979,
oil paint on fibreglass strips mounted on wood sections.

from text to image. Likewise for *ut musica pictura*. Lessing had refuted the possibility of the former, and saw no need to stop at the latter, except to say that 'colours are not sounds, and ears are not eyes', thus disqualifying painting from treating musical themes.[84] At the opposite extreme from this purism, Castel's 'musical tapestry' and his 'auricular harpsichord' were precisely designed to 'translate' sounds into colour. This exercise, which was based on the principle of sound-colour synaesthesia, inspired several compositions of 'colour music', by Hector and Laszlo, for example.[85] It also guided the Corradini brothers in their experiments with the chromatic piano: 'After a few necessary adjustments, we translated a Venitian Barcarole by Mendelssohn, a Rondo by Chopin and a Sonata by Mozart.'[86] And the 'translation' of these same composers is also the subject of one of the brothers' first films. Laszlo, Fischinger and later McLaren, to name but a few, likewise turned to the medium of film. And the American dancer Loïe Fuller, who was also drawn to film, had planned visual transpositions of the music of Mendelssohn, Berlioz, Grieg, Debussy, Scriabin and Stravinsky.[87]

But painting was the artform which explored most fully the translation of music. The 'Musicalist Painters' (*les Peintres Musicalistes*), a group founded in 1932, made this their speciality,[88] publishing a Manifesto and holding a series of *Salons*: the 'Belles infidèles' held centre stage once more. Their main theoretician, Charles Blanc-Gatti – who used the terms 'translation' or 'transposition' interchangeably – transcribed various pieces of music, including Saint-Saëns's *Rouet d'Omphale* and Ravel's *Bolero*. Olivier Messiaen, who worked with him and owned several of his paintings, described him as 'painting what he heard – and I transformed what I had seen into sound and rhythm.'[89] Blanc-Gatti referred to numerous artistic and scientific sources,[90] but he seems not to have been aware that this practice, which was in fact inaugurated by D. D. Jameson in 1844,[91] already existed at the beginning of the century among the Italian Symbolists.[92] When Russolo gave an interpretation of his painting of 1911 called *La Musica*, he used the term 'translation' three times.[93] And the anthroposophists were also interested, believing that 'notes of music correspond to glowing colours.' This is what was shown by the illustrated *Thought-forms* (1901) of Annie Besant and Charles W. Leadbeater, for whom sound, 'always associated with colour . . . produces forms as well as colours'.[94] These ideas subtended a whole series of experiments between the two World Wars: in North America, Marsden Hartley, Arthur Dove and Georgia O'Keeffe depicted jazz music in the spirit of a nationalistic quest for identity,[95] and in Vienna the circle around Oskar Rainer and the Institut für musikalische Graphik explored the pedagogical virtues of such correspondences.[96] Paul Klee[97] and Henri Nouveau[98] transcribed Bach, and, in 1928, Kandinsky transposed Mussorgsky into forms, colours and lights in Dessau, after translating the theme of Beethoven's Fifth Symphony into dots.[99] We should also mention the names of Walter Behm,[100] Max Gehlsen, Hilde Kaul, Rudolph Gahlbeck,[101] Trevor Bell,[102] Judith Rothschild,[103] Ira Jean Belmont,[104] Dessa (Deborah Petroz-Abeles) and Rachel Sebba,[105] among many others.[106] This tradition was revived by Luigi Veronesi, Robert Strübin, Jakob Weder[107] and Jack Ox, who painted a series of visualizations of music by Bach, Debussy, Stravinsky and Bruckner.[108] And quite recently, Laszlo's music gave rise to a whole range of visual transpositions.[109]

Is Middle C Red or Blue?

Some people claim that when Van Gogh took piano lessons, he linked the notes to colours.[110] More generally, the numerous systems of correspondences invented to match the musical scale to the colour spectrum supposed some fundamental belief in a hidden affinity between the visible and the audible. Yet when we look at the sheer variety of systems of equivalence – somewhat similar to the case of the colour of vowels, which so irritated Etiemble – we begin to sense how subjective the analogies were. One need only compare, for example, the coloured scales of Scriabin and Rimsy-Korsakov, despite the fact that they were contemporaries and from a similar cultural background.[111]

It is difficult to compare the different findings because the systems' modes of construction and results are so heterogeneous.[112] There are many causes for this, for example, the conflict between the numbers six and seven (six primary and secondary or complementary colours, seven notes in the diatonic scale), which creates problems at the end of the cycle (between violet and red, and between B and C); or the naming of colours, since each language differs in this,[113] and the terminological imprecision is magnified when adjectives are added (cornflower blue, sea green, and so on.).[114] Musical classifications are similarly variable, with absolute values (the notes of the scale) being used alongside relative ones (degrees, tonal functions or intervals, as well as keys, modes and chords). There are also competing ways of organizing the series of elements: for music, the chromatic scale versus the cycle of fifths; for colour, the spectrum (from red to violet) versus values or degrees of luminosity (from yellow to violet). This is why the theories focused variously on measuring the relation between spectrum bandwidths and Pythagorean proportions (Newton[115]), on the numerical relation between string and frequency lengths, or even on the relation between the rainbow and the system of natural harmonics (Haug[116]). Although, given the vogue for synaesthesia, the foundation for the system tended to be located in psychology, certain authors attempted to find a compromise between reasoning or measurement, and a subjective, hence necessarily individualistic, approach.[117] Schopenhauer, for instance, tried to reconcile 'the rationality of numerical relations' with 'feeling alone'.[118] Even the argument of frequencies was not straightforward: Blanc-Gatti claimed that 'colours are notes 50 octaves higher', whereas Vitinghoff, using the same calculations, arrived at the figure of 41 octaves!'[119] This is a good example of the arbitrariness of this type of speculation, which, moreover, made no distinction between sound and light waves.[120] To demonstrate this, we have borrowed Etiemble's idea of 'a table of discordances'[121] in order to survey some forty systems of correspondences between notes and colours, spanning more than three centuries (Appendix 5).[122]

Additionally, certain artists such as the composer Jean d'Udine maintained that a sound's pitch was related to values or degrees of luminosity (rather than to a particular colour), and different timbres were related to different hues.[123] But the range of timbres proved as disparate as the correspondences between the notes of the scale and colours. And linking colours with musical instruments, as J. L. Hoffmann was the first to do, in 1786[124] – followed by musicians,[125] painters[126] and critics[127] – yielded results which were as incoherent as those of psychologists. The colour blue, for example, was associated with all the stringed instruments, with the flute (five times out of eleven), the trumpet (twice) and the organ (twice), while the colour red conjured up the flute, the oboe, the basset horn, the trumpet (six times out of eighteen), the trombone (twice), the bass saxophone, cymbals, drums and the human voice. Quite a symphony!

So we can see, if proof were needed, how arbitrary these results were, and indeed the incoherence of the whole project, regardless of whether the system was based on rational or intuitive criteria.[128] And at the risk of setting the town ablaze again on the subject of the spirit or 'character' of different keys,[129] we should also not forget that concert pitch varied not only historically but even at the same moment, with sometimes as much as a whole tone between religious and profane music, or in different venues of the same town.

But such unruliness should not demoralize the historian, since every disorder has a meaning, and examining mistakes or misunderstandings can be highly instructive. Moreover, certain correlations, such as those between a musical note and a colour, have a relative fixity within the apparent chaos. Thus one can draw a diagonal line – corresponding to a statistical frequency – from c as red to b as violet. Far from being there by chance, this regularity points to the association of red, as one end of the visible spectrum, with the 'bottom' of the musical scale, its traditional starting point, and so as the natural equivalent of 'c'. Also, the easiest scale to play on a keyboard instrument is the scale of c major, because it uses only the white keys. These remarks may appear anecdotal, but they actually show three types of mediation at work in the comparisons between musical notes and colours: theoretical (music theory), technical (how the instruments were made) and linguistic (the term '*infra*-red', for example, situates colour spatially, on a scale similar to that of the keyboard).[130] Another factor is the weight of tradition, which we see in the frequent association of the timbre of the trumpet with scarlet, an association clearly influenced by the canonical example of Locke's blind man and the colour he sees.

We should also note the importance of the religious symbolism of numbers, which led Newton to divide the spectrum into seven sections.[131] Three and twelve are also highly significant, and have equivalents in music: when Castel mapped the chromatic triangle of blue-yellow-red onto the 'perfect' chord C-E-G in 1740, he was embodying the idea of divine perfection, represented by the figure of the circle and the Trinity, and also that of the created world, since he held that each 'primitive' colour incarnated a kingdom (red for the animal, blue for the vegetable and yellow for the mineral kingdom).[132] His influence on the history of the music of colours was substantial, and especially on Gustave de La Moussaye,[133] who adopted Castel's two triads in 1853, but reversed their order (red = C, blue = G). He endowed the figure of the circle with the same symbolic force, as suggested in his conclusion:

> From these various comparisons it ensues that the harmonic laws of the universe are linked together by identical relations, that they together form a vast homogeneous whole, and that all converge along their radius towards their common centre, the godhead.

In the same year, he published a second article in the same journal, *L'Artiste*, in which he enlarged his 'dodecaphonic' [*sic*] system of correspondences to the other senses, which now totalled seven after the addition of 'generation' and 'magnetic vision.'[134] In the 1820s, Brès, whom we mentioned above, had likewise shaped his system of correspondences around the number seven, which in his view corresponded to the number of vowels, the notes of the scale, the number of colours and degrees of luminosity, the number of tastes, smells, planets, periods of human life – and more.[135]

Similarly, Castel's choice of 'c' = blue had a theological dimension, insofar as blue is the colour of the sky, and thus associated with God, who is the origin of all things, just as 'c' is the fundamental note of the major scale. When it became possible to measure frequencies and compare the wavelengths of sound and light,[136] the order was reversed, with 'c' becoming red, and violet having the highest frequency (the equivalent of 'b' on the musical scale). But quantification did not eliminate the weight of symbolism, as we shall see.

A Feast for the Senses

Every synaesthetic system, whether it is constructed on intuitive or rational principles, is rooted in ideological suppositions. Thus equivalences are not part of a natural order, as some have claimed, nor do they derive from a sovereign individual subjectivity, as just as many others have maintained. Rather, they are geographically and temporally specific cultural constructions which as such can be interpreted in historical terms. And although we should take into account the artwork's internal logic, as Sergei Eisenstein, among others, has emphasized,[137] we should also consider its determinant contexts.

In this respect, it is important to bear in mind that colour hearing is simply a particular case within a much larger whole, the idea of a synaesthesic universe. This was an inexhaustible source of poetic invention and scientific investigation,[138] and once again it was Castel who blazed the trail: 'I shall extend my demonstrations', he boasted, 'to all the other senses.'[139] He imagined a 'harpsichord for the senses', whose instructions opened with the following lines: 'Put some 40 incense-burners full of different perfumes side by side; put valves on them, and make sure that the movement of the keys opens the valves.'[140] The idea met with some success. The composer Grétry, declaring that 'each of our five senses can have its own harpsichord', mused on the 'guttural harmonies' which a harpsichord of flavours would produce: 'what a pleasure it would be for the discerning palate to prelude on this harpsichord!', he exclaimed. Convinced of 'the analogy which exists between all natural phenomena', he listed 'the colours in music, as in painting, which indicate different passions and characters'.[141]

Again, this idea was centuries old. Aristotle had thought of applying to flavours the same musical proportions as he had applied to colours.[142] Athanasius Kircher followed suit in placing the issue '*sub quinque sensibus*' (under the five senses).[143] Moses Mendelssohn pondered the correlation between the senses, and their potential harmony,[144] and Herder was nagged by the same question: 'How are sight and hearing, color and word, scent and sound, connected? ... We are a single thinking *sensorium commune*.'[145] For Senancourt, 'melody, if we take the term in its broadest possible sense, can also result from a series of colours or a series of scents.'[146] In 1818 André Morellet formulated the idea of 'the correspondence between different organs',[147] long before his homonym François Morellet's essay of 1964, *Mise en condition du spectateur*.[148] The works of Brès, Jean d'Udine and Blanc-Gatti,[149] among others, also testify to this persistence of the utopian idea of a total synaesthesia.

Rimbaud, the author of the sonnet *Voyelles*, prided himself on having invented 'a poetic language which will one day be accessible to all the senses'.[150] And Symbolists like Ghil held similar beliefs.[151] His tables of 'concordances' were actually used for a staging of Paul Napoléon Roinard's adaptation of the 'Song of Songs' at the Théâtre d'art in Paris on 10 December 1891, attended by many musicians and poets.[152] The scenery was devised by Roinard himself, and the musical setting was by a certain Madame Flamen de Labrély. Paul Fort appealed implicitly to the authority of Ghil and Rimbaud in describing 'the orchestration of the first scene: Speech: i-blue illuminated with o-white; Music: in C; Colour: in pale purple; Scent: incense'.[153] This experiment did not pass unnoticed. One critic praised it: 'the music and scents, harmonizing with the subject-matter of the scenes represented, primed and then crowned the spectator's impressions';[154] but another wrote mockingly that 'the silence was broken

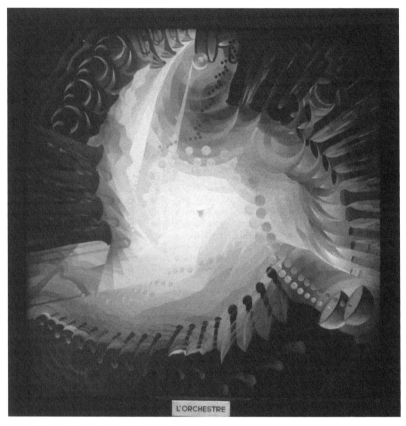

L'ORCHESTRE

Charles Blanc-Gatti, *L'Orchestre chromophonique*, 1932, painting.

by sneezing; we could not have imagined that the public was so refined, and so particular about the quality of its perfumes', ending with a jibe about the music: 'Maybe the vaporizers had not been tuned.'[155] This was not the last such experiment: F. Khnopff had perfume released in an exhibition, as did Scriabin for the 1915 production in New York of his *Prometheus*, along with projections of coloured light.[156]

Taste–smell synaesthesia intrigued Sibelius,[157] and Valentine de Saint-Point's declamatory poems, the '*Métachories*' – accompanied by music and dance – aspired to 'a fusion of all the arts', including scents.[158] Kupka maintained that because 'making an artwork requires the collaboration of all the sense organs',[159] one should 'add to the activity of the optic nerve that of the olfactory, acoustic and sensitive nerves'.[160] The pianist Marie Jaëll, who based her teachings on the analogy and correspondences between sounds, scents and sensations of touch, declared that one must 'listen with one's hands', and she also maintained that the way we perceive colours influences how we perceive musical timbre.[161] The Bauhaus never tired of experimenting with interactions between the senses, particularly the sense of touch, for example in Gertrud Grunow's pedagogy,[162] which inspired the teaching of Itten's and Moholy-Nagy's *Vorkurs*; and equally in the way Kandinsky encouraged a total synaesthetic experience in his teaching,[163] writing in 1938: 'don't think that you receive painting solely through your eyes. No, although you may be unaware of it, you receive it through all five senses.'[164]

This idea of total synaesthesia also attracted the Futurists. Boccioni wrote in 1914: 'The day may come when the painted canvas is not enough. . . . Then paintings will perhaps be a giddying architecture of sounds and scents.'[165] In *La Peinture des sons, des bruits et odeurs*, Carlo Carrà imagined a 'total painting which requires the active cooperation of all the senses'.[166] Russolo called one of his canvases *Profumo*, and Enrico Prampolini sought to 'highlight in a single synthesis sensations linked to form, colour, architectonics, movement, noise, scent, and so forth'.[167] In 1921 the manifesto on *Musical improvisation* by Bartoccini and Mantia announced that it was preparing for 'the ideal fusion of all the arts' through 'musical commentaries on poems, thoughts, canvases, scents, tactile boards, etc.'[168] Marinetti's movement, Tactilism, planned 'accompaniments of music and light' for 'tactile theatre', since 'the distinction between the five senses is arbitrary.'[169] Karel Teige's Poetism likewise endorsed a total art, and Nicolas Schöffer's 'Centre for sexual recreation' (*c.* 1960) involved all the senses, as did many happenings of the time.[170] Eisenstein's theory of 'vertical montage' advocated the 'synchronization' of all the senses.[171] And in 1970 Man Ray mused that 'if I made a film now, it would be in colour and in 3-D . . . It would have to give off scents as well as sounds, and hot and cold.'[172]

The Baser Senses

Hearing and sight, as traditionally the noblest senses, took pride of place in the hierarchy, overshadowing the others.[173] Diderot, in the footsteps of Locke and Condillac, explored the relation between the senses of sight and touch,[174] but excluded from his notion of relation, on which he based his idea of Beauty, the most material ones: 'I exclude from this the qualities of taste and smell.'[175] But these two could also be invested with aesthetic qualities, as the double sense of the word 'taste' suggests. Segalen, for example, was interested in 'smells you can hear', 'audible tastes', 'taste counterpoint' and even 'optico-gustatory counterpoint'.[176] Rémy de Gourmont admonished René Ghil for 'not daring to include the hallucinatory sense of smell'.[177] But these vulgar senses could be rehabilitated only by assimilating them to the art of sounds. In 1570 Cardanus established parallels between tastes and musical intervals,[178] and in the ensuing century Fénelon depicted a 'music of scents' created 'in the same way as we assemble sounds', and producing 'a harmony which awakens the sense of smell just like our concerts caress the ear with sounds by turns low and high'.[179] Synaesthetic symphonies punctuate Zola's novels, not least the cheese symphony in the *Ventre de Paris* and the 'strange music of scents' which attends the death of Albine in *La Faute de l'abbé Mouret*, itself echoed in the whites sale episode of *Au Bonheur des dames*.[180] A work of the time devised a 'scale of smells' in which violet corresponded to 'D in the key of G major', orange blossom to 'G in the key of G major' and so forth.[181] In 2004 Pascal Desarzens devised a Scented Concert in collaboration with a chemist, illustrating eight scents musically. Christian Morgenstern had the idea of a 'scent organ',[182] and Kurt Lasswitz, a contemporary of Jules Verne, imagined a 'scents piano' called '*Ododion*', which starred in a 'scented concert' performed in an '*Odoratorium*'. It would usher in

– with a discreet nod to Wagner – the 'smells drama of the future'.[183] Lasswitz took the idea even further, and envisaged a brain organ (called a '*Gehirnsorgel*' or a '*Psychokinet*') capable of conveying emotions just like music, except that it did so directly, without the mediation of the five senses.[184]

Another theory which was to produce the most surprising applications was Aristotle's organization of tastes and colours numerically, in order to makes analogies between them. Thus in 1755 Polycarpe Poncelet declared that 'For liqueurs to chime agreeably together, their flavours must be mixed in harmonic proportions.' He added that the

> different flavours are produced by the more or less intense vibrations of the salts which act on the sense of taste, just as sounds are produced by the more or less intense vibrations of the air which acts on the sense of hearing.

Echoing Castel, Poncelet outlined an 'organ of flavours' for 'deliciously tasty music', which he called 'music for the tongue and the palate', made of 'consonances and dissonances' in 'harmonic proportion'. He devised a scale of seven flavours corresponding to the degrees of the diatonic scale, and deduced from this that 'a composer of stews, preserves, or ratafia is, in his own way, a composer of symphonies.'[185] We can perhaps find an echo of this in Huysmans's *A Rebours* (1884), where the 'art of perfumery', and the grammar and syntax of fragrances, are described in the musical terms of 'chords of fragrances, themes, orchestration, intervals'.[186] It was during this period that Castel was rediscovered, as suggested by an allusion in the *Mercure de France* to his 'harpsichord for the senses', presented as prefiguring Jean Des Esseintes's mouth organ.[187] Colin's 'pianoktail' imagined by Boris Vian[188] and, later still, Karl Gerstner's '*Taste Perceptor*' (1970) prolong this tradition.[189] Man Ray experimented with a scented version:

> We were testing it for Poiret in 1926. There was a boat on the Seine with an organ which released scents. One could play it and have all the scents.[190]

Continuing these analogies, Debussy described Grieg's music as an 'orchestral cuisine in which the scent of the harps blends with the citrus tang of the oboe, all of this bathed in the juice of the strings . . . a sort of very white song . . . music' (1903).[191] Some years later, C. F. Ramuz said that he and Stravinsky had pooled gastronomic and musical memories, and made associations between them, both of them

> agreeing conclusively . . . that music and cookery are one and the same thing, and that composing a successful dish is like composing an orchestral piece or a sonata.[192]

The Futurists were particularly interested in cookery, often linking it with music.[193] More recently, Philippe Beaussant, an expert in Baroque music, has shown his command of culinary metaphors.[194] But the most fabulous example of gourmet synaesthesia remains to this day a letter from Kandinsky to Elisaveta Ludwigovna, written on 7 December 1925, to thank her for a dish of polenta she had prepared for him:

> polenta contains a synthesis of pleasures for me because, curiously, it arouses three senses in a perfectly harmonious way: first the eyes see the marvellous yellow, then the nose apprehends a smell which unquestionably bears that yellow within it, and lastly the palate takes delight in a flavour in which this yellow and this scent are united. Then come associations for the fingers (the fingers of the spirit), polenta is gentle to its deepest depths (its surface too has gentle moments), and lastly for the ear – the middle-range notes of the flute. A quiet, muted sound, but strong . . . and the polenta I received had a little touch of pink in its yellow . . . unquestionably the flute.[195]

Cosmic Music

> O métamorphose mystique
> De tous mes sens fondus en un!
> Son haleine fait la musique,
> Comme sa voix fait le parfum!

These lines by Baudelaire are an invitation to pass into a higher, cosmic dimension, since the synaesthetic process is conceived as extending to the whole universe.[196] Balzac's *Séraphîta* describes ecstasy in terms of 'light [giving] birth to melody, melody [giving] birth to light, colours were light and melody'[197] and P. S. Ballanche wrote: 'All the senses enliven each other by reciprocal action. It is like onomatopoeias of colours, since everything is so harmonious in man and the universe.'[198] Cardanus was already associating planets, colours and tastes in 1550,[199] and a century later Athanasius Kircher created an impressive table of universal correspondences, in which musical intervals, colours, stars, minerals, plants and animal species were all linked to each other.[200] This encyclopaedic vein continued into the nineteenth century, as we have seen with Brès and de La Moussaye. From a quite different perspective, that of neurological research, Hermann Bahr arrived at 'the mystical union of the senses,'[201] while Charles Fourier, with his table of the 'seven passions of the soul', linked the notes of the scale, feelings, colours, logical operations, geometrical figures and various metals.[202] Anthroposophists such as Helena Blavatsky and Rudolf Steiner added further systems of analogy.[203]

Nineteenth-century psychological enquiries sometimes came to similar conclusions, but the associative chains were born of such a colourful imagination that they often ended up resembling the Surrealist game of 'one in the other'.[204] If one follows the associative chain link by link, one can pass from the colour of notes, of composers,[205] of musical instruments, vowels and even of the cries of animals[206] to the colour of scents and flavours, then the colour of numbers, hours, days,[207] months, epochs or signs of the zodiac;[208] and on to the colour of the elements, and of metals and planets, which brings us to the colour of body parts, the temperaments and the humours.[209] And ever since Goethe's *Farbenlehre*, and its sixth section devoted to the ethical and sensory effects of colour, the latter has been systematically related to scales of emotion and palettes of feelings.[210] René Ghil produced a table of correspondences between vowels, consonants, colours and timbres, which he related to feelings.[211] The concept of *Stimmung* thus extended the classical doctrine of the affects, or equally Poussin's theory of modes, on the basis of a theory of musical expressivity which was ultimately completely circular.

At the same time, the obsessive recurrence of terms such as 'synthesis'[212] and 'correspondence' signalled a powerful revival of analogical thought, renewed by the paradigm of vibration. It was the mathematician Leonhard Euler who laid the foundations for future developments when he updated a theory already outlined by several seventeenth-century thinkers, that the ether 'quivered' or 'rippled' like a wave, in a similar way to how air moves when strings vibrate.[213] He invented a sound-colour chromatic scale, which he explained as follows:

> since colours and sounds can both be expressed in numbers . . . two colours or two notes, one of which has precisely twice the number of vibrations as the other, after increasing the interval by an octave, seem to be the same colour and they bear the same name.

This idea met with great success. One of Balzac's characters maintains that

> the nature of sound is identical to that of light. Sound is light in a different form: both proceed by vibrations which, when they reach man, are transformed by him into thought in his nerve centres.[214]

For Gauguin and his contemporaries, colour was 'vibration, just like music'.[215] As an interface between sound and light, and an omnipresent and unifying element,[216] the notion of vibration could also function as a link between physics (the measurement of the frequencies of specific wavelengths), occultism ('aura', 'thought waves' and the anthroposophists' 'cosmic vibrations'[217]) and psychology (Kandinsky's 'psychical' or 'internal' vibration).[218] Vibration could even constitute a common denominator between the different senses. Carrà believed that 'sounds, noises and smells are different forms and intensities of vibration.'[219] Charles Henry's *Introduction à une esthétique scientifique* (Introduction to a Scientific Aesthetics) linked vibration to rhythm and proposed a general theory of correspondences based on the idea of a synaesthetic totality, in which positivism and mysticism could at last be reconciled.[220] Henri Rovel's approach was similar:

> The human being is one; all the sensations of harmony we experience are the result of vibrations; consequently, whether these sensations are perceived by the eyes or the ears, the laws governing them must be the same.[221]

Louis Favre depicted humankind as 'lost in an ocean of vibrations',[222] while in Segalen's view, 'we are immersed in a sea of unidentified waves.'[223]

As stage lighting and the use of coloured light projectors developed, electricity became the star of the music of colours, as perfected in Loïe Fuller's stagings.[224] Along with the notion of vibration, electricity revived the centuries-old ideal of universal transparency. Frédéric Kastner's book, tellingly entitled *Singing Flames: A Theory of Vibrations and Considerations on Electricity*, proved so popular that three new editions were published in the space of one year (1875–6). It foretold that 'the arts and industry will reach their apogee' through implementation of the analogy between light waves and sound waves. Half a century later, Mauro Montalti expressed a similar enthusiasm in his manifesto *For a New Electro-vibrating-luminous Theatre* (1920), in which he sought to 'translate' his ideas into 'colour and light vibrations'.[225] According to Raoul Hausmann, the inventor of the 'optophone', 'light is vibrating electricity, as is sound.'[226]

And on 25 April 1930 a recital by Leon Theremin at the Carnegie Hall was publicized as 'Ether-Wave and Electrical Music',[227] while Rimington claimed that the 'vibrations' of sound were 'translated' into colour through electricity.[228]

So the notion of translation emerges here too, and not only, as we have seen, around the Musicalists' transpositions. This search for bridging elements, achieved first by mathematics (through Pythagoras' aesthetics of harmonic proportions), then by physics (measuring frequencies), then by physiology and psychology (synaesthesia), received a new impetus from the technological advances found in electronics and computing, which again embodied the principle of reversibility seemingly capable of abolishing all frontiers.[229] After all, is our future digital universe not an unambiguous response to ancient monist ideology? R. Hausmann, whose optophone 'changes images ... into sounds', expressed his conviction as follows: 'if we reverse the process, sounds become images again.'[230] The metamorphoses of Mussorgsky's *Pictures of an Exhibition* provide a good illustration of this translatability: Mussorgsky's music 'translated' Hartmann's watercolours, was later given theatrical form and colours by Kandinsky in Dessau, in 1928, then, in 1975, K. P. Brehmer made a series of engravings from the sound recording of the Mussorgsky piece, and these in turn inspired the composer Philip Corner in 1976–80 to create his *Pictures of Pictures from Pictures of Pictures* . . .[231]

The new tools resulting from technological progress could thus revive the old dream of a multi-sensory unity. In 1904 Félix Le Dantec, a recognized scholar with significant influence in artistic circles, noted that 'thanks to the improvements imagined by human endeavour, the territory [*le canton*] reserved for investigations into one sense is frequently overstepped, and impinges more and more on neighbouring fields.' He quoted an old Breton tale 'about a character who could hear the wheat sprout, as though this were an unbelievable wonder', and praised the faculty of vision, musing on the possibility that 'the territory of sight will totally cover over those of sound, scent, taste, hot and cold, and so forth.' After representing the phonograph as a reciprocal 'translation' between line and sound,

Le Dantec concluded as follows: 'Using the eyes to study sound . . . now that is proper science!'[232]

On this subject, Voltaire speculated that 'The secret analogy between light and sound makes one suspect that all things in nature have hidden relations, which will perhaps be discovered one day.'[233] Almost two centuries later, Louis Favre echoed his words with 'Everything is inter-connected in this world.'[234] We cannot but be struck by the persistence of this *Weltanschauung*, which affirms the unity of the cosmos, and by the reappearance across the centuries, including the twentieth, of cosmological systems which date back to antiquity or the Renaissance.[235] The notion of the harmony of the spheres (*musica mundana*[236]) can be found in Scriabin, Wychnegradsky and Gerstner, for example.[237] A passage from Nerval's *Aurélia* suggests that synaesthesia is the prime operator of this rebirth:

> from colours, scents and sounds I saw as yet unknown harmonies emerge . . . Everything lives, everything acts, everything corresponds; the magnetic rays emanating from myself and others pass through the infinite chain of created things without obstacle; it is a transparent network laid over the world, whose loose threads are propagated by degrees to the planets and the stars. Although at present a captive on this earth, I converse with the choir of the stars.[238]

And Maupassant stated: 'I did not really know if I was breathing in music or hearing perfumes, or if I was sleeping among the stars.'[239]

But the most spectacular example of this legacy is a book long forgotten today, but which has its claim to fame, with three editions in 1903, 1906 and 1911. It was written by the Marquis Saint-Yves d'Alveydre, Papus's teacher, and was entitled *The Musical Archaeometrist*. Its sub-title is worth quoting in full: 'Key to all the religions and all the sciences of Antiquity. A synthetic reform of all the contemporary arts.'[240] No ambition lacking there! Saint-Yves d'Alveydre, a self-styled 'chromological archaeometrist', who saw his role as interpreting 'the language of colours', explored colour equivalences as part of a system he called the 'science of cosmological correspondences', which incorporated all the series devised by previous generations. This was no small feat. Everything is in everything – and vice versa! Although d'Alveydre was an extreme, and even a caricatural, case, he was by no means alone. His 'universal *rapporteur*' – the term recalls Charles Henry's *Rapporteur esthétique* – is a 'scientific and factual portrayor of the greatest mysteries of religions'.[241] This claim can be read as symptomatic of the Symbolists' attempt to reconcile scientific positivism and occultism.[242] After all, did Ghil not draw on Helmholtz's experiments,[243] and Kandinsky transpose Fechner-style experimental aesthetics into his theosophist framework?[244]

The influences could also work the other way round, with scientists pursuing the same utopias as artists, even if they criticized their untrustworthiness.[245] For example, the article 'retina' in the *Dictionnaire encyclopédique des sciences médicales* (1876) claimed that if one managed to cross the optical with the acoustic nerve, 'one would see thunder and hear lightning'.[246] Max Nordau's famous condemnation of Symbolism as 'degenerate' was accurate,[247] at least on one point: in criticizing sound-colour synaesthesia as a desire to regress to the state of the lower animals, with their single sense organ, he highlighted the contemporary fascination with biological origins (as suggested also by Odilon Redon's iconography). Although we cannot accept Nordau's value judgement,[248] he deserves recognition as the first to have drawn attention to the paradox of modernism's attraction to the archaic. Wagner's 'artwork of the future' saw itself as resuscitating the ancient ideal of Greek tragedy. The fascination for colour hearing, and the numerous attempts to correlate sounds and colours, thus stemmed from a profound nostalgia for lost unity, a desire to return to roots, in the same way as the explorations of originary synaesthesias (*Ursynästhesien*[249]) undertaken by historians, linguists and psychologists.

6
BACH THROUGH THE PRISM
OF PAINTING

In the wake of Romanticism, music became the primary model for the pictorial arts. And of the many composers to have inspired painters in the twentieth century, none is more frequently cited than J. S. Bach. Since this is well known and amply documented,[1] we shall simply ask three questions in this chapter, with a view to exploring the causes of this privileged position and its implications: who are the key figures in this return to Bach? Why Bach rather than another composer? And, lastly, how did painters 'translate' his music?

Who?

Among the many artists who displayed their admiration for Bach in some form or other are Ludwig Richter, Arnold Böcklin, Auguste Renoir, Odilon Redon, Maurice Denis, Aristide Maillol, Georges Braque, Frantisek Kupka, Adolf Hölzel, Johannes Itten, Franz Marc, Paul Klee, Lyonel Feininger, Oskar Kokoschka, Hans Richter, Duncan Grant, Oskar Fischinger, Oskar Schlemmer, Felice Casorati, Willi Baumeister, Piet Mondrian, Henri Nouveau, Joan Miró, Ossip Zadkine, Steven-Paul Robert, Auguste Herbin, Maurice Estève, Max Beckmann, Wols, Max Ackermann, Rafael Soto, Victor Vasarely and Yaacov Agam.

This is a long list, which makes the absences even more significant. The most surprising of them is the (relative) absence of Delacroix: Bach gets only three mentions in his *Diaries* (against 67 for Mozart[2]). Matisse and Kandinsky are also curiously silent, at least in their writings.[3] By contrast, Bach is a cult figure within certain movements

Steven-Paul Robert, *Still-life,* 1936, oil painting.

such as Cubism and its heirs – the *Blaue Reiter*, the Bauhaus, Constructivism and abstraction.

Paul Klee is a special case. In his *Diaries* one can find no less than twelve references to Bach, the most revealing of which are his statements concerning his 'growing love of music . . . I play Bach Sonatas, what is Böcklin worth in comparison? It makes me smile' (10 November 1897).[4] He mentions Bach's 'great musical sovereignty'[5] and remarks that 'the counterpoint between the artistic and human spheres is organic, as in one of J. S. Bach's *Inventions*'[6] (1903 and April 1905 respectively). In the summer of 1915, when holidaying in Bern, Klee received the visit of Jawlensky and Werefkin. As he wrote afterwards, 'We felt inspired to make music, so we dragged Bach into a Wedekind-style world'.[7] In November of the same year, Klee showed Jawlensky's *Variations* to Franz Marc:

> We were playing Bach, and he placed his *Variations* in front of him on the ground. That was very much the way he was

– looking at paintings while listening to music. Previously, he had often taken out his sketch book to paint from the music.[8]

And on 28 June 1918:

> The admirable effect of my holidays is that I am simply revelling in art. My senses are enlivened by playing Bach day and night. I had never lived his music so intensely until now, nor identified with him so completely. What concentration, and what an extraordinarily enriching personal experience.[9]

He had already written to his wife barely a week previously (22 June) that

> I live art in every cell of my body, and my wits are also sharpened by playing Bach frequently. I have never lived and played this music so intensely before. I feel at one with this god, and this will doubtless bear fruit.[10]

His son Felix describes how his father celebrated the demobilization after the First World War by playing Bach Sonatas with his wife Lily, who gave piano lessons to Maria Marc and taught her the *Suites françaises*.[11]

Feininger, another painter-musician, was also a loyal devotee of Bach, and Bach's name crops up all over his correspondence. 'I often sit down at the organ and take refuge in the powerful tones of Bach.'[12] On 18 May 1918 he wrote:

> I did not study the piano, but the violin . . . And yet in the past I often spent six to eight hours a day on the *Well-tempered Clavier*; and I could play by heart (and still can today, but with nothing like my previous skill) the *48 Preludes and Fugues*.[13]

This explains his profession of faith: 'I play Bach and Buxtehude on my Estey harmonium: music is as much my life as the air I breathe and my painting.'[14] For Feininger, Bach's counterpoint embodied the crystallization of space, and cosmic rhythms.

Hölzel and his students were also fervent admirers of Bach. Referring to the stained-glass window he made in Hanover depicting the *Resurrection* (1916), he wrote: 'Bach's *Art of the Fugue* accompanied me throughout this blessed period of creativity.'[15] Schlemmer similarly thought Bach had a determinant influence on his style, as we shall see later. And Itten had a special, lifelong relationship with Bach's works. At sixteen, he was a pupil of the music teacher Hans Klee, the painter's father, and hesitated between painting and music. He summarized a visit there, on 11 November 1919 in Munich, with the words 'He played Bach and I listened',[16] and his memoirs present another telling scene:

> Once when . . . Professor Adolf Hölzel entered my studio with a Viennese student and introduced her to me, he said: 'We are painters and we paint, but Itten is a painter and plays Johann Sebastian Bach.' Later, for years on end, I could stand no other music.[17]

When painting the *Bachsänger* (1916), which represented the singer Lindberg with whom he organized a Bach concert, Itten said that 'every day, before getting down to work, I played Bach fugues and his 2-part *Inventions*.'[18] Itten's *Diaries* confirm at several points how intensively he played. And in a letter to Anna Höllering, he wrote that 'I spend days on end working my way through Bach scores – the most beautiful thing on this earth . . . If only I could, just once in my life, create a work that could stand alongside Bach' (31 December 1918).[19] His many expressions of admiration for Bach show that he was seeking in Bach's music a model for an abstract, objective, spatial, organic and cosmic art.[20]

This early twentieth-century phenomenon of painters performing Bach went hand in hand with many painted homages to the musician. Braque, who played the flute, painted six such tributes between 1912 and 1914.[21] Those of August Macke (*Farbige Komposition 1 – Hommage à J. S. Bach*, Ludwigshafen, Wilhelm-Hack-Museum) and Marsden Hartley (*Musical Theme no. 2 – Bach Preludes and Fugues*, coll. Thyssen-Bornemisza) also date from 1912. Thereafter came Augusto Giacometti in 1914 (*Chromatische Fantasie*, Zurich, Kunsthaus), Nadezhda Udaltsova in 1915 (*At the Piano*, Yale Univ. Art Gall.), Hölzel (*Fuge über ein Auferstehungsthema*, Oldenburg, Landesmuseum) and Itten in 1916 (*Der Bachsänger*, Stuttgart, Galerie der Stadt), Klee in 1919 (*Im Bachschen Stil*, private coll.), Ossip Zadkine in 1936[22] and 1942[23] (*Homage to Bach*), Maurice Estève in 1938 (*Cantata for J. S. Bach*, galerie Nathan), Raoul Dufy in 1950[24] and Torolf Engström in 1973 (*Homage to Bach*).

Although prior to 1912 we find no such works, except for some commemorative monuments or insignificant representations of Bach, such as Ernst Würtenberger's woodcuts (1906), thereafter Bach enjoyed immense popularity, a phenomenon we attempt to explain below.

Why?

Of course, the groundwork had been laid in today's Austria and Germany by the many 'returns to Bach' of Mozart, Beethoven, Mendelssohn, Schumann, Brahms and Max Reger.[25] The collaboration between painters and musicians intensified in 1916, when Busoni met up with Max Oppenheimer (MOPP), Hans Richter and Boccioni in Zurich, and later with Henri Nouveau in Berlin. Busoni's pupil Leo Kerstenberg played Bach for Kokoschka. France also had its Bach enthusiasts, with the musicians Alexandre Boëly, Charles Valentin Alkan, César Frank, Camille Saint-Saëns and Vincent d'Indy at the Schola Cantorum. The J. S. Bach Foundation was created in 1903, and the Bach Society in 1905. Albert Schweitzer's monograph on Bach went through six editions between 1904 and 1928. And if we look at how frequently Bach was played in the music programmed for the year 1912–13 in Paris, he comes sixth out of 83 composers. A similar enthusiasm is evident in Catalonia, with large numbers of performances and publications. Stewart Buettner has a tempting theory that Braque might even have attended the second Bach festival in Barcelona.[26] With the Neoclassical movement, the return to Bach became a return to order, both in music (Stravinsky, Hindemith, Casella, for example), and in the visual arts.[27] The illustrations by Demetrios Galanis of a special issue of the *Revue musicale* in 1932 show this clearly.

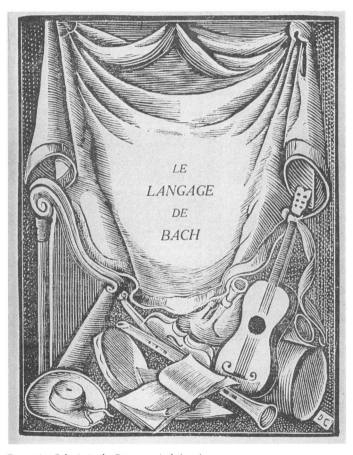

Demetrios Galanis, in the *Revue musicale* (1932).

In order to understand why Bach found such favour with painters, we shall try to elucidate the different facets of their image of him. We shall look at painters' writings as well as their works in order to identify the projections, associations and mediations which made it possible for the figure of Bach to become a rallying point and a model. We shall also reconstruct the contexts and particular logics of these associations, in order better to situate these readings – or constructions – of Bach.

Broadly, we find two types of reading, representing two opposed aesthetics, which can be defined schematically as 'expression' and 'construction'. In France, the former was represented by a book by André Pirro, *L'Esthétique de J. S. Bach* (The Aesthetics of J. S. Bach, four editions between 1907 and 1913). Here, Bach is full of 'pathos', he is a 'commanding orator' whose music is linked to 'ideas and feelings', and whose 'style is always informed by allegory'. Bach seeks to 'speak to us, to touch us'.[28] Pirro focused in particular on the expressivity of the vocal works and the words. The second, and opposite, aesthetic position was represented by an article revealingly entitled '*Bach et l'art pour l'art*' (Bach and Art for Art's Sake). Its author, Jean Marnold, was close to Hanslick's position,[29] and prefigured Stravinsky's *Poétique musicale*:[30] 'The singer could, without detriment, be replaced by an instrument.' Marnold denied any relation 'between the subject or the feeling and how it is interpreted musically', and he saw Bach's music as incarnating a beauty 'absolutely independent of the subject', and its polyphonic composition as a 'new form, freed . . . from the alien yoke of speech and subject', a 'complete and autonomous musical organism'.[31]

Painters overwhelmingly adhered to this latter vision of Bach, with the exception of Kokoschka and his series of lithographs from 1914 on the *Cantata* BWV 60, '*O Ewigkeit – Du Donnerwort*'.[32] However, in order to circumscribe Bach's position within the oppositional network structuring this system of values and set of associations, we should also examine how other musicians were perceived, particularly Beethoven, who at the time embodied the 'expressionist' pole. In 1915, Oskar Schlemmer noted in his *Diaries*: 'When it comes down to it, I have to choose between Cézanne and Van Gogh, the Classical and the Romantic, Ingres and Delacroix, Leibl and Böcklin, Bach and Beethoven.' And: 'The artist should have nothing to do with the sentimental, with "*Stimmung*"'. Later (23 September 1918), he wrote that

> I can easily situate Beethoven and Hölderlin in terms of the opposition between Apollonian and Dionysiac. . . . The term 'expressionism' is an even better term for this specifically Dionysiac element. In my view, a *largo expressivo* by Bach can embody the luminous ideal of permanence, its inner plenitude.[33]

One can find the same opposition between Bach and Beethoven in Henri Nouveau, who founded the superiority of Bach on the following conviction: 'Music had not yet been profaned, and been used to express feelings.'[34]

These examples show what a pivotal role the figure of Bach had in countering Romantic and Symbolist subjectivism, represented among others by Wagner.[35] This was one of the aims of Jaques-Dalcroze's production in Hellerau in 1912, in which he had dancers dance to Bach's *Fugues and Inventions*.[36] Klee noted in his *Diaries*, in 1917, that 'a quintet from *Don Giovanni* is closer to us than the epic movement of *Tristan*. Mozart and Bach are more modern than the nineteenth century.'[37] In 1921 Albert Jeanneret declared that he preferred 'Bach and Mozart, [who] give us architectures', to Beethoven and Wagner, who embody 'individualistic romanticism';[38] and the pianist Eduard Erdmann set Bach's '*Es-Musik*' against the '*Ich-Musik*' of Schönberg and the Romantics.[39] The fact that Bach was often twinned with Mozart, particularly by Braque and Dufy, is also revealing.[40] Miró felt they both had had a determinant influence on his development, while the sculptor François Simecek saw them as a matching pair, at once similar and opposed to each other.[41]

Ever since Stendhal, 'comparison fever' had spread like wildfire, and the twinning of Mozart with Raphael, or Beethoven with

François Simecek, *Rythme selon Bach*, 1928–32, sculpture.

François Simecek, *Rythme selon Mozart*, 1928–32, sculpture.

Michelangelo, had become a commonplace.[42] Likewise for Bach and Dürer, with a further dimension, that of nationality. In 1798, Friedrich Rochlitz called Bach 'the Dürer of German music',[43] a position echoed more than a century later by Hans Thoma's statement that 'what the name of Dürer represents for German painting the name of Bach represents for German music.'[44] The same stereotype existed in France, and inspired the graphic style of a decorative monogram in the *Revue musicale* (1932). Odilon Redon also likened Bach to Dürer and to his 'remarkable *Melancholy*', adding that 'although I do not enjoy listening to Bach very much, I accept the analogy.'[45] In Germany, the matching of these two figures, who were heroes for the Romantics, often had nationalistic overtones: for Max Reger, 'To champion Bach is to be authentically German, unwavering',[46] and W. Pinder associated Bach's polyphony with ornamentation, adding that 'were it not for the reference to Northern music, especially Bach, German ornamentation would be hard to bear.' Further on he wrote: 'If we want to understand ornaments as part of a whole, we must decipher them in detail with as much attention as for a Bach fugue.'[47]

Bach's pairing with Dürer was but one of many anachronistic comparisons, including his association with the 'old style' and his qualification as 'Gothic' (by Liszt). This label gave rise to a new, typically Romantic *topos* around the metaphor of the cathedral, which was used to describe Bach's major works, especially the *St Matthew's Passion* (Marnold). E.T.A. Hoffmann declared that the resemblance of Bach's works to cathedrals mirrored that of Italian composers to St Peter's Basilica in Rome.[48] Philipp Veit described how

> When I am listening serenely to a Bach fugue . . . gradually forms appear, pillars rise up and come together in mighty arcs . . . and from these lofty vaults the voice of God resounds.[49]

Busoni also considered Bach to be an 'architect of cathedrals', and called his works 'Gothic in sound',[50] like Camille Mauclair, who labelled

Bach a 'great builder of cathedrals in sound'.[51] This analogy was medi-
ated by the figure of the organist, and by the image of stained glass
(Hölzel, Kupka and Van Doesburg).

Bach's music was thus described as 'monumental' and 'architec-
tural' (Henri Nouveau).[52] These epithets – which could have inspired
Schlegel's famous phrase, 'music is frozen architecture' – were illus-
trated by Heinrich Tischler in his sketch *Bach* (1937),[53] and in the
churches painted by Feininger. Gris's works reminded Kahnweiler
of 'the majestic musical architecture of J. S. Bach',[54] and Miró, in an
interview with Georges Duthuit, declared that 'Bach . . . gives me
lessons in great architecture' (1937).[55] This theme, associated with that
of Bach as an embodiment of the German spirit, led Bach to be
represented by using straight lines, as for example in Charles Blanc-
Gatti's painting *Concerto by Bach*, whose chequered pattern sets it
apart from Blanc-Gatti's other pictorial transcriptions of music, all
of which use curved lines.

In the same period, Louise Janin wrote that Bach's music 'is sug-
gestive of . . . a sort of rectangular construction'.[56] And Schlemmer
(23 September 1936) wondered whether

> my abstract symmetries could be the equivalent of the
> chorale in music. Are they not similar to the chorales in
> Bach's *Passions*, built as solidly as square towers, which take
> over from the fine tracery of the arias? And what would be
> the equivalent of the recitative?[57]

The classical opposition between a straight-lined Bach and a
curvilinear Mozart seems to live on (Bach was quite recently called
a 'geometrical composer'[58]), and it has even influenced confectionery,
with Salzburg's square-shaped '*Bachwürfel*' and spherical '*Mozart-
kugel*'![59]

So, for painters, Bach was a Constructivist, his music determined
by geometry, structure, order, symmetry, rigour and logic. It had a
certain austerity, with a concentration and economy of means char-
acteristic of chamber music. This is well represented in Braque's

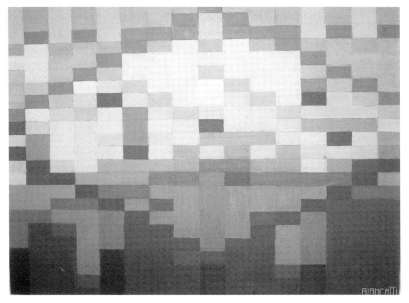

Charles Blanc-Gatti, *Concerto by Bach*, 1931, oil on canvas.

famous *Aria de Bach* (1912, Washington, DC, Nat. Gall.), which is virtually a manifesto for Synthetic Cubism.

But we should not forget that the Romantics had already reacted against intuitionist approaches. Delacroix, for example, commenting (*Diaries*, 7 April 1849) on a conversation he had had with Chopin, wrote that

> art is not what the common people think, that is, a sort of inspiration which comes from heaven knows where, which arrives by chance, and presents only the picturesque exterior of things. It is reason itself embellished by genius, but following a necessary course and checked by higher laws.

This passage was quoted by Hölzel,[60] who wrote in 1919: 'In composing a particular painting, . . . I always try to find the obligatory [*gesetzmässig*] sequence it requires to achieve its necessity, as with

Bach; one tone calls forth the next.'[61] The key word here is *Gesetz*, law, as with Schlemmer's assertion that 'the greats – Mozart, Bach, Leonardo, Dürer – obeyed laws.'[62] In a letter to Elisabeth Erdmann of 14 July 1907, Macke had expressed a similar goal of 'integrating colours into a system, just like notes'.[63]

In this search for rules, it was, unsurprisingly, the laws of counterpoint which served as a model. Polyphony was a key concept for Klee, as is well known,[64] and Itten subtitled his *Diaries* 'Contributions to a Visual Counterpoint' (1930). Twenty years later, he wrote:

> The abstract and concrete painters have attempted – and still attempt – to create, out of non-figurative forms and colours, visual organisms which are as beautiful and true as is a Bach fugue in the domain of sound.[65]

Delaunay echoed this: 'I played with colours as one might express oneself in music through a fugue of coloured, fugal phrases.'[66] Delacroix reported Chopin's description of the fugue as 'pure logic in music, and knowing about fugues means understanding the matrix of all rationality and all consequence in music'.[67] The fugue was a form often applied to painting: Goethe boldly called Leonardo's *Last Supper* 'the first complete pictorial fugue in the visual arts',[68] and Runge echoed this in his description of his *Lesson of the Nightingale*.[69] Redon, who saw in Gauguin's paintings 'an analogy with the fugue',[70] wrote with reference to Dürer's *Melancholia*, 'Ever since I came of age I have had this sort of linear fugue before my eyes.'[71] In the twentieth century, the paradigm of the fugue replaced that of the symphony, which had dominated the nineteenth-century 'musicalist' aesthetic.[72] And the ideal of rationality it represented was of course incarnated precisely by Bach. 'At the end of each of Bach's works, one could write "*quod erat demonstrandum*"', was Henri Nouveau's formulation. In this light, the many references to Bach in the writings of the proponents of Concrete Art, particularly Max Bill, should come as no surprise.

Having started as a simple metaphor,[73] the fugue thus became an actual compositional principle, and the search for '*Fugengesetzlichkeit*', to borrow Schlemmer's term, inspired many an artist. Čiurlionis drew his famous *Fugue* in 1908, and some four years later Macke painted his homage to Bach, or *Fugenbilder*. Thereafter, among others, came Kandinsky (*Fuga – Beherrschte Improvisation*, 1914, New York, Guggenheim Museum, and *Grosse Fuge*), Hölzel (*Fuge über ein Auferstehungsthema*, Oldenburg, Landesmuseum, 1916, and the stained-glass window for Hermann Bahlsen's biscuit factory in Hanover, 1916–18), Van Doesburg (*Komposition IV*, Alkmaar, Haus De Lange, 1917), Klee (*Fuge in rot*, Bern, coll. Felix Klee, 1921), Hans Richter (New York, Museum of Modern Art, 1923), Joseph Albers (Basel, Kunstmuseum, 1925), Felix del Marle (*Prélude, fugue, finale*, coll. Thyssen-Bornemisza, 1925) and Alexander Jawlensky (*Fuge in blau und rot*, coll. Maria Jawlensky, 1936). After the Second World War the series continues, with among others Richard Lohse (*Thema für optische Fuge*, 1945), Theo Eble (1947), Camille Graeser (1948), Henri Valensi (*Fugue en jaune*, 1948), Ernst Wilhelm Nay (*Fugale Bilder*, 1949–51), Adolf Fleischmann (*Fuge in blau*, 1963), Jannis Kounellis (*Fugue de Bach*, 1972), Peter Loew (*Die grüne Fuge*, 1983), Maurice Estève (*Fugue*, 1992) and Thomas Huber (*Thema Raum und Fuge*, 1995). Sculptors also contributed to the trend, for instance Albert Schilling's *Fuga* (1959, bronze, Münchenstein). Even when Bach's name is not explicitly mentioned, he is the tutelary figure, as shown by Feininger, who composed thirteen fugues, and who, after playing one by Bach, remarked that the essence of this music 'has found expression in my paintings'.[74]

Kupka painted the first abstract painting ever exhibited in Paris, called *Amorpha, Fugue in Two Colours*, in 1912. He noted in his auto-biography, written in 1926–7, that in 1911 he was often visited by an accomplished performer of Bach fugues, Morse-Rummel, at a time when he was trying to establish an analogy between the fugue and Seurat's and Signac's painting.[75] He also himself visited many Gothic cathedrals in that period. As painting abandoned figuration and turned to music for new principles of composition, polyphony became viewed as the equivalent of abstraction. In an interview given on 19 October 1913 to the *New York Times*, Kupka stated that 'music is simply the art of sounds which are not in nature and which are almost entirely fabricated.' Stressing the importance of relations between forms, he added:

> it is the same with colours, which must all belong either to the major or to the minor scale . . . I think I can find something between sight and hearing, and I can create a figure in colours like Bach has done in music.[76]

Bach was thus felt to be a totally contemporary figure, incarnating the idea of pure form. Klee described Delaunay's *Fenêtres* in 1912 as 'the prototype of an autonomous painting . . . which has a totally abstract formal existence, without any motif borrowed from nature . . . like a Bach fugue'.[77] Paul Erich Küppers, the director of the Kestner-Gesellschaft in Hanover, described 'the absolute music of space. One experiences this transcendant energy as though it were the counterpoint of a Bach fugue, removed from any concrete reality' (1920).[78] Van Doesburg, for whom Bach represented non-expressive music (a view shared by Stravinsky), compared his windows in the Salle de l'Aubette in Strasbourg to a fugue.[79] Schlemmer maintained that Bach's music 'should be called abstract . . . because it develops out of the means specific to each instrument, and it must obey mathematics and counterpoint'.[80] Ezra Pound, the mouthpiece of the Vorticists, remarked that 'some of Lewis's works have something in them which is to painting what certain qualities of Bach are to music.' And he continued: 'A new Vorticist music would arise not from mimetic representation, but from paying greater attention to the mathematics of harmony.'[81] And Itten declared, in a conference of 1958 on abstract painting, that 'A fugue by J. S. Bach . . . is abstract music.'[82]

The Vienna School also promoted this purist interpretation of Bach. Schönberg acknowledged a debt to Bach for his 'spirit of counterpoint,'[83] and Webern said in a conference of 1932 that *The Art of the Fugue* contained 'such a wealth of totally abstract relations; it is the most abstract music there is.'[84] When J. R. Soto, a faithful subscriber to the *Domaine musical* concerts in Paris, wanted to 'give painting this level of genuinely universal language possessed by music and mathematics', it was again 'the knowledge and the genius of Bach' that served as a model: 'Western music is an art-science, and Bach, a great creator of structures.'[85] The artists of Zurich Concrete Art were likewise inspired by Bach in their use of the idea of series.

How?

The number of artworks inspired by Bach's music is considerable, across the whole range of the visual arts, including film (Hans Richter, Viking Eggeling, Walt Disney (*Fantasia*) and Oskar Fischinger (*Motion Painting No. 1*, 1947, from the *Third Brandenburg Concerto*), among others). An exhaustive list is impossible here, so we shall simply mention some of the many attempts to 'translate' particular pieces. Only Bach, it would appear, generates so many 'translations' of this sort.[86]

Chronologically, our first example could be Bernardus Boeckelmann's series *Acht Fugen aus J. S. Bachs Wohltemperierten Klavier durch Farben analytisch dargestellt* (Leipzig, 1890–1905), followed by his *Inventionen* (1900–1912). One could also mention T.A.F. Knorr's *Fugen des wohltemperierten Klaviers von J. S. Bach in bildlicher Darstellung* (1912) and Klee's visual transcription of the *Adagio* of Bach's *Sonate G-dur für Violine und Cembalo* (1922).[87]

The most important figure in this respect is Henri Nouveau, who combined multiple talents as a painter, sculptor, poet and musician. After studying the piano under Busoni at the *Hochschule für Musik* in Berlin from 1921 to 1923, he moved to Paris to study composition with Nadia Boulanger. In 1927 he was with the Bauhaus at Dessau, and a year later he decided to make a visual transcription of a few bars (52 to 55) of the Eighth Fugue, in E flat minor, of *Das Wohltemperierte Klavier Teil 1*. His choice seems to have been determined by Busoni's opinion, in his edition of the work, that this was Bach's most important piece in the collection. His analysis of the score took the form of a 'scientific' transcription on graph paper, which aimed to show

Jack Ox, *Bach Canata no. 80*, 1979, oil on fibreglass
mounted on wood.

'the determinism of [the piece's] construction'.[88] After this linear ver-
sion of 348 cm long, published in the Bauhaus magazine, Nouveau
moved on to a three-dimensional version called *Monument to Bach*,
which was built after the war in the park of the Leverkusen Clinic.
In 1954, in his *Notes* on Bach, Nouveau talked of 'architecture in time'
– in a radical reworking of Schlegel's formula – and used Bach to
'demonstrate architectural thought', in which the structure symbol-
izes the music.[89] In his search for precision he was doubtless
influenced by Wilhelm Werker's research into the role of symmetry
in the Fugues (Werker's *Bachstudien* were published in Leipzig in
1922) and Wolfgang Graeser's studies on the importance of mathe-
matics in Bach's works (published in the *Jahrbuch der Bachgesellschaft*
in 1924).[90]

Other works inspired by Bach included those made in the context
of Oskar Rainer's teachings in Vienna;[91] a transcription, in the style
of Klee, of a *Fugue for Organ*[92] and Boris Bilinsky's rendering of the
Chorale BWV 727. Also Franz Rederer's *Selbstbildnis genannt 'Bach'*

(1946);[93] Serge Charchoune's *Composition inspirée par la Variation no. 5 pour clavecin* (1957, Paris, galerie Roque), Robert Strübin's *Prélude et Fugue en do mineur* (1957) and *si mineur* (1958),[94] Yaacov Agam's *Hommage à J. S. Bach* (1965), Luigi Veronesi's *Visualisazione cromatica: J. S. Bach contrapunto no. 2 dell'Arte della fuga* (1971), Karl Duschek's *Sonata in G moll, visualisiert in Tonhöhen und Tempoabläufen* (1977, Stuttgart, the artist's collection), Linda Schwarz's *Bach-Projekt – Notenbilder zu Bachs Präludium B.W.V. 1007* (1991),[95] and Farhad Ostrovani's *Études pour les Variations Goldberg* (1997 onwards). Lastly, two spectacular creations deserve a special mention. In 1979, Jack Ox designed and painted a three-sided pyramid to represent the trinitarian symbolism of the *Cantata* no. 80.[96] And in 1980–81, Jakob Weder painted a *Farbsymphonie* over a series of large panels, based on Bach's *Third Suite for Orchestra*. Each of the movements – *Ouverture*, *Air*, *Gigue*, *Bourrée*, *Gavotte* – was transcribed in mosaic-like patterns, whose units were determined by a highly precise system of correspondences between sounds and colours, calculated to the third decimal place.[97]

As we have seen, Bach's music attracts such a broad spectrum of interpretations – from the most conservative to the most avant-garde – that the corpus ultimately lacks any formal unity. What, after all, do Raoul Dufy's commemorative emblems, with their neo-Baroque decorative charm, have in common with the fragmentation of Cubist works, in which the method of collage is conceived as mirroring the principle of polyphony in music? And what similarities can we find between Braque's austere palette and Macke's or Itten's generous range of colours? Of course this diversity reflects, first and foremost, the rich resources of Bach's works themselves. It is hardly surprising that his vocal music, his orchestral works and his works for solo instruments should elicit different responses; and that a Cantata, the *Chromatic Fantasia*, the *Well-tempered Clavier*, the *Art of the Fugue* or the *Musical Offering* will, again, give quite different results on the canvas.

Moreover, the relation between the music, and the paintings or sculptures it inspires, depends on the artistic genre chosen and the artist's intention, which may be simply an allusion or a full homage, a suggestive representation or a rational analysis, or even a literal transcription. Sometimes the inspiration is a whole work, but it can be just a short passage; and sometimes the idea is simply to capture a style or a period, emblematized by the name of 'Bach'. This name is often actually written on the canvas, like an echo of Bach's insertion of his own signature as a theme for variations in the *Art of the Fugue*.

More importantly, the subjective dimension of the visual works raises the more general question of the permeability between different means of expression and the relativity of synaesthetic correlations. Are the traditional correspondences made between colours and key signatures, lines and melodies, musical and visual rhythms any more than simple metaphors? What, for example, would be the equivalent of a straight line in music? Moving from time to space is itself problematic, as suggested by the range of mediations, and hence the diversity of results. Klee's *Im Bachschen Stil*, one could argue, has more in common with Klee's other paintings from 1919 than it has with Bach's music, and only six years later, another of Klee's homages to Bach, the *Alter Klang* (1925), looks quite different, with its chequered composition characteristic of the Bauhaus years. In other words, there are as many Bachs as there are painters and listeners.

Ultimately, the only common denominator of all these experiments seems to be the conviction, expressed by Klee in 1917, that this music is more 'advanced' than painting: 'Mozart and Bach are more modern than the 19th century.'[98] This paradox could well be rooted in the organicist dogma – important to Marnold and Klee, as we have seen – which underpins modern speculations on visual forms,[99] and which is superbly summarized in Itten's image of Bach: 'With him it is only ever a question of the organic completeness of the living being.'[100]

7
'COMPARISON FEVER': TRUE OR FALSE FRIENDS?

At several points in his *Haydine*, published in Milan in 1812, Giuseppe Carpani seeks to highlight the qualities of his favourite composer Haydn by comparing him to certain visual artists. The line-up includes Palladio, Ariosto, Claude Lorrain, Berchem, Jacques Courtois ('il Borgognone'), Van Huysum, Titian, Giovanni Benedetto Castiglione ('il Grechetto') and Rembrandt, culminating with 'the Tintoretto from Rohrau'. For good measure, he goes on to list no less than 32 *paragoni*, pairing Pergolesi with Raphael, Piccini with Titian, Sacchini with Correggio, Durante with Leonardo, Hasse with Rubens, Handel with Michelangelo, and Gluck with Caravaggio. 'More great names could be added,' he remarks, 'but I think that is enough for a joke.'[1]

Yet this little game – which Carpani also called 'a diversion' (*gingillo*) and a 'past-time' – reappeared in print three years later in what was to be one of the most famous cases of plagiarism in literary history. Stendhal, using the pseudonym of Louis-Alexandre-César Bombet, published his own *Letters on Haydn*, which annexed part of Carpani's list, dismissed the rest and changed three of the pairs: Cimarosa, Mayer and Mozart, previously paired with Veronese, Poussin and Giulio Romano, were now united with Raphael, Carlo Maratta and Domenichino respectively.[2]

'Comparison fever will be my downfall' was Stendhal's cry. And the least one can say is that this ailment proved particularly contagious. Ever since Stendhal, the most varied authors have found themselves drawn to coupling Roland de Lassus with Quentin Metsys, Agostini with Tintoretto, Campra, Couperin or Mozart with Watteau, Scarlatti with Tiepolo, Pergolesi with Correggio, Haydn with Fragonard, Beethoven with Michelangelo or Segantini, Berlioz with John Martin, Brahms with Klinger, Saint-Saëns or César Franck with Puvis de Chavannes, Wagner with Turner, Delacroix or Courbet, Richard Strauss with Böcklin, Mahler with Klimt, Stravinsky with Picasso, Bartok with Brancusi, Webern with Segantini or Mondrian, Alban Berg with Munch, Earle Brown with Vordemberge-Gildewart, John Cage with Rauschenberg or Duchamp – and the list goes on.

This trend was of course not of Stendhal's making, and 'inter-disciplinary' comparisons go back to antiquity. Dionysius of Hali-carnassus drew parallels between Isocrates' talent for oratory and Phidias' and Polyclitus' sculpture, and likewise between Lysias' oratory and the sculpture of Calamis and Callimachus.[3] In 1567 Cosimo Bartoli matched Josquin des Prez with Michelangelo,[4] in 1778 Philipp Christoph Kayser called Gluck the 'Shakespeare of music',[5] and Carpani himself appealed to Mattei's comparisons between the great artists of his time and the great poets of antiquity.[6] Montesquieu made some twenty comparisons between writers and painters or musicians.[7] But it was in the Romantic period that comparison fever reached epidemic proportions – and it has been claiming new victims ever since.

When we take a closer look at this vast corpus, it becomes clear that it covers a huge range of different situations and motives. Most comparisons emerge posthumously, but some are declared by the interested parties themselves. Anton Raphael Mengs, for example, claimed to have whistled a Sonata by Corelli while working on his *Annunciation* for the Royal Chapel at Aranjuez because he wanted to paint 'in the style of Corelli'.[8] Sometimes, however, the real situation belied the stated connection: for instance, Delacroix is known to have had little feeling for Berlioz's music.[9]

Another feature are the anachronisms – such as when Bach is described as 'Gothic' – which are frequent, not to say endemic, in Carpani's work. Yet parallels drawn between contemporaries are not necessarily any more convincing. Haydn and Fragonard were born in the same year, 1732: does this really give them something in common?[10] The connection suggested between Beethoven and Goya,[11] simply because they had vaguely similar facial features, or were both deaf, is no less problematic. And whereas the links between Böcklin and Wagner might seem more plausible, and are corroborated by a number of Bayreuth productions which quote the *Isle of the Dead*,[12] we also know that Wagner's music was not to Böcklin's taste, and Giorgio de Chirico later put paid to the myth of Böcklin's Wagner-worship.[13] On the other hand, who could have guessed, just by looking at Cézanne's paintings, or indeed those of the Impressionists, that they felt tremendous admiration for Wagner? Cézanne even devoted a painting to the master, *The Tannhäuser Overture* (St Petersburg, State Hermitage Museum).

The most convincing cases are those based on a personal relationship. A well-known example is Delacroix's and Chopin's friendship.[14] The *Ballets Russes*' production of *Pulcinella*, which opened in 1920, brought together Stravinsky and Picasso, whose portraits of each other grew out of their mutual admiration.[15] Their similar trajectories, as with Webern and Mondrian, or Kandinsky and Schönberg – in the latter case, attested by a correspondence[16] – also play a role. To be entirely convincing, however, parallels should be based on structural analogies derived from detailed analysis of the works themselves – an approach too rarely undertaken. The comparative analysis of Filippo Brunelleschi's architectural designs for the Santa Maria del Fiore dome in Florence, and Guillaume Dufay's music at its inauguration in 1436 is exemplary in this respect.[17]

That said, however persuasive the arguments justifying the correlation, its limits need to be addressed. Comparisons never proved anything. A first pitfall consists of making a purely metaphorical association, as with Camille Mauclair's[18] subsequently much-debated coupling of the two Claudes, Monet and Debussy.[19] Debussy's 'impressionism' is still debated,[20] and vague notions such as a 'vibratory essence' (G. Boudinet), to qualify the relation between the two artists, will not get us very far.[21] Even Carpani relied on word-play, when he justified calling Haydn the 'Tintoretto of music' because of 'Robusti's Michelangelesque robustness, combined with fervour, eccentricity, novelty and abundance'.[22]

A further indication that these correspondences are tenuous is their inconsistency. As we have seen, Carpani himself had no qualms generating ever more of them, for Haydn. Likewise for Mozart, when Stendhal twins him variously with Domenichino, Correggio and Raphael,[23] while Th. De Wyzewa chooses Fragonard or Watteau.[24] Beethoven, who is generally paired with Michelangelo, keeps company with Rembrandt, but also with Rubens, Goya, Runge, Rodin and Le Sidaner. And this fluctuating list is by no means complete.

These proliferating parallels were quick to be challenged, especially since they were often flimsy and subjective, rarely supported by reasoned argument, and vulnerable to the still powerful critiques of the comparative approach and the *Geistesgeschichte* voiced by Karl Vossler and Kurt Wais in the name of the specificity of each expressive medium.[25] These objections in turn raise the thorny issue of the possibility and, indeed, the value of making connections between the fields of sight and sound. Drawing parallels on the basis of the formal analysis of an individual work or its component parts is problematic enough, how much more so, then, is relating the entire oeuvre of a painter to that of a composer! So are we condemned to accept Pierre Boulez's judgement that 'all the comparisons which have been attempted are confused, forced, and no more than empty equivalences'?[26] We consider it more worthwhile, for our part, to explore why they were made, and to try to grasp how they originated and functioned.

A closer look at these analogies reveals the variety of uses to which they were put. Sometimes the aim was simply to help memorize or classify, at other times it was more clearly pedagogical, as with Théophile Gautier's association of the three Romantics – Berlioz, Delacroix, Hugo. In a famous open letter to Berlioz, Liszt wrote that

> Raphael and Michelangelo make me understand Mozart and Beethoven better. John of Pisa, Fra Beato, and Francia explain Allegri, Marcello, and Palestrina; Titian and Rossini seem to me to be like two stars with similar rays. The Coliseum

and the Campo Santo are not so foreign to the *Heroic Symphony* and the *Requiem* as one might believe.[27]

Schumann likewise saw the instructive potential of the visual arts: 'The cultured musician benefits as much from studying a Raphael Madonna as does the painter from listening to a Mozart Symphony.'[28]

In most cases, however, the comparison contained a value judgement. It could be negative – Beethoven was 'the Kant of music' for Carpani[29] – but it was mostly effusively positive: comparing Bach to Homer, Virgil or Newton[30] was a way of marking Bach's historical importance, his poetic inspiration or his theoretical (or even scientific) rigour. Such eulogies sometimes had nationalistic overtones, as when Bach was called the 'Albrecht Dürer of German music'.[31]

Parallels could also illustrate aesthetic convictions. This was the case for the Neoclassicist Carpani,[32] who instrumentalized the drawing/colour debate in order to glorify Italian music, deemed to be essentially melodic, in opposition to harmony. 'The cantilena or melody is the soul of music', he said, echoing Rousseau, 'the cantilena is to music what drawing is to painting', adding that 'where melody is lacking, so is thought'[33] – a conclusion which the advocates of ideal imitation would not have rejected. Influenced by the doctrine of *mimesis*, Carpani also praised the 'descriptive genre' in music; this was behind the comparison he made between Claude Lorrain and Haydn, termed a 'landscape painter' for the scene of the sun's appearance in the *Creation*.[34] On the issue of expressivity, Carpani praised the eclecticism of the School of Bologna, claiming that 'had Haydn painted the passions and the emotions as well as images and things, he would have been at once the Raphael, Titian and Michelangelo of musical painting.'[35]

The theme of the *arti sorelle*, which had emerged from the *paragone* debate, developed spectacularly in the course of the eighteenth century, illustrated by a large number of comparisons between music and painting.[36] In the Romantic period, a new social space emerged, corresponding to the extended meanings of the term 'art'. The frontispiece of the review *L'Artiste*, designed by Célestin Nanteuil, is emblematic in this respect: it shows a painter, sculptor, writer and musician all together in the same workshop.[37] Yet an opposite movement was also at work, one which privileged the *specificity* of each artistic language, and which regained momentum with Lessing's *Laocoon*. This was certainly Stendhal's frame of reference when he wrote of 'the boundaries of the art of music',[38] and its mimetic and expressive possibilities.[39] However, he also made comparisons between painters and musicians, in the context of the tradition stretching from the Romantics to the Symbolists, in which music had the status of an exemplary art for painting – later a model of abstraction – in reaction to Lessing's distinctions. This explains Mauclair's allusion to Beethoven as 'not mimetic music' when referring to Henri Le Sidaner's paintings.[40] Stendhal also claimed that 'the subject-matter plays no part in the merit of the painter; it is a bit like the words of a *libretto* for music.'[41] This connects with another debate, in which vocal music was set against instrumental or 'absolute' music,[42] which should serve as a model for 'pure painting'.

We have seen that, depending on his argument, Carpani compared Haydn to any number of different painters. Likewise Gautier, who filled the descriptive passages of his travel writings or novels with references to the visual arts. The names of Jacques Callot, Rembrandt, Piranese, Goya, John Martin and many others are used to qualify an atmosphere or a colour, like a sort of suggestive palette, based on synaesthesia. So are such comparisons simply reducible to individual psychology and subjective taste?

If we look more closely at the mechanism of comparison, we see that it bears a certain resemblance to the process of communication, in which one of the terms plays the role of signifier (Tintoretto, for Carpani), the other, that of signified (Haydn). A structuralist approach can help us understand this communicative process better, by reconstructing the implicit context of each term. Ernst Gombrich has argued that neither expression nor communication can function in a vacuum, and that all transmission of information is based on a coherent network of associations.[43] He concludes that the problem of synesthetic equivalences will cease to look embarrassingly arbitrary and subjective if here, too, we fix our attention not on likeness of elements but on structural relationships within a scale or matrix.[44]

Umberto Eco[45] and Georges Roque,[46] grappling with a similar problem – colour symbolism – appealed to Hjelmslev's theory of the double articulation of the planes of expression and of content, and concluded, like Gombrich, that it is the position of each term within the whole structure that determines its sense. This would mean, for Carpani, the position of Haydn in the field of music, and that of Tintoretto in the field of painting.

Martin Staehelin provides a revealing analysis of the duos Raphael/ Mozart and Michelangelo/Beethoven in this respect.[47] There is a double relation at work here, with Raphael opposed to Michelangelo and Mozart to Beethoven. The *topos* of twinning Mozart and Raphael started with F. X. Niemetschek in 1798, and was taken up by Rochlitz two years later.[48] It won support both in Germany (Goethe, Schumann, Grillparzer, Otto Jahn and Hermann Grimm) and in France (Ingres, Lamartine, Bizet). Mozart thereafter underwent a transformation from a tragic figure (the *Requiem*) to an angelic and luminous one, in contrast to the sombre Beethoven. By the time we come to Berlioz, there was 'the spirit of Beethoven, which is of Saturn' in opposition to Mozart 'who is of Jupiter'.[49] This polarity was mirrored in the Romantic rehabilitation of Michelangelo, his *terribilità* and bad temper, versus the Apollonian Raphael. Delacroix associated Michelangelo with Beethoven through their shared aesthetic of irregularity, suffering and melancholy.[50] This image persisted into the twentieth century, through Camille Mauclair and E. Herriot for example.[51]

What counts in these comparisons is therefore not the similarities in the protagonists' lives or works, but the equivalent position each figure occupies in their respective fields. When Heinrich Heine called Chopin 'the Raphael of the piano', in the context of praising Liszt, he was implicitly assimilating Liszt to Michelangelo.[52] Likewise, the return to Bach in Cubist musical iconography signified a condemnation of Symbolism's infatuation with Wagner.

For the varied images of Mozart, a good source is Stendhal's *Voyages en Italie*, where comparison fever reaches epidemic proportions. Whereas Carpani compared Mozart to Giulio Romano, Stendhal in 1814 compares him to Domenichino, reserving for Pergolese and Cimarosa the epithet of 'the Raphael of music'. It was only later, in 1824, in the *Vie de Rossini*, that Stendhal twinned Mozart with Raphael:[53] 'Raphael had precisely some of the qualities of tenderness and the modest perfections which Mozart had.'[54] A comparison three years later preserved something of this first reception of Mozart: 'Raphael and Mozart are similar: every Raphael figure and every Mozart melody is both stirring and charming.'[55] On the other hand, in 1814, *Don Giovanni* still represented 'Shakespeare-like terror,'[56] and Mozart remained full of 'passions'[57] and depth,[58] comparable to Corneille[59] and Correggio (1816–18).[60] The link with Correggio led to the idea of Mozart's melancholy,[61] which Stendhal had already suggested in the *Vies de Haydn, de Mozart et de Métastase*, echoing Carpani.[62] In 1827, by contrast, it was Mozart's simplicity which enchanted Stendhal,[63] and a year later the 'delicate and sublime pleasure' afforded by his music.[64] This was because the other pole had in the meantime acquired a sharper outline: Beethoven had an 'impetuous ardour akin to Michelangelo's' (*Vie de Rossini*).[65]

Stendhal drew the following conclusions from his comparisons:

> I have often thought that the effect of the symphonies of Haydn or Mozart would be much increased if they were played in a theatre and if, during their performance, the most exquisite scenery, reflecting the principal ideas of the different pieces, were to be presented on stage. Beautiful scenery, representing a calm sea and an immense cloudless sky would, I feel sure, enhance the effect of any Haydn *andante* depicting a joyful calm.[66]

Ricciotto Canudo saw things similarly, but the other way round:

if we look at a picture while listening to a piece of music with the same rhythm and colours, the emotion it conveys to us is ten times more intense than what each could have conveyed to us separately.[67]

Louis Martinet had already formulated this idea in 1861. It was central to the ideal of the *Gesamtkunstwerk*, and found expression in film and in Bauhaus theatrical productions, as well as in a number of museographical experiments. To take but two examples: the Strindberg exhibition at the Museo Correr in Venice in 1980, and the Monet exhibition at the Centre culturel du Marais in Paris in 1983 where, respectively, Schönberg's music (*Verklärte Nacht*) and Debussy's *Jeux* were played. Although the idea is interesting because it can intensify our vision, it has the disadvantage of orientating, and hence necessarily limiting, the way we see.

Should we therefore abandon comparisons between painters and musicians? The question emerged explicitly in 1917.[68] If the answer is 'no', what use can they be to us? As we have seen, the meaning of each association is dependent on its particular context. Consequently, if we reconstitute the networks of relations implicit in each comparison, we may be able to neutralize this relativity, and salvage the treasures of *Geistesgeschichte* and the comparative approach which Riegl developed with such talent in the conclusion to his study on Late Rome.[69] Needless to say – and at the risk of resuscitating the determinist myth of the *Zeitgeist* – an inter-disciplinary approach is vital here, as it is for any understanding of the development of the arts.[70] It remains to be seen, however, to what extent the hopes placed by F. Sabatier in the 'comparative principle' as a 'future companion to history' is grounded (even if the comparative approach 'does not yet constitute a genuine science today').[71] Clearly, the case is far from closed.

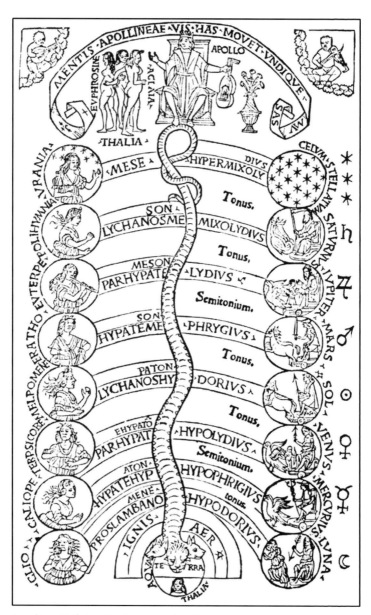

Franchinus Gaffurius, *Practica musicae* (1496).

8
MODERN VARIATIONS ON AN ANCIENT THEME: THE MUSIC OF THE SPHERES

In 1928 Schönberg gave a lecture in Breslau to coincide with a performance of his *Glückliche Hand*. He evoked the 'starry vault' and the paths of the planets, and then the relations which may be established between sounds, colours and light 'in accordance with the laws of a world built by its creator on measure and number'.[1] Some three centuries earlier Descartes had written:

> In inquiries in which order and measure are examined, everything must be considered to be mathematical, and it matters not whether one seeks that measure in numbers, figures, sounds or stars.

This coincidence between two authors who otherwise appear to have nothing in common, is but one sign of the fascination exerted over the centuries by the aesthetics of numerical proportions.[2]

This enduring interest reflected the idea that numbers provide a common denominator between the audible and the visible, a view dating back at least to 1581 and Vincenzo Galilei.[3] The works of Rudolf Wittkower, John Onians and Ann Moyer,[4] among others, have shown how important Pythagoras was for the visual arts in the Renaissance, and we can no longer ignore the influence of music theory on Italian painting and architecture. From Leon Battista Alberti to Daniele Barbaro, Giangiorgio Zorzi and Andrea Palladio, architectural forms were often designed in accordance with regulatory ideas derived from the mathematical principles of music. The personal contacts between Piero della Francesca, Luca Pacioli, Franchinus Gaffurius, Leonardo da Vinci and Bramante helped disseminate these ideas, and Tintoretto is thought to have composed his *Concerto di giovani donne* (Dresden) in the light of the *Institutioni harmoniche* partly because he knew their author, Zarlino.[5] But beyond this, artists of the time regarded the doctrine of numerical proportions as particularly prestigious, because it had a Classical pedigree (Pythagoras,[6] Plato,[7] Cicero,[8] Vitruvius,[9] Philo of Alexandria, St Augustine, Macrobius, Martianus Capella, Fulgentius, Johannes Scotus Eriugena, and others); it endowed the artist with the added social value linked to intellectual activities; and it also had a claim to being a 'natural' foundation, in the macrocosm, since it was the basis of the *musica mundana*. This idea of *musica mundana*, which was first formulated by Boethius, was later christianized by the Church Fathers,[10] the Gnostics and the medieval mystics (Hildegard von Bingen), and it underwent further changes as it circulated from Marsilio Ficino to Franchinus Gaffurius,[11] Cornelius Agrippa,[12] Gioseffo Zarlino,[13] Johannes Kepler,[14] Robert Fludd,[15] Athanasius Kircher,[16] Marin Mersenne,[17] Dante,[18] Shakespeare,[19] Milton,[20] Metastasio, Mozart[21] and Goethe, and right up to our own times with Hans Kayser's theories on harmonics.[22]

Music and Astronomy

Pythagoras' influence did not stop at structures and forms, however. It extended to iconography, particularly in the pictorial genres of the allegory and the still-life, and was also evident in speculations on the music of colours. A universe governed by the harmony of the spheres became a common representation from the Middle Ages onwards,[23] especially to illustrate philosophical treatises, and some of its indirect descendants survive to this day. These are the ones we shall focus on below.

As a result of the *paragone* debate in the Renaissance,[24] the arts won a certain autonomy, and were reorganized along new lines. This produced a flourish of iconographical representations of the 'liberal arts'.[25] Painting tried to shake off its status as a 'mechanical' art, in order to belong with the disciplines of the *quadrivium* – music, astronomy, arithmetic and geometry. We see this clearly in Pollaiuolo's introduction of a fifth figure, representing Perspective, into the ensemble of the tomb of Pope Sixtus IV in the Vatican (1489–93). Architecture was later admitted within the liberal arts, where it was positioned between Perspective, Astrology and Music, as illustrated in an etching by Étienne Delaune.[26] The traditional kinship[27] between Astrology and Music had been established long before – Plato had called them 'sisters'[28] – and it was illustrated in a variety of media: a painted allegory inspired by Frans Floris (Brussels[29]); a tapestry from Bruges (*c.* 1675, Musée Gruuthuse[30]); and the two wings of an organ decorated by Jan Soens, representing Astronomy and Music,[31] are but a few examples.

Alongside the system of the liberal arts, the representation of the Muses – associated since antiquity with the movement of the spheres[32] – played a strategic role in achieving autonomy for painting. The representation of this autonomy in the form of a tenth Muse joining in the choir gathered before Apollo came later,[33] but in the meantime artists paid close attention to the nine canonical ones. Not only were Mount Parnassus and Mount Helicon frequent themes,[34] but more significantly, the arrangement of the figures often stressed the importance of the Muse of Astronomy, and her association with music, particularly through the figure of Euterpe. Tintoretto's paintings (Museo di Castelvecchio, Verona, and Neuilly, private collection) are good examples of this. Urania, whose usual attributes are a sphere, an astrolabe and a compass, was often also shown with a musical instrument – a lute in the Reims Pontifical,[35] a lyre on the back of the medal of Giovanni Pontano attributed to Adriano Fiorentino (Naples, Capodimonte[36]), a shawm in Adriaen Collaert's engraving *Orpheus and the Muses*,[37] and a viola da gamba in Marten de Vos's allegory and in Jacopo Zucchi's ceiling in the Villa Medicis.[38] In a drawing by Marcus Gheeraerts of the painter in his studio (1577, Paris, Bibliothèque Nationale), a violin lies alongside the traditional sphere and compass. The ceiling above the *Venus Urania* in the Sanssouci Palace, Potsdam, shows an angel-musician

VRANIA.

VRANIA cœli motus scrutatur ♏ ♌ astra.

Philips Galle, after Marten de Vos, Urania
from *The Muses*, 16th-century engraving.

Odilon Redon, *L'Art céleste,* 1894, lithograph.

and a zodiac, and the figure of Astronomy decorating a clock by Ch. G. Manière has a lyre as her attribute.[39]

The affinity between music theory and cosmological mechanics thus left an enduring mark on iconography. Cesare Ripa, for example, recommended that Music be represented seated on a blue-coloured sphere.[40] In the Saronno cupola (1534), the frescoes of Gaudenzio Ferrari show the orchestra of angels arranged in concentric circles according to the classical schema of the *musica mundana,*[41] which was later imitated by Isidoro Bianchi in the cupola of S. Maria dei Ghirli at Campione (1628–38).[42] A study by Charles Hope of Veronese's paintings on the ceiling of the Libreria vecchia di S. Marco in Venice propose a new reading of the central medallion as Astronomy listening to the music of the spheres.[43] Philippe de Champaigne surrounds God the Father with angel-musicians in his painting *La Création du monde* (*c.* 1633, Musée de Rouen), and Boullée's plan for Newton's cenotaph (1784) uses a similar cosmic symbolism. Even Odilon Redon places a winged violinist among the heavenly clouds (the lithograph *L'art céleste*, 1894).

In many compositions, musical instruments were additionally placed next to instruments connected with astronomy – the astrolabe, the celestial globe or the zodiac. Examples include the allegory *Peace* by Marten de Vos,[44] a *Love Triumphant* by Caravaggio (1602, Berlin) and variants by Astolfo Petrazzi and Rutilio Manetti,[45] a *Vanitas* by Wilhelm Bartsius (1635–40, Geneva Museum), an *Atelier* by Job Adriaenszoon Berckheyde (1659, the Hermitage) and an engraving by Sadeler, *Litterae* (1597, after Stradanus), in which the lute is framed by an armillary sphere and a treatise on astronomy. In the following century, a portrait of the Marquise de Pompadour by Boucher (*c.* 1750, Louvre) shows a celestial globe at the foot of her harpsichord. In an *Allegory of the Arts* by Francesco de Mura (*c.* 1750, Louvre), a sphere is placed above a violin and a score by Haydn, the *Divertimenti primi* written for the King of Naples. The portrait *Giovanni Borgherini with His Tutor* (Washington, DC, Nat. Gall.), attributed to Giorgione,[46] has a flute close to the sphere and compass. Similar compositions can be found in allegories of the attributes of the arts, in still-lifes (Guilliam Gabron[47]) or *trompe l'oeil* pieces (Sebastiano Lazzari, Benedetto Sartori). Sébastien Stoskopff in his *L'Été ou Les cinq sens* (Summer, or the Five Senses, 1633) and his *Grande Vanité* (1641, Strasbourg, Musée de l'Oeuvre Notre-Dame), arranged the sphere and the musical instruments contiguously, or symmetrically.[48] But it was Evaristo Baschenis and Bartolomeo Bettera[49] who brought these two types of instruments together most consistently – generally interpreted as symbols of *Vanitas*.[50]

Sébastien Stoskopff, *Summer, or the Five Senses*, 1633, oil on canvas.

In the Pratolino Gardens,[51] the presence of an observatory and of musical automata signals this affinity between music and astronomy. It could take other forms too, for example the eminent music theorist Vincenzo was the father of Galileo Galilei, who discovered sun spots and the mountains on the moon, while the accomplished lute-player Constantin was the father of Christian Huygens, who discovered the Orion Nebula. The astronomer Nicolaas Witsen (1676–1715) collected musical instruments,[52] and William Herschel, who was the first to describe the moons of Saturn, was initially an organist in Bath. Nearer to us, the musician Charles Koechlin initially wanted to be an astronomer, and Alexandre Dénéréaz, who was likewise a composer, an author of a treatise on harmony and a typical representative of neo-Pythagorean musical experiments between the two wars, had initially hesitated between the Fine Arts and astronomy. In his treatise entitled 'The Harmonies of the World' (unpublished),[53] as in his conference on 'Music and its Relation to the Harmony of the Spheres' (1928), he used the Golden Section to demonstrate analogies between musical intervals and the movement of the planets.[54]

A Rainbow of Music

The affinity between music and colour, a traditional Venetian theme,[55] is also relevant in this context. Ripa swathed Harmony in a robe of seven colours corresponding to the notes of the scale,[56] and seven was also the number of divisions of the spectrum chosen arbitrarily by Newton after his experiments with prisms,[57] just as it was the number of strings represented on Apollo's lyre.[58] Newton's successors closed the scale of colours back on itself to make the chromatic circle, or equally the rainbow, which also has a circular form. The circle represented divine perfection, the perfection of the universe of Creation, partaking of both time and space. The popularity of circular canons in the Baroque period testifies to its symbolic importance,[59] as do Castel's *L'Optique des couleurs*, in which the figure of the circle was used to prove the parallel between the orders of sight and sound,[60] and the schemas of Giuseppe Tartini's *Trattato di musica*[61] and Francis Webb's *Panharmonicon*.[62] In 1810 Philipp Otto Runge transformed the circle into a sphere of colours, giving it the outward appearance of a planet. And the notion of cycle, which was at the heart of the classical tonal system, could also be linked to chromatic schemes: the structural analogy of the cycle was precisely the one chosen by Hauer and Itten in 1919 as the basis of their system of audio-visual correspondences.[63] Thus the harmony of the spheres could reappear in support of a syntax of colours.

This notion, the music of the spheres, stood the test of time partly through its association with mystical currents.[64] Thus Saint-Martin wrote that 'I could hear all the parts of the universe form into a sublime melody.'[65] The metaphor found favour in the nineteenth century, for example in the writings of Germaine de Staël, Balzac, Chateaubriand and George Sand,[66] while Lamartine made a number of allusions to 'the harmony of the heavens' in a poem he addressed to a woman singer.[67] In *Aurelia*, Nerval claimed to converse with 'the choir of the stars',[68] and Victor Hugo praised 'the deaf man who could hear the infinite. Stooped over the shadows, this mysterious seer of music listened to the spheres. There, noting down the zodiacal harmony which Plato had professed – was Beethoven.[69] Berlioz, also referring to Beethoven, mentioned 'the music of the star-studded spheres'.[70] Monet's paintings were a 'universal symphony' (Clémenceau),[71] and Thomas Mann used the same metaphor in *Dr Faustus*.[72]

Here we should recall the importance, for the German Romantics, of this '*menschliche schöpferische Musik des Weltalls*' (human creative music of the universe) so dear to Novalis.[73] August Wilhelm Schlegel,[74] Schelling,[75] Tieck[76] and Wackenroder,[77] Rochlitz,[78] Jean Paul, Goethe, E.T.A. Hoffmann,[79] Schopenhauer[80] and Rudolf Steiner[81] all referred to the age-old harmony of the spheres, as did Runge and Friedrich to a lesser extent.[82] Their influence was decisive in reviving this theme and transmitting it to the twentieth-century avant-gardes, and even further to New Age utopias.[83] Alfred Stieglitz, for example, called his photographs of clouds *Songs of the Sky* (1923–7), and the symbolism of the stars seems to have inspired Robert Delaunay's *Formes circulaires*, which bear the sub-title *Soleil no. 1* (1912–13, coll. Hack). Delaunay had written to Kandinsky a little earlier that 'I am still waiting for the laws I have found to be relaxed, those based on researches into colour transparency, comparable to notes in music.'[84] Kandinsky's variations on the theme of the circle draw on these ideas also.[85] Stanton MacDonald-Wright's series *Conception Synchromy* (1915) also has a circular rhythm; in a treatise of 1924 he compared the relations between colours and keys to the movement of 'the planets around the sun'.[86] Franz Kupka's series *Disks of Newton* (1911–12, Paris, Musée National d'Art moderne), which, like *Creation* and *Cosmic Spring*, is part of the preparatory studies for *Amorpha, Fugue in Two Colours* (1912, Prague, Národní-Galerie (National Gallery)), can be regarded as a homage to Newton's theory of gravitation, but also to his experiments with prisms. Here again we find the link between the chromatic circle and the cosmic sphere.[87]

Other examples also illustrate the vitality of this theme of celestial harmony. Planets were to serve as decoration for the music room which Albert Trachsel designed for the Countess of Béarn's private residence (1897).[88] Čiurlionis, an avid reader of Camille Flammarion, organized his triptychs in the form of symphonies in three movements, true to his twin vocation as painter and composer.[89] After painting a cycle called *Zodiac* (1907), he undertook a *Sonata of the Sun* and *Sonata of the Stars* (1908). Wenzel Hablik's *Starry Sky* (1909, Itzehoe, Fondation Hablik) recalls Schinkel's scenery for the Queen of the Night in the *Magic Flute*, not forgetting Giacomo Balla's series *Mercury Passes in Front of the Sun* (1914, Milan, coll. Mattioli and Paris, Musée National d'Art Moderne), a *Futurist Composition* by Emilio Pettoruti in the same year (Paris, coll. Ullmann) and Johannes Itten's *Bachsänger* (1916, Stuttgart, Stadtgalerie), in which the presence of a globe reinforces the cosmic dimension of the music.[90] The imagery could take many forms, for example in Albert Gleizes' *Portrait of Florent Schmitt* (1915, Centre Pompidou, Paris), where the 'wave-like curves' were, in his view, 'reminiscent of the music of the spheres', while the inspiration for Miro's *Constellations* (1940) – in which, according to Breton, 'all the signs of the celestial score are harmoniously integrated'[91] – was 'the night, music and the stars'.[92] In 1965 the Basel-born painter (and initially pianist) Robert Strübin called a gouache he painted *Musica Mundana*.[93] And Timm Ulrichs called the second canvas in his series *Sphärenmusik* (1982), 'Nachtlied'.[94] Even the astro-physicist Trinh Xuan Thuan chose to call a book of his *The Secret Melody* (English edn, 1994).[95] These examples give some measure of how greatly the modern imagination of celestial objects remains linked to the world of music.

The survival of metaphors of celestial harmony is also borne out by the writings of many musicians, painters, poets and critics. Jean-Georges Kastner entitled his hybrid work *La Harpe d'Eole et la musique cosmique* (1856), J. M. Guyau compared the rhythmic regularity of poetry to 'a concert which has a distant analogical affinity with what the ancient philosophers called the music of the spheres',[96] and Marie Jaëll referred to Liszt's touch at the piano in these terms;[97] Victor Segalen, quoting Pythagoras, mentioned 'the vast song of the planets';[98] and Sibelius believed there were 'musical notes and harmonies on every planet'.[99] Gustav Mahler declared to Clémenceau: 'People will only understand my music long after my death, because what I tried to compose is a music of the spheres.'[100] Scriabin, who like Čiurlionis and Kandinsky read the works of Camille Flammarion, wished to recreate in music 'the planetary systems of the stars (the cosmos)',[101] while Ferruccio Busoni considered that 'everything resonates', and exhorted people to listen to the universe, in which 'every star has its rhythms and every world, its cadence'.[102] Kandinsky, who likewise considered that '*die Welt klingt*' (the world rings out),[103] wrote that 'every work is born . . . in exactly the same way as the cosmos . . . through catastrophes which, starting with a chaotic growling of instruments, ends up creating a symphony which we call the music of the spheres'.[104] For the film critic Paul Ramain, 'rhythm is what the Ancients called

George Crumb, *Makrokosmos 12, Spiral Galaxy, Aquarius,* 1972.

the music of the spheres';[105] Max Oppenheimer, listening to the Mozart Violin Concerto in A major, noted that '*Wie Sphärenmusik klang es*' (It sounded like the music of the spheres);[106] and, in conversation with Claude Samuel, Olivier Messiaen referred to 'the resonance of the planets', and claimed, quoting Job, that 'the stars sing.'[107]

Modern musical theory sometimes took the metaphor literally. For example, Joseph Hauer, the inventor – before Schönberg – of the duodecaphonic system, linked the chromatic circle with the cycle of fifths, defining the 'absolute music' to which he aspired as 'the original language of the universe, the harmony of the spheres and cosmic order.'[108] Paul Hindemith, who was a draughtsman as well as a composer, and whose admiration for Kepler is well known (as the hero of his symphony (1952) and his opera (1957) called *Harmonie der Welt*), compared the hierarchical principle of the tonal system to the solar system governed by the laws of gravitation, in his treatise on composition.[109] The same image can be found in Frank Martin[110] and Hans Haug.[111] A similar cosmic symbolism is present in Edgar Varèse's *Gesamtkunstwerk*, *The One-all-alone*, also called *L'Astronome*. Lastly, there is Bruno Walter's *credo*, based on Pythagoras and Goethe, concerning the harmony of the spheres and *Urmusik*.[112]

One could also cite the numerous examples of musical works clearly inspired by astronomy: Joseph Strauss's waltz *Sphärenklänge* (Opus 235), Gustav Holst's *The Planets* (1916), Roberto Détrée's *Architectura Celestis* (1940), Olivier Messiaen's *Des canyons aux étoiles* (1971–4), John Cage's *Atlas eclipticalis* (1961) and *Études australes* (1975), George Crumb's *Makrokosmos* (1972–3), Karlheinz Stockhausen's *Zodiac* (1975–7), Gérard Grisey's *Pulsars* (1997), Pierre-André Bovey's *Arcturus* (1997) and Dominique Dousse Leibzig's *Les sept planètes sacrées* (1998), to name but a few. *Constellations* is the title of the first movement of Henri Dutilleux's quartet *Ainsi la nuit* (1976), in which the cosmic atmosphere prefigures its sequel, *La Nuit étoilée* (1978), inspired by Van Gogh's famous painting, *Starry Night* (New York, Museum of Modern Art).

Lastly, this utopian cosmic harmony was often associated with the doctrine of synaesthesia,[113] as summarized in the words of Jean d'Udine, for whom 'the pealing of the seven solar bells continues constantly, in an echo of universal appearances.'[114] Charles Blanc-Gatti, 'the painter of sounds', quoted him frequently, for instance the tenet that 'any music which does not put its composer, its performer and its listener into direct contact with the harmony of the spheres is only an empty game of patience.'[115] The theory of the *Gesamtkunstwerk* and experiments in multi-media breathed fresh life into this *topos*, from Scriabin's *Mysterium* to Wychnegradsy's *Temple de lumière* (1943–4), from Stockhausen's *Konzertkugel* (1956) to Otto Piene's *Lichtballett* (1960), and from the installations of the Prometheus group at Kazan,[116] to Manfred Kelkel's *Music of the Worlds* (1988). Allusions to the music of the universe abounded in *Klangkunst*, a major exhibition in Berlin of 1996,[117] while the Basel-born Karl Gerstner expressed his passion for audio-visual synaesthesia in the creation of an imagined 'Dome of colours' in which every sound-colour 'must be seen, and heard, like the harmony of the spheres emitted by the cosmos of colours'.[118]

'If only I could, with an instrument like radar, capture the music of the spheres!', Takis exclaimed.[119] In 1994 the 'Art and Public' gallery in Geneva displayed a poster '*Musique des sphères & Zen Records présentent Christian Marclay*', and a similar tradition lay behind the release of musical balloons into the sky of Yverdon on 9 May 2005, in an installation by Luke Jerram entitled *Sky Orchestra*. Although we may be surprised to see the avant-gardes champion this centuries-old vision of the world, and still today, for example in the work of Claudio Parmiggiani,[120] this paradox is not unusual, since modernity often looked to historically distant traditions for its roots.[121] The re-emergence of the ancient ideal of universal harmony can be interpreted as a reaction to the 'demusicalization' and desacralization of the world since the Enlightenment,[122] and even as the expression of a nostalgia which we have had occasion to mention already in this study: the nostalgia for a lost unity.

9
A SURVEY OF ARCHITECTURE AND MUSIC

'I have always loved passionately music and architecture,' Chateaubriand declared.[1] Linking these two arts could be considered a commonplace, and the dialogue which developed between them, in different periods, has already generated a lengthy bibliography.[2] The common denominators between the two have for centuries been rhythm, measure and proportion. Today there seems to be nothing paradoxical about 'listening to space' or 'constructing sound'.

Theme and Variations

Philostratus the Younger described the construction of the city walls of Thebes in his *Imagines* (*Eikones*) as follows:

> Amphion . . . talked the language of melody to the stones, and they responded willingly, and came running all together . . . Attracted by the music, they listened, and assembled to raise the ramparts.[3]

This enduringly popular legend was illustrated, among others, by Dosso Dossi, Primaticcio, Antoine Caron, Sébastien Leclerc, Charles Coypel, Giambattista Tiepolo, Élisabeth Vigée-Le Brun and Henri Laurens. Amphion's lyre – a paradoxical proof of the efficacy of the trumpets of Jericho[4] – was evoked by Horace, Apollodorus, Apollonius of Rhodes, Dante, Le Camus de Mézières, Friedrich Schelling, August Wilhelm Schlegel, Friedrich Overbeck, Heinrich Heine, Ludwig Gotthard Kosegarten, Joseph von Eichendorff, Rudolf Steiner and

Claude Ramey, *Architecture and Music*, project for the Pantheon, 1793.

Frank Lloyd Wright, and it was also the theme of a melodrama by Valéry dating from 1891 and set to music by Honegger in 1929–31, for the dancer Ida Rubinstein.[5]

Goethe, in a curtain-raiser written in 1802 for the opening of the new theatre in Lauchstädt, brought in other legendary musicians to display music's power:

> As though summoned by Apollo's lyre
> The stones assemble into walls;
> As though enthralled by Orpheus' notes
> A forest approaches, and transforms itself into a temple.[6]

It was again Orpheus whom Goethe, perhaps inspired in this by Euripides' *Iphigenia in Aulis* (verse 1212), imagined building a whole town with the sounds of his lyre, just like Amphion.[7] The town's inhabitants experience, in Goethe's words, how '*das Auge übernimmt Funktion, Gebühr und Pflicht des Ohres*' (the eyes fulfil the function, role and duty of the ear). August Wilhelm Schlegel disagreed with this transfer, arguing that the eye can only measure proportions approximately,[8] but the Romantics still used the metaphor frequently. Friedrich Schlegel conceived architecture as musical sculpture (*musikalische Plastik*), and in *Faust II*, Goethe wrote that '*der ganze Tempel singt*' (the whole temple sings) (verse 6448). Valéry was treading in their footsteps when he maintained that 'a façade can sing!'[9]

Bach's work was sometimes compared to a cathedral, and he himself was described as an architect, a *topos* which has withstood the test of time:[10] for example, Miró, in conversation with Georges Duthuit, declared in 1937 that 'Bach teaches me . . . great architecture,'[11] and for Kahnweiler, Gris' works recall Bach's 'majestic musical architectures.'[12] Théophile Gautier described the architecture of St Isaac's Cathedral in St Petersburg as 'a magnificent musical phrase' and a 'symphony of marble', and even as having the 'exact inversions of a fugue.'[13] Oswald Spengler, who claimed that the development of polyphony was 'inseparable from the architectural history of the cathedral', noted that the invention of the flying buttress coincided with that of counterpoint. He described Bach's 'Faustian' music as 'a cathedral of sounds.'[14] Valéry discovered 'an inexpressible correspondence' between *Tannhäuser* and the façade of Reims Cathedral,[15] and György Kurtág mentioned Reims and Chartres when discussing the close links between visual and acoustic perception.[16]

Architecture was also called 'frozen music' (*erstarrte Musik*),[17] a phrase with an impressive posterity, right into the twentieth century, employed by Goethe, Germaine de Staël,[18] Schopenhauer,[19] Liszt and Ruskin, among others.[20] It is sometimes (wrongly) attributed to Friedrich Schlegel, but was actually forged by Schelling.[21] Stravinsky wrote that

> we cannot better describe the sensation produced in us by music than by comparing it with the sensation we have when gazing at the interplay of architectural forms. Goethe

Comte de Caylus, etching of Charles Coypel, *Amphion*, 1730.

Bernard Picart, *Amphion*, in Michel de Marolles,
Le Temple des muses (c. 1733).

understood this well, when he said that architecture is petrified music.[22]

The comparison also met with criticism, however. Byron challenged it head on: 'Someone has said that the perfection of architecture is frozen music – the perfection of beauty to my mind always presented the idea of living music', adding that he came across this formulation thanks to Germaine de Staël.[23] Moritz Hauptmann suggested merely a variation, in 1853, whereby music was a '*flüssige Architektur*' (flowing architecture) – prefiguring in this Michael Hopkins's 'fluid architecture'.[24] Later still, Xenakis wrote that 'Goethe said that Architecture is petrified music. From the viewpoint of the composer, one could turn the sentence round and say that music is mobile architecture.'[25] But Goethe himself preferred to qualify architecture as '*verstummte Tonkunst*'[26] (a melody fallen silent) rather than as *erstarrte Musik*, in his comparison between the '*Stimmung*' ('mood') produced by architecture and the effects produced by music. And in his *Italian Journey*, he played on Simonides' famous formula of painting as silent poetry, speaking of architecture as '*stumme Musik*' (mute music).[27]

Affinities

Friedrich Weinbrenner, in his criticism of Goerres's continued reference to 'architecture as frozen music', pointed out that the architect does not always make a good musician, nor vice versa.[28] He is certainly not wrong about that, even if the incidence of architect-musicians is very high. We could cite Gunzo, the creator of Cluny III, Bramante,[29] Karl Friedrich Schinkel,[30] Victor Horta (a great Wagner enthusiast), Erich Mendelsohn, Charles Sarazin, Frank Lloyd Wright, Iannis Xenakis, Peter Eisenman and Daniel Libeskind. And also Jean Weinfeld, a Bauhaus architect who made musical instruments he called '*Fonics*'. Many architects have been inspired by music, for example Toyo Ito by Takemitsu, or Libeskind by Schönberg. But the other way round is also true: Guillaume Dufay's motet *Nuper rosarum flores*, performed for the inauguration of the cupola of Santa Maria del Fiore the Cathedral of Florence, in 1436, was based on the proportions in Brunelleschi's designs.[31] And in 1628, at the consecration of the new Salzburg Cathedral, Orazio Benevoli distributed choirs and musicians around the inner space, which was probably designed with this in mind. In Stravinsky's *Canticum sacrum* (1956), the five parts correspond to the five domes of the Basilica of St Mark in Venice, and reconnect with the tradition of Adrian Willaert's *Cori spezzati*[32] and Giovanni Gabrieli's *Sacrae symphoniae*.[33] In a work published in 1593, Girolamo Diruta mentions a two-organ duel played there between Claudio Merulo and Andrea Gabrieli.[34]

Some affinities actually led to real partnerships, such as Daniel Libeskind with Simon Bainbridge. The composer Luigi Nono dedicated a composition for orchestra in 1984 'A Carlo Scarpa, Architetto, Ai suoi infiniti possibili'. Renzo Piano also worked with Nono (*Prometeo* in the Church of San Lorenzo in Venice in 1984), and also with Pierre Boulez ('Espace de projection', Institut de recherche et coordination acoustique musique (IRCAM), 1989) and Luciano Berio. At the Osaka Universal Exhibition of 1970, Fritz Bornemann built a spherical building for a work by Karlheinz Stockhausen, *Spiral*. We have seen how music could be composed for a particular architectural space, and now, with audio-video installations, we see the inverse, with spaces designed for particular works, for example, Peter Zumthor's Pavilion at the Hanover Universal Exhibition of 2000, called 'Corps sonore'. Bernhard Leitner's *Sound Architectures,* or his *Cylindre sonore* in the Parc de la Villette in Paris, also build spaces, but virtual ones. An exhibition in San Francisco on 'Sound Environments' was devoted to these sorts of experiments in 2010. Advances in computing and electro-acoustics have extended the possibilities of sight–sound interactivity, and opened up new ways of combining sound and the built environment.[35] Mobile sound sources, listeners who move around, and multi-directional listening scenarios are some of the changes resulting in architecture no longer being a receptable for music but actually produced by it, as in Xenakis's *Diatope* and *Polytopes*.[36] Some

Francesco di Stefano, detto il Pesellino, *Construction of the Temple of Jerusalem, c.* 1445, painting.

performances even manage to 'inhabit a musical object' or 'play an architectural instrument'.[37]

Vitruvius, Athanasius Kircher, Marin Mersenne and Adolf Loos, among others, were keen explorers of acoustics, a discipline which came into its own with the building of concert halls, particularly in the late nineteenth century – such as the Vienna Musikverein (1870), the Leipzig Gewandhaus (1884), Zurich's Tonhalle, Amsterdam's Concertgebouw (1888), the Carnegie Hall in New York (1891) and so on – and again in the 1950s.[38] The parallels made between the propagation of sound and of light, both of which obey the rules of physics, mark a continuity between Marin Mersenne and Le Corbusier.[39] The spectacular nature of the ever-increasing number of opera houses, auditoria and music complexes built today is a sign of the prestige that music seems to confer upon architecture all over the world, from Sydney to London, Glyndebourne, Rome, Paris, Lyon, Strasbourg, Hamburg, Bremen, Copenhagen, Luxembourg, Porto, Los Angeles, Atlanta, Rio, Montreux, Lucerne, Beijing, Taichung and Qingdao. Already much earlier, music inspired Berlage's designs for his Beethoven House (1908) and a Wagner Theatre (1910), and the spirit of Wagner permeated all these projects, from the original Festspielhaus in Bayreuth to Barcelona's Palau de la Música.

Architects were also concerned with how concert halls were decorated, particularly Schinkel, and later, at the time of Art Nouveau, Van de Velde, Guimard, Behrens and Olbrich. In 1931 at the Berlin Deutsche Bau-Austellung, Kandinsky's plans for a space built by Mies van der Rohe revived this tradition.

The close relations between architecture and music also inform iconography. Pesellino's *Construction of the Temple of Jerusalem* has King Solomon holding a psaltery. The emblems of both arts figure on the frontispiece of Giovanni Battista Caporali's commentary on Vitruvius (Perugia, 1536), and, on Rameau's *Code de la musique pratique*, the woman with the lute is measuring a length of string with a compass.[40] Some still-lifes juxtapose the emblems of the builder with those of the musician, as do some (self-)portraits of architects. Thus Joseph Ziegler, the director of a school of architectural drawing, represents himself at a table with a ruler, a set square, an architectural drawing and a cello, holding a compass in his right hand and a flute in his left (1831, watercolour, Historisches Museum der Stadt Wien (Vienna Museum)).

Architectural theory is peppered with references to music, most strikingly in Peter Zumthor's claim that 'contemporary architecture should have foundations as radical as those of contemporary music.'[41] The comparison also works the other way round, such that the model is now music, now architecture. Cesariano, who wrote a treatise on architecture, quotes the composer Gaffurius,[42] Le Corbusier quotes Rameau,[43] Gaffurius himself mentions Alberti[44] and Vitruvius,[45] as does the composer and music theorist Zarlino, and later Mersenne; Rameau refers to Briseux,[46] and Boulez to Frank Lloyd Wright.[47] Jacques de

Plan des Werkes

A. Analytischer:

1. Choral - Variationen (Einleitung — Choral und Variationen — Übergang)
2. Fuga I. 3. Fuga II. 4. Fuga III. 5. Intermezzo. 6. Variatio I. 7. Variatio II.
8. Variatio III. 9. Cadenza. 10. Fuga IV. 11. Corale. 12. Stretta.

B. Architektonischer:

Ferrucio Busoni, structure of the *Fantasia contrappuntistica*, 1910.

Liège uses an architectural comparison to explain the relation between different voices,[48] and Busoni analyses the structure of his *Fantasia contrappuntistica* using an architectural method.[49] For Joseph Matthias Hauer, composers were 'musical architects',[50] Brian Ferneyhough's *Carceri d'invenzione* (1984–7) were inspired by Piranese, and Edgar Varèse referred to Saint-Philibert de Tournus.[51]

Viollet-le-Duc regarded music and architecture as 'twins'.[52] Although the attribution to St Augustine of the two arts as 'sisters' is apocryphal, as we show in the next chapter, that was how the Renaissance still depicted the relation. In the famous *paragone* debate, in which different arts vied for social recognition, architecture laid claim to being a liberal art alongside astronomy and music, due to its kinship with arithmetic and geometry. In 1509, Luca Pacioli wanted to extend the exclusive realm of the *quadrivium* to include Perspective, because it too was essentially mathematical, he argued, and similar to architecture.[53] An allegorical composition by Etienne Delaune, and *Le Cabinet des Beaux Arts* (1690) by Charles Perrault, expressed this idea.[54] And Mersenne wrote that 'Masons do not deserve [the name of] Architects, because they do not know the reasons for the concerts they give.'[55]

A Certain Worldview

Under the prestigious patronage of the Ancients – Pythagoras, Plato,[56] Aristotle,[57] Vitruvius, Ptolemy[58] and Boethius[59] – architecture and music found common ground in numerical relations. Vitruvius's was of central importance here,[60] echoed as late as 1821 in an essay entitled 'the music of the eye'.[61] The works of Rudolph Wittkower,[62] Franco Borsi,[63] John Onians,[64] Paul Naredi-Rainer[65] and George L. Hersey[66] have shown the importance of speculations on proportion.[67] Brunelleschi sought to 'rediscover the method of those excellent builders of antiquity, and their musical proportions,'[68] and Alberti declared that 'the whole principle of delimitation will thus draw on musicians' teachings, since it is they who have studied numbers most extensively.'[69] In 1454 he warned Matteo de' Pasti, who headed the construction work on the *Tempio Malatestiano*, that any change in the proportions 'puts all the music out of tune' ('*discorda tutta quella musica*').[70] Serlio's arguments on *simmetria* took a more complex view: 'On this façade, the windows are not equally spaced . . . but this is a concordant discord, as in music when the soprano, bass, tenor and alto appear to move in different directions.' He added that 'the composer's art makes this harmony agreeable to the ear.'[71]

Discussing his pedagogical recommendations – which were adopted by, among others, Francesco di Giorgio Martini,[72] Jacopo de' Barbari,[73] Philibert de l'Orme[74] and even Gioseffo Zarlino[75] – Vitruvius decreed that 'As for music, [the architect] must be very accomplished in it, in order to grasp canonical and mathematical proportions.'

Etienne Delaune, *Liberal Arts*, before 1573, wood engraving.

Although he did not say much more on the subject, evoking practical reasons (military, acoustic and even hydraulic) for the requirement of 'musical proportion',[76] his followers were quick to develop this 'divine analogy' (to cite Valéry[77]), which reappeared regularly in theories of both architecture and painting.[78] Cesare Cesariano devoted a whole chapter of his commentary to the *'musicale scientia'* or *'musica ratione'*,[79] and Daniele Barbaro declared that 'this excellent method, in music as in architecture, is called eurythmy', and he provided all sorts of comparisons with the zither and with singing, in order to define consonance and harmony.'[80] Francesco Colonna,[81] Fra Giocondo, Francesco Giorgi (Zorzi),[82] Giovanni Battista Caporali,[83] Giacomo Soldati, Vignola, Andrea,[84] Juan Bautista Villalpando[85] and Vincenzo Scamozzi all devised variations on the theme of 'harmonic architecture', based on musical proportions.[86] They were followed in this by Charles Etienne Briseux,[87] La Font de Saint-Yenne[88] and Bernardo Antonio Vittone.[89] Similarly, Nicolas Le Camus de Mézières stated that music 'has the most intimate relations with Architecture:

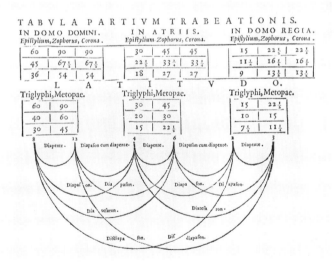

Juan Bautista Villalpando, 'Musical Proportions of the Temple of Salomon', in *Ezechielem explanationes* (1596–1604).

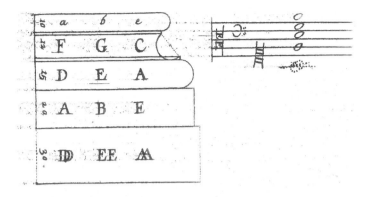

François Blondel, *Musical Proportions of the Base of a Column*, in *Cours d'architecture* (1657–83).

they have the same consonances and the same proportions.'[90] And in the *Encyclopédie*, Diderot referred to the 'relations' (*rapports*) that music and architecture share.[91]

François Blondel, in his *Cours d'architecture*, devoted a whole chapter to praising a work called *l'Architecture harmonique ou application de la doctrine des proportions de la Musique à l'Architecture*, written by a certain 'Monsieur Ouvrard, Music Master at the Sainte-Chapelle'.[92] In this treatise, published in 1679, Ouvrard explored the analogy in greater detail:

> And since in Music all sounds which are not linked by proportion or ratio are disagreeable to the ear and offend it, so we maintain that in Architecture all the dimensions or measurements which are not within these proportions, or which lack conformity, will offend the eye and have no pleasing effect.

This recalls Palladio, who wrote in 1567 that 'proportions between voices are harmony for the ear; proportions between measurements are harmony for the eye'.[93] Blondel gave even more concrete examples, commenting on the dimensions of the base of a column as follows:

Robert Fludd, *Templum musicae*, in *Utriusque cosmi . . . historia* (1618).

'Perhaps it is for this same reason that when the bands of the Ionic architrave are divided according to the numbers 5, 4, 3, it appears beautiful to us, because in Music it produces a consonance.'[94] Charles Perrault, however, refuted this analogy: 'The comparison between ornaments in architecture and harmony in music does not pass muster' (*Parallel between the Ancients and the Moderns*).[95] His brother Claude, who likewise defended the Moderns, also refuted the dogmatism of canonical proportions in favour of a relativistic, empirical approach.[96]

The notion of *ratio* was also important for giving music the role of a paradigm of unity, whether of a work or of the universe. The human body and the cosmos were supposedly governed by the same system of harmonic proportions.[97] At two points Blondel cites Pythagoras' adage, 'nature is always the same in all things.'[98] Rameau also appealed to Pythagoras, in claiming that 'the principle of everything is one.' And in the Middle Ages the doctrine of the music of the spheres, the *musica mundana*, produced the notion of God the Architect who ensures the harmony of creation through the interplay of proportions. Johannes Kepler recorded celestial consonances,[99] and certain plates from the treatises of Robert Fludd (*Utriusque mundi*, 1618)[100] and Athanasius Kircher (*Musurgia universalis*, 1650) represent the musical essence of the universe as buildings. In the twentieth century, this cosmic dimension reappeared as the 'Temple' in Scriabin's utopia, which was concretized by Ivan Wyschnegradsky's plan for the dome of his *Temple of Light* (1943–4), made out of a mosaic of colours corresponding to the twelve semi-tones of the chromatic scale. Hermann Finsterlin, Bruno Taut, Wassili Luckhardt and Wenzel Hablik from the *Gläserne Kette* group (1919) imagined the possibilities of a cosmic architecture, which influenced the design of some concert halls, namely Hans Poelzig's in Dresden and Salzburg (1921) and Hans Scharoun's Philharmonia in Berlin (1963).

Parallelisms

The image of music has always been double, as August Wilhelm Schlegel noted.[101] On the one hand music was conceived as a system of proportions based on Pythagorean mathematics, with a 'natural' grounding through the theory of harmonics (Zarlino and Rameau). On the other hand, it was envisaged as a subjective, emotional and vague form of expression, where the listener's imagination can roam freely through the play of associations. Music in this sense was part of rhetoric or even psychology. Architecture found correspondences in both camps.

Often characterized as a model of scientific rigour, music epitomized 'the light of reason' for Rameau,[102] as it did for Valéry, who considered that it provided architecture with an example of 'a structure and a duration which are not those of beings but of forms and laws'.[103] And Fausto Melotti claimed that 'Greek architecture, Piero della Francesca's painting, Bach's music and rational architecture are all "exact" arts.'[104]

Theories of the expressivity of genres (or *genera dicendi*)[105] and of characters[106] were often associated with the theory of architectural orders – which Vitruvius also called *genera*[107] – and with the theory of musical modes, which Poussin codified.[108] The commentary on Abraham Bosse's illustrations for Denis Gaultier's *Rhétorique des dieux* (1652) specifies that

> since each of these modes provokes certain passions . . . there is represented in each the actions which the mode arouses . . . and the author has taken care to make Architecture conform to these modes.[109]

Thus the Doric order translated the Dorian mode, as was the case in one of the *Intermedi* of the comedy *La Pellegrina*, performed for the wedding of Ferdinand de Medicis and Christine de Lorraine[110] in Florence in 1589, as well as in Girolamo Cardano's *De musica* (1574).[111] Architecture and music could both be assimilated to an art of rhetoric because both were concerned with harmonizing form and content: Zarlino's treatise had a chapter entitled 'How the Harmonies are Adapted to the Words', and he prescribed that 'all things should be made in proportion.'[112]

The notion of rhythm, linked to that of eurythmy,[113] was another concept deployed in comparisons between the visible and the audible. Adolphe Appia's *Espaces rythmiques* are a particularly good example,[114] as is the 'Congress of Rhythm' which Émile Jaques-Dalcroze organized in Geneva in 1926, bringing together musicians and visual artists.[115] Three years earlier, Moisei Yakovlevich Ginzburg published his essay *Rhythm in Architecture*, in which he declared that 'the laws of rhythm . . . define the true essence of every architectural work' and that 'architecture, like music, is in this sense the purest of all the arts.'[116] The persistence of the critical category of 'rhythm' in architectural analysis is illustrated, for example, by Y. Pauwels, who uses the term 'rhythm' no less than 23 times in a few pages devoted to Philibert de l'Orme.[117] Schelling, who called architecture 'music in space', described an 'architectural rhythm' (concerning triglyphs and intercolumniation) based on an equivalence between spatial and temporal distances,[118] which Geymüller's 'rhythmic bays' also embodied.[119] August Schmarsow also employed this concept of rhythm, which originated in music. But the division between the arts of space and of time, which Lessing had introduced, seems nevertheless to have held firm throughout the nineteenth century. Schopenhauer, while supporting the opposition developed in Lessing's *Laocoon*, and reaffirming it by refusing to envisage that music had any spatial dimension, nevertheless stated that '*Der Rythmus ist in der Zeit, was im Raume die Simmetrie ist*' (rhythm is in time what symmetry is in space), thus pinpointing what he thought to be the only overlap between music and architecture.[120]

As the spectator's movements began to be taken into account, an aesthetics of reception developed. Soufflot in 1741, J. D. Leroy in 1764 and A. Schmarsow in 1897 explored this dynamic aspect and introduced a temporal dimension into their works.[121] The integration of time into architecture was mirrored by the integration of space into music, as suggested in Proust's description of Swann's experience of listening to the Sonata by Vinteuil:

> [Swann] was able to picture to himself its extent, its symmetrical arrangement, its notation, the strength of its expression; he had before him that definite object which was no longer pure music, but rather design, architecture, thought, and which allowed the actual music to be recalled.[122]

Baudelaire regarded Wagner's music as 'a vast horizon' and 'an immense space'.[123] Spengler talked of 'an infinite space of sound',[124] and Peter Zumthor, who conceived architecture as an instrument for gathering sound, wrote that 'I enter into music when I listen to it. It is a space.'[125] This interpenetration gave rise to new practices, such as, in 2005, the performance of Rebecca Saunders's *Chroma* by musicians dispersed across the different floors of the Geneva Museum, while the listeners moved around freely.[126]

Lastly, we should not forget the role played by the great debate on instrumental music. In the eighteenth century, Chastellux and Chabanon developed aesthetic theories which were critical of the dogma of *mimesis*, and likened architecture to music, considered to be a model of autonomy.[127] Schopenhauer's thesis that music requires no words led him to defend its independence and condemn all imitative practice.[128] With the arrival of non-figurative painting, architecture, alongside music, again came to incarnate abstraction and purism. Kupka and Kandinsky put forward this view,[129] as did Ben Nicholson:

> the kind of painting which I find exciting . . . is both musical and architectural, where the architectural construction is used to express a 'musical' relationship between form, tone and colour.[130]

Towards the *Gesamtkunstwerk*

'Music is: time and space, like architecture', Le Corbusier declared.[131] He was not only an architect, but a painter, and from a musical family: his mother taught the piano, and his brother, Albert Jeanneret, was a violinist and composer.[132] He designed the cover of one of his brother's scores,[133] and was an accomplished and enthusiastic music lover. He often used musical metaphors,[134] talking of the 'consonances' of forms, of a 'symphony' for Chandigarh and of 'visual acoustics' for Ronchamp,[135] a building which he qualified elsewhere as 'counterpoint and fugue,

Music great music'.[136] He regarded architecture as 'the synthesis of the arts . . . form, volumes, colour, acoustics, music'.[137] When he formulated his conception of architecture as 'a pure creation of the mind', in 1923, it was by comparison with music. In this he revived the *paragone* debate,[138] and Leonardo's characterization of painting as a '*cosa mentale*', as well as Schelling's advocacy of architecture as a 'fine art' freed from any utilitarian contingency.[139] The theme of harmonic proportions inspired both the writings and the practice of Le Corbusier. His *Modulor* – used by Xenakis in *Metastaseis* in 1955 – was a manifesto for cosmic unity, as suggested by its subtitle, *Essai sur une mesure harmonique à l'échelle humaine applicable universellement à l'architecture et à la mécanique* (Reflections on a harmonic measure on a human scale universally applicable to Architecture and Mechanics).

Le Corbusier/Xenakis, *Philips Pavillon* at Expo 58, Brussels, 1958.

In this work, Le Corbusier started with a reference to Pythagoras, and proceeded to list music and musicians, ranging from Gregorian chant to 'the latest atonalities', via Bach, Mozart, Beethoven, Debussy, Ravel, Satie and Stravinsky, declaring that 'music is always present' to him, because 'music and architecture depend on measurement.'[140] Some twenty years earlier, at a conference, he mentioned the same list of composers, ending with the statement that 'architecture and music are sisters who are very close to each other . . . architecture is in music and music in architecture.'[141]

The 'musical' sections of glass in the facade of Le Corbusier's Sainte Marie de La Tourette illustrate perfectly the 'tangent between architecture and music' dear to his collaborator Xenakis, who commented that

> arcs can be drawn between music and architecture. The wave-like glass sections are a concrete example of the passage from rhythm, musical series (the ear), to architecture, just as later there is the passage from mass *glissandi* by the strings to defining the form of the shells of the Philips Pavilion.

And he added: 'This approach, this experience which I acquired alongside and together with Le Corbusier . . . helped me conceive my music also as an architectural project.'[142] Le Corbusier worked with another musician, Edgar Varèse, whom he had met in 1935 in New York at a concert Varèse was conducting. In 1951, Le Corbusier asked him to compose music for his 'Unité d'habitation' in Marseilles, and in 1956, at Ronchamp, after contacting Olivier Messiaen, he commissioned Varèse to invent an electronic musical system to be placed under the bells of the chapel, a project he would return to eight years later.[143] The Brussels or Philips Pavilion was another collaboration with Xenakis, for the World Fair of 1958. Called a *Poème électronique*, it was described by Xenakis, who was responsible for carrying out the whole project, as a 'vast audiovisual synthesis' and 'a total electronic gesture', in a fusion of architecture, cinema and the projection of coloured lights and sound.[144] It was a modern instance of the

Gesamtkunstwerk, whose origins go back to the Romantic era, and particularly to Runge's cycle *The Times of Day*, which was conceived as 'an abstract painterly fantastical-musical poem with choirs, and a composition for all the three arts together, to which Architecture should contribute a special building'.[145]

Honoré Daumier, *Les Paysagistes, Charivari* (1865), lithograph.
The first copies nature, the second copies the first.

10

MAGISTER DIXIT, OR THE HISTORY OF A MISUNDERSTANDING

It has sometimes been said that for generations after Aristotle, spiders had six legs: the authority of the master was enough to cloud the vision of the entomologist. This is doubtlessly apocryphal,[1] but in the first dialogue of the famous *Parallel of the Ancients and the Moderns*, devoted to criticizing 'Partiality in favour of the Ancients', Charles Perrault cheekily put the following words into the mouth of the Abbott, his mouthpiece:

> In the past all you had to do was to quote Aristotle in order to reduce to silence someone who had dared make a remark contrary to the sentiments of that philosopher.[2]

One could venture to say that something similar goes on in the human sciences today. A particularly eloquent example is a quotation attributed for the last half-century by historians to St Augustine, to the effect that architecture is the sister of music. It is an attractive idea, of course, and, as the proverb says, *se non è vero, è ben trovato*. But it is perhaps just a little too attractive, and above all St Augustine (who did indeed publish a treatise on music, *De musica*) never wrote anything of the sort! Moreover, he never wrote on architecture, and the term does not even appear in his texts.[3] Although the words *aedificium* and *architectus* appear in passing within digressions on symmetry in *De ordine* (II, 34) and *De religione* (XXII, 59), music is never discussed. And in the *De Trinitate* (II–XIV, VII, 9) – a passage referred to by Tanja Ledoux[4] – it is music and geometry that are linked, not architecture, which is not even mentioned.

One might well ask why Augustine never discussed architecture directly. Perhaps simply because, as Dominique Iogna-Prat has shown, Augustine considered that a church is merely 'a frame and a container in which a content can be held . . . What is essential is not in the stone.'[5] But there may also be a more general reason: architecture was not part of the *quadrivium* at the time, and had the status of a mere mechanical art. Making it into a sister of music would have been to infringe the *doxa* codified by Martianus Capella, which ordained that Architecture, associated as it happens with Medicine, had no place among the select 'sciences of the stars': '*his mortalium rerum cura terrenorumque sollertia est nec cum aethere quicquam habent superisque confine*' (the interest in all that is mortal and the attention paid to earthly things have nothing in common with the higher spheres).[6] Tanja Ledoux has interpreted the *Triumph of Saint Augustine* in the Bracciolini Chapel, S. Francesco al Prato, Pistoia, as an allegory of Architecture. But Gabriele Frings has shown convincingly that the two columns represented there are actually the traditional attributes of Jubal.[7] Besides, the representation of the Liberal Arts has a general function here and does not imply a relation to each art singly. It is a similar case with regards to the *Triumph of Saint Thomas Aquinas* in the Spanish Chapel, Santa Maria Novella, since the person honoured has no privileged link with music. It was only much later, when the art of construction was admitted into the Liberal Arts, that the theorist of 'harmonic architecture', René Ouvrard, referred to St Augustine.[8]

So whodunnit? If we work back along the chain of references to find out who first perpetrated this anachronistic attribution of 'architecture as the sister of music' to St Augustine, the culprit seems to be Otto von Simson's classic work on Gothic cathedrals, which refers to two texts by Augustine.[9] To our great surprise we discovered that not only does neither of these two texts contain the famous statement on the sibling bonds between the two arts, but in fact the subject-matter is quite different. One text deals with grammar, versification, rhythm, geometry and astronomy;[10] the other, with dance.[11] As for the passage in *De musica* which is sometimes cited in this context, it discusses the beauty of proportion with respect to sound, light, scents, tastes and touch.[12] No trace of architecture, despite the insistence of Simson who, in no less than seven mentions over two paragraphs, attributes to St Augustine a major interest in the discipline! Could the high priest of Gothic have lost his memory? Or was this wishful thinking? Whatever the reason, no one after him seems to have gone back to check the source, not even in order to understand the context; all defer to the authority of the Master, and simply give that single reference. This misplaced trust affects quite a crowd: Herbert von Einem,[13] Georg Germann,[14] Karen Michels,[15] Tanja Ledoux,[16] Ulrike Steinhauser[17] and Vasco Zara,[18] to name but a few. Wilhelm Perpeet, who devotes a whole chapter to Augustine's aesthetics, and cites his sources with precision for every argument, nevertheless refers to Simson for the famous twinning of the two arts.[19] And even Paul Naredi-Rainer, an acknowledged specialist in the field, maintains on three occasions in an article of 1985 that Augustine was interested in architecture, on the basis of references to Simson and to Perpeet (who himself was citing Simson).[20] Curiously enough, Naredi-Rainer even adds a further reference to Augustine (*De musica*, vi, xii, 38), where there is a discussion of beauty in numbers, but no more mention of architecture than in the first two texts. He returned to the theme in the fifth edition of his classic work, *Architektur und Harmonie*, with predictably Simson and Perpeet for references.[21] Is there no end to this hall of mirrors?

11
THE PARADOX OF MUSIC WITH SCULPTURE

Much has been written on the relations between music and painting, and music and architecture, but no similar attention of any scope seems to have been devoted to the relations between music and sculpture. This chapter sets out to begin to fill that gap, and complete the triptych. The association of music and sculpture is certainly paradoxical, or even a kind of oxymoron, since nothing seems to link the two arts, and they have long been diametrically opposed, as heavy to light, static to dynamic, space to time, and sight (or touch) to hearing. Although the myths of Amphion's lyre or the trumpets of Jericho show, each differently, a close relation between music and architecture, they also show the triumph of one over the other, of immaterial sound over the heaviness and resistance of stone.

August Wilhelm Schlegel, stressing this same opposition between matter and spirit, assigned the representation of bodies to sculpture and the expression of thoughts to poetry.[1] The traditional divide in Western aesthetics between a privileged *disegno* and a second-class *colorito* was reconfigured by the victory of the colourists and their manifold references to music. Germaine de Staël, in reaction to the School of Jacques Louis David, declared that 'painting loses most of its charm when it gets closer to sculpture',[2] and Van Gogh wrote to Theo that 'painting as it is now promises to become more subtle – more music and less sculpture.'[3] Valéry contrasted the two, from a different perspective, stating that 'statues make one think of statues, but music does not make one think of music.'[4]

This new hierarchy affected how the history of the arts was conceived. In 1814, E.T.A. Hoffmann wrote that 'the two opposing poles of the ancient world and the modern world . . . are sculpture and music', and he considered music to be the expression of the 'inner spirituality of man'.[5] For Hegel, who associated every art with a particular historical period, music was opposed to sculpture, and corresponded to the last stage of spiritualization.[6] Similarly for Carl Gustav Carus, who saw music as succeeding sculpture.[7] As for Heinrich Heine, who thought he lived in 'the most brilliant period of music . . . which could well be the last word in art', he also consigned sculpture to the past: 'The spirit found stone too hard'.[8] These theories influenced French artists, for example Delacroix in his statement that

> One can say of painting, as of music, that it is essentially a modern art . . . In sculpture, the Ancients seem already to have done what can be done.[9]

A similar path of progress, leading from sculpture to music and from sensation to emotion, was traced by Teodor de Wyzewa,[10] and Oswald Spengler's Nietzschean system placed 'the naked statue . . . in the Apollonian camp', whereas 'Faustian music . . . banishes the statue's sculptural quality . . . The Faustian group is formed around a pure spatial infinity, with instrumental music at its centre'.[11] This was the reason why Anton Hanak finally did not make a monument to Gustav Mahler: he abandoned the project with a paraphrase of Schelling's formula on architecture as 'frozen music' (*erstarrte Musik*[12]), asking 'But does music let itself be turned to stone?'[13]

As we have seen, comparisons between the arts evolved over the centuries in a sort of pendulum movement. The centrifugal movement, best illustrated by Lessing's *Laocoon*, stressed differences and sought to define specificities. The reaction of Romanticism, which sought the unity of *Ars Una* and universal correspondences, did not, however, bring music and sculpture any closer together. Sculpture at the time was not rated highly and was unhelpfully associated with Neoclassicism. Baudelaire, who found it boring, wrote that 'colour is a melodious science which is not taught by handling marble.' He ended with 'we could understand a musician wanting to imitate Delacroix – but a sculptor, never!'[14]

The two arts were not reconciled until the emergence of the Symbolist aesthetic, which was resolutely 'centripetal', on the side of reciprocal relations between the arts. J. P. Armengaud has shown how closely Camille Claudel's sculpture resembles Debussy's music, despite their painful separation in the real world. Rodin recounts how

> lately, a journalist criticized my *Victor Hugo* in the Palais Royal, saying that it was not sculpture, but music. And he added naively that the work made him think of a Beethoven symphony. If only that were the case![15]

The cult of Beethoven was indeed in its heyday.[16] Rodin thought one of Michelangelo's *Slaves* bore 'the mask of Beethoven',[17] and that John the Baptist in Max Klinger's *Pietà* also had Beethoven's features.[18] Jean-Désiré Ringel d'Illzach drew his inspiration from Beethoven's nine symphonies, as did Auguste de Niederhäusern (called Rodo) in his *Temple de la mélancolie* (1909) and his *Andante,* which was to decorate a temple to music (1910).[19] Antoine Bourdelle made some hundred sculptures of Beethoven, mentioning that 'while listening recently to one of his magnificent trios, it seemed to me that instead of seeing, for once I was hearing sculpture.'[20]

Representations of Music

Of course sculpture could, like painting, and without overstepping the limits of its medium, represent musicians and their instruments. It certainly exploited this possibility to the full. We can find many medieval examples, from church portals to capitals to the misericords under choir stalls. Musical iconography was used in all of sculpture's traditional genres, for example allegorically in Falconet's *La Musique* (1740), Henri Ding's *La Muse de Berlioz* (1890) and the reliefs of the Théâtre des Champs-Élysées by Bourdelle (1913). In representations of myth, Orpheus had a privileged role, from Canova to Rodin,

Jacques Froment-Meurice, monument to Chopin, 1906, marble.

Zadkine and Walter Linck; but *Apollo* was also represented (Alberto Giacometti, 1929), *Terpsichore* (Canova, 1808–18) and *Amphion* (Henri Laurens, 1937). There was also a religious repertory, such as *David* (Pablo Gargallo, 1934) or *Cécile* (Emmanuel Fremiet, 1883–96), while angel-musicians and *putti* abound in Donatello,[21] the Della Robbia brothers and in Baroque decoration.

Monumental sculpture often depicted music or musicians. This can be seen particularly in cemeteries, as in Père Lachaise in Paris, or in public parks, especially in Paris (the Parc Monceau boasts Alexandre Falguière's *Ambroise Thomas* (1900), Antonin Mercié's *Charles Gounod* (1902) and Jacques Froment-Meurice's *Frédéric Chopin au piano* (1906)), and in Vienna (with statues of Haydn, Mozart, Beethoven and Johann Strauss). This fashion was at its height

Louis-François Roubiliac, *Handel,* 1738, sculpture.

in the belle époque, but there were predecessors: Louis-François Roubiliac, who made a portrait bust of *Farinelli*, is better known for his two monuments to Handel, one in Westminster (1761–2), which conforms to official sculptural rhetoric,[22] and the other in Vauxhall Gardens (1738; today in the Victoria and Albert Museum), an early example of a sculpture in homage to a living artist. It presents a curious mixture of allegory and intimacy. Handel is identified with Apollo, through the sun which decorates his lyre, but he also wears slippers and a night cap! Entirely different is the majestic *Beethoven* (1902) of the Vienna Secession, which unites Christian hagiography with classical mythology.[23] Max Klinger apparently had the idea for this statue while at the piano. As a great music lover, he also made busts and monuments to Liszt, Brahms, Strauss and

Wagner.[24] Jean-Joseph Carriès' homage to Wagner, the *Porte de Parsifal* (1889–94), remained unfinished, unlike Debussy's consecration by the Martel brothers (1919–33)[25] and by Maillol (1929–33).

Portrait busts of musicians were also enduringly popular, as shown by, among others, *Cimarosa* by Canova, *Paganini* by David d'Angers, *Beethoven* by Étienne Hippolyte Maindron (*c.* 1850) and Josef Danhauser,[26] *Rossini* by Lorenzo Bartolini and Antoine Etex, *Fauré* by Fremiet, *Mahler/Mozart* by Rodin, *Furtwängler* by Alexander Archipenko and *Schönberg* by Fritz Wotruba. Jean-Baptiste Carpeaux's *Gounod* (1873), which was made in London while Gounod was improvising at the piano, recalls Delacroix's famous *Chopin* at the Louvre. Carpeaux's portrait of his brother Charles, a violinist, shows his close – familial and familiar – relationship with music. Caricatures were also popular, for example, Dantan's statuettes of *Rossini*, *Paganini* and *Berlioz* – just three of his thirty-odd musician sculptures.[27]

So musicians were often taken as models, and also singers, for example by Rodo (1912),[28] Ernst Barlach,[29] Joseph Bernard and Henri Chapu (*La cantate*). Sculptors and painters represented instruments for the beauty of their forms, and Cubist iconography had quite a collection of still-lifes (otherwise rarely found in three dimensions), with its guitars, mandolins, banjos and violins by Picasso, Ossip Zadkine, Henri Laurens, Otto Gutfreund and Jacques Lipchitz, and its music-playing Pierrots and Harlequins. The Martel brothers represented various instrumentalists playing the musical saw (Gaston Wiener), the accordion, the lute, the viol – and even a whole orchestra. String instruments, an unceasing source of inspiration, were particularly popular, sometimes undergoing strange metamorphoses, as in Germaine Richier's *La Mandoline ou la cigale* (1954–5). The violin was invariably associated with the female body,[30] as in Man Ray's famous *Violon d'Ingres* (1924). The emblematic value of this instrument is suggested by the following anecdote narrated by Constantin Brancusi, who crafted his own artistic myth in the process:

> It is thanks to a violin that I came to be a sculptor. I was eleven, and I was working in a dyeing works. I had organized

and tidied the place so well that the owner said to me: 'There is one thing you don't know how to do, and that is make a violin.' I discovered Stradivarius's secret, I hollowed out the wood and boiled it: the violon sounded magnificent. When he saw it, my boss said to me: 'you must become a sculptor.'[31]

The instrument itself can become a sculpture, when it is treated as a surface to be carved – for example, the necks of viols decorated with narrative scenes, or the serpents one can see in museums – or an instrument may even be invented from scratch: the Bauhaus architect and instrument-maker Jean Weinfeld (1905–1992) invented 'Fonics' ('*Formes nouvelles pour instruments à cordes*' – New forms for stringed instruments). Some new designs, such as Ernst F. Chladni's (1756–1827) *euphon* and *clavicylinder*, Benjamin Franklin's *harmonica* (1761) and Luigi Russolo's *intonarumori* (1913) were not concerned with the instrument's sculptural qualities, but others were, such as the Baschet Brothers' *Instrumentarium*,[32] including the Cristal, first built in 1955.

From Dada to Fluxus, a vein of irony also developed. Duchamp fired the first shot, in 1916, with *A Bruit secret* (With Hidden Noise). The parodic dimension is even more visible in Man Ray's *Emak Bakia* (1927), where loose horse hair taken from a bow hangs down the neck of a violin. His *Espoirs et illusions optiques* (1938) likewise uses collage, this time a banjo whose resonance chamber is a mirror. This piece probably inspired Christian Marclay's *Grand piano* (1994), in the Geneva Museum, and another incongruous piece of his, *Cor de chasse* (Hunting Horn), transformed into a commode chair. Marclay used worn records, discarded instruments and photos to explore the relationship between seeing and listening, although the works themselves remained paradoxically silent, as did those of Sarkis, whose primary materials in his installations were often recorded tapes. John Armleder's trombones on a sofa (*Seafoam*, 1989) and Beuys' felt-wrapped pianos were also soundless. The different versions of Nam June Paik's *Piano intégral* (1958–63) suggest on the contrary a hubbub which Jean Tinguely achieved in 1955 with his mechanical creations busy creating drawings and concrete music, in his *Reliefs Méta-mécaniques sonores*, *Sculptures radiophoniques* and the four *Méta-harmonies* (1978–85), which he sometimes called 'acoustic mixing machines'. The works of Arman, that great leveller of violins, are nothing if not iconoclastic. Anselm Stalder's *Concert de flûte du roi* (1976–87) – probably a reference to Frederick the Great – is a minimalist moulding of the flute-player's lips and fingertips, while with *Boîte à musique* (1980), a simple perforated scroll, and *Pavillon* (1985), a fragment of a gramophone, Sylvie and Cherif Defraoui took this mocking reductionism to its limits.

The Ideal of Pure Form

The vast movement leading from the Enlightenment's *ut pictura musica*[33] to the avant-gardes' *ut musica pictura* saw the transition from painting as an ideal for (descriptive) music to ('pure') music as an ideal for non-figurative painting. A similar change affected sculpture, as we can see in an abstract polychrome bas-relief by the architect H. R. Von der Mühll, entitled *La Musique* (1928). The works of the Baschet Brothers, Bernard and François, also provide a good example of the close relationship between music and sculpture: the musical instruments they constructed appear to be abstract sculptures, but they can also be played, as indeed they were, in the group they formed called 'Sound Structures'.

In the absence of colour, sculpture's references to music were couched in terms of pure form – volumes, structures, rhythms and proportions. Musical terms were often borrowed for the titles of sculptures, and could take the form of catalogue references (the proponent of Musicalism, Étienne Beothy's *Opus 76* or *Opus 79*, 1936–7),[34] of tempo markings (Julien Dillens, *Allegretto*, 1894), of vertical – chord – functions (*Dreiklang* by Rudolph Belling, 1919, *Zweiklang* by Albert Schilling, 1956) or horizontal – melodic – ones (Schilling, *Melodie*, 1956).[35] Naming the sculpture after traditional musical forms was also common (Baranoff-Rossiné, *Symphonie*, 1913, or Patrick Honegger,

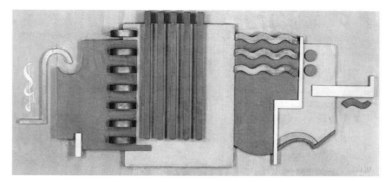

Henri Von der Mühll, *La musique,* 1928, painted plaster.

Chaconne, 1992), and for sculptors as for painters, the fugue epit-
omized musical structure (Schilling, 1959, Antoine Poncet, 1982–5).
Eduardo Chilida gave many of his sculptures eloquent titles: *Musica
callada* (1955, Music Fallen Silent), *Canto esparo* (1960–61), *Musica de
la esferas* (1953, Music of the Spheres), *Musica de la constelaciones*
(1954, Music of the Constellations), *Petit palais de musique* (1992),
and the series *De Musica* (1988–99). Walter Linck, after a figurative
phase in which he represented flautists and violinists, returned to
musical themes in his Constructivist works (*Piano rythmique, Harpe
animée, Glasharfe, Son d'acier, Lyrique,* among others).[36]

Pythagoras, the patron saint of relations between music and
mathematics, is sometimes represented holding the hammers with
which, as legend has it, he discovered harmonic proportions (which
is why he has sometimes been confused with the representation of
Jubal or Tubalcain, the blacksmith who features in the Old Testament).[37]
Although Pythagoras' influence was much greater in architecture
than in sculpture, his discoveries lay behind Pomponius Gauricus'
comparison between the proportions of the human body and 'har-
monic proportions in musical instruments'.[38] One could say that
Rafael Soto, in his search for 'the level of truly universal language
which music and mathematics possess', was, *mutatis mutandis,* an
heir to this Renaissance scientific aesthetic when he maintained that
'dodecaphonic music and its immediate consequence, serial music,

have helped me discover how . . . to bring a rigorously objective codification to the visual arts.'[39] He was inspired by Bach's science of counterpoint,[40] calling him a 'great creator of structures', and was close to the contemporary music scene, creating, for example, his *Pénétrables musicaux*. We have seen how influential Bach was on painting, and he was similarly admired by sculptors. Henri Nouveau, a pupil of Nadia Boulanger, made *Monument à Bach*, which was rebuilt after the war in the park of the Leverkusen Clinic, Germany. Zadkine created *Hommage à Bach* (1936) and Chilida created two such sculptures (1979 and 1981).

The case of Melotti, who declared that Bach's music was an 'exact' art,[41] is particularly interesting. His hesitation between a career as an organist and a sculptor is reminiscent of Paul Klee, initially a violinist. And on numerous occasions he declared his 'very profound relationship with music', as confirmed by his nephew the pianist Maurizio Pollini. 'For me', Melotti said, 'music was my starting-point. . . . Slowly music brought me – with its laws, its digressions and its meanderings – to a balanced approach.'[42] He summarized his explorations in a striking formula: 'Sculpture is saved through counterpoint.' Here

Albert Schilling, *Fuga*, 1959, bronze.

again, the titles of his works stress the importance of this musical source of inspiration: in a *catalogue raisonné* of Melotti's works, we find 58 items called *Contrappunto*, 39 *Tema e variazioni*, 13 *Canone*, 5 *Dissonanze armoniose* and a plethora of other musical references such as *Modulazione, Dissonanze armoniose, Toccata, Fuga, Ritmo, Basso continuo, Cadenza, Scala musicale, Chiave di violino*, and so on, and various allusions to Bach, Beethoven, Wagner, Debussy, Stravinsky, Schönberg, Bartok and Petrassi.[43]

Once again we encounter the fascination of artists and psychologists for synaesthesia, from Romanticism to today, a sensibility which most probably inspired Boleslas Biegas's sculptures on the music of Beethoven, Chopin and Wagner,[44] and Étienne Hadju's *Hommage à Béla Bartok* (1949). This work, with its hammered copper, expresses Hadju's subjective appreciation of the composer's work.[45] To each his Bartok! A similar subjective force is perceptible in François Simecek's sculptures carried out in the same year, *Rythmes selon Bach* and *Rythmes selon Mozart* (1932).

However, relative to painting, there are few sculptures explicitly inspired by musical works (or vice versa),[46] even when one is dealing with sculptors who have a passion for music, or fully fledged musician-sculptors. Some exceptions prove the rule nonetheless. James Pradier, who held musical evenings in his workshop, himself played the piano, the organ, the harp and the guitar, as well as composing music.[47] Emmanuel Fremiet was a relative of Gabriel Fauré, and Marguerite de Saint-Marceaux's salon attracted the musical elite of the time, and other artists (her husband was the sculptor René de Saint-Marceaux).[48] Max Klinger's studio had a grand piano in it.[49] Auguste de Niederhäusern (Rodo), a fervent supporter of Wagner and admirer of Schumann, was a friend of Jaques-Dalcroze and Scriabin, and played the alpenhorn.[50] The Martel brothers were knowledgeable music lovers, and themselves played the piano, the cello and the accordion, and hosted concerts in their studio. Jacques Lipchitz had a subscription to the Salle Pleyel concerts, Rafael Soto attended those of the *Domaine musical*,[51] and Christian Marclay had musical training before becoming a disc jockey.[52]

Lastly, we should mention the inter-disciplinary contacts, collaborative projects and cross-pollinations, which today are more common than ever. Earle Brown, who worked with Vassilakis Takis in 1963 on the *Sound of the Void*, said he was inspired by Calder's mobiles, one of which he even incorporated into a composition (*Calder Piece*, 1963).[53] Francis Miroglio's *Ping Squash* for percussion (1979) was also a homage to Alexander Calder. Toshi Ichianagi composed a piece in 1963 from the sounds produced by Jean Tinguely's sculptures, and Thierry Blondeau created a *Musique Taïngli* (2000). The composer Jean-Marc Chouvel and the sculptor Laurent Golon also worked together.[54]

Sound Sculpture

In 1963 Takis began creating 'musical sculptures', three years later he made a 'luminous musical telesculpture', and since 1974 he has been devising 'musical spaces'.[55] The notion of sound sculpture is, admittedly, difficult to define; its inventor is sometimes given as Fortunato Depero (for his invention of a '*complesso plastico-colorato-motorumorista di equivalenti in moto*' (coloured plastic compound motorumorista of moving equivalents) in 1915), and sometimes as László Moholy-Nagy or Harry Partch.[56] Duchamp defined it as 'sounds lasting and leaving from different points and forming a sound sculpture which lasts'.[57] However, installations, environments, *happenings* and other types of performance have long blurred the categories, and what we call *Klangkunst* or *sound sculpture* is a hybrid and fluctuating field, a frontier zone which challenges traditional taxonomies.[58]

Everything depends on the definition used, and the task of circumscribing the limits of each form of expression is made more difficult by today's developments: where, for example, does music end and noise begin? How to distinguish sculpture from arts such as sculpto-painting, Op-art, or Kinetic Art? Are Nicolas Schöffer's *Tours spatiodynamiques* sculpture or architecture? And where should we situate John Cage's transparent, virtual and invisible *Sculptures musicales*, whose text-based scores are reminiscent of Mallarmé's *Coup de dés*?[59] Since we shall never have answers to these questions, and rather than cling dogmatically to some pedantic *distingo*, we shall take a historical approach. This new territory is so vast that we shall merely suggest the current state of affairs by mapping some more recent exhibitions devoted to the 'musical sculpture' theme: in Vancouver (*Sound Sculpture*, 1975), Los Angeles (*Sound Sculpture*, 1979), Düsseldorf (*Sehen um zu hören*, 1975), Berlin (*Für Augen und Ohren*, 1980), Paris (*Écouter par les yeux. Objets et environnements sonores*, 1980), New York (*Sound/Art*, 1983), Würzburg (*Klangskulpturen*, 1985), Stuttgart (*Vom Klang der Bilder*, 1985), Aix-la-Chapelle (*Klangobjekte*, 1990), Basel (*Geräusche*, 1993), Koblenz (*Klangskulpturen, Augenmusik*, 1995), Berlin (*Klangkunst*, 1996), Vienna (*Sounds & Files*, 2000), Paris (*Sons et lumières*, 2004), Washington, DC (*Visual Music*, 2005), Zurich (*Sound, Performance and Sculpture*, 2005, and *Beyond the Sound, Klangskulpturen* by Yuri Kalendarev, 2010), and the *Ostseebiennale der Klangkunst* (2004–8).

In the field of audio-visual correspondences, timbre was often taken as an equivalent of texture. The sculptor Oscar Wiggli explored the relations between volumes of metal and synthesized sounds. He was both a blacksmith and a composer – he trained at IRCAM, Paris – and he drew and sculpted sounds, sometimes using material recorded while he was working the metal. His graphic scores partake both of the visual and the acoustic,[60] and in his various installations, he organized 'dialogues' between his sculptures and different sounds, alternating with periods of silence, which he broadcast over loud-speakers positioned in the installation space. At a retrospective of Wiggli's work in Bern, a film projected his 'sound reliefs' accompanied by a soundtrack he had composed.[61] His musical fountain *Arethusa* (Hahnloser coll.) produced sounds through drops of water falling on the sculpted bronze. These sounds inspired him to compose an electronic piece, which he then recorded, and the 45 rpm record accompanied the monograph devoted to Wiggli's work.[62] In another exhibition, where he displayed his photographs of the sky taken from a moving train, and linked them with a tape recording, he stated that 'For me, there is a great similarity between clouds and sounds, because for both, time is important.' By working both on a solid volume of metal – iron or bronze – and on the immaterial substance of electro-acoustic music, by uniting the heavy (for example his monumental cast-iron sculptures created in the Swiss Von Roll workshops between 1988 and 1994) with the ethereal, and the concrete with the virtual, Wiggli seems to have successfully brought together two media which for centuries had appeared irreconcilable – music and sculpture – as *Partition forgée* and *Rêve de forgeron*, a recorded piece, suggest in their titles alone.

CODA

Throughout this study, our historical and systematic approach has enabled us to tease out continuities in the relations between music and the other arts. Seemingly disparate phenomena have been brought into contact, such as onomatopoeia, hieroglyphs and colour hearing, synaesthesia and cosmic music, or primitivism and modernity. However, our working categories have been challenged by this emphasis on the *longue durée*, and the inter-disciplinary approach of our work has raised a number of methodological issues.

Comparative study is never simple, and comparing the specific languages of music and painting, for example, or equally matching up artists, as Stendhal did, will always be problematic, and sometimes fraught with inconsistencies, as when Rousseau wished to 'put some vision into hearing' while also railing against 'the false analogy between colours and sounds'.[1] Although the arts have always been compared to each other, this process is not unproblematic; we need only recall the bewildering diversity of images used to characterize Bach's music.

Moreover, the continuities we have teased out are paradoxical, consisting of breaks and returns. They tend to mimic the musical form of the *rondo*, in which the principal theme would be a quest for originary unity, while the contrasting theme, which introduces an inverse movement, emphasizes the diversity and hermetic closure of each expressive medium. Overall, historically, we can note a pendulum-like movement, alternating between centripetal and centrifugal tendencies, movements of convergence and divergence, claims of homogeneity and heterogeneity, identity and differentiation, fusion of forms and claims to specificity. This tension informs aesthetic thought and practice in the West right up to the poetics of the avant-gardes.

In 1954 Boulez analysed the contemporary trends of the art world in the following terms:

> As for the comparison between the 'arts', in other words, music and poetry, or music and painting, the failure of total art, of the *Gesamtkunstwerk*, had made everyone very circumspect . . . But it would seem that, without returning to Romantic dreams of unity, contemporary thinking is more confident in reciprocal relations, based on the notion of structure as a founding principle.[2]

Could we apply this to the situation today? Does post-modernism mark the return of a fantasy of unity? And is this nostalgia symptomatic? The revival of myths of origin coincided with the first cracks in the edifice of knowledge, as its sheer accumulated volume required divisions and specialization. This situation is truer than ever today, as the proliferating bibliography on our subject suggests.

A defining feature of classicism, its doctrine of decorum (or fittingness), and its dogma of conformity, which modernism so utterly rejected, was its wish to believe that correspondences can be transparent and univocal: *ut pictura poesis*. In the different artistic media, an organically coherent system prevailed, whether in the tonal hierarchy organized around the privileged tonic – dominant relation, or in the syntax of Albertian perspective, founded on a central vanishing point and distance points. Prokofiev's and Stravinsky's polytonal compositions, Hauer's and Schönberg's twelve-tone technique and the multiple viewpoints of analytical Cubism were the first breaches in these classical ramparts. The leitmotif thereafter would be discontinuity.

So modernity seemed to throw its weight behind an aesthetics of rupture and distance. Originally from Chevreul, but adopted by Delaunay, the notion of 'simultaneity', which also implies contrast, was put to use extensively in collage. Surrealism's theory of the image derived from the same structural principle: it was the distance between the two poles that produced the Surrealist spark. 'The more the relationship between the two juxtaposed realities is distant and true,' Breton maintained, quoting Reverdy, 'the stronger the image will be – the greater its emotional power and poetic reality' (*Nord-Sud*, 1918).[3] Disjunction, dislocation, dissociation, the role of chance – these forms or strategies all sought to valorize heterogeneity or even anarchy, a term explicity championed by the composer Th. von Hartmann,[4] and used twice by Kandinsky,[5] who theorized his art as 'a combinatory logic based on dissociation'.[6] He opted for an 'anti-geometric' and 'anti-logical'[7] approach – as did his compatriots Malevich, Kruchonykh and Khlebnikov, who had worked together on the Futurist adventure of the *Victory over the Sun* – whereas the Florentine 'Cerebrists' went further still, claiming the right to 'every sort of incoherence'.[8] A good example of this tendency is a 'theatrical synthesis' by Corra and Settimelli, aptly entitled *Dissonance* (1915), in which a character interrupts a knight's declaration of love with the question, 'You got a light?'[9]

The tension between line and colour (already familiar to Degas) was a precursor of that between form and content. Kandinsky spoke of expressive dissonance ('*Gemütsdissonanz*') in relation to combining the colour red with a sad note.[10] The titles of works, whose poetic possibilities were explored in depth by Paul Klee and Max Ernst,[11] and theorized by Redon,[12] also encoded disparity. Experiments were made with divergent sense impressions, as when Kandinsky, in his *Gelber Klang*, combined a crescendo of bright yellow light with bass notes. Schönberg, in his reflexions on the links between music and speech, imagined the possibility of a contradictory relation between the two.[13] Eisenstein rebelled against the 'doubling effect', and so dissociated sound from image. But this dread of redundant repetition and parallels also had negative effects. Philippe Beaussant, the musicologist and academician, criticized what could be called schizophrenic productions, where text and music were utterly disconnected; he considered them to be perversions by Brecht's followers of the master's notion of 'distance'.[14]

So these were the terms of the great debate on 'dissonance', that watchword of modernity. The dialogue between painting and music had much to say on the subject, most intensely in the correspondence between Schönberg and Kandinsky. And the term, in its original, musical sense, was soon applied to all aesthetic issues (see for example Nikolai Kulbin[15]), and often misapplied too.[16] A. W. Schlegel perhaps sensed what the future held for 'dissonance' when he mused: 'Who knows whether genius does not fashion humanity into a great masterpiece, in which even dissonances have a place?'[17] We should recall that it was the painter Kandinsky who raised this question in his first letter to Schönberg. He also addressed the issue in his work *On the Spiritual in Art*, quoting Schönberg.[18] But Schönberg refused to acknowledge the dilemma, in his *Theory of Harmony*: 'the terms consonance and dissonance, which define an opposition,' he stated, 'are not relevant.'[19] And in the same year, Pratella declared that 'the values of consonance and dissonance are absolutely inconsistent.'[20]

Reflections on dissonance were thus contemporary with the movement to differentiate expressive media, which culminated in the Cubist theory of the 'painting-object' and the development of abstraction. This development energized the quest for the specificity of painting. But it also revived its polar opposite, as a redeeming compensatory force: the Wagnerian ideal of a totalizing reintegration of the fragments, in the *Gesamtkunstwerk*.

As we have seen, this ideal of unity was also central to the psychological theory of associationism. Senancourt, reflecting on the power of the senses, privileged hearing because 'the sounds heard in sublime places produce a deeper and more lasting impression than their forms.' He illustrated this with an anecdote concerning the famous song *Ranz des vaches*, 'which not only brings back memories, it actually paints'. The close connection between sound and image was what, in his view, guaranteed inter-subjective communication: 'two people, who were looking through the *Tableaux pittoresques de la Suisse* independently, on seeing the image of the Grimsel Pass both exclaimed: "this is where one should listen to the *ranz des vaches*."'[21] Proust's famous madeleine, and the links he makes between place names and colours, likewise draw on synaesthetic associations based on taste and sound respectively, and suggest the interpenetration and unity of sense impressions.[22]

The renewed interest today in colour hearing might have a similar cause – nostalgia for unity. Kandinsky saw in Schönberg's *Theory of Harmony* an 'organic continuity', and this desire to link back to a tradition which runs deeper than any rifts might explain the paradox that Hölzel, Itten, Feininger and Klee looked to classical polyphony rather than to contemporary music for their musical models: the *basso continuo* had weathered all revolutions. The word 'nostalgia' – *Sehnsucht* – even appears verbatim in Kandinsky's writings on the hope and consolation provided by Mozart's music, although he quickly returned to the 'principle of contrast' on which, he claimed, 'our harmony rests'.[23]

'Harmony' – a term which may sound anachronistic to our ears. Yet some need for unity, or thirst for correspondences, continues to haunt today's critical literature and what are called 'multi-media' artworks. Reflecting on how texts relate to music, Schönberg imagined that a divergence might be resolved organically into a parallel at some higher level.[24] And Franz Marc, in a much-quoted letter to August Macke, spoke of 'a more distant consonance'.[25] For Kandinsky too, distance could be redeemed by a projection into the future: 'Today's dissonance in painting and music is tomorrow's consonance.'[26] History, we would suggest, has proved him right – so far.

Appendix 1
FRIEDRICH MAHLING'S BIBLIOGRAPHY, STUDIES ON SYNAESTHESIA, 1635-1926

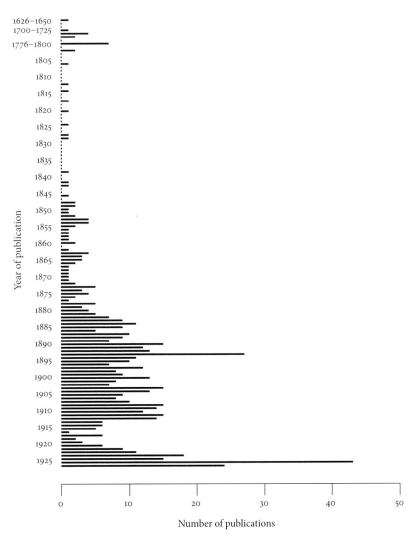

Appendix 2
MAJOR MULTI-MEDIA WORKS AND EVENTS, 1861-2006

1861	*Tannhäuser* in Paris
1874	Modeste Mussorgsky, *Pictures at an Exhibition*
	Wagner's Festspielhaus opens in Bayreuth
1885	The *Revue wagnérienne* is founded
1889	Louis Favre, *The Music of Colours* and *Illuminated Fountains* at the Universal Exhibition
	Nicolai Rimsky-Korsakov, *Mlada*
1891	*The Song of Songs*, 'synthetic theatre' at the Théâtre d'art, Paris
1894	Max Klinger, *Brahmsphantasie*
1895	First concert of *colour music* in London by A. W. Rimington
	Esposizione internazionale di elettricità, Turin
1900	Loïe Fuller Pavilion at the Universal Exhibition
1902	Gustav Klimt, *Beethoven Frieze* at the Wiener Secession
1906	Paul Dukas, *Ariane et Barbe bleue*
1908	Mikalojus Konstantinas Čiurlionis, *Fugue*
1909	Serge Diaghilev founds the Ballets Russes
	Arnold Schönberg, *Farben*, op. 16
1910	First abstract films by the Corradini brothers
1911	Granville Bantok, *Atlanta in Calydon Symphony*
	Béla Bartók, *Bluebeard's Castle*
	The Corradini brothers make an abstract film on Mendelssohn's *Song of Spring*
	Wassily Kandinsky paints *Impression III (Concert)*
	Beginning of Kandinsky's correspondence with Schönberg
1912	Adrian B. Klein, *Compositions in Colour-music*
	Frantisek Kupka, *Amorpha, fugue en deux couleurs*
	Wassily Kandinsky, *Gelber Klang*
	Kandinsky and Franz Marc publish the Almanach of the *Blaue Reiter*
	Lecture by Bruno Corra: abstract film and chromatic music
1913	Alexei Kroutchonykh, Mikhail Matiouchine and Kasimir Malevich, *Victory over the Sun*
	Valentine de Saint-Point creates 'Métachorie' (poetry, music and dance)
	Arnold Schönberg, *Die glückliche Hand*

Wassily Kandinsky, *Klänge*

Exhibition of the Synchromists at the Galerie Bernheim, Paris

1914   Duncan Grant, *Abstract Kinetic Collage Painting with Sound*

Loïe Fuller, *Synaesthetic Symphonies* at the Théâtre du Châtelet, Paris

Luigi Russolo, great Futurist concerto of *intonarumori*

Léopold Survage, *Rythmes colorés*

1915   Scriabin's *Prometheus: The Poem of Fire* performed at Carnegie Hall,
New York, with a *clavier à lumières* (colour organ)

1916   Arturo Ciacelli makes an 'abstract and simultaneous' film on the music
of colours

Claude Bragdon presents *Cathedral without Walls* in Central Park,
New York

Robert and Sonia Delaunay plan a 'simultaneist' exhibition for the Dalmau
Gallery, Barcelona

Fortunato Depero, *Colori,* an 'abstract theatrical synthesis'

The 'Prometheans' group founded, New York

1917   Guillaume Apollinaire, *Les mamelles de Tiresias*

Giacomo Balla, stage design for Stravinsky's *Fireworks* in Rome
(Ballets Russes)

Serge Charchoune presents his Ornamental Films at the Dalmau Gallery,
Barcelona

Cocteau, Picasso and Satie stage *Parade* (Ballets Russes)

Fortunato Depero, stage design for Stravinsky's *Song of the Nightingale*

1919   The Bauhaus founded

Joseph Matthias Hauer and Johannes Itten meet in Vienna

1920   Achille Ricciardi, *Teatro del colore* in Rome (design by Prampolini)

1921   Viking Eggeling, *Symphonie diagonale*

First musical film by Fischinger

Walter Ruttmann, *Lichtspiel,* op. 1

1922   Arthur Bliss, *Colour Symphony*

Mikhail Matiouchine, *Naissance de la lumière, de la couleur et du volume*

Kurt Schwitters, *Ursonate*

Francis Picabia, *Optophone*

The Mayson Opera Singers demonstrate the sound–colour correspondences
developed by Edith Tudor-Hart

Thomas Wilfred, first recital on the *clavilux*

Symphony for sirens, hydroplane, artillery and choir of spectators
in Baku

1923   Ludwig Hirschfeld-Mack, *Farbensonatine*

Kurt Schwerdtfeger, *Reflektorische Lichtspiele*

Oskar Schlemmer, *Ballet triadique* at the Bauhaus

1924	Lewis Barnes, recital of *Music in Colour* at Selfridges in London
	George Gershwin, *Rhapsody in Blue*
	Fernand Léger, *Ballet mécanique*
	Satie, Picabia and René Clair stage *Relâche* and *Entracte* at the Ballets Suédois
1925	The November group organizes 'Der absolute Film' in Berlin
	Ludwig Hirschfeld-Mack, *Farbenlicht-spiele*
	Alexander Laszlo founds the *Gesellschaft für den Synchromismus* in Munich and gives his first recitals of *Farblichtmusik*
	László Moholy-Nagy, *Mechanische Exzentrik*
	Paul Poiret installs the *clavilux* (colour organ) on his barge in Paris during the *Arts déco* exhibition
	Hans Richter, *Rythmus 21*
	Thomas Wilfred, *clavilux* recital in London and Paris
1927	First *Farbe – Ton – Forschungen* Congress in Hamburg
	Alexander Laszlo, *Pacific 231* (film)
	Walter Ruttmann, *Berlin – Symphonie einer Grossstradt*
1928	Wassily Kandinsky, *Pictures at an Exhibition* (Mussorgsky), Dessau
1929	Roman Clemens, *Spiel aus Form, Farbe, Licht und Ton*
	Rudolph Pfenninger invents the *Tönende Handschrift*
	Arnold Schönberg, *Begleitmusik zu einer Lichtspielszene,* op. 34
1929–34	Oskar Fischinger, *Studien*
1930	Second *Farbe – Ton – Forschungen* Congress in Hamburg, where Oskar Fischinger presents his synaesthetic film *R. 5*
	Lev Theremin, recital of *Color Music* at Carnegie Hall
	Dziga Vertov, *Dornbass-sinfonie*
1931	Oskar Fischinger, *Jazz*
1932	First *Salon des peintres musicalistes*, Paris
1933	Third *Farbe – Ton – Forschungen* Congress, Hamburg
	Henri Mauvoisin, *La palette musicale* (demonstration of the colours of the orchestra), Paris
	Musicolor, concert-display in Neuchâtel
1934	Nikolai Volnov, *Rachmaninov's Prelude* (film)
1935	Les cinéphonies
	Charles Blanc-Gatti exhibits his *Décors lumineux, polychromes et dynamiques* (light projections) at the Salon de la lumière, Paris
1936	Fourth *Farbe – Ton – Forschungen* Congress, Hamburg
	Oskar Fischinger, *Allegretto*
1937	Display by Autan-Lara on *Les Voyelles et leur synchronisation sonore et chromatique* (Vowels and Their Sound and Colour Synchronisation) at the *Arts et techniques* exhibition, Paris

1938	Serge Eisenstein and Serge Prokofiev, *Alexander Nevsky*
	Norman McLaren, *Money a Pickle*
1939	Charles Blanc-Gatti, *Chromophony*
	The American Color-Light Music Society founded
1940	Walt Disney, *Fantasia*
1942	Ivan Wychegradsky, *Mosaïque lumineuse de la coupole du Temple*
1943–5	*Five Film Exercises* by the Whitney brothers
1945	Franciska and Stefan Themerson, *The Eye and the Ear,* music by K. Szymanowski
1949	Arthur Honegger, Ernest Klausz and Serge Lifar, *The Birth of Colours*
	Norman MacLaren, *Begone Dull Care*
1952	John Cage, Merce Cunningham and Robert Rauschenberg, *Untitled Event* at Black Mountain College
1955	Norman MacLaren, *Blinkity Blank*
	Nicolas Schöffer, *Tour spatiodynamique cybernétique de Saint Cloud*
	James Whitney, *Yantra*
1957–9	Jordan Belson and Henry Jacobs, *Vortex concerts* at the San Francisco planetarium
1958	Jean Tinguely, *Mes Etoiles – concert pour sept peintures*
	Varèse, Xenakis and Le Corbusier create the *Poème électronique* at the Philips Pavilion at the Brussels International Exhibition
1959	Allan Kaprow, *18 happenings*, Reuben Gallery, New York
1960	Jean Dubuffet and Asger Jorn, first musical improvisations
	Yves Klein, *Symphonie monotone*
	Olivier Messiaen, *Chronochromie*
	Jean Tinguely, *Hommage à New York*
1962	'Prometheus' Group created in Kazan
	Fluxus internationale Festspiele, Wiesbaden
1963	Olivier Messiaen, *Couleurs de la Cité céleste*
	Nam June Paik, *The Exhibition of Music-electronik Television* at Wuppertal
	Fluxus Festival, Nice
1966	Takis, *Télésculpture lumineuse*
	Andy Warhol + The Velvet Underground, *Up-tight,* New York
	9 Evenings: Theatre and Engineering, New York
1967	Mark Boyle and Pink Floyd, *Music in Colour*
	Iannis Xenakis, *Polytope*, Montreal Universal Exhibition
	First *son et lumière* Congress in Kazan
	Lumière et mouvement exhibition in Paris
	First concert of the Joshua Light Show, Toronto

1968	John Cage and Marcel Duchamp play chess in Toronto
	Stanley Kubrick, *2001: A Space Odyssey,* with *Atmosphères* by Ligeti
	Rodion Chtchedrin, *Poetoria*
1969	Second *son et lumière* Congress in Kazan
	Steve Reich, *Pendulum Music* at the Whitney Museum (with B. Naumann, R. Serra)
1971	Norman MacLaren, *Synchromy*
	Bob Wilson, *Le regard du sourd*
1972	Takehisa Kosugi, *Wave Code*
	Iannis Xenakis, *Polytope de Cluny*
1973	Jean Dubuffet, *Coucou Bazar* in New York and Paris
1975	Third *son et lumière* Congress in Kazan
1976	*Die Verfransung der Künste. Festival Intermedialer Kunst,* Hamburg
	Bob Wilson and Philip Glass, *Einstein on the Beach*
1977–2003	Karlheinz Stockhausen, *Das Licht*
1978	Jean Dubuffet, remake of *Coucou Bazar* in Turin
1979	Jan Tinguely, *Métaharmonie II*
1981	Jakob Weder paints Bach's *Suite in D Major*
1983	Laurie Anderson, *United States*
	Elektra exhibition in Paris
1984	Creation in Venice of Luigi Nono's *Prometeo*
1985	Michael Torke, *Ecstatic Orange*
1986	Fourth *son et lumière* Congress, Kazan
	Symposium in Hanover: *Stum – Film – Musik – Video. Die Konkurrenz von Auge und Ohr*
1987	Fifth *son et lumière* Festival, Kazan
1988	Jack Ox paints Bruckner's *Eighth Symphony*
1990	Sofia Gubaidulina, *Alleluia*
1991	Christian Marclay, *One Hundred Turntables*, Tokyo
1993	Beryl Korot and Steve Reich, *The Cave*
	Jack Ox paints the *Ursonate de Schwitters*
1994	Jenö Takacs, *Klänge und Farben*, op. 95
1995	*Augenmusik, Ohrkunst,* Baden-Württembergische Musikhochschultage
1996	Dominique Dousse Leibzig, *Les sept couleurs du spectre*
1997	Dominique Barthassat, *Mandalas sonores*, Dehli
	Peter Greenaway and Jean-Baptiste Bazzière, *100 Objects to Represent the World*, Salzburg
	Mit den Augen hören / Mit den Ohren schauen (Hearing with one's eyes/ Seeing with one's ears) course at the Volkshochschule, Solothurn, Switzerland

1999	Regula Sibi, *Son et couleur*, concert for piano and projections, Paris, Centre culturel suisse
2000	Prometheus Congress, Kazan
	Sculpted Sound in Concert, London, ICA
2001	The American Synesthesia Association founded
	Images and sounds at the Archipel Festival, Geneva
2002	Symposium *Farbe – Bild – Klang* at the Hochschule für Musik und Theater, Zurich
2003	Jim Hodges, *Corridor* (*Installation in Colorsound)*
	Kronos Quartet, *Visual Music*
2004	*Farblichtmusik im 20. und 21. Jahrhundert*, Zurich, Musikhochschule (with a reconstitution of the *Sonatina für Klavier und Farblicht*, op. 11, by A. Laszlo)
2005	*Klang und Bild – Musik Sehen – Klingende Bilder*, events at the Aargauer Kunsthaus
	Arte y sinestesia Congress, Almeria
	Symposium *Der gelbe Klang. Synästhesie, Gesamtkunstwerk, Interdisciplinarität*, Basel
2006	*An Exhibition about Sound, Performance and Sculpture*, Zurich, Migros Museum

Appendix 3
AUDIO-VISUAL INSTALLATIONS, UTOPIAN PROJECTS AND MACHINES

1591	*gravicembolo* by Mauro Cremonese (according to Comanini, *Il Figino*)
1725	ocular harpsichord by Père Louis-Bertrand Castel
1739–43	*Generalbass-Maschine* by Lorenz Christoph Mizler
1743	*Farbenclavecymbel* by Johann Gottlob Krüger
1769	ocular music by Edme-Gilles Guyot
1781	*eidophysikon* by Philippe Jacques Loutherbourg
1783	*Augen-Leyer* by Johann Samuel Halle
1787	vibrating plates (*Klangfiguren*) by Ernst Chladni
1788	*Farbenklavier* by K. von Eckartshausen
1819	kaleidoscope by David Brewster (shortly afterwards with musical accompaniment)
1844	keyboard by D. D. Jameson
1863	*Farben-instrument* by F. W. Philippy
1873	pyrophone by Frédéric Kastner
1877	colour organ by Bainbridge Bishop
1880	photophone by Graham Bell
1881	spectrophone by Graham Bell
1883	mouth organ by Des Esseintes (Huysmans, *À rebours*)
1889	colour organ by Louis Favre
1891	eidophone by Mme Watts-Hughes
1893	colour organ by Alexander Wallace Rimington
	plans for a colour organ by William Schooling
1898	light organ by H. Beau and Bertrand-Taillet
	harmonium interprète by William Nicati
	phonograph by Dr Rosibus
1900	plan for an instrument by E. G. Lind
1901	photographophone by Ernst Ruhmer
1903	*phonochrôme* by Edmond Tardif
1909	piano with coloured keys, by the Argentinian painter Oscar Agustin Alejandro Schulz Solari
1911	chromatic keyboard by the Corradini brothers

1912	colour organ by Alexander Burnett Hector
	optophone by Dr Fournier d'Albe
	Orgues lumineuses by Abel Gance
	mobile colour machine by Van Deering Perrine
1912–26	optophonic piano by Vladimir Baranoff-Rossiné
1914	three-colour organ by M. Luckiesh
1915	*complexe plastique moto-bruitiste* by Fortunato Depero
	pianola or *chromola* by Preston S. Millar
1916–23	kinetic light machine or light organ by Morgan Russel
1919	chromophone by Louis Artus
	sarabet by Mary Hallock Greenewalt
	first clavilux by Thomas Wilfred
1920	projector by Gregory Gidoni
	Licht-Raum-Modulator by László Moholy-Nagy
	keyboard by Leonard Taylor
1921	colour projector by Adrian Klein
	thermenivox, illumovox or etherophone by Léon Theremin
1922	phonochromograph by Carol-Bérard
	optophone by Raoul Hausmann
	projector by R. Lovstrom
1922–4	*Reflektorische Farbenlichtspiele* by Ludwig Hirschfeld-Mack
1924	mutochrome by C. F. Smith
1924–8	spectrophone or *Farbe-т on-Klavier* by Zdeněk Pešánek
1925	*Farblichtklavier* or *Sonchromatoskop* by Alexander Laszlo
	colour music by Richard Lovstrom
	Orgues lumineuses by Paul Poiret
1927	light-colour play console by Mary Hallock Greenewalt
1928	light piano by Gregory Gidoni
1929	chromatophore by Anatol Vietinghoff-Scheel
1930	musichrome by George Hall
1931	colour organ by E. B. Patterson
1932	colorophone by Smith
1934	chromophonic orchestra by Charles Blanc-Gatti
	kinemachrome at the Palace of the Soviets
1936	*Mobilcolour IV* by Charles Dockum
1937	light console by Frederick Bentham
1938	chromaton or symphochrome by Tom Douglas Jones
1943–4	Light Temple by Ivan Wyschnegradsky
c. 1945	colour organ by W. Christian Sidenius
1946	pianoktail by Boris Vian (L'écume des jours)
1950	lumigraph by Oskar Fischinger

1956	installation project by Vladimir Borisenko at the Scriabin Museum
	Kinetic theatre by Carole Schneemann and Jordan Belson
1957	vortex concerts at the San Francisco Planetarium by Henry Jacobs
1958	*Space Theater* by Milton Cohen
1960	optophonium by Hermann Goepfert
	musiscope by Nicolas Schöffer
1960–69	*Synchrome Kineidoscope* by Stanton MacDonald-Wright
1962	Chromie by Frank Malina
1963	electromedia theatre -14 by Aldo Tambellini
1965	projector by Yuri Pravdyuk
1968	music with balls by Terry Riley
1969	HPSCHD by John Cage and Ronald Nameth
	music/kinetic art workshop at Karkov
	colour organ by Karl Gerstner
	Electronic Light Ballet by Otto Piene
1973	installation by Bulat Galeyev
1983	sonoscope by Alexander Vitkin
1994	sonochromovideo, chromosonograph or ocular piano
	by Louis Boffard and Daniel Paquette
2001	phonokinetoscope by Rodney Graham
2004	*Farblichtflügel* by Natalia Sidler
2005	light organ by Peter Coffin

Appendix 4
THEORETICAL WORKS AND MANIFESTOS

1725	B. Castel, *Clavecin pour les yeux avec l'art de peindre les sons*
1735	J. Ch. Le Blon, *Colorito*
1739	L. C. Mizler, *Anfangs-Gründe des Generalbasses*
	G. Ph. Telemann, *Beschreibung der Augenorgel oder Augen-clavicimbels*
1740	B. Castel, *Optique des couleurs*
1742	Debate at the Imperial Academy of St Petersburg
1743	J. G. Krüger, *De novo musices, quo oculi delectantur, genere*
1744	J. Harris, *A Discourse on Music, Painting and Poetry*
1752	Ch. Avison, *On the Analogies between Music and Painting*
1753	D. Diderot, *Clavecin oculaire*
1755	M. Mendelssohn, *Über die Empfindungen*
1756	G. Hussey, *System of Colours*
1759	G. A. Will, *Der Ton und die Farbe*
1761	L. Euler, *Lettres à une princesse d'Allemagne*
1770	E. G. Guyot, *Musique oculaire*
1778	C. L. Junker, *Betrachtungen über Mahlerey, Ton- und Bildhauerkunst*
1780	J. J. Engel, *Über die musikalische Malerei*
1784	K. von Eckartshausen, *Augenmusik oder Harmonie der Farben*
1786	Ch. F. Hellwag, *Über die Vergleichung der Farben des Regenbogen mit den Tönen der musikalischen Oktave*
	J. L. Hoffmann, *Versuch einer Geschichte der malerischen Harmonie*
1800	P. di G. Gonzaga, *Musique oculaire*
1801	Th. Young, *On the Theory of Light and Colours*
1802	F. Chadni, *Klangfiguren*
1806	Ch. F. D. Schubart, *Ideen zu einer Ästhetik der Tonkunst*
	Anonymous, *Die Melodie der Farben*
1807-8	Ph. O. Runge, *Gespräche über Analogie der Farben und Töne*
1812	G.T.L. Sachs, *Historia naturalis duorum leucaethiopum*
1814	F. Webb, *Panharmonicon*

1817   G. Field, *Chromatics: An Essay on the Analogy and Harmony of Colours*

1819   D. Brewster, *A Treatise on the Kaleidoscope*

1820   G. Field, *Aesthetics*

1821   A. Majer, *Discorso sulla origine, progressi e stato attuale della musica italiana*

1825   Dr Busby, *Assimilation of Colours to Musical Sounds*

1839   G. Field, *Outlines of Analogical Philosophy*

1840   J. Becker, *Ideen über Makerei und Musik*

1844   D. D. Jameson, *Colour-Music*

1845   D. R. Hay, *Tke Principles of Beauty in Colouring Systematized*

1853   G. de La Moussaye, *Les couleurs et les sons*

1863   L. Ch. Matthias, *Farben-musik*

1869   J. D. MacDonald, *Sound and Colour: Analogies and Harmonies*

1870   W. Barrett, *Light and Sound*

1874   C. E. Smith, *The Music of Color*

1875   H. R. Haweis, *Music and Morals*

        F. Kastner, *Les flammes chantantes*

        J. Plath, *Über die Versuche einer Farbenharmonie nach akustischen Prinzipien*

1979   Ayrton and Perry, *On the Music of Colour and Visible Motion*

Appendix 5
CORRELATIONS BETWEEN NOTES AND COLOURS

Frequency of Correlations between Notes and Colours
(taken from approximately 40 systems of correspondence)

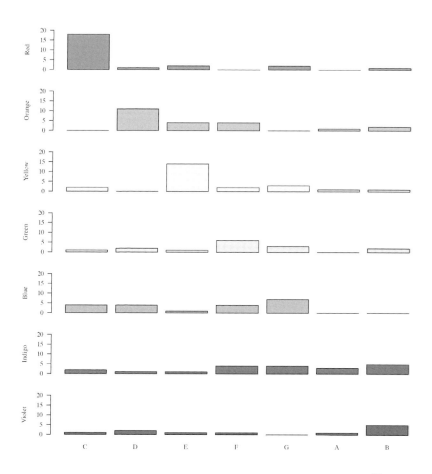

Appendix 6
MULTI-MEDIA EXHIBITIONS, 1961-2006

1961   Milan, *Musica e segno. Esposizione di grafica musicale contemporanea*, Galleria Blu

1971   Amsterdam, *Sound–Sight*, Municipal Museum

1972   Hagen, *Musikalische Graphik – Graphische Musik*, Karl-Ernst-Osthaus-Museum

1973   Paris, *Rétrospective des Salons musicalistes*, Galerie Hexagramme

1974   Berlin, *Homage to Schönberg. Der Blaue Reiter und das Musikalische in der Malerei der Zeit*, Nationalgalerie

Bern, *Noten. Musikalische Schriftbilder und ihre Ausführung*, Kunsthalle

Lugano, *Pittura e musivca dalla fine del '800 a oggi*, Villa Malpensata

1975   Düsseldorf, *Sehen um zu hören. Objekte und Konzerte zur Visuellen Musik der 60 ter Jahre*, Kunsthalle

Vancouver, *Sound-Sculpture*, Art Gallery

1979   Baden-Baden, *Hans Otte. Visuelle Musik*, Staatliche Kunsthalle

Los Angeles, *Sound: An Exhibition of Sound Sculpture, Instrument Building and Acoustically Tuned Spaces*, Institute for Contemporary Art

1980   Berlin, *Für Augen und Ohren, von der Spieluhr zum akustischen Environment*, Akademie der Künste

Paris, *Ecouter par les yeux. Objets et environnements sonores*, Musée d'art moderne de la ville

1981   Bochum, *Hommage à Picasso. Kubismus und Musik*, Museum, Haus Kemnade

Geneva, *Images 33 tours. Couverture et pochettes de disque*, Cabinet des estampes

Leipzig, *Musik im Bild. Malerei, Graphik und Plastik aus 5 Jahrhunderten*, Museum der bildenden Künste

New York, *Soundings*, Neuberger Museum

1982   London, *Artists and Sound*, Tate Gallery

Rimini, *Sonorità prospettiche. Suono, ambiente, immagine*

1983   New York, *Sound/Art*, Sculpture Center

Mönchengladbach, *Hast du Töne? Eine Ausstellung zum Sehen und Hören*, Städtisches Museum

Paris, *Electra*, Musée d'art moderne de la Ville

1985	Charleroi, *L'oeil musicien. Les écritures et les images de la musique*, Palais des Beaux-Arts
	Plymouth Arts Centre, *Sound / Vision*, Arts Centre
	Prague, *Musica picta*, Nationalgalerie
	Rome, *Cinque secoli di stampa musicale in Europa*, Palazzo Venezia
	Stuttgart, *Vom Klang der Bilder*, Staatsgalerie
	Würzburg, *Klangskupturen*, Städtische Galerie
1986	Brussels, *Capriccio, Musique et Art au xxe siècle, convergences, rencontres, affinités*, Palais des Beaux-Arts
1987	Bern, *Der gelbe Klang*, Kunstmuseum
	Bremen, *Klanginstallationen*, Gesellschaft für Aktuelle Kunst
	Eindhoven, *Echo. The Images of Sound*
	Mainz, *Aspekte visueller Poesie und visueller Musik*, Gutenberg-Museum
1988	Saarbrücken, *Klangräume*, Stadtgalerie
	L'Aquila, *Altenative attuali '88*, Convitto nazionale
1989	Darmstadt, *Musik und Raum*, Mathildenhöhe
1990	Marseilles, *Peinture, cinéma, peinture*, la Vieille Charité
	Paris, *Qu'est-ce que le musicalisme?*, Galerie Drouart
1991	Nice, *La musique et la peinture, 1600–1900*, Musée des Beaux-Arts
1993	Basel, *Geräusche. Eine Austellung*, Museum für Gestaltung
1994	Anvers, *Muziek and Graphiek*, Hessenhuis
	The Hague, *Music and Painting in the Golden Age*, Hoogsteder Galerie Ottenstein, *Klingende Dinge – Sounding Things*, Château Pfäffikon, *Sound and Vision. Musikvideo und Filmavantgarde*, Seedamm-Kulturzentrum
	San Antonio, *Synesthesia: Sound and Vision in Contemporary Art*, Museum of Art.
	Tourcoing, *Les métamorphoses d'Orphée*, Musée des Beaux-Arts
1995	Anvers, *Divertimento. La musique dans l'art*, Musée des Beaux-Arts
	Koblenz, *Klangskulpturen, Augenmusik. Grenzgänge zwischen Musik und Plastik im 20. Jh.*, Ludwig Museum
	Olten, *Bilder vom Hören, Bilder zum Hören*, Stadthaus
1996	Basel, *Canto d'amore. Klassistische Moderne in Musik und bildender Kunst*, Kunstmuseum und Paul Sacher Stiftung
	Berlin, *Klangkunst*, Akademie der Künste
	Serravezza, *Ascoltare l'immagine. L'esperienza del suono negli artisti della visualità*, Palazzo Mediceo
	Vevey, *De l'archet au pinceau. Rencontres entre musique et arts visuels en Suisse romande*, Musée Jenisch
1997	Martigny, *Ragamala. Ecouter des couleurs, peindre des sons*, Manoir de la Ville de Martigny

1998	Basel, *Farben – Klänge. Kandinsky, Bilder. Schönberg, Konzerte*, Fondation Beyeler
	Vienna, *Crossings. Kunst zum Hören und Sehen*, Kunsthalle
1999	Chambéry, *La musique dans la peinture du xvie au xixe siècle*, Musée des Beaux-Arts
2000	Cremona, *Dipingere la musica. Strumenti in posa nell'arte del Cinque e Seicento*, Santa Maria della Pietà
	Langenthal, *Farbklavier und Formorgel* (Colour-piano and Form-organ), Kunsthaus
	Lyons, *Musiques en scène*, Musée d'art contemporain
	Rome, *Colori della musica. Dipinti, strumenti e concert tra Cinque e Seicento*, Palazzo Barberini
	Vienna, *Schönberg / Kandinsky, Blauer Reiter und die Russische Avantgarde*, Arnold Schönberg Center
	Vienna, *Sounds and Files*, Künstlerhaus
2001	Moscow, *Schönberg, Kandinsky*, Galerie Tretiakov
	Paris, *Figures de la passion*, Musée de la musique
	Paris, *Musique et arts plastiques*, la Sorbonne
	Payerne, *Peinture et musique. L'oeil écoute . . . l'oreille voit* (Painting and music. The eye listens . . . the ear sees)
	Sion, *Encore, la force de la répétition*, Musée d'art
	Vienna, *Schönberg und Kandinsky. Malerei und Musik im Dialog*, Schönberg Center
2002	Bolzano, *Musicaxocchi / Augenmusik / Eye-music*
	Colmar, *Jean Dubuffet: Coucou Bazar*
	Paris, *L'invention du sentiment. Aux sources du romantisme*, Musée de la musique
2003	Buffalo, *The Composer's Eye: M. Feldman, G. Gershwin, P. Hindemith, A. Schoenberg, E. Varèse*, Music Library
	Madrid, *Analogias musicales. Kandinsky y sus contemporaneos*. Madrid, Museo Thyssen-Bornemisza
	New York, *Schönberg, Kandinsky and the Blue Rider*, Jewish Museum
	Paris, *Aux origines de l'abstraction, 1800–1914*, Musée d'Orsay
2004	Paris, *Sons et lumières*, Centre Pompidou
2005	Rovereto, *La danza delle Avanguardie. Dipinti, scene e costumi da Degas a Picasso, da Matisse a Keith Haring*, MART
	Washington, DC, *Visual Music*, Hirshhorn Museum
	Zurich, *An Exhibition about Sound, Performance and Sculpture*, Migrosmuseum
2006	Basel, *Edgar Varèse Komponist, Klanforscher, Visionär*, Tinguely Museum and Paul Sacher Foundation

Geneva, *Audio*, Cabinet des estampes

Genoa, *Suoni e visioni. Un viaggio emozionale attraverso la musica
e la fotografia negli ultimi cinquant'anni*, Museo d'arte contemporanea

Perugia, *Sound and Vision*, Museo della Città

Siena, *Good Vibrations. Le arti visive e il rock*, Palazzo delle Papesse

Zug, *Harmonie und Dissonanz. Gerstl – Schönberg – Kandinsky. Malerei
und Musik im Aufbruch*, Kunsthaus

REFERENCES

*All references with an asterisk are primary
sources listed in the Bibliography*

Prelude

1   See 'Jack Ox' at https://en.wikipedia.org, accessed 28 June 2017.

1 The Polyphony of Music and Painting

1   *Neuhaus (1995), De la Motte (1999).
2   *Higgins (1984). Earlier, *Blanc-Gatti (1958), p. 170.
3   Fink (1988); see also Helga de la Motte-Haber, 'Klänge nach Bildern', in Schneider (2000), pp. 37–51.
4   Fink (1991).
5   Cf. Gröger (1964), Jung-Kaiser (2003), pp. 141–69.
6   Jung-Kaiser (2003), pp. 185–9.
7   *Die Maler und das Theater im 20. Jahrhundert*, exh. cat. (Frankfurt, 1986).
8   Kochno (1973).
9   Weddigen (1984).
10 Renato Meucci, 'Domenichino "musicologo" e le origini della sonata a tre', in *Domenichino, 1581–1641* (Rome, 1997), pp. 311–17.
11 Brenneman (2005).
12 Christian Meyer and Therese Muxeneder, *Arnold Schönberg. Catalogue raisonné* (Los Angeles, CA, 2005), II, pp. 7–55.
13 *M. K. Čiurlionis, Die Welt als grosse Sinfonie* (Cologne, 1998).
14 Salmen (1984).
15 *Strawinsky. Sein Nachlass. Sein Bild*, exh. cat. (Basel, 1984).
16 Volker Mertens, 'Maler, Bilder, schwankende Gestalten. Der Künstler als Opernheld', in Schneider (2000), pp. 87–103.
17 Brugnolo (1993).
18 Emanuel Winternitz, *Instruments de musique du monde occidental* (Paris, 1966) and *Musical Instruments and Their Symbolism in Western Art* (New Haven, CT, 1979).
19 On this subject, see the many works by Albert Pomme de Mirimonde.
20 Mirimonde (1974), Staiti (2002).
21 *Pater (1877), p. 111.

22 Hugo Wolf, *Chroniques musicales, 1884–87*, introd. Georges Starobinski (Geneva, 2004).

23 *Albèra (1995).

24 Paul Naredi-Rainer, *Architektur und Harmonie. Zahl, Mass und Proportion in der abendländischen Baukunst* (Cologne, 1982).

25 Simson (1966).

26 Wittkower (1967), Onians (1984), Barthelmes (1985).

27 Bienz (1998). See also the review *Daidalos*, no. 17, devoted to relations between architecture and music.

28 Anne-Marie Mathy, 'La consécration de la cathédrale de Florence par le pape Eugène IV: musique, poésie, architecture', in Brumana (1993), pp. 87–108.

29 *Plastik + Musik. Werke der Brüder Baschet*, exh. cat. (Cologne, 1971).

30 *Takis*, exh. cat. (Paris, 1993).

31 *Komponisten der 20. Jh. in der Paul Sacher Stiftung*, exh. cat. (Basel, 1986).

32 *Stockhausen (1960).

33 *Robert Strübin (1987–1965). Retrospektive. Musikbilder und andere Werke*, exh. cat. (Lucerne, 1970).

34 *Apollinaire (1917), pp. 3–4.

2 Musical Analogies in Theories of Painting

1 *Kircher (1650), II, pp. 240–41.

2 *Richardson (1725), p. 154.

3 *Castel (1763), pp. 282 and 309ff.

4 On the reactions to Castel, see Franssen (1991), Mortier (1995), pp. 95–103, Jewanski (1999) and Caduff (2003).

5 Denis Diderot, 'Clavecin oculaire' (1753), in *Oeuvres complètes*, ed. Roger Lewinter, XV (Paris, 1973), p. 191.

6 *Rousseau (1755), (1974), p. 159.

7 Hausmann, cited in *Sons et lumières* (Paris, 2005), p. 205.

8 '*Oculis cum admiratione audimus, et auribus spectamus*', *Kircher (1650), II, p. 367.

9 'Lettre à Mr. Rameau' (1738), in *Voltaire's Correspondance*, ed. Theodore Besterman, VII (Geneva, 1954), p. 478.

10 Louis Bertrand Castel, review of Newton's *Optics*, *Journal de Trévoux*, VIII (1723), pp. 1428–50. See also *Castel (1740), p. 304, where the issue is 'the analogy . . . between colour and sound'.

11 *Runge (1840), I, pp. 168–70.

12 Leonid Sabanejew, 'Analogie von Ton und Farbe' (1911), rpt. quoted in Christiane Bauermeister et al., *Sieg über die Sonne. Aspekte russischer Kunst zu Beginn des 20. Jh.* (Berlin, 1983), pp. 286–90.

13 Stanton MacDonald-Wright, 'The Analogy between Color and Sound', in *Treatise on Color* (1924), rpt. in David W. Scott, *The Art of Stanton MacDonald-Wright* (Washington, DC, 1967), p. 14. See also Harrell (2000).

14 Gombrich (1979).

15 Jean Mitry, *Esthétique et psychologie du cinéma* (Paris, 1963), I, pp. 332–7; Bordwell (1980). See Guido (2006), who quotes many examples of the use of musical analogies, particularly in Abel Gance (the cinema as a 'music of light'), Léon Moussinac, Germaine Dulac, Louis Delluc, Paul Ramain and Émile Vuillermoz.

16 Jewanski (1999).

17 *Blanc-Gatti (1958), pp. 136 and 150.

18 *Kepler (1619), V, ch. V–VIII.

19 *Castel (1740), pp. 71ff., associated the 'perfect' chord and the primary colours with the Trinity.

20 For example, the paradox of the seven colours (the number corresponding to the degrees of the diatonic scale), which Newton, Young and other scientists held to. On the fetishism around the number seven and the problem of indigo cf. Georges Roque, *Art et science de la couleur. Chevreul et les peintres, de Delacroix à l'abstraction* (Paris, 1997), pp. 84–6, and Jewanski (1999), pp. 88, 106ff. and 252–62.

21 The number twelve, which corresponds to the degrees of the chromatic scale, was used in many chromatic circles. *Mersenne (1636), pp. 100–101, emphasized this 'analogy', and maintained that 'if one makes songs from twelve degrees in the octave, by dividing it into semi-tones, one will have the hues of twelve colours.' Castel's colour harpsichord with its twelve hues was likened to an organ spanning twelve octaves of twelve semi-tones each.

22 *Castel (1740), p. 478.

23 Howat (1983), Nectoux (2005).

24 *Lavignac (1895), p. 214.

25 Charles Blanc, 'Eugène Delacroix', *Gazette des Beaux-Arts* (1864), rpt. in *Les artistes de mon temps* (Paris, 1876), pp. 23–88 (62).

26 *Van Gogh (1990), II, p. 742.

27 *Mauclair (1904), p. 258.

28 'James Ensor' (1908), in *Verhaeren (1997), II, p. 915.

29 *Sérusier (1921), pp. 97–8 and 30.

30 *Matisse (1972).

31 'El Pitor venezian, musico esperto, Ben sona un istrumento e ben l'acorda', *Boschini (1660), p. 324.

32 Malmanger (1992).

33 *Félibien (1669), p. 41.

34 *Van Gogh (1990), III, p. 574.

35 *Matisse (1972), p. 213.

36   '*Die Farbe ist die Taste. Das Auge ist der Hammer. Die Seele ist das Klavier*', *Kandinsky (1911), p. 64.

37   For example *Klee (1988), p. 300, no. 873, March (1910): 'One day I must be able to freely invent on the colour piano of my juxtaposed watercolour pans' ('*Ich muss dereinst auf dem Farbklavier der nebeneinander stehenden Aquarellnäpfe frei phantasieren können*'). See also Hans Joachim Albrecht and Rudolph Koella, *Hans Hinterreiter* (Zürich, 1982), pp. 19ff. *MacDonald-Wright (1924) went so far as to position colours according to the arrangement of the keys on a piano. The Xul Solari Museum in Buenos Aires (Oscar Augustin Alejandro Schulz Solari, 1887–1963) displays a piano and a harmonium with coloured keys.

38   Klein (1926), pp. 256–61.

39   '*El Pitor venezian . . . / Forma fughe, passazi, bizarie / Tocade, recercari, fantasie / E fa trasporti da una chiave a l'altra*', *Boschini (1660), p. 324.

40   On the importance of the notion of polyphony in Klee, cf. Kagan (1983), pp. 76ff.

41   See for example the many comparisons between colours and instruments in *Kandinsky (1911).

42   '*Il Mantegna si è appigliato ad un lume pronto e minuto, ma graziato armonicamente e con somma melodia riflessato*', *Lomazzo (1590), p. 288.

43   *Castel (1763), p. 310.

44   Daniel Arasse, *Léonard de Vinci. Le rythme du monde* (Paris, 1997), p. 222.

45   Germaine Dulac in *Les cahiers du cinéma*, 1925, quoted by Jean Mitry, *Esthétique et psychologie du cinéma* (Paris, 1963), I, p. 333. On these questions, see Guido (2006).

46   *Walzel (1917), pp. 5–8.

47   '*La scultura è salva nel contrappunto. La pittura si giustifica più facilmente con l'arabesco diatonico e l'orchestrazione cromatica*' ('Sculpture is saved by counterpoint. Painting is closer to diatonic arabesques and chromatic orchestration'), quoted in Germano Celant, *Fausto Melotti* (Milan, 1990), no. 9.

48   Eigeldinger (1989).

49   Paul Souriau, *L'imagination de l'artiste* (Paris, 1901), p. 60.

50   'We spoke about melody and line: Bach and Meister Franke; about harmony and colour: Schönberg und Van Gogh', *Itten (1978), p. 61.

51   '*corrispondenza . . . a guisa di perfetta musica che rende la sua armonia proporzionata in tutte le voci*', Gabriele Paleotti, *Discorso intorno alle imagini sacre e profane* (1582), in *Barocchi (1961), II, p. 371.

52   '*Breve Instruzione per intendere in qualche modo le maniere degli autori veneziani*', in *Boschini (1660), p. 733.

53   *Félibien (1669), p. 56.

54   *André (1763), II, p. 67.

55   *André (1763), p. 171.

56   *Diderot (1766), p. 678.

57   Anton Webern, *Chemin vers la nouvelle musique* (Paris, 1980), p. 47 (*The Path to the New Music*, trans. Leo Black (Bryn Mawr, PA, 1963)).

58   William Nicati, *La psychologie naturelle* (Paris, 1898), p. 49.

59   Christian von Ehrenfels, 'Über Gestaltqualitäten', *Vierteljahrsschrift für wissenschaftliche Philosophie*, XIV (1890), pp. 249–92.

60   Roger de Piles, *L'Idée du peintre parfait* [1699] (Paris, 1993), p. 62.

61   'Du coloris', in *de Piles (1708), pp. 142–64 (154). Georges Roque, 'Harmonie des couleurs', *48/14*, no. 12 (Spring 2001) has shown how the analogy with music could function as a social or political allegory, from Roger de Piles to the Neo-Impressionists.

62   *André (1763), p. 33.

63   '*Chè, siccome gli orecchi restano offesi da una musica che fa strepito o dissonanza o durezza . . . cosi restano offesi gli occhi da' colori troppo carichi o troppo crudi*', *Vasari (1906), I, p. 180. English trans., *Vasari on Technique*, trans. Louisa S. Maclehose, ed. G. Baldwin Brown (London, 1907), pp. 219–20.

64   '*nasce un'armonia e musica, dirò così, pittoresca*', *Borghini (1564), p. 120.

65   '*le ragioni dell'armonia nella musica sono per intendere quelle del colorire*', Elisabeth Cropper, *The Ideal of Painting. Pietro Testa's Düsseldorf Notebook* (Princeton, NJ, 1984), p. 137.

66   *Félibien (1707), p. 9. The Abbé of Marsy similarly demanded 'concord and harmony in the tones and colours; just as in a concert, the musician by his art knows how to . . . marry the dissonances of several voices'. There follows a homage to Castel's harpsichord, described as a 'pleasant rêverie', in Claude Henri Watelet, *L'art de peindre*, enlarged edition (Paris, 1761), p. 285.

67   *Félibien (1707), p. 40, ch. XX: 'De l'accord des couleurs'.

68   '*compartiva le qualità de' colori con le loro proporzioni . . . acciochè tutti li colori insieme avessero tra di loro concordia e unione, senza offendersi l'un l'altro; e diceva che si come la melodia delle voci diletta l'udito, cosi ancora la vista si ricrea della consonanza de' colori accompagnata dall'armonia de' lineamenti. Chiamava però la pittura musica*', *Bellori (1672), p. 206.

69   '*Seppe con li muti colori dipingere il suono ed esprimere li gradi della musica . . . per tal modo aggiunse l'udito alla pittura*', *Bellori (1672), p. 313.

70   *Castel (1740), p. 314.

71   *Carpani (1812): '*Accompagnamenti sono alla melodia ciò che è alla pittura il colorito*' (p. 36). '*La cantilena è alla musica ciò che alla pittura è il disegno*' (p. 38). '*La cantilena, ossia la melodia è l'anima della musica*' (p. 33). '*Dove non v'è cantilena non v'è pensiero*' (p. 39).

72   See for example *Lomazzo (1584), pp. 26–7, who associates perspective with the liberal arts.

73   *Castel (1740), p. 19.

74   *Castel (1763), p. 350.

75 'Es fehlt an einer aufgestellten und approbierten Theorie, wie sie die Musik hat, in der keiner gegen den Generalbass schlegeln darf, ohne dass die Meister es rügen und unsere Ohren es mehr oder weniger empfinden', Goethe, 1807, quoted by Jewanski (1999), p. 564. On this issue, see also Schönjahn (1999).

76 Francisco de Hollanda, *Colloqui con Michelangelo* (Milan, 1943), p. 47: '*La buona pittura è una musica e una melodia . . . che solo l'intelligenza può percipere.*'

77 Brenno Boccadoro, 'Musique et mathématique entre 1300 et 1500', *Revue musiacle suisse* (March 2000), pp. 7–12.

78 *Salon de 1859*, in *Baudelaire (1954), p. 778. *Signac (1899), p. 51, significantly attributes this declaration to Delacroix.

79 *Debussy (1971), p. 206.

80 *Castel (1740), pp. 249–50.

81 Plotinus, *An Essay on the Beautiful*, trans. Thomas Taylor (London, 1917).

82 Leon Battista Alberti, *De re aedificatoria* (1485), English trans., *On the Art of Building in Ten Books*, trans. Joseph Rykwert, Neil Leach and Robert Tavernor (Cambridge, MA, 1991), p. 305.

83 Aristotle, *De Sensu* 439 b, English trans. by J. I. Beare, *On Sense and the Sensible*, in *The Works of Aristotle* (London, 1931).

84 'Ist nicht die Tonleiter in der Musik das, was die Abstufung der Farben in Weiss und Schwarz?', *Runge (1840), p. 168.

85 'quell'arte apunto che Pitagora inventò le medesime proporzioni armoniche', Gregorio Comanini, *Il Figino overo del fine della pittura*, 1591, in *Barocchi (1962), III, pp. 237–379 (368). On this much-debated issue, cf. A. B. Ceswell, 'The Pythagorism of Arcimboldo', *Journal of Aesthetics and Art Criticism*, XXXIX/2 (1980–81), pp. 155–61; Pavel Preiss, 'Farbe und Klang in der Theorie und Praxis des Manierismus', in *Mannerism and Music of the XVIth and XVIIth Centuries*, Colloquium Musica Bohemica et Europaea, ed. R. Pecman (Brno, 1970), pp. 163–70; and Tornitore (1985), pp. 58–77.

86 'avendo saputo temperare i mezzi con gli estremi, e con le ragioni del grave e dell'acuto di una perfetta musica . . . perdendosi li contorni nel fondo soavemente, e generandosene il numero e la consonanza', *Bellori (1672), p. 323.

87 Marcel Baumgartner, *Jakob Weder. Farbordnung und Malerei als Sinnbild kosmischer Gesetze* (Zürich, 1981).

88 Paul Verlaine, 'Art poétique' (1882), in *Oeuvres poétiques complètes* (Paris, 1962), p. 326.

89 *Hoffmann (1985), p. 39.

90 'Die Analogie des Sehens . . . mit der Grunderscheinung des Gehörs, führt auf sehr schöne Resultate für eine zukünftige Vereinigung der Musik und Malerei', *Runge (1840), II, p. 388.

91 *Gauguin (1974), p. 138.

92 *Cahier pour Aline* (1892), in *Gauguin (1974), p. 94.

93 Letter to Fontainas, March 1899, ibid., p. 222.

94 *Racontars de rapin* (1902), ibid., p. 256.

95 Friedrich Schlegel, *Description des tableaux de Paris* (1805), in Edouard Pommier, *Histoire et théories de l'art, de Winckelmann à Panofsky, Revue germanique internationale*, II (1994), pp. 221–46 (240).

96 *Becker (1840).

97 *Hanslick (1854).

98 On this point, see the magnificent summary by de Brenno Boccadoro, 'Eléments de grammaire mélancolique', *Acta musicologica*, LXXVI (2004), pp. 25–65.

99 *Lettre à Chantelou* (24 November 1647), in *Poussin (1964), pp. 123–4. On the various interpretations of the *Letter on Modes*, cf. Mirimonde (1975), I, pp. 52–62; Oskar Bätschmann, *Dialektik der Malerei von Nicolas Poussin* (Munich, 1982), pp. 48–9, and 'Diskurs der Architektur im Bild. Architekturdarstellungen im Werk von Poussin', in *Architektur und Sprache*, ed. Carlpeter Braegger (Munich, 1982), pp. 29–33; Puttfarken (1985), pp. 29–37.

100 Quoted in Eric Franz, *Signac et la libération de la couleur. De Matisse à Mondrian* (Grenoble, 1997), p. 248.

101 *Survage (1914), p. 25.

102 *Matisse (1972), p. 204. The term 'analogy' appears four times in these few pages.

103 Klaus Lankheit, 'Die Frühromantik und die Grundlagen der "gegenstands losen" Malerei', *Neue Heidelberger Jahrbücher*, new series (1951), pp. 55–90; Stelzer (1964).

104 '*Der Musiker nimmt das Wesen seiner Kunst aus sich – auch nicht der leiseste Verdacht von Nachahmung kann ihn treffen*', Novalis, *Vermischte Fragmente III*, in *Schriften* (1977–88), II, p. 574.

105 *Hegel (1976), III, p. 80.

106 Théophile Gautier, *Emaux et camées* (1852), in *Poésies complètes*, ed. Rene Jasinski (Paris, 1970), III, p. 40.

107 Théophile Gautier, *Guide du musée du Louvre* (1867) (Paris, 1893), p. 41.

108 Van Gogh, *Correspondance générale* (1990), II, pp. 742–5.

109 Alexander Wallace Rimington, *A New Art: Colour Music*, quoted by Jewanski (1997), p. 17.

110 *Albèra (1995). For a prehistory of this relation, cf. André Charak, 'Perception de la tonalité et vision perspective à l'âge classique', in Kintzler (2002), pp. 93–104.

111 *Valensi (1973), p. 176.

112 Quoted in David W. Scott, *The Art of Stanton MacDonald-Wright* (Washington, DC, 1967), p. 12. Charles H. Caffin, 'Of Verities and Illusions', *Camera Works*, no. 14 (1906), pp. 41–5 (44) presented the 'abstract' essence of music as a model for painting.

113 '*möglichst objektiv gesetzmässige Gestaltung*', *Itten (1978), p. 31.

114 *Matisse (1972), p. 204.

115 *A Théo*, 6 June 1888, in *Van Gogh (1990), III, p. 132.

116   Anton Webern, *Journal*, 6 November 1904, quoted by Günter Metken, 'L'élévation en musique. Anton Webern et Segantini', *Revue de l'art*, no. 96 (1992), p. 83.

117   *Zarlino (1573), p. 181.

118   *Darwin (1791), p. 129.

119   Boulez (1989).

120   *Satie (1977), p. 69.

121   Quoted by Harry Halbreich, *Arthur Honegger, un musicien dans la cité des hommes* (Paris, 1992), p. 737.

3 The New *Paragone* Debate: Paradoxes and Contradictions

1   Ausonius, *Epigrammata*, XIII, 11, verse 8, *The Works of Ausonius*, ed. R.P.H. Green (Oxford, 1991), p. 9.

2   *Viardot (1859). Kagan (1986) has stressed the importance of this text, pp. 86–91.

3   Von Maur (1985). The most important works before this exhibition are by Lockspeiser (1973), Würtenberger (1979) and Hammerstein (1984).

4   Cf. for example, Perrier (1995); Dieter Daniels, 'Der Multimedia-paragone', in Kneisel (1996), pp. 246–50; for a list of audio-visual events in the twentieth century, cf. Davies (1997).

5   For Eastern Europe, where such movements were particularly important, see the anthology of texts selected by R. Stanislawski and Ch. Brockhaus, 'Synthese der Künste und Entmaterialisierung', in *Europa Europa. Das Jahrhundert der Avantgarde in Mittel- und Osteuropa* (Bonn, 1994), vol. III, pp. 80–121.

6   *Boschini (1660), pp. 324, 731, 753 and 755. On the importance of this text, cf. Philip Sohm, *Pittoresco: Marco Boschini, His Critics, and Their Critiques of Painterly Brushwork in Seventeenth- and Eighteenth-century Italy* (Cambridge, 1991).

7   *Bellori (1672), p. 206.

8   *Félibien (1669), 'Préface', and (1707), pp. 9, 40 and 41.

9   *De Piles (1699), ch. XXI, and (1709), p. 154.

10   Bott (1997).

11   Marc-Antoine Charpentier, *Les Arts florissants* (composed 1685–6), 'Idyle en Musique'.

12   *Galilei (1581), p. 86, speaks of the '*comparatione*' between colours and harmonies.

13   *Mersenne (1636), p. 100: 'One can compare simple sounds to simple colours, the intervals between the sounds to mixtures of the said colours, and songs to paintings'.

14   Athanasius Kircher, *Ars magna lucis et umbrae* (Rome, 1646), p. 131: '*Parallela comparatio luminis ad sonum*'.

15   Nicolas de Malebranche, *Eclaircissements sur la recherche de la vérité* (1678), in *Oeuvres* (Paris, 1979), I, p. 1020: 'It is with light and the various colours as it is with sound and the different tones'.

16 On Castel, see Franssen (1991) and Mortier (1995). On Hoffmann, who is less well known, see Rainer Cadenbach, 'Tonmalerei als Farbenkunst. J. H. Hoffmanns Versuch einer wechselseitigen Erläuterung von malerischer Harmonie und Tonkunst', in Schmierer (1995), pp. 93–112.

17 Cf. Mras (1963) and (1966); Günter Busch, 'Synästhesie und Imagination. Zu Delacroix's kunsttheoretischen Äusserungen', in H. Koopmann, Beiträge zur Theorie der Künste im 19. Jh. (Frankfurt, 1971), I, pp. 240–55; Revault d'Allonnes (1989).

18 'Die polyphone Malerei ist der Musik dadurch überlegen, als das Zeitliche hier mehr ein Räumliches ist', Paul Klee wrote in July 1917 (Tagebücher, p. 440). Robert Delaunay stated that 'Auditory perception is insufficient for a knowledge of the Universe because it does not remain over time', in Du cubisme à l'art abstrait, ed. Pierre Francastel (Paris, 1957), p. 147. On this issue, cf. Christian Geelhaar, 'Paul Klee', in Von Maur (1985), pp. 424ff. and De la Motte-Haber (1990), pp. 185–9.

19 Babbitt (1910).

20 Mendelsohn (1982); Farago (1992); Fallay d'Este (1992); Marco Collareta, 'Le arti sorelle. Teoria e pratica del paragone', in La pittura in Italia. Il Cinquecento, ed. Giuliano Briganti (Milan, 1988), pp. 569–80; Ekkehard Mai and Kurt Wettengl, ed., Wettstreit der Künste. Malerei und Skulptur von Dürer bis Daumier (Wolfratshausen, 2002); Jacqueline Lichtenstein, La tache aveugle. Essai sur les relations de la peinture et de la sculpture à l'âge moderne (Paris, 2003).

21 Schueller (1953); Hagstrum (1958). Leonardo's terminology was long-lived. Cf. for example *Morse (1826). Liszt, in 1865, used the expression 'arti sorelle' to refer to poetry, painting and music, which he wished to bring together within the same Academy. Gauguin, in his Cahier pour Aline, described painting as the 'sister of music', and Wagner also mentioned the 'drei urgeborene Schwester' ('three sisters, originarily') in 'Tanzkunst, Tonkunst und Dichtkunst', Gesammelte Schriften und Dichtungen (Moers, 1976), III, p. 67.

22 Cf. Heidrich (1997).

23 Jean-Etienne Liotard, Traité des principes et des règles de la peinture (Geneva, 1781), rpt. Minkoff (1973), p. 24. The same expression can be found in Tieck (1798), p. 202.

24 Louis-Claude de Saint-Martin, L'homme de désir (Lyons, 1790), rpt. in Oeuvres majeures, ed. R. Amadou, vol. III (Hildesheim, 1980), p. 79.

25 Rensselaer W. Lee, Ut Pictura Poesis: The Humanistic Theory of Painting [1942] (New York, 1967); Niklaus Rudolf Schweizer, The Ut Pictura Poesis Controversy in Eighteenth-century England and Germany (Bern, 1972).

26 'Poetry is for the ear and painting for the eye', Wilhelm Heinse, Ardinghello und die glücklichen Inseln [1787] (Stuttgart, 1975), p. 698. For the paragone, see also pp. 12 and 171–80.

27 'One of the surest signs of the decadence of art is the mixing of its different forms', Johann Wolfgang von Goethe, 'Einleitung in die Propyläen' [1798], Werke, Hamburger Ausgabe XII: Schriften zur Kunst (Hamburg, 1967), p. 49.

28 'Space cannot be made into time, nor time into space, the visible cannot be made audible, nor can the audible become visible', *Herder (1800), pp. 187–8. Lessing had paid little attention to music, and Herder explicitly refused to take seriously the analogy between sounds and colours.

29 Ludwig Fernow, 'Über das Kunstschöne', in *Römische Studien*, I (Zürich, 1806), pp. 308–9.

30 *Quatremère (1823), pp. 38, 72–6 and 341–5.

31 Paul Böckmann, 'Das Laokoonproblem und seine Auflösung in der Romantik', in *Bildende Kunst und Literatur. Beiträge zum Problem ihrer Wechselbeziehungen im 19. Jh.*, ed. Wolfdietrich Rasch (Frankfurt, 1971), pp. 59–78; Alain Montandon, 'Castel en Allemagne. Synesthésies et correspondances dans le romantisme allemand', in Mortier and Hasquin (1995), pp. 95–103. On the influence of German Romanticism, cf. also Hugh Honour, 'Frozen Music', in *Romanticism* (Harmondsworth, 1979), pp. 119ff.; Vergo (1994).

32 'Lessing sah zu scharf und verlor darüber das Gefühl des undeutlichen Ganzen, die magische Anschauung der Gegenstände zusammen in mannichfacher Erleuchtung und Verdunklung' ('Lessing's perception was too sharp, and so the intuition of the indeterminate whole escaped him, the magical vision of things together in their manifold illumination and darkening'), *Novalis (1981), II, p. 557.

33 *Schelling (1802), pp. 379–80.

34 *A. W. Schlegel [1801–2] (Stuttgart, 1963), pp. 100ff.

35 *Klee (1976), pp. 29, 119, 143 and 173.

36 The allusion to *Laocoon* is explicit in *Wagner (1851), I, p. 199: 'Whenever Lessing drew borders and set limits on poetry, he did not mean *the dramatic work of art . . .* which unites in it all the moments of the visual arts.'

37 *Baudelaire (1861), p. 1049.

38 This was the programme of the *Revue wagnérienne* in which Edouard Dujardin advocated the 'necessary union of the arts' (15.VIII.1887). The terms 'union', 'fusion' and 'totality' are a recurrent leitmotif in *Wyzewa (1895), pp. 11, 20, 29, 50 *et passim*. See also Debussy's criticism of Wagner's 'fusion of the arts', *Debussy (1971), p. 193.

39 Henderik R. Rookmaker, *Synthetist Art Theories: Genesis and Nature of the Ideas on Art of Gauguin and His Circle* (Amsterdam, 1959); Helga de la Motte-Haber, 'Die Idee der Kunstsynthese', in Perrier (1995), pp. 13–18. The vogue for the concept of 'synthesis' reached its peak with *Kandinsky (1923).

40 *Rousseau (1755), p. 160.

41 *A. W. Schlegel, *Die Kunstlehre* (1801–2), pp. 100ff.

42 *Baudelaire (1861), p. 1052.

43 Ansermet, quoted by Bablet (1971), p. 804.

44 *Debussy (1971), p. 46.

45 There are too many recent studies on this theme to cite them at length. See in particular Bayer (1981), Bräm (1986) or Makis Salomos, 'Notes sur la spatialisation

de la musique et l'émergence du son', in Genevois (1998), pp. 105–25. But the interest in this issue is by no means recent. Cf. Max Schneider, 'Raumtiefenhören in der Musik', *Vierter Kongress für Ästhetik und allgemeine Kunstwissenschaft*, Hamburg 7–9 October 1930 (Stuttgart, 1931), pp. 207–15.

46 Olivier Revault d'Allonnes, *Xenakis. Les polytopes* (Paris, 1975), p. 128.

47 Bienz (1998), pp. 89 and 92.

48 *Nono (1993), pp. 125ff., 193 *et passim*.

49 Christian Martin Schmidt, 'Zum Aspekt des musikalischen Raums bei Ligeti', in Otto Kolleritsch, *G. LIgeti. Personalstil – Avantgardismus – Popularität* (Vienna, 1987), pp. 60–74.

50 Cf. De la Motte-Haber (1999), pp. 244ff.

51 *Neuhaus (1995).

52 *Leitner (1998).

53 Pierre Mariétan, *Musique paysage* (Paris, 1979).

54 Oscar Wiggli, *Guarec. Les sons dans la caverne* (Muriaux, 1998).

55 Cf. Jewanski (1997), p. 21.

56 Cf. 'Les écrivains-dessinateurs', *Revue de l'art*, 44 (1979), and Würtenberger (1979), pp. 50ff.

57 *Viardot (1859), p. 26.

58 *Leonardo (1993), ch. 29: 'Come la musica si dee chiamare sorella e minore della pittura'.

59 Paul Gauguin, 'Cahier pour Aline' (1892), in *Oviri, Ecrits d'un sauvage*, ed. Daniel Guérin (Paris, 1974), p. 94.

60 Kagan (1986). On music as an inspiration for painting in Romanticism, cf. Klaus Lankheit, 'Die Frühromantik und die Grundlagen der "gegenstandlosen" Malerei', *Neue Heidelberger Jahrbücher*, new series (1951), pp. 55–90; Paul Hadermann, 'De l'évasion à la prise de conscience. Littérature et arts contemporains', *Revue de l'Université de Bruxelles*, no. 2–3 (1971), pp. 317–31. See also Rauhut (1956); Stelzer (1964); Hadermann (1992 ('Die Musikalisierung') and 1994); Bentgens (1997), pp. 40ff.

61 Ludwig Tieck, *Franz Sternbalds Wanderungen. Eine altdeutsche Geschichte* (1798), in *L. Tiecks Schriften* (Berlin, 1843), XVI, pp. 301–2.

62 *De Staël (1813), IV, p. 204.

63 Alphonse de Lamartine, *Cours familier de littérature*, VI (Paris, 1858), pp. 398 and 400.

64 Auguste Rodin, *L'Art*, conversations selected by Paul Gsell [1911] (Paris, 1967), p. 126.

65 *Kupka (1913), p. 198.

66 *Apel (1806), pp. 451ff.

67 '*dem Maler wird das Gedicht zum Bild, der Musiker setzt die Gemälde in Töne um*', *Schumann (1891), p. 34.

68 *Baudelaire (1861), p. 1051.

69 Théophile Gautier, *Les dieux et demi-dieux de la peinture* (Paris, 1864), p. 24.

70 Emile Zola, *Au bonheur des dames* [1883] (Paris, 1964), p. 769. For other examples, cf. Jean Kaempfer, *Emile Zola, d'un naturalisme pervers* (Paris, 1989), pp. 239–45.

71 Théophile Gautier, *Emaux et camées* (1852), in *Poésies complètes*, ed. Rene Jasinski (Paris, 1970), III, p. 22.

72 '*Wäre ich Beethoven, so würde ich es in Musik sagen*', *Stifter (1842), p. 594.

73 Victor Hugo, *Notre-Dame de Paris* (1832), III, ch. II (Paris, 1975), pp. 136–7.

74 '*in poetischer, musikalischer und malerischer Form*', Liszt, quoted by Salmen (1986) p. 157.

75 Wolfram Steinbeck, 'Musik nach Bildern. Zu Franz Liszts *Hunnenschlacht*', in Schmierer (1995), pp. 17–38.

76 Cf. W. Salmen (1988); J. Bellas (1986); and Jean-Jacques Eigeldinger, '"Anch'io son pittore" ou Liszt compositeur de *Sposalizio* et *Penseroso*', in Junod and Wuhrmann (1996), pp. 49–74. On these issues, see also 'Gemälde als Programm neuer musikalischer Formen', in De la Motte-Haber (1990), pp. 80–102.

77 Kandinsky, in a lecture published in Moscow in 1921 and quoted by Hahl-Koch (1984), p. 109. *Blanc-Gatti (1958), p. 57, likewise boasted of the fact that his friend Jean d'Udine immediately recognized the musical subjects of his transpositions.

78 *Hoffmann (1985), p. 222.

79 '*Man sollte plastische Kunstwerke nie ohne Musik sehn – musikalische Kunstwerke hingegen nur in schön dekorirten Sälen hören*' (One should never look at works of art without music – but musical works should only be listened to in beautifully decorated rooms), Novalis, *Schriften*, II (Darmstadt, 1981), p. 37.

80 *Delacroix (1932), 9. IV.1856 (II, p. 439).

81 *Stendhal (1814), p. 98.

82 Dezsö Legany, 'Liszt in Rom – nach der Presse', *Studia Musicologica*, XIX (1977), p. 39. *L'Osservatore Romano* of 2 December 1865 commented: '*Cosi la galleria dantesca sarà inaugurata col concorso delle tre arti sorelle, la Poesia, la Pittura e la Musica*' (Thus the Dantesque gallery will be inaugurated with the help of the three sister arts of Poetry, Painting and Music).

83 '*damit Musik und Malerei richtig zueinander sich verhalten und eins das andere unterstütze*', C. D. Friedrich, letters to Joukowski of 14 October and 12 December 1835, in *C. D. Friedrich in Briefen und Bekenntnissen,* ed. Sigrid Hinz (Berlin, 1968), pp. 65–70.

84 Moritz von Schwind, *Briefe,* ed. Otto Stoessl (Leipzig, n.d.), pp. 114, 253–4 and 268. See also Würtenberger (1979), pp. 64–7.

85 *Tieck amd Wackenroder (1799), pp. 42–6. See also *Becker (1840), p. 129.

86 '*eine abstrakte malerische phantastisch-musikalische Dichtung mit Chören, eine Komposition für alle drei Künste zusammen, wofür die Baukunst ein eigenes Gebäude aufführen sollte*', Runge, letter to his brother, 22 February 1803.

87 Lingner (1983), pp. 52–69; Silvia Bordini, 'Pittura come spettacolo: le *Ore del giorno* tra paesaggio romantico e nuove tecnologie', in *Ricerche di storia dell'arte*, no. 25

(1985), pp. 5–16; Wolfgang Dömling, 'Wiedervereinigung der Künste, Skizzen zur Geschichte einer Idee', in Schmierer (1995), pp. 119–26. On the misunderstandings arising from the use of this term, cf. Vergo (1993); and 'Wagner – Van de Velde – Kandinsky', in Kropfinger (1995), pp. 431–48.

88   *Scriabin (1979).

89   *Schelling (1802–3), p. 380.

90   Bisanz-Prakken (1977 and 1982); Bouillon (1986); Karl Schawelka, 'Klimts Beethovenfries und das Ideal des "Musikalischen"', in Jürgen Nautz et al., *Die Wiener Jahrhundertwende* (Vienna, 1993), pp. 559–75.

91   Düchting (1996).

92   Hans Christoph von Tavel, *Der gelbe Klang* (Bern, 1987).

93   '*Le Arti andranno sempre più fondendosi*', Francesco Cangiullo, *Poesia pentagrammata* (Napoli, 1923), p. 10.

94   Ricciotto Canudo, *Le livre de l'évolution – l'Homme* (Paris, 1907), pp. 303–4.

95   Guido (2006).

96   '*Allein die Einheit ist überall im Menschen früher als die Trennung*' (In the human being, unity alone is everywhere earlier than separation), *A. W. Schlegel, *Die Kunstlehre* (1801–2), p. 106.

97   '*Alle Künste entspringen gleicher Quelle*', *Liszt (1882), p. 193. Goethe had used the image of rivers flowing from the same mountain, but in order to stress that they diverge, *Farbenlehre, Didaktischer Teil*, v, 'Verhältnis zur Tonlehre' (Munich, 1970), p. 164.

98   '*Alle Künste kommen aus der gleichen und aus einer einzigen Wurzel . . . aus demselben Stamm*', *Kandinsky (1938), p. 217. Castel had maintained that 'originally, all the arts were together and came forth one from the other like flowers and fruits from the same stem', article in the *Mercure de France* (1751), quoted in Mortier (1995), p. 121.

99   *Blanc-Gatti (1958), p. 128.

100   *Morice (1889), p. 287.

101   Albert Gos, 'Avec Henri Bergson à Saint-Cergue', in *Souvenirs d'un peintre de montagne* [1942] (Geneva, n.d.), p. 167.

102   Étienne Bonnot de Condillac, *Essai sur l'origine des connaissances humaines* [1746] (Paris, 1973), p. 229.

103   'Zukünftige Vereinigung der Musik und Malerei', letter of 27 September 1809, in *Runge (1840), II, p. 388.

104   *Schuré (1876), p. 5.

105   *Schuré (1904), pp. 301 and 305. The same idea can be found in Henry van de Velde, *Aperçus en vue d'une synthèse d'art* (Bruxelles, 1895).

106   Leonid Sabanejew, 'Prometheus von Skrjabin', in *Der Blaue Reiter* [1912] (Munich, 1965), p. 110: '*Es ist die Zeit der Wiedervereinigung dieser sämtlichen zerstreuten Künste gekommen*' (The time has come to reunite these various dispersed arts).

107 'die bildende Kunst in ihrer höchsten Vollendung muss Musik werden', *Schiller (1795), p. 84.

108 'Wie die Musik zu werden ist das Ziel jeder Kunst', Arthur Schopenhauer, Werke (Zürich, 1977), x, p. 329.

109 *Pater (1877), p. 111.

110 *De Staël (1813), III, p. 360.

111 *Hegel (1944), III, p. 301.

112 *Carus (1835), pp. 81–3. The same idea can be found in Delacroix, 'Variations du Beau' (1857), in Ecrits sur l'art (Paris, 1988), pp. 33–49 (43).

113 *Van Gogh (1990) (August 1888, Letter 528). One can find the same opposition between music and sculpture in *Baudelaire (1954), p. 577 (Salon de 1845).

114 *Wyzewa (1895), pp. 16–19.

115 Heinrich Heine, 24 April 1841, Pariser Berichte, 1840–1848, in Werke, Säkularausgabe, x (Berlin, 1979), p. 99.

116 *Viardot (1859), p. 22; *Canudo (1921).

117 *Valensi (1932, 1934 and 1936).

118 *Tieck and Wackenroder (1799), p. 74.

119 *Runge (1840), I, p. 44. On the influence of occultism, cf. Heinz Matile, Die Farbenlehre Ph.O. Runges. Ein Beitrag zur Geschichte der Künstlerfarbenlehre (Munich, 1979), p. 183.

120 Charles Avison, 'On the Analogies between Music and Painting', in An Essay on Musical Expression, quoted by Kagan (1986), p. 88. For an earlier attempt to relate painting and music, term for term, see *Ménestrier (1681), pp. 73–5.

121 A. B. Ceswell, 'The Pythagorism of Arcimboldo', Journal of Aesthetics and Art Criticism, XXXIX, no. 2 (1980–81), pp. 155–61; Preiss (1970); Tornitore (1985). Unlike his successors, however, Arcimboldo linked dark colour tones with high-pitched notes.

122 *Runge (1840).

123 *Castel (1740), p. 300.

124 *Töpffer (1848), p. 172.

125 Christian von Ehrenfels, 'Über Gestaltqualitäten', Vierteljahrsschrift für wissenschaftliche Philosophie, XIV (1890), pp. 249–92. George Sand, Impressions et souvenirs (Paris, 1873), p. 81. *Baudelaire (1954), Salon de 1845, p. 613. Kagan (1983), pp. 77ff.

126 *Rousseau (1755), p. 149.

127 *Viardot (1859), p. 25.

128 Peisse, Le Constitutionel (31 May 1853).

129 *Berlioz (1862), p. 8.

130 George Sand, Impressions et souvenirs (Paris, 1873), p. 81.

131 *Baudelaire (1954), Salon de 1845, p. 613.

132 Kagan (1983), pp. 77ff.

133 *A. W. Schlegel, *Die Kunstlehre* (1801–2), p. 205. See also *Rochlitz (1800), p. 385.

134 *Morse (1826), p. 50.

135 *Diderot (1751), *Lettre à Mademoiselle De la Chaux*, p. 128.

136 Frédéric Melchior Grimm, *Correspondance littéraire*, July 1761 (Paris, 1878), rpt. Kraus (1968), IV, p. 430.

137 *De Staël (1813), III, p. 361.

138 *Stendhal (1815), pp. 98 and 101.

139 *Quatremère de Quincy (1823), p. 100.

140 *E.T.A. Hoffmann (1985), pp. 101 and 40.

141 Franz Liszt, Foreword to *L'Album d'un voyageur* [1842] (Vienna, n.d.).

142 *Delacroix, *Journal*, 26 January 1824.

143 *Deschanel (1864), p. 204.

144 On the meaning of this opposition between music and literature, cf. Kearns (1989), pp. 56 and 79ff.

145 *Gauguin (1951), p. 49, and 1950, p. 182.

146 *Redon (1961), p. 67. For the connotations of music for the Symbolists, cf. A. G. Lehmann, *Symbolist Aesthetic in France, 1885–1895* (Oxford, 1968), pp. 149–75, and Rookmaaker (1959), pp. 210–20.

147 Ambroise Vollard, *Souvenirs d'un marchand de tableaux* [1937] (Paris, 1957), p. 179.

148 For example, *Kandinsky (1970), pp. 54 and 130. [English trans., *Point, Line and Plane* [1926] (New York, 1947). See also the contradictions analysed by Laurence Ferrara, 'Schopenhauer on Music as the Embodiment of Will', in *Schopenhauer, Philosophy and the Arts,* ed. Dale Jacquette (Cambridge, 1996), pp. 183–99.

149 On the influence of music theory on the visual arts in the Renaissance, see among others Wittkower (1967), Onians (1984), Weddigen (1984) and Brugnolo (1993). The two traditions – the expressive or rhetorical tradition, and the Pythagorean tradition – cohabit in Poussin's theory of modes.

150 *Baudelaire (1954), p. 778 (*Salon de 1859*). Earlier, Novalis had written that 'Music has much in common with algebra' ('*Die Musik hat viel Ähnlichkeit mit der Algeber*'), *Schriften* (Darmstadt, 1977–88), III, p. 519.

151 *Debussy (1971), p. 171. On these questions, cf. Howat (1983).

152 On the fate of this phrase, cf. *Walzel (1917), pp. 5–8.

153 Cf. for example *Runge (1840), I, pp. 33, 36 and 223.

154 Wassily Kandinsky and Franz Marc, *Der Blaue Reiter* [1912] (Munich, 1965), p. 87.

155 Adolf Hölzel in *Hess (1981), p. 98: '*Ich meine, es müsse, wie es in der Musik einen Kontrapunkt und eine Harmonielehre gibt, auch in der Malerei eine bestimmte Lehre über künstlerische Kontraste jeder Art und deren notwendigen harmonischen Ausgleich angestrebt werden.*' (I mean, just as in music we have counterpoint and a theory of harmony, so in painting we should attempt to create a theory of artistic contrasts of all sorts, and their necessary harmonic balancing.)

156 *Albera (1995), p. 141.

157 *Lavignac (1895), p. 441.

158 Richard Kostelanetz, *John Cage* (Cologne, 1973), p. 107. See also *Higgins (1984), pp. 94–5, who traces back this 'centripetal' tendency in the relations between the arts to Coleridge and Giordano Bruno.

159 Bulat M. Galeyev, 'The New Laokoön: A Periodic System of the Arts', *Leonardo*, XXIV/4 (1991), pp. 453–6.

160 Vossler (1940).

161 Adorno (1967).

162 Greenberg (1940 and 1960). In 1981 Greenberg again mounted an attack on the 'invasion' of the art scene by multi-media works, arguing for restoring the purity of the arts of space, pp. 91–3.

163 Ibid., 'But only when the avant-garde's interest in music led it to consider music as a *method* of art rather than a kind of effect did the avant-garde find what it was looking for.'

164 Kristeller (1951).

165 *De Piles (1708), pp. 142–64.

166 *Diderot (1751), p. 81.

167 This chapter contradicts other statements by Rousseau, for example, that 'sounds never have more energy than when they produce the effect of colours': *Essai sur l'origine des langues* [1755] (Paris, 1974), p. 91.

168 *Reynolds (1975), p. 240.

169 *Quatremère (1823), pp. 19, 68, 96, 332 *et passim*. English trans., *An Essay on the Nature, the End, and the Means of Imitation in the Fine Arts* (London, 1837).

170 'Darin eben zeigt sich der vollkommene Stil in jeglicher Kunst, dass er die spezifische Schranken derselben zu entfernen weiss, ohne doch ihre spezifischen Vorzüge mit aufzuheben', *Schiller (1795), p. 85.

171 I elaborated on this point in my *Transparence et opacité. Essai sur les fondements théoriques de l'art moderne* (Lausanne, 1976), ch. V and VI.

172 *Redon (1923), p. 33.

173 *Delacroix (1996), pp. 86–9, and (1923), II, p. 62.

174 'It is striking to observe with what consummate skill the painter, like a great musician, has varied his touch and execution', *Constable (1970), p. 48.

175 *Redon (1961), pp. 156–7.

176 Frédéric Melchior Grimm, *Correspondance littéraire* [July 1761] (Paris, 1878), rpt. Kraus (1968), IV, p. 432.

177 *Viardot (1859), p. 26.

178 Germaine de Staël, *Corinne ou l'Italie* (1807), ed. Simone Balayé (Paris, 2000), p. 210.

179 *Baudelaire (1954), p. 856 ('L'oeuvre et la vie de Delacroix', 1863).

180 Charles Baudelaire, 'L'art philosophique', ibid., p. 926.

181 *Pater (1877), pp. 111 and 107.

182 Ibid., p. 110.

183 *'Reinheit der Kunstart wird daher das erste Erfordernis für ihre Verständlichkeit. Wogegen Mischung der Kunstarten die Verständlichkeit nur trüben kann . . . Wenn der Musiker . . . zu malen versucht, so bringt er weder Musik noch ein Gemälde zustande'*, Richard Wagner, *Oper und Drama* (1851), Second Part (Berlin, 1914), p. 102; English trans., ed. W. Ashton Ellis, *Opera and Drama* (Lincoln, NE, 1995). Cf. Salmen (1986), p. 153.

184 Victor Segalen, *Oeuvres complètes* (Paris, 1995), I, p. 759. On this point, cf. Barilier (1998).

185 *Kandinsky (1911), French trans. 1969, pp. 65, 137 and 76. And again, *Kandinsky (1912), p. 49: *'Jede Kunst hat eine eigene Sprache, das heisst die nur ihr eigenen Mittel. . . . Im letzten innerlichen Grunde sind diese Mittel vollkommen gleich.'* See also Hadermann (1988).

186 *'Die Würde der Kunst erscheint bei der Musik vielleicht am eminentesten, weil sie keinen Stoff hat'*, Goethe, *Maximen und Reflexionen*, no. 769, in *Werke* (Hamburg, 1967), XII, p. 473.

187 *'Sie ist Geist'*, *Herder (1800), p. 187.

188 *E.T.A. Hoffmann (1985), p. 38.

189 *'Blosse Form, ohne den Stoff'* and *'innerste Seele, ohne Körper'*, *Schopenhauer (1818), p. 160.

190 Panofsky (1954).

191 For example in *E.T.A. Hoffmann (1985), pp. 40 and 101. Cf. Dahlhaus (1978); Klaus-Dieter Dobat, *Musik als romantische Illusion. Eine Untersuchung zur Bedeutung der Musikvorstellung E.T.A. Hoffmanns für sein literarisches Werk* (Tübingen, 1984), pp. 15ff., 46ff. and 61ff.; John Neubauer, *The Emancipation of Music from Language: Departure from Mimesis in Eighteenth-century Aesthetics* (New Haven, CT, 1986); Wolfram Steinbeck, 'Musik über Musik. Vom romantischen Sprachproblem der Instrumentalmusik zu Liszts Symphonischer Dichtung *Orpheus'*, *Schweizer Jahrbuch für Musikwissenschaft*, new series S.15 (1995), pp. 163–81.

192 *Hanslick (1854).

193 *Viardot (1859), p. 25.

194 *Signac (1899), p. 108.

195 *Töpffer (1848), p. 231.

196 *Rousseau (1755), p. 151.

197 *'so ist die Musik . . . auch von der erscheinenden Welt ganz unabhängig . . . könnte gewissermassen, auch wenn die Welt gar nicht wäre, doch bestehen'*, *Schopenhauer (1818), p. 156.

198 Antoine Chrysostome Quatremère de Quincy, *Dictionnaire historique d'architecture* (Paris, 1832), p. 502 (v. 'Décorateur').

199 Gombrich (1979).

200 Redon, quoted by Robert Coustet 'Solitude et clairvoyance d'un collectionneur bordelais, Gabriel Frizeau', *Gazette des Beaux-Arts* (May–June 1988), pp. 325–34 (328).

201 'im Beginn der Entwicklung einer ganz neuer Kunst . . . mit Formen, die nichts bedeuten und nichts darstellen und an nichts erinnern, unsere Seele so tief, so stark zu erregen, wie es nur immer die Musik mit Tönen vermag', *Endell (1898), p. 75.

202 Cf. Hahl-Koch (1997), pp. 72 and 79.

203 Charles H. Caffin, 'Of Verities and Illusions', Camera Work, II/14 (1906), pp. 41–5 (44).

204 Vergo (1980), pp. 41–63.

205 Stelzer (1964). Kagan (1983), p. 89, has shown the importance of Adam Smith in this move from theory to practice.

206 *Rochlitz (1800), pp. 383 and 390–91.

207 'Der Musiker nimmt das Wesen seiner Kunst aus sich – auch nicht der leiseste Verdacht von Nachahmung kann ihn treffen', *Novalis (1977–88), II, p. 574. See also III, p. 559: 'Die eigentliche sichtbare Musik sind die Arabesken, Muster, Ornamente.'

208 *Stendhal (1829), p. 634.

209 *Morse (1826), p. 112.

210 *Coleridge (1907), p. 261.

211 *Hegel (1836–8), III, p. 258.

212 Germaine de Staël, De l'Allemagne [1813] (Paris, 1869), p. 480.

213 *Delacroix (1923), I, p. 66.

214 Paul Gauguin, letters to Schuffenecker, 14 August and 8 October 1888, in Oviri (1974), pp. 40 and 42.

215 Letter to Fontainas of March 1899. Gauguin used musical metaphors on several occasions, when interviewed by Jean Tardieu (Echo de Paris, 13 May 1895) in Avant et après, the Notes synthétiques and in his commentaries on the painting Manao Tupapau, cf. Gauguin (Paris, 1989), p. 280.

216 'These abstract relations . . . whether of colours or sounds, form what we may properly term the musical or harmonic element in every art . . . [and] are pleasant to the human senses or instincts, though they represent nothing and serve for nothing', *Ruskin (1870), p. 207.

217 *Whistler (1890), p. 127.

218 Cf. Arnaldo (2003).

219 *Apollinaire (1912), p. 14. Apollinaire was evidently so satisfied with this formulation that he used it again on two occasions in the same year, in a column 'Les Futuristes' (Le Petit Bleu, 9 February 1912), and in 'Art et curiosité. Les commencements du cubisme' (Le Temps, 14 October 1912), rpt. in Chroniques d'art, 1902–1918, ed. L.-C. Breunig (Paris, 1960), pp. 277 and 343. It can also be found in an article entitled 'Le commencement du cubisme. Réalité, peinture pure', rpt. in Robert Delaunay, Du cubisme à l'art abstrait, ed. Pierre Francastel (Paris, 1957), pp. 151–4 (153).

220 Peter-Klaus Schuster, 'In Search of Paradise Lost: Runge – Marc – Beuys', in Keith Hartley et al., The Romantic Spirit in German Art, 1790–1990 (London, 1994), pp. 62–81.

221 Cf. Reck (1991).

4 Synaesthesia, Convergence and Correspondence:
  Yearnings for a Lost Unity

1 Lussac (2004).

2 Szeemann (1983).

3 *Castel (1763).

4 On the classification of the arts, and comparative aesthetics, cf. Souriau (1947) and Munro (1949).

5 Jean Massin, *La lettre et l'image, la figuration dans l'alphabet latin du 18e siècle à nos jours* (Paris, 1970); René Etiemble, *L'écriture* (Paris, 1973). *Schreibkunst in der deutschsprachigen Schweiz 1548 bis 1980* (Zürich, 1981); *Naissance de l'écriture, cunéiformes et hieroglyphs* (Paris, 1982).

6 Rensselaer W. Lee, *Ut Pictura Poesis: The Humanistic Theory of Painting* [1940] (New York, 1967); Robert J. Clements, *Picta Poesis: Literary and Humanistic Theory in Renaissance Emblem Books* (Rome, 1960); M. Praz, *Mnemosyne: The Parallel between Literature and the Visual Arts* (Princeton, NJ, 1970); 'Ut pictura poesis', *Cahiers du Musée National d'Art Moderne*, no. 38 (1992); *Poésure et peintrie, 'd'un art à l'autre'* (Marseilles, 1993).

7 Jean H. Hagstrum, *The Sister Arts: The Tradition of Literary Pictorialism and English Poetry from Dryden to Gray* (Chicago, IL, 1958).

8 Gisbert Kranz, *Das Bildgedicht in Europa. Zur Theorie und Geschichte einer literarischen Gattung* (Paderborn, 1973); *Id., Das Bildgedicht. Theorie, Lexikon, Bibliographie* (Frankfurt, 1981).

9 Von Maur (1985).

10 André Breton, 'Surrealist Comet' (1947), in *Free Rein*, trans. Michel Parmentier and Jacqueline d'Amboise (Lincoln, NE, 1995), pp. 88–98; 95. Original in *La clé des champs* (Paris, 1973), pp. 159–60.

11 *Le message automatique* (1933), in *Breton (1992), p. 382.

12 For the relations between literature and painting in Surrealism, see the exhibition catalogue *Eluard et ses amis peintres* (Paris, 1982) and Jean Charles Gateau, *Eluard et la peinture surréaliste* (Geneva, 1982).

13 Ferdinand Alquié, *Philosophie du surréalisme* (Paris, 1955).

14 Baudelaire, 'My Heart Laid Bare', in *Baudelaire: His Prose and Poetry*, vol. XXVII, ed. T. R. Smith (New York, 1919). Original: 'Mon coeur mis à nu', in *Baudelaire (1954), p. 1217.

15 André Breton, 'Introduction to the Discourse on the Paucity of Reality', trans. Richard Sieburth and Jennifer Gordon, *October*, LXIX (Summer 1994), pp. 133–44. Original: *Introduction au discours sur le peu de réalité* (1925), in *Breton (1992), p. 273.

16 André Masson, 'Peindre est une gageure', in *Ecrits* (Paris, 1976), p. 13.

17 Breton, 'Silence Is Golden' (1944), in *What Is Surrealism?: Selected Writings*,

ed. Franklin Rosemont (New York, 1978), p. 265–9. Original: 'Silence d'or' (1944), in *La clé des champs* (Paris, 1967), p. 120.

18 André Breton, *Manifestos of Surrealism*, trans. Richard Seaver and Helen R. Lane (Ann Arbor, MI, 1969), p. 123 [translation slightly modified]. Original: *Seconds manifestes du surréalisme* (1930), in *Breton (1988), p. 781.

19 Albert Béguin, 'L'androgyne', *Minotaure*, XI (1938), pp. 10f; Jérôme Peignot, *Les jeux de l'amour et du langage* (Paris, 1974). See also Whitney Chadwick, *Myth in Surrealist Painting, 1929–1939* (Ann Arbor, MI, 1980).

20 Gabriel Bergounioux, 'L'origine du langage: mythes et théories', in *Aux origins des langues et du langage*, ed. Jean-Marie Hombert (Paris, 2005), pp. 14ff. See also Marco Pasi and Philippe Rabaté, 'Langue angélique, langue magique, l'énochien', in *Les langues secrètes, Politica Hermetica*, no. 13 (1999), pp. 94–126.

21 Jean Roudaut, *Poètes et grammairiens du XVIIIe s.* (Paris, 1971).

22 André Chervel, 'Le débat sur l'arbitraire du signe', *Romantisme*, IX, no. 25–6 (1979), pp. 3–33. On the link between onomatopoeia and motivation, cf. Tzvetan Todorov, *Théories du symbole* (Paris, 1977), pp. 164ff.

23 Auguste Le Flamanc, *Les utopies prérévolutionnaires et la philosophie du XVIIIe s.* (Paris, 1934); 'Mythe de l'origine des langues', *Revue des Sciences humaines*, no. 166 (1977); 'Le mythe de la langue universelle', *Critique*, no. 387–8 (1979), pp. 14–39. Chantal Grell and Christian Michel, ed., *Primitivisme et mythe des origines dans la France des Lumières, 1680–1820* (Paris, 1989); Umberto Eco, *The Search for the Perfect Language (The Making of Europe)* (Oxford, 1997); M. Pasi and Ph. Rabaté, 'Langue angélique, langue magique, l'énochien', *Politica Hermetica*, no. 13 (1999), pp. 94–123.

24 Charles de Brosses, *Traité de la formation méchanique des langues et des principes physiques de l'étymologie* [1765] (Paris, 1801).

25 Daniel Droixhe, 'Le primitivisme linguistique de Turgot', in C. Grell and C. Michel, *Primitivisme et mythe . . .* [see note 23], pp. 59–86.

26 Copineau, *Essai synthétique sur l'origine et la formation des langues* (Paris, 1774). Copineau mentions natural signs, 'silent', 'mimicking' and 'pathetic' language.

27 *Herder (1770), pp. 113–23. Cf. Walter Moser, 'Herder et la toupie des origines', *Revue des sciences humaines*, XLIII, no. 166 (April–June 1977), pp. 205–26.

28 Friedrich Schlegel, 'On the Language and Wisdom of the Indians', in *The Aesthetic and Miscellaneous Works of Friedrich von Schlegel*, trans. E. Millington (London, 1808), ch. V: 'On the Origin of Language'. August Wilhelm Schlegel also refers to the 'origin of languages': cf. 'Betrachtungen über die Metrik' (1800), in *Sämtliche Werke*, ed. Eduard Böcking, VII (Leipzig, 1846), p. 162.

29 Antoine Court de Gébelin, *Monde primitif* (Paris, 1773); *Histoire naturelle de la parole ou origine du langage, de l'écriture et de la grammaire universelle* (Paris, 1776) and *Dictionnaire étymologique et raisonné des racines latines* (Paris, 1780).

30   John Bulwer argued that gesture, 'the only speech and general language of human nature', had managed to escape the Babelian confusion of tongues: *Chirologia: Or the Natural Language of the Hand and Chironomia: Or the Art of Manual Rhetoric* [1644] (Carbondale, IL, 1974), p. 6.

31   *A. W. Schlegel (1800), p. 105, considered dance to be a primitive form of expression, an '*einzige Ur-Kunst*' situated between time and space.

32   Etienne Bonnot de Condillac, *Essay on the Origin of Human Knowledge*, trans. and ed. Hans Aarsleff (Cambridge, 2001), p. 194. Original: *Essai sur l'origine des connaissances humaines* [1746] (Paris, 1973), p. 267.

33   Giambattista Vico, *The New Science* [1725], trans. Thomas Bergin and Max Fisch (New York, 1948).

34   Jonathan Swift, *Gulliver's Travels* (Oxford, 1965), pp. 185–6.

35   *Morellet (1818), pp. 366–413.

36   'On Poesy or Art' (1818), in *Coleridge (1907), II, p. 253. Swift likewise condemned monosyllables, which he considered barbarous, calling them the 'disgrace of our language' (ibid., II, p. 175).

37   Charles Nodier, *Dictionnaire des onomatopées* [1806] (Paris, 1828), pp. 10–11, 29 and 31. On the etymology of verbal roots, see also Honoré Joseph Chavée, *La part des femmes dans l'enseignement de la langue maternelle* (Paris, 1859).

38   Charles Nodier, *Notions élémentaires de linguistique ou Histoire abrégée de la parole et de l'écriture*, in *Oeuvres complètes* (Paris, 1834), XII, pp. 12, 15, 34 and 91.

39   Gérard Genette, *Mimologics*, trans. Thaïs E. Morgan, Foreword by Gerald Prince (Lincoln, NE, 1995).

40   *Les mots anglais* (1877), in *Mallarmé (1956), pp. 886ff.

41   *René Ghil, *De la poésie scientifique* (Paris, 1909), p. 43, refers to the origin of language and the 'primordial cry, of the same essence as gesture'. See also Ghil (1904), pp. 47–50.

42   *D'Udine (1910), p. 31.

43   Helena Blavatsky, *La doctrine secrète* [1907] (Paris, 1955), III, pp. 247–8. See also Alain Mercier, *Eliphas Lévi et la pensée magique XIXe s.* (Paris, 1974), who cites *L'arche sainte et le feu sacré*: 'The first writing was made of images, and the first language of man must have been composed of analogies.'

44   Paul Valéry, 'Introduction à la méthode de Léonard de Vinci' (1894), in *Oeuvres*, I (Paris, 1957), p. 1184.

45   Jean Paulhan, *La preuve par l'étymologie* (Paris, 1953).

46   Jean-Pierre Brisset, *La grammaire logique* [1883] (Paris, 1970), or *Les origines humaines* (Angers, 1913). Cf. Michel Pierssens, *La tour de babil* (Paris, 1976).

47   Filippo Tommaso Marinetti, *Destruction of Syntax – Imagination without Strings – Words-in-Freedom: Futurist Manifesto* (May 1913), in *Documents of 20th Century Art: Futurist Manifestos*, ed. Umbro Apollonio, trans. Robert Brain, R. W. Flint, J. C. Higgitt and Caroline Tisdall (New York, 1973), pp. 95–100.

48 Velimir Khlebnikov, *Collected Works of Velimir Khlebnikov: Selected Poems*, ed. Ronald Vroom, trans. Paul Schmidt (Cambridge, MA, 1997).

49 Kurt Schwitters, '*Anregungen zur Erlangung einer Systemschrift*', VIII–IX (1927), pp. 312–16.

50 Jack Ox attempted a visual translation of the *Ursonate, Die Sonate in Urlauten von Kurt Schwitters* (Cologne, 1993).

51 Cf. Maurice Lemaître, *La plastique lettriste et hypergraphique* (Paris, 1956); *Grenzgebiete der bildenden Kunst, Konkrete Poesie* (Stuttgart, 1972). See also Vincent Barras, 'Poésie post-sonore: paysage fin-de-siècle', *Nouvelle revue musicale suisse* (February 1998), pp. 20–23.

52 R. Hausmann, 'Introduction à une histoire du poème phonétique', in R. Hausmann (Saint-Etienne, 1994), pp. 238–9.

53 Raoul Hausmann, 'Optophonétique' (1922), ibid., pp. 240–42.

54 Raoul Hausmann, 'Origine et évolution du poème optophonique', ibid., p. 250.

55 Antonin Artaud, 'Letters on Language, Second Letter to J. P. Paris, September 28, 1932', in *The Theater and Its Double*, trans. Mary Caroline Richards (New York, 1958), pp. 110–11. Original: 'Théâtre de la cruauté' (1932–3), in *Le théâtre et son double* [1938] (Paris, 1964), pp. 167–8.

56 William Warburton, *Essai sur les hiéroglyphes des Egyptiens, où l'on voit l'origine et le progrès du langage et de l'écriture* [Paris, 1744] (Paris, 1977), pp. 98 and 144, translation of part of William Warburton, *The Divine Legation of Moses Demonstrated on the Principles of a Religious Deist* (1738–1741); and Condillac, *Essay . . .* [see note 32].

57 Bulwer, *Chirologia . . .* [see note 30], pp. 94 and 142.

58 Denis Diderot, 'Letter on the Deaf and Dumb', in *Diderot's Early Philosophical Works*, trans. and ed. Margaret Jourdain (Chicago, IL, and London, 1916), p. 195.

59 *Rousseau (1755), pp. 95, 101 and 105.

60 Charles Nodier, *Notions élémentaires de linguistique, ou histoire abrégée de la parole et de l'écriture* (Paris, 1834), pp. 75 f. and 92.

61 Jacques Damase, *Révolution typographique depuis Mallarmé* (Geneva, 1966); *L'espace et la lettre, écritures, typographies*, Cahiers Jussieu 3 (Paris, 1977).

62 Pierre Garnier, 'Manifesto for a New Poetry Visual and Phonic' (1962). Original: *Manifeste pour une poésie nouvelle visuelle et phonétique* (Paris, 1962); and Garnier, *Spatialisme et poésie concrète* (Paris, 1968); M. Lengellé, *Le spatialisme selon l'itinéraire de P. Garnier* (Paris, 1979).

63 Reinhard Döhl, 'Poesie zum Ansehen, Bilder zum Lesen?', in *Gestaltungsgeschichte und Gesellschaftsgeschichte*, ed. H. Kreuzer (Stuttgart, 1969), pp. 554–82; Klaus Peter Dencker, *Text-Bilder, Visuelle Poesie international von der Antike bis zur Gegenwart* (Cologne, 1972); Milton Klonsky, *Speaking Pictures: A Gallery of Pictorial Poetry from the 16th Century to the Present* (New York, 1975); *La lettre, la figure, le rébus dans la poétique de la Renaissance*, in *Revue des Sciences humaines*, CLXXIX (1980); Sophie de Sivry and Laurent Beccaria, *L'art et l'écriture* (Paris, 1998).

64   Cf. Ellen McCracken, *Schrift und Bild* (Baden-Baden, 1962); *International Calligraphy Today* (London, 1982); Francine Claire Legrand, 'Peinture et écriture', *Quadrum*, XIII (1962), pp. 4–48; Anne-Marie Christin, ed., *Ecritures, systèmes idéographiques et pratiques expressives*, Colloque international de l'Université de Paris VII, 1980 (Paris, 1982).

65   William Willets, *Chinese Calligraphy: Its History and Aesthetic Motivation* (Oxford, 1981); McCracken, *International Calligraphy Today*; Jean-François Billeter, *L'art chinois de l'écriture* (Geneva, 1989). For its influence in the West, cf. *Weltkulturen und moderne Kunst* (Munich, 1972), pp. 186 f. and 389 f.

66   Juan Miró replying to Georges Duthuit in *Cahiers d'art*, VIII–X (1936), p. 263. See also Raymond Queneau, *Bâtons, chiffres et lettres* [1950] (Paris, 1965), pp. 311ff.

67   Robert Benayoun, 'Le mot et l'image', in *Le Surréalisme même* (Paris 1958), p. 35.

68   Cf. Guillaume Apollinaire, *Le guetteur mélancolique* (Paris, 1952), pp. 142–4; J. Peignot, *De l'écriture à la typographie* (Paris, 1967).

69   *Apollinaire (1917), rpt. (Paris, 1946), pp. 3–4.

70   Pierre Garnier, quoted by Jérôme Peignot, *Du calligramme* (Paris, 1978), p. 39.

71   Wolfgang Max Faust, *Bilder werden Worte, Zum Verhältnis von bildender Kunst und Literatur im 20. Jh. oder vom Anfang der Kunst am Ende der Künste* (Munich, 1977).

72   André Leroi-Gourhan, *Gesture and Speech* [1964], trans. Anna Bostock Berger (Cambridge, MA, 1993), p. 192.

5 Hearing in Colour: The Transformations of a Myth

1   *Kircher (1650), p. 367.

2   Igor Markévitch, *Le testament d'Icare* (Paris, 1984), p. 157.

3   *Messiaen (1986); Bernard (1986); Fink (2004).

4   Ove Nordwall, *G. Ligeti, eine Monographie* (Mainz, 1971), pp. 16–18; '*Träumen Sie in Farbe?*', György Ligeti in *Gespräch mit Eckhard Roelcke* (Vienna, 2003), pp. 16–19. See also Budde (1987).

5   Cf. *Segalen (1902), p. 41.

6   Maurice Merleau-Ponty, *Phenomenology of Perception* [1945], trans. Colin Smith (London and New York, 1962).

7   Etiemble (1968), p. 137. For a structural analysis of Rimbaud's sonnet, cf. Lévi-Strauss (1993), pp. 132ff. On its success, Kearns (1989), pp. 69ff. On its influence, Bernard (1960).

8   One by Oskar Pfister, the other by Hermine von Hug-Hellmuth, 'De l'audition colorée, essai d'explication du phénomène par la méthode psychanalytique', republished in *Essais psychanalytiques* (Paris, 1991), pp. 49–94.

9   For example, *Messiaen (1986), pp. 65–9 *et passim*.

10   Cytowic (1989) and (1993), Böhme (1991), Hadermann (1992), Günther (1994), Kienscherf (1996), Adler (2002), Paetzold (2003), Kalisch (2004) and Jewanski

(2006), among others. Also the numerous Internet forums and websites devoted to synaesthesia, where one can also find Michael Haverkamp's paper, 'Visualisation of Synaesthetic Experience during the Early 20th Century, an Analytic Approach', International Conference on Synesthesia, Hanover, Medizinische Hochschule, March 2003.

11 Cf. De la Motte-Haber (1985), pp. 307–28; (1990), pp. 61–71 and 138–75; and (1999); Genevois (1998). For the many exhibitions on this theme, see the list in Appendix 6, 1961–2006.

12 *Ghil (1885). See also *Galton (1883).

13 *Kandinsky (1911), pp. 85–8, 122ff. *et passim*, and his teachings at the Bauhaus in *Kandinsky (1926), p. 381. His sources are identified by Clark V. Poling, 'Synaesthesia and the Inner Effect of Color', in *Kandinsky's Teaching at the Bauhaus: Color Theory and Analytical Drawing* (New York, 1982), p. 49 and note 20.

14 *Satie (1977), p. 141.

15 'Les mots sans rides', *Littérature* (1 December 1922), republished in *Les pas perdus*, *Breton (1988), p. 285.

16 *Eisenstein (1947), p. 90.

17 *Gerstner (1986), p. 178.

18 *Kupka (1913), p. 140.

19 Cf. Rousseau (1997), p. 26 and note 38.

20 Cf. *Paris-Paris* (Paris, 1981), p. 276.

21 Paola Vasselli et al., *E. Delessert* (Rome, 1992), p. 142.

22 Claire Nydegger, *Voyelles d'Arthur Rimbaud* (Saint-Prex, 1995).

23 Vladimir Nabokov, *Alphabet in Color,* illus. by Jean Holabird (New York, 2005).

24 Jacques Lipchitz, *My Life in Sculpture* (London, 1972), p. 123.

25 Aichele (1986), pp. 459–60, interprets this painting as an allusion to the *Rosenkavalier* by Richard Strauss, whose initials figure in capital letters. See also Will-Levaillant (1985) and Bauschatz (1996).

26 Diderot, 'Additions à la Lettre sur les aveugles' (1782), in *Oeuvres philosophiques* (Paris, 1964), p. 156.

27 [Copineau], *Essai synthétique sur l'origine et la formation des langues* (Paris, 1774), p. 34. For other examples, see Schrader (1969), p. 18.

28 '*Vokal-Farbenleitern*' and '*Tonleitern der Vokale*', *A. W. Schlegel (1800), pp. 175 and 168.

29 '*Die Vokale sind das Gefühlausdrückende in einer Sprache*' and '*i himmelblau ist der Vokal der Innigkeit und Liebe*', *A. W. Schlegel (1800), p. 175.

30 Rudolph Steiner, *Eurythmie curative* [1921] (Saint-Prex, 1979), p. 19. English trans., *Curative Eurythmy*, trans. Kristina Krohn and Dr Anthony Degenaar (London, 1983).

31 *Kircher (1650), p. 422, devotes a chapter to '*Symphonismus patheticus sive de musica variarum affectionum animi*'.

32   *Herder (1770). Cf. Albert Welleck, 'Das Laut-Sinn-Problem unter dem Gesichtpunkt der FarbeTon-Forschung und die Synesthesien der Sprache', in Anschütz (1931), pp. 240–53.

33   *Court de Gébelin, *Monde primitif*, 1773, *Histoire naturelle de la parole ou origine du langage, de l'écriture et de la grammaire universelle*, 1776, and *Dictionnaire étymologique et raisonné des racines latines*, 1780.

34   *Ghil (1909), p. 43.

35   *Brès (1828).

36   Pierre-Simon Ballanche, *Palingénésie sociale* (1832), quoted by René Wellek, *Concepts of Criticism* (New Haven, CT, 1969), pp. 175–6.

37   *Rossigneux (1905), p. 209.

38   Jacob Ludwig Grimm, *On the Origin of Language* (1851), trans. Raymond A. Wiley (Leiden, 1984).

39   Grimm, ibid. Cf. André Chervel, 'Le débat sur l'arbitraire du signe', *Romantisme*, IX, (1979), no. 25–6, pp. 3–33.

40   Honoré Joseph Chavée, *La part des femmes dans l'enseignement de la langue maternelle* (Paris, 1859), pp. 26 and 17–19.

41   Jewanski (1999).

42   On Castel, cf. Wellek (1935), pp. 354–69; Chouillet (1976); Franssen (1991); Mortier (1995); Warszawski (2000); and Jewanski (1999), pp. 267–449, and (2006), pp. 147–58.

43   *Diderot (1753). See also *Les bijoux indiscrets* (1743), in *Oeuvres* (Paris, 1951), pp. 62, 63 and 67.

44   Cf. Chouillet (1976).

45   *Voltaire (1738), pp. 393–4.

46   Le Camus de Mézières, *Le génie de l'architecture ou l'analogie de cet art avec nos sensations* (Paris, 1780), p. 10.

47   Alain Montandon, 'Castel en Allemagne. Synesthésies et correspondances dans le romantisme allemand', in Mortier (1995), pp. 95–103.

48   On the importance of synaesthesia in the Romantic period, see Stephen Ullmann, *The Principles of Semantics* [1951] (Oxford, 1967), pp. 272–89; see also Brown (1953); Rauhut (1956–7); Schrader (1969); ch. I, Marks (1978), ch. VIII; Utz (1990); and Franssen (1991).

49   *Darwin (1789), p. iii.

50   *Darwin (1799), pp. 127–30. Note the allusion to the importance of vowels and metaphors in primitive languages.

51   John Locke, *Essay Concerning Human Understanding* (1690), III, 4, ed. Peter H. Nidditch (Oxford, 1975), p. 425. No one has pointed out the paradox that this much-cited passage concerns 'simple ideas', and that any permeability between the senses is dismissed as 'a sort of philosophy worthy only of Sancho Panza'!

52   Charles Nodier, *Notions élémentaires de linguistique, ou histoire abrégée de la parole et de l'écriture* (Paris, 1834), p. 43.

53 Germaine de Staël, *De l'Allemagne* (1810), III, ch. x.

54 *Tieck and Wackenroder (1799).

55 '*so dass der Klang hier Farbe kennet . . . sich Farbe, Duft, Gesang, Geschwister nennet!*', in Ludwig Tieck, *Prinz Zerbino, oder die Reise nach dem guten Geschmack* (Vienna, 1819), p. 248. ('Their colours sing, their forms resound . . . Colour, fragrance, song, proclaim themselves one family', *Prince Zerbino or, The Quest for Good Taste,* a Comedy in six acts.)

56 Baudelaire, *Salon de 1846*, *Baudelaire (1954), p. 615. The original text can be found in *Hoffmann (1814–15), pp. 29–30. Charles Baudelaire, *Art in Paris, 1845–1862*, trans. Jonathan Mayne (Oxford, 1965).

57 'Richard Wagner et Tannhäuser', *Baudelaire (1976), p. 1051. Charles Baudelaire, *The Painter of Modern Life and Other Essays*, trans. Jonathan Mayne (New York, 1964).

58 '*les sons et les parfums tournent dans l'air du soir*', 'Harmonies du soir', in *Les fleurs du mal*, *Baudelaire (1954), p. 121. English trans., Richard Howard, *Les Fleurs du mal*, (Boston, MA, 1983).

59 'Exposition universelle de 1855', ibid., p. 690.

60 Gautier, 'Le hachich' (1843), in *L'orient* (Paris, 1884), p. 52.

61 '*Düfte singen, Töne duften, Farben tönen*', *Bahr (1895), p. 63.

62 Pierre Quercy, *Les hallucinations* (Paris, 1936), II, pp. 35–40, ch. III: 'Les opsiphonies'. In *L'hallucination. Études cliniques* (Paris, 1930), pp. 97–103, Quercy mentions the case of Rimbaud.

63 Mahling (1927), pp. 317–47.

64 *Flournoy (1893), p. 3.

65 Klein (1926).

66 Mahling (1927), pp. 416–32.

67 Annelies Argelander, *Das Farbenhören und der synästhetische Faktor der Wahrnehmung* (Jena, 1927).

68 Wellek (1931 and 1954); Kienscherf (1996).

69 Wellek (1926–7), Anschütz (1931), Jewanski (1997 and 2002). The Hamburg Congresses are often referred to in *Blanc-Gatti (1958), whose book contains an extensive specialist bibliography (pp. 166ff.). But artists' interest in this research started much earlier, as shown by the chronology written at their request by Gérôme-Maësse, 'L'audition colorée', *Les Tendances nouvelles,* no. 33 (November 1907), republished (New York, 1980), pp. 655–63.

70 For other neologisms, suggested by Th. Wilfred, cf. Rousseau (2004), p. 35. Further details on some of these strange machines can be found in Jones (1972); Moritz (1987); Peacock (1988); and Jewanski (1999 and 2006). See also *Laszlo (1925) and Wellek (1930). On the survival of these experiments, cf. Galeyev (1976 and 1988); Roberta Reeder, '*Gesamtkunst* and Technology in the USSR', in Günther (1994), pp. 201–39; Evers (1997), pp. XI–XVII and Jewanski and Sidler (2005). For the relation to the cinema, Moritz (1985 and 1986).

71 Gregorio Comanini, *Il Figino* (1591), in *Barocchi (1962), III, p. 370. On this issue, Tornitore (1985).

72 The theoretical debates were particularly lively in the review *Leonardo*, with contributions from both artists and scientists, especially in the years 1968, 1970, 1972, 1975, 1976, 1978 and 1979.

73 Cf. the studies by Fechner (1876), Bleuler and Lehmann (1881) and Claparède and Millet (1892), discussed in *Flournoy (1893).

74 Düchting (1996 and 2002).

75 *Rimington (1895), p. 257.

76 On Alexander Laszlo, cf. Jewanski and Sidler (2006), pp. 131–374.

77 De la Motte-Haber (1990), pp. 199ff.; Brenez and McKane (1995); Brougher (2005); Lista (2006); pp. 241–88, and Guido (2006).

78 Hans Richter, 'Musik und Film', in *Dada-Monographie einer Bewegung*, ed. Willy Verkauf (Teufen, 1957), pp. 64–71.

79 Kurt Früh, 'Film et musique', *Vie, Art, Cité*, no. 5 (1942), n.p.

80 Guido (2006).

81 'La naissance d'un sixième art. Essai sur le cinématographe' (1911), and 'Manifeste des septarts' (1923), in *Canudo (1995), pp. 32–40 and 41–3.

82 Youngblood (1970), II, pp. 75ff.

83 Hapkemeyer (2000), pp. 126–7. The prototype is perhaps the famous *Prose du Transsibérien* by Cendrars and Delaunay.

84 '*dass die Farben keine Töne, und die Ohren keine Augen sind*', *Lessing (1766), p. 112.

85 Cf. Klein (1926), p. 170.

86 *Corradini (1912), p. 294 (1984, p. 160).

87 Margaret Haile-Harris, *Loïe Fuller: Magician of Light* (Richmond, VA, 1979), pp. 28ff. See also Gabriele Brandstetter and Brygida Maria Ochaim, *Loïe Fuller. Tanz, Licht-Spiel, Art Nouveau* (Freiburg, 1989), and Giovanni Lista, *Loïe Fuller, danseuse de la Belle Epoque* (Paris, 1994).

88 *Valensi (1936); Souriau (1963); Flamand (1973); and Schidlower (1990).

89 *Messiaen (1994), p. 68.

90 *Blanc-Gatti (1958), pp. 160ff.

91 D. D. Jameson, *Colour Music* (London, 1844). Cf. Jewanski and Sidler (1995), col. 359, and 2006, p. 169.

92 Deuchler (2003), p. 119.

93 *Russolo (1916), pp. 15–16.

94 *Besant (1905), p. 62. See also Friedrich Mahling, 'Das Farbe-Ton-Problem und die Anthroposophie', in Anschütz (1931), pp. 336–47.

95 Cf. Brougher (2005).

96 *Rainer (1925) and Loef (1980), p. 175.

97 *Klee (1964), p. 286.

98 *Nouveau (1960).

99 *Kandinsky (1926), p. 46. His painting *Promenade* (1920, Centre Pompidou) is perhaps an allusion to Mussorgsky, as *Feuervogel* is supposedly to Stravinsky (1917, priv. coll. Zurich).

100 Walter Behm, 'Erläuterungen zu meinen synoptischen Bildern und zu den Schülerarbeitenaus meinem synoptischen Kunstunterricht', in Anschütz (1931), pp. 414–15; Steiert (1995), pp. 94–7.

101 Anschütz (1927), pl. i-v, and (1931), pp. 413 and 416.

102 Loef (1980), p. 171.

103 *Rothschild (1970), p. 281.

104 *Belmont (1944).

105 *Sebba (1991).

106 A series of other examples can be found in the brochure published by Philips' Phonographic Industries with the title *Klang im Bild – Musique sur toile – Sound into Sight* (Baarn, n.d.).

107 S. Wittwer, *Jakob Weder. Die Wahrheit der Farbe* (Studen, 2006).

108 Jack Ox and Peter Frank, 'The Systematic Translation of Musical Compositions into Paintings', *Leonardo*, xvii/3 (1984), pp. 152–8; Von Maur (1985), pp. 281 and 444; and *Auf ein Wort! Aspekte visueller Poesie und visueller Musik* (Mainz, 1987), pp. 132–43.

109 Cf. Jewanski and Sidler (2006), pp. 373–421.

110 Schmunk (2000), p. 185.

111 See the comparative table made by Harrison (2001), p. 123.

112 For a typology of the different systems, cf. Klein (1926), pp. 116 and 122–3. See also Pütz (1995), p. 144, who compares associations between colours, feelings, instruments, *Stimmungen*, and so on, in Scriabin, Kandinsky, Rudolf Steiner and Schönberg.

113 *Flournoy (1893), p. 100, rightly notes that the associations made are also affected by the names of the notes (which vary from one language to another) and may be influenced by the colour attributed to the vowel. We should not forget, on this issue, that Scriabin and *Myers (1915) were obliged to communicate in French, which was their only common language.

114 See for example the table of correspondences between colours and vowels in *De Rochas (1891).

115 Cf. John Gage, 'Newton and Painting', in *Common Denominators in Art and Science*, ed. Martin Pollock (Aberdeen, 1983), pp. 20–23.

116 Hans Haug, *Considérations sur l'harmonie naturelle des sons,* a duplicate loaned to the *Archives musicales de la Bibliothèque cantonale à Lausanne*. Haug (1900–1967) takes the analogy to its limits, mapping colour terminology onto the classification of intervals, which he calls 'primary' and 'secondary', and onto that of chords, which may be 'hot' or 'cold' (p. 22). Similarly, *Messiaen (1986), p. 65, sees an analogy between the simultaneous contrast of complementary colours and the phenomenon of natural resonance.

117   For recent examples, cf. Loef (1980) or Seba (1991).

118   *Schopenhauer (1816), p. 64.

119   See the exhibition catalogue *Blanc-Gatti, le peintre des sons* (Paris, 1931), which presents a comparative table of sound and light frequencies; and Anatol Vietinghoff-Scheel, 'Das neue Chromatophon', in Anschütz (1931), pp. 389–96 (391).

120   On the many criticisms made of the sound–light analogy, cf. Jewanski and Sidler (2006), pp. 162–8.

121   Etiemble (1968), pp. 119, 125, 129 and 130.

122   For a similar set of correlations, cf. Mattis (2005), p. 213.

123   *D'Udine (1897), pp. 18 and 22. Similarly for *Slawson (1985).

124   Johann Leonhard Hoffmann, *Versuch einer Geschichte der malerischen Harmonie* (Halle, 1786).

125   Joachim Raff in 1855, or the Schönberg of *Farben* (op. 16) and of the *Klangfarbenmelodie*.

126   *Kandinsky (1911). The correspondences between colours and instruments can be found in 'Art concret' (1938), in *Écrits*, II, p. 370.

127   Jean d'Udine, or René Ghil and his 'verbal instrumentation'. See also *Lavignac (1896), pp. 211–13, and Klein (1926), p. 44.

128   See for example Garner (1978).

129   Cf. the criticism of Schubert by *Schumann (1854), I, pp. 180–82, and Denéréaz (1921), pp. 308–9. See also Wolfgang Auhagen, *Studien zur Tonartcharakteristik in theoretischen Schriften und Kompositionen vom späten 17. Jh. bis zum Beginn des 20. Jh.* (Bern, 1983).

130   Cf. Berlioz, who criticized the purely conventional association between high and low in general, and high-pitched and low-pitched in music. See *Berlioz (1862), p. 216.

131   David Topper, 'Newton on the Number of Colours in the Spectrum', *Studies in History and Philosophy of Science*, XXI (1990), pp. 269–79.

132   *Castel (1740), pp. 116 and 161ff. *Rovel (1908) took up this logic of the 'perfect chord' of colours and attempted to adapt it to the scientific calculation of frequencies.

133   *De La Moussaye (1853), pp. 189–90.

134   Ibid., 'Harmonie des sensations' (1 September 1853), pp. 33–4.

135   *Brès (1828).

136   Young, *On the Theory of Light and Colours* (1801).

137   *Eisenstein (1947), p. 150.

138   See, for example, the study by Dr Louis Appia, *De la corrélation physiologique entre les cinq sens et de leurs rapports avec les mouvements volontaires. Application à l'éducation des aveugles* (Paris, 1879).

139   Castel, in *Mercure de France* (February 1726), p. 277. See also March 1726, p. 459.

140   *Castel (1763), pp. XXI and 369–70.

141   *Grétry (1796), pp. 235–8.

142   Aristotle, *De sensu*, 442 a.

143   *Kircher (1650), p. 422: '*Sic ergo constituetur juxta naturam propriam musicae proportionesapor jucundissimus . . . Quod de saporibus dictum est, prorsus simile ratione de odoribus et tactu dici debet, cum in omnibus eadem sit ratio . . . Nobis mirandam quandam harmoniam . . . sub quinque sensibus.*'

144   *Mendelssohn (1755).

145   Johann Gottfried Herder, 'Treatise on the Origin of Language', in *Philosophical Writings*, trans. Michael N. Forster (Cambridge, 2002), pp. 65–167.

146   Etienne Pivert de Senancourt, *Obermann* [1804] (Paris, 1931), II. p. 68. See also I, p. 147: 'The harpsichord of colours was ingenious; the harpsichord of smells would have been more interesting.'

147   *Morellet (1818), p. 376.

148   Cf. Lista (2005), p. 188.

149   *Brès (1828); *D'Udine (1910), pp. x–xi; *Blanc-Gatti (1958), pp. 151ff.

150   'Alchimie du verbe', in *Rimbaud (1972), p. 106.

151   *Ghil (1978). Cf. Kearns (1989), p. 70.

152   Rousseau (2006).

153   Paul Fort, *Mes mémoires. Toute la vie d'un poète, 1872–1943* (Paris, 1944), pp. 34–7.

154   *Echo de Paris* (30 December 1891), quoted in *Nabis, 1888–1900* (Zürich/Munich, 1993), p. 402. The performance was also described in *Fénéon (1970), II, p. 836 ('Au Théâtre d'art', *La Paix*, 15 December 1891), *Binet (1892), p. 611, and Rémy de Gourmont, *Promenades littéraires*, IV (Paris, 1920), p. 50. The 'scented stage-set' was also mentioned by Maurice Denis in *Sérusier (1921), p. 65.

155   Julien Leclerq, *Mercure de France* (January 1892), p. 84.

156   Pütz (1995), pp. 135ff. The idea was roundly criticized by John F. Runciman, 'Noises, Smells and Colours', *Musical Quarterly*, I (1915), pp. 149–61.

157   Santeri Levas, *Sibelius: A Personal Portrait* (London, 1972), ch. v, 'The Sixth Sense', pp. 36–50.

158   Cf. Lista (1989), p. 95.

159   Frantisek Kupka, interview in the *New York Times* (1913), in *L'année 1913*, ed. Liliane Brion-Guerry (Paris, 1973), III, p. 231.

160   *Kupka (1913), p. 161.

161   Marie Jaëll, *L'intelligence et le rythme dans les mouvements artistiques* (Paris, 1904), p. 96, and *Les rythmes du regard et la dissociation des doigts* (Paris, 1906), pp. 3ff. and 143. See also Hélène Kiener, *Marie Jaëll: 1846–1925, problèmes d'esthétique et de pédagogie musicale* (Paris, 1952), p. 155. On her influence, Pierre (2003), and Lawrence Joseph, *Catherine Pozzi. Une robe couleur du temps* (Paris, 1988), pp. 62–5.

162   Düchting (1996), pp. 41–7.

163   *Kandinsky (1975), *Écrits*, III, pp. 206 and 381.

164   *Kandinsky (1970?), 'Art' [1938], in *Écrits*, II, p. 371.

165   *Boccioni (1914), p. 106.

166   *Carrà (1913), p. 185.

167   'avvalorare in un'unica sintesi queste sensazioni plastiche, cromatiche, architettoniche, dimoto, rumore, odore, ecc', 'Un'arte nuova? Costruzione assoluta di moto-rumore', 1915, in E. Prampolini (Modena, 1986), p. 24. See also Lista (1989), pp. 185ff.: 'The Futurist synthesis'.

168   *Lista (1973), p. 321.

169   Ibid., pp. 344–5.

170   *Teige (1928), pp. 97–8.

171   *Eisenstein (1947).

172   Pierre Bourgeade, Bonsoir Man Ray (Paris, 1990), p. 69.

173   Chapeaurouge (1983), ch. I.

174   Denis Diderot, 'Letter on the Blind for the Use of Those Who See' (1749), in Diderot's Early Philosophical Works, ed. and trans. Margaret Jourdain (Chicago, IL, 1916). Contemporary speculations on the relations between sight and touch clearly draw on Lockian empiricism; cf. John W. Davis, 'The Molyneux Problem', Journal of the History of Ideas, XXI/3 (1960), pp. 392–408. There are many other allusions to the tactile vision of the blind, for example Francesco Algarotti, Dialogues on Newton's Optics, in Works (Berlin, 1772), I, p. 187.

175   *Diderot (1752), p. 418.

176   *Segalen (1902), pp. 72–3.

177   Rémy de Gourmont, Promenades littéraires, IV (Paris, 1920), p. 50.

178   Hieronymus Cardanus, Opus nuvum de proportionibus numerorum, quoted by Jewanski and Sidler (2006), p. 136.

179   François Fénelon, Voyage dans l'île des plaisirs, c. 1690 (Fables composées pour l'éducation de Mgr. le Duc de Bourgogne), in Oeuvres, I (Paris, 1983), pp. 203–4.

180   Émile Zola, Les Rougon-Macquart (Paris, 1960–64), I, pp. 826–9; and III, pp. 769–70. Cf. Jean Kaempfer, Émile Zola. D'un naturalisme pervers (Paris, 1989), pp. 239–45.

181   Septimus Piesse, Histoire des parfums, 1890, quoted by Rousseau (2006), p. 160.

182   Chistian Morgenstern, Palmström [1910] (Munich, 1961) 4th edn, p. 31.

183   Kurt Lasswitz, 'Bis zum Nullpunkt des Seins. Erzählung aus dem Jahre 2771', in Bilder aus der Zukunft. Zwei Erzählungen aus dem 24. und 39. Jahrhundert (Breslau, 1878), I, pp. 6, 12 and 45.

184   Lasswitz, 'Gegen das Weltgesetz', ibid., II, pp. 31, 33 and 37.

185   *Poncelet (1755), pp. xviii–xxii.

186   *Huysmans (1884), pp. 70–71 and 168–76.

187   Mercure de France (October 1892), pp. 185–6.

188   *Vian (1946), pp. 29–30.

189   Henri Stierlin, ed., L'art de Karl Gerstner (Paris, 1981), p. 21.

190   This was probably the same barge on which Poiret had installed a colour organ (clavilux) the previous year.

191   *Debussy (1971), p. 150.

192 Charles Ferdinand Ramuz, 'Souvenirs sur Igor Stravinsky' (1928), in *Oeuvres complètes*, XVIII (Lausanne, 1968), p. 119.

193 Filippo Tommaso Marinetti, *La cuisine futuriste*, trans. and presented by Nathalie Heinich (Paris, 1982).

194 Philippe Beaussant, *Mangez baroque et restez minces* (Paris, 1999), pp. 7–15.

195 Quoted in *Hommage à W. Kandinsky* (Paris, 1974), p. 131.

196 'Tout entière', in *Les Fleurs du mal*, XLI, *Baudelaire (1954), p. 116. English trans., Roy Campbell, *Poems of Baudelaire* (New York, 1952): 'O mystic fusion that, enwreathing / My senses, fuses each in each, / To hear the music of her breathing / And breathe the perfume of her speech.'

197 *Balzac (1835), p. 292.

198 Pierre-Simon Ballanche, *Palingénésie sociale*, see note 36.

199 Jewanski (1999), p. 583, and (2006), p. 136. The Chinese associated colours, sounds, planets, tastes, elements and seasons: cf. Jewanski (1995), col. 346, and (2006), p. 133.

200 *Kircher (1646), p. 67, and (1650), p. 393.

201 '*diese mystische Union der Sinne*', *Bahr (1895), p. 234.

202 Charles Fourier, *Théorie de l'unité universelle*, in *Oeuvres complètes* (Paris, 1843) 2nd edn, II, p. 145. See also Rousseau (2004), p. 29.

203 Joscelyn Godwin, *Harmonies of Heaven and Earth* (London, 1987).

204 On the game of 'one in the other' (1954), cf. Jean-Paul Clébert, *Dictionnaire du surréalisme* (Paris, 1996), p. 324.

205 *Binet (1892).

206 *Flournoy (1893), pp. 98 and 102.

207 Cf. for example Ferdinand Suarez de Mendoza, *L'audition colorée. Étude sur les fausses sensations* (Paris, 1890); *Souriau (1895), pp. 849–70, and (1901), ch. IV.

208 *Messiaen (1986), p. 45.

209 Dauven (1961), p. 46. See also pp. 34, 61–2 and 73.

210 *De La Moussaye (1853), p. 34, devised a system of equivalences between colours and temperaments, and *Favre (1900), pp. 7ff. and 48, stressed their expressive value, as did *Kandinsky (1911), *Brand (1914) and Pratella, among others, cf. Lista (2006), p. 167. *Blanc-Gatti (1958), p. 19, created a table of correspondences between musical intervals and 'emotional impressions'.

211 *Ghil (1904), p. 57.

212 See for instance the Manifesto (by Marinetti et al.) of the *Futurist Synthetic Theatre* (1915) and this movement's 'theatrical syntheses', cf. Lista (1989), pp. 136 and 146.

213 *Euler (1760), pp. 271–3. *Castel (1725), p. 2557, mentioned the 'imperceptible quiverings of bodies of light and sound'.

214 *Balzac (1837), pp. 502–3.

215 Letter to Fontainas, March 1899, in *Gauguin (1974), p. 222. *Blanc-Gatti (1958) dwells at length on this idea, pp. 73, 92, 133 *et passim*.

216   Cf. Georges Roque, 'This great world of vibrations which is the basis of the universe', in Duplaix (2004), pp. 51–67.

217   Rudolph Steiner and the theosophist Alexandra Zacharina-Unkovskaya established their system of sound-colour correspondences on precisely these cosmic vibrations, and A. Besant referred to the Chladni plates (p. 20). On the interpenetration of science and occult practices, see Linda Henderson, 'Kupka, les rayons X et le monde des ondes électromagnétiques', in F. *Kupka ou l'invention d'une abstraction* (Paris, 1989), pp. 51–7.

218   *Kandinsky (1911), pp. 85 and 105.

219   *Carrà (1913), p. 183.

220   *Henry (1885). Cf. Alain Mercier, 'Charles Henry et l'esthétique symboliste', *Revue des sciences humaines*, no. 38 (April–June 1970), pp. 251–72.

221   *Rovel (1908), p. 721. See also p. 753: 'Life is characterized by vibrations. Without vibrations, there is no life. The entire world obeys this law.'

222   *Favre (1900), p. 1. See also *Gerstner (1986), p. 164.

223   *Segalen (1902), p. 90.

224   Cf. *Licht* (Basel, 1990); Wolfgang Schivelbusch, *Licht, Schein und Wahn. Auftritte der elektrischen Beleuchtung im 20. Jh.* (Berlin, 1992); and Andreas Blühm and Louise Lippincott, *Light! The Industrial Age, 1750–1900. Art and Science, Technology and Society* (London, 2000), pp. 29ff.

225   Mauro Montalti, 'Pour un nouveau théâtre électro-vibro-lumineux' (1920), in *Lista (1973), pp. 275–7. See also the Manifesto by F. Depero on complexity in the three-dimensional arts (1914), which champions 'a volitional electric transcendental sensibility' (ibid., p. 198).

226   *Hausmann (1922), p. 241.

227   Another concert of 'electrical music' took place on 1 April 1932 in the same venue, performed by the Theremin electrical symphony orchestra, with 'light and sound phenomena'.

228   *Rimington (1895), pp. 257–9 and 264–65. Previously *Kastner (1875), and later *D'Udine (1910), p. viii. Cf. Frank Popper, 'L'électricité et l'électronique dans l'art au xxe siècle', in *Electra* (Paris, 1983), pp. 19–77.

229   Hans Ulrich Reck, 'Der Streit der Kunstgattungen im Kontext der Entwicklung neuer Medientechnologien', *Kunstforum International*, cxv (September–October 1991), pp. 81–98 (87–8).

230   *Hausmann (1922), p. 241.

231   De la Motte-Haber (1990), pp. 138–48.

232   Félix Le Dantec, *Les lois naturelles. Réflexions d'un biologiste sur les sciences* (Paris, 1914), pp. 30–31. Book I is entitled *Les cantons sensoriels et le monisme*. It is quoted by *D'Udine (1910) and *Blanc-Gatti (1958), among others.

233   *Voltaire (1738), p. 391.

234   *Favre (1900), p. v. This theme can be found in *Gerstner (1986), p. 164.

235 Cf. Henri Morier, *Dictionnaire de poétique et de rhétorique* (Paris, 1981), 'Correspondances', pp. 311–38.

236 On the historical connection between synaesthesia, the colour of sounds and the harmony of the spheres, cf. Wellek (1929), pp. 32–3; (1931), pp. 538–43, 557–60 *et passim*; (1935), pp. 351 and 371; and (1963), pp. 167 and 169. See also Schrader (1969), ch. VII; and Lawrence E. Marks, *The Unity of the Senses: Interrelations among the Modalities* (London, 1978), p. 248.

237 On Scriabin, cf. L. Verdi (1996), and on Wychnegradsky, Von Maur (1985), pp. 218–20. The theme of the celestial dome seems to derive here from *Scriabin's *Mysterium* (1979), p. 121, and can be found in *Gerstner's *Color-Dome* (1986), pp. 160 and 168.

238 *Nerval (1853), p. 740.

239 Guy de Maupassant, quoted by *Segalen (1902), p. 75.

240 *Saint-Yves d'Alveydre (1911). Compare with the title of a work by Helena Blavatsky, *The Secret Doctrine: The Synthesis of Science, Religion and Philosophy* (1888). Blavatsky was also interested in sound-colour correspondence.

241 *Saint-Yves d'Alveydre (1911), pp. 273 and 319.

242 Ringbom (1966 and 1970); Tuchman (1986); and Loers (1995); see also Linda Dalrymple Henderson, 'Mysticism and Occultism in Modern Art', *Art Journal*, XLVI/1 (Spring 1987).

243 *Ghil (1909), p. 44. On his sources of inspiration and scientific pretentions, cf. the excellent introduction by Tiziana Goruppi to *Ghil (1885).

244 Particularly in his study of form-colour correspondences. See his conference paper, 'On Working Methods for Synthetic Art', (1921), Experiment, VIII/1 (2002), pp. 187–92 ('De la méthode de travail sur l'art synthétique'), given at the Russian Academy of Artistic Sciences, French trans. by Christian Derouet and Jessica Boissel, *Kandinsky, Oeuvres* (Paris, 1984), pp. 158–9.

245 Zilczer (1987) has convincingly shown the convergence between these two, scientific and mystical, traditions.

246 J. Nuel, quoted by Tornitore (1986), p. 45.

247 Max Nordau, *Entartung*, 1892–3 (2 vols). Nordau equated the 'mysticism of colours' with 'intellectual decline' (p. 32).

248 See the reaction of *Segalen (1902).

249 Wellek (1930 and 1931), pp. 535 sq.

6 Bach Through the Prism of Painting

1 A. Schmoll, also called Eisenwerth, 'Hommage à Bach. Ein Thema der bildenden Kunst des 20. Jh.', in *Convivium Musicorum, Festschrift Wolfgang Boetticher* (Berlin, 1974), pp. 325–37; Würtenberger (1979), ch. 21, pp. 172–83: 'Die Verehrung von J. S.

Bach. Der Begriff der Fuge bei den Kunsthistorikern und ihre Vorbildlichkeit bei den Malern'; Wilhelm Weber and Fritz Kaiser, *Hommage à Bach* (Mainz, 1980); Walter Salmen, 'Leuchte des Erstrebenswerten'. Bach und die bildende Kunst im 20. Jh'., *Neue Zürcher Zeitung*, 16/17 March 1985, p. 68; Von Maur (1985), pp. 28–47; Friedrich Teja Bach, 'J. S. Bach in der klassischen Moderne', ibid., pp. 328–35; Walter Salmen, 'Reflexionen über Bach in der bildenden Kunst des 20 Jh., *Bach-Jahrbuch*, LXXII (February 1986), pp. 91–102; Gerhard Schumacher, 'J. S. Bach und eine "Harmonielehre der Malerei". Musikalisch-kunstästhetische Reflexion und Gestaltung bei Braque, Klee und Kandinsky', in *Musica privata. die Rolle der Musik im privaten Leben* (Innsbruck, 1991), pp. 357–77; Suzanne Fontaine, 'Ausdruck und Konstruktion. Die Bach-Rezeption von Kandinsky, Itten, Klee und Feininger', in *Bach und die Nachwelt*, ed. Michael Heinemann and Hans Joachim Hinrichsen (Laaber, 1997), III, pp. 397–426.

2   On painters' acclamation of Mozart, cf. Jung-Kaiser (2003).

3   The name of Bach is curiously absent from the painter's writings, *Matisse (1972); yet the importance music had for him is well known.

4   *Klee (1988), no. 52.

5   Ibid., no. 540.

6   Ibid., no. 618.

7   Ibid., no. 963.

8   Ibid., no. 964.

9   Ibid., no. 1024.

10   *Klee (1979), p. 924: '*ich bin voll Kunst, und auch die Erkenntnis ist durch das mehrmalig Bachspielen wieder vertieft. Noch nie hab ich mit solcher Intensität Bach erlebt und wohl auch gespielt. Ich fühlte mich eins mit diesem Gott, und das muss ja Früchte tragen.*'

11   Letter from Franz Marc to August Macke of 12 May 1913.

12   Fontaine, 'Ausdruck und Konstruktion', p. 416. See also Karin von Maur, 'Feininger und die Kunst der Fuge', in *Lyonel Feininger. Von Gelmeroda nach Manhatten*, ed. Roland März (Berlin, 1998), pp. 272–84.

13   Florens Deuchler, 'Malerei und Musik', in *Lyonel Feininger. Sein Weg zum Bauhaus-Meister* (Leipzig, 1996), pp. 173–9 (176).

14   Fontaine, 'Ausdruck und Konstruktion', p. 415.

15   Quoted by Wilhelm Weber and Fritz Kaiser, *Hommage à Bach*, p. 18.

16   *Itten (1978), p. 65.

17   Ibid., p. 7.

18   Ibid., p. 31. See also pp. 26, 62 and 68, *et passim.*

19   Ibid., p. 62.

20   Ibid., pp. 17, 19, 31, 53, 61, 254, 265.

21   Cf. Nicole Worms de Romilly / Jean Laude, *Braque, le cubisme. Catalogue de l'oeuvre, 1907–1914* (Paris, 1982), nos 122, 161, 165, 180 and 199, to which should be added a

papier collé of 1912 entitled *Bal* (William Rubin, *Picasso et Braque. L'invention du cubisme* (Paris, 1990), p. 248). Each of these paintings has the name 'Bach' encoded within it. One could add the no. 222, *Verre et bouteille* (1913–14, New York, Museum of Modern Art), where the mention of 'Joh' could be read as Bach's first name, truncated.

22   Ionel Jianou, *Zadkine* (Paris, 1979), nos 235 and 236.

23   Marie-Claude Dane, *Musée Zadkine* (Paris, 1982), no. 104.

24   Dufy painted five 'Homage to Bach' canvases between 1950 and 1952 (Maurice Laffaille, *Raoul Dufy, catalogue raisonné* of the painted works, Geneva, 1972–7, IV, nos 1506–1510) to which should be added no. 2022 of the *Supplément* (Paris, 1985) and two watercolours (Fanny Guillon-Laffaille, *Raoul Dufy*, catalogue raisonné of the watercolours, Paris, 1981–2, II, nos 1645 and 1646). By comparison, he painted twenty 'Homage to Mozart' canvases between 1915 and 1952.

25   Michael Heinemann and Hans-Joachim Hinrichsen, ed., *Bach und die Nachwelt* (Laaber, 1997); John Maxwell Coetzee, 'What Is a Classic?', in *Stranger Shores: Essays, 1886–1999* (London, 2002), pp. 1–19 (9ff.)

26   Stewart Buettner, 'Catalonia and the Early Musical Subjects of Braque and Picasso', *Art History* (1996), no. 1, pp. 102–27.

27   Cf. Boehm (1996).

28   André Pirro, *L'esthétique de J. S. Bach* (Paris, (1907) , 1913, 4th edn, pp. 354, 382 and 476.

29   *Hanslick (1854), which had two French editions, Paris 1877 and 1893.

30   *Stravinsky (1942).

31   Jean Marnold, 'Bach et l'art pour l'art', *Mercure de France* (October–December 1903), pp. 529–36.

32   Spielmann (1996), pp. 77–91. A self-portrait (a lithograph) from the same year is entitled *Bachkantate*.

33   *Schlemmer (1977), pp. 21 and 32.

34   *Nouveau (2002), pp. 77–80.

35   See for example *Dukas (1948), p. 662, who compared Wagner unfavourably to 'the marvellous reawakening of J. S. Bach'.

36   Richard Hamann and Jost Hermand, *Stilkunst um 1900 (Epochen deutscher Kultur von 1870 bis zur Gegenwart, Band 4)*, 2nd edn (Munich, 1972), p. 162.

37   *Klee (1988), no. 1081.

38   Albert Jeanneret, 'L'intelligence dans l'oeuvre musicale', *L'Esprit nouveau*, no. 7 (April 1921), p. 842. See also Amédée Ozenfant and Charles-Edouard Jeanneret, 'Vers le cristal', ibid., no. 25 (July 1924), n.p., where Bach is associated with Cubism due to its 'geometrical' and 'organic' organization.

39   Fontaine, 'Ausdruck und Konstruktion', p. 402.

40   Jung-Kaiser (2003), pp. 171ff.

41   'I have always loved music, and in that period it began occupying for me the role which poetry had occupied in the 1920s – especially Bach and Mozart'; a statement from 1948 quoted by Jean-Louis Prat in *Miró* (Martigny, 1997), p. 106.

42 *Stendhal (1815), p. 224.

43 Quoted by Hammerstein (1984), p. 9.

44 Hans Thoma, Dürervortrag, 1903, quoted by Hammerstein, ibid.

45 *Redon (1961), pp. 109–10.

46 Hamann and Hermand, *Stilkunst um 1900*, pp. 431 and 113. For the ideological context of the cult of Bach, see also Fontaine, 'Ausdruck und Konstruction'.

47 Wilhelm Pinder, *Aussagen zur Kunst* [1949] (Munich, 1993), pp. 52 and 53.

48 *Hoffmann (1931), p. 49.

49 Quoted by Würtenberger (1979), p. 179. The association 'Bach – cathedral – Gothic' persisted far into the 20th century, as suggested by a poster for the 'Ulmer Bachkonzerte 1966' – designed by Peter Polland, reproduced in *Art* (September 2003), p. 43.

50 *Ferruccio Busoni (1910), quoted by Salmen (1986), p. 94.

51 *Mauclair (1928), p. 151.

52 *Nouveau (2002), p. 85.

53 Von Maur (1985), p. 174. According to Erich Mendelsohn, Frank Lloyd Wright was another creative artist fascinated by Bach's music (ibid., p. 173).

54 Daniel Henri Kahnweiler, *Juan Gris. Sa vie, son oeuvre, ses écrits*, 4th edn (Paris, 1964), p. 214.

55 *Cahiers d'Art*, rpt. in *Miró (1995), p. 163.

56 *Janin (1933), p. 26.

57 Schlemmer (1977)

58 Wolfram Goertz, 'Der geometrische Komponist', *Du*, no. 764 (March 2006), pp. 28–35 (30).

59 The illustrator and caricaturist Hansi's contribution to the debate on the form of the Haut-Koenigsbourg Tower after its restoration provides another amusing example of the association between the German national character and the square: 'German art and German science have decided that the tower was originally square . . . every truly beautiful and truly German thing is square from its birth. Just look at a German's skull, what further proof do you need.' (Quoted by Elisabeth Castellani Zahir, 'Echt falsch und doch schön alt. Die Wiederherstellung der Hohkönigsburg im Elsass 1900 bis 1908', *Zeitschrift für Schweizerische Archäologie und Kunstgeschichte*, LIV (1997), book 2, p. 148.)

60 Cf. Würtenberger (1979), p. 179.

61 Wolfgang Venzmer, *Adolf Hölzel, Leben und Werk* (Stuttgart, 1982), p. 140.

62 *Schlemmer (1977), 4 April 1916.

63 Quoted by Vergo (1994), p. 584.

64 Cf. Kagan (1983).

65 *Itten (1978), p. 256.

66 Robert Delaunay, *Du cubisme à l'art abstrait*, ed. Pierre Francastel (Paris, 1957), p. 81.

67 *Delacroix (1932), I, p. 284 (7 April 1849).

68 Johann Wolfgang von Goethe to Friedrich Zelter, 31 December 1817, *Briefe 1814–1832*, in *Goethes Werke, Gedenkausgabe vol. 21* (Zurich, 1951), p. 257.

69 He wrote to his brother Daniel on 4 August 1802: 'This painting will be exactly what a fugue is in music', *Runge (1840), p. 223: '*dieses Bild dasselbe wird, was eine Fuge in Musik ist.*'

70 *Redon (1987), p. 86.

71 *Redon (1961), p. 110. See also p. 26.

72 De la Motte-Haber (1990), p. 188.

73 Its first mention is probably by *Boschini (1660), p. 324, who wrote that '*Pitor venezian, musico esperto . . . forma fughe*' ('The Venetian painter, an accomplished musician, knows how to tune and play his instrument').

74 L. Feininger quoted by Hans Sündermann, 'Musikalische Graphik', *Alte und moderne Kunst*, book 74 (1964), p. 42.

75 *Frank Kupka, 1871–1957* (Zurich, 1976), p. 142.

76 Frantisek Kupka, 'Le véritable rôle de l'art', in *L'année 1913,* ed. Liliane Brion-Guerry (Paris, 1973), III, p. 161.

77 'Die Ausstellung des Modernen Bundes im Kunsthaus Zürich' (1912), rpt. in *Klee (1976), p. 108. Klee returned to this comparison between Delaunay's painting and the form of the fugue in 1917 – *Klee (1988), no. 1081.

78 *Der Kubismus, ein künstlerisches Formproblem unserer Zeit* (Leipzig, 1920), quoted by Von Maur (1985), p. 374.

79 Nancy J. Troy, 'Theo van Doesburg: From Music into Space', *Arts Magazine* (February 1982), pp. 92–101 (100).

80 Oskar Schlemmer, 'Abstraction in Dance and Costume' (1928), in *Oskar Schlemmer Man: Teaching Notes from the Bauhaus*, ed. Heimo Kuchling, trans. Janet Seligman (London, 1971).

81 Ezra Pound, 'Vorticism' (1914), in *Ezra Pound and the Visual Arts,* ed. Harriet Zinnes (New York, 1980), pp. 199–209 (199).

82 *Johannes Itten, Künstler und Lehrer* (Bern, 1985), p. 11.

83 'Du nationalisme en musique II' (1931) in *Schönberg (1977), p. 139.

84 *Webern (1960), p. 36.

85 Soto, quoted by Marc Collet, 'Le domaine musical de Soto', in *Jesus Raphael Soto* (Paris, 1997), pp. 36–7.

86 Transcribing Bach's fugues into visual form seems even to have been a technical exercise in schools. For examples, cf. Loef (1974), pp. 171 and 175.

87 *Klee (1964), pp. 285–7.

88 'A Bach fugue represented in space', in *Nouveau (1960), p. 9. This text was published for the first time in the *Bauhaus Review* in 1929.

89 Ibid., pp. 12ff.

90 Heinrich Poos, 'Henrik Neugeborens Entwurf zu einem Bach-Monument (1928). Dokumentation und Kritik', in Schmierer (1995), pp. 45–57.

91 *Rainer (1925), pp. 71–3 and 84–5.

92 Hans Sündermann, 'Musikalische Graphik', *Alte und moderne Kunst*, 74 (1964), p. 43, pl. 13.

93 *Franz Rederer (1899–1965), Musikerportraits* (Bregenz, 1994), p. 12.

94 Cf. Arthur Godel, 'Musik und Farbe', in *Robert Strübin (1897–1965). Retrospektive. Musikbilder und andere Werke*, ed. Jean-Christoph Ammann (Lucerne, 1970); Thomas Lehner, *Die phantastische Erfindung des Basler Maler-Pianisten Robert Strübin. Der Kunstkonverter. Über die Verwandlung von Musik in Malerei und wieder zurück* (Nuremberg, 1973), pp. 27 and 35.

95 Werner Grünzweig, 'Handwerk, Analyse, Bild und Ton. Zu Linda Schwarz' Bach-projekt', in Schmierer (1995), pp. 223–8.

96 Jack Ox, with Peter Frank, 'The Systematic Translation of Musical Compositions into Paintings', *Leonardo*, XVII, no. 3 (1984), p. 153.

97 Marcel Baumgartner and Karl Gerstner, *Jakob Weder, Farbordnung und Malerei als Sinnbild kosmischer Gesetze* (Zurich, 1981), pp. 30–39.

98 *Klee (1988), no. 1081.

99 Georg Germann, 'Das organische Ganze', *Archithese*, 2 (1972), pp. 36–41.

100 *Johannes Itten, Künstler und Lehrer*, p. 11.

7 'Comparison Fever': True or False Friends?

1 '*Potrei produrre avanti questa galleria; ma parmi che basti per uno scherzo*', *Carpani (1812), pp. 54, 106, 129, 181, 183, 212 and 219–21.

2 *Stendhal (1814), pp. 141–2. On this plagiarism, cf. the Preface by Henri Martineau to the *Vies de Haydn, de Mozart et de Métastase* (Paris, 1928). For the history of its various editions, cf. *Stendhal a Roma* (Rome, 1983), pp. 63–5.

3 Dionysius of Halicarnassus, *Isocrates*, 4, 6.

4 Cf. Annibaldi (1968), p. 26.

5 Quoted in Staehelin (1977), who mentions yet further precedents.

6 *Carpani (1812), p. 220.

7 Montesquieu, *Essai sur le goût*, ed. Ch.-J. Beyer (Geneva, 1967), pp. 154–5 and 91.

8 As reported by Giuseppe Nicola de Azara, quoted by Steffi Roettgen, *A. R. Mengs, 1728–1779. Das malerische und zeichnerische Werk* (Munich, 1999), p. 35.

9 As suggested by the various remarks in his *Diaries*, *Delacroix (1932), I, pp. 290, 342 and 455, II, and III, p. 290.

10 As Denizeau claims, Denizeau (1998), p. 40.

11 *Champfleury (1861), or Edouard Herriot, *La vie de Beethoven* [1929] (Paris, 1933), pp. 241–3. See also Hans Hollander, 'Beethoven und Goya. Parallelen und Gegensätze', *Das Orchester*, no. 28 (1980), pp. 803–5.

12 *Hommage à l'Ile des morts de Böcklin* (Paris, 2001), p. 76.

13   Giorgio de Chirico, *Il meccanismo del pensiero. Critica, polemica, autobiografia, 1911–1943* (Turin, 1985), p. 171. See also J.-M. D. Douiller in Paul Lang (2005), pp. 104–5.

14   Juliusz Starzynski, 'Delacroix et Chopin', *Académie polonaise des sciences,* fasc. 34 (Paris and Warsaw, 1962), pp. 3–21.

15   The portraits made of Stravinksy by Picasso are famous, but the sketch of Picasso by Stravinsky is less well known. It is reproduced in Robert Craft, *Conversations with Igor Stravinsky* (London, 1959), p. 65.

16   *Albèra (1995).

17   Anne-Marie Mathy, 'La consécration de la cathédrale de Florence par le pape Eugène IV', in *Musica e arti figurative* (Turin, 1968), pp. 87–8; Charles W. Warren, 'Brunelleschi's Dome and Dufay's Motet', *The Musical Quarterly* (January 1973), pp. 92–105; and Hans Ryschawy and Rolf W. Stoll, 'Die Bedeutung der Zahl in Dufays Kompositionsart: *Nuper rosarum flores*', *Musik-Konzepte*, no. 60 (April 1988), pp. 3–73.

18   'The music of Mr Debussy is an auditory impressionism, and the painting of Mr Monet, a fugue of colours', *Mauclair (1904), pp. 260-61.

19   See, among others, Arnold Werner-Jensen, 'Malerischer und musikalischer Impressionnismus. Gegenüberstellung von Monet und Debussy', *Musik und Bildung*, IX, (1977), pp. 402–7.

20   Stefan Jarocinski, *Debussy, impressionnisme et symbolisme* [1966] (Paris, 1970); François Lesure et al., *Debussy e il simbolismo* (Rome, 1984); Howat (1983); Sabatier (1995), pp. 325–35 and 383–4; Bentgens (1997), pp. 114–63; Jörg Jewanski, 'Annäherungen. Debussy und die bildenden Künste', in Schneider (2000), pp. 53–73; Nectoux (2005), pp. 209–27.

21   Boudinet (1998), p. 27.

22   '*quella robustezza Buonarrotesca che possedeva il Robusti, unita al fuoco, alla bizzarria, alla novità e copia*', *Carpani (1812), p. 219.

23   *Stendhal (1829), pp. 885 and 607–8. *Viardot (1859) compares Mozart with Albert Cuyp.

24   *Wyzewa (1895), p. 23.

25   Vossler (1935); Wais (1936), pp. 79–95.

26   Boulez (1989), p. 44.

27   *Liszt (1995), p. 187. See also Eigeldinger (1996), pp. 49–74.

28   '*Der gebildete Musiker wird an einer Raphaelschen Madonna mit gleichem Nutzen studieren können wie der Maler an einer Mozartschen Symphonie*', *Schumann (1891), p. 34.

29   *Carpani (1812), p. 252.

30   Gilles Cantagrel, *Bach en son temps* (Paris, 1982), pp. 314 and 326.

31   Johann Ferdinand Rochlitz, in *Allgemeine Musikalische Zeitung*, 21 November 1798, quoted in *Bach en son temps*, p. 330.

32 Giorgio Pestelli, 'Giuseppe Carpani e il neoclassicismo musicale della vecchia Italia', in *Musica e arti figurative* (Turin, 1968), pp. 105–21; Galliano Ciliberti, '"Le passioni degli dei": musica e pittura tra Gluck e David', in *Musica e immagine tra iconografia e mondo dell'opera, Studi in onore di Massimo Bogianckino* (Florence, 1993), pp. 177–95.

33 '*La cantilena, ossia la melodia, è l'anima della musica . . . La cantilena è alla musica ciò che alla pittura è il disegno. . . . Dove non v'è cantilena non v'è pensiero*', *Carpani (1812), pp. 33, 38 and 39.

34 Ibid., pp. 129 and 181–2.

35 '*Se l'Haydn nel dipingere le passioni e gli affetti fosse stato quell'uomo che era nel dipingere le immagini e le cose, egli sarebbe insieme il Raffaele, il Tiziano e il Michelangelo della pittura musicale*', ibid., pp. 218–19.

36 Cf. Heidrich (1997), note 7.

37 Similarly on the frontispieces of *La Plume* towards the end of the century.

38 *Stendhal (1815), pp. 73–4.

39 Helmut C. Jacobs, 'Musik, Bild, Text – Stendhals literarische Visualisierung von Musik', in Stendhal, *Image et texte*, ed. Sybil Dümchen and Michael Nerlich (Tübingen, 1994), pp. 145–57, and Chris Rauseo, 'Das musikalische Malen. Stendhals klangliche Bildvermittlung', ibid., pp. 158–64.

40 *Mauclair (1902), p. 301. This is clearly in reaction to the traditional association of Beethoven with 'descriptive' music, on the basis of his Pastoral Symphony.

41 *Stendhal (1829), p. 634.

42 Dahlhaus (1978).

43 Ernst H. Gombrich, 'Expression and Communication', in *Meditations on a Hobby Horse* (London, 1963), pp. 56–69; see also his *Art and Illusion* (London, 1959), p. 314.

44 Gombrich, 'Expression and Communication', p. 457.

45 Umberto Eco, 'How Culture Conditions the Colours We See', in *On Signs*, ed. Marshall Blonsky (Baltimore, MD, 1985), pp. 157–75.

46 Georges Roque, 'La symbolique des couleurs est-elle arbitraire?', in *La vie nous en fait voir de toutes les couleurs* (Lausanne, 1998), pp. 145–59.

47 Staehelin (1977). See also *Salmen* (1988), and *Freiburger Universitätsblätter*, XXXVI, 136, pp. 43–56, Jung-Kaiser (2003), pp. 11–26.

48 *Rochlitz (1799–1801), pp. 641–53.

49 *Berlioz (1862), p. 84.

50 Eugène Delacroix, 'Questions sur le beau' (1854), in *Écrits sur l'art* (Paris, 1988), pp. 24–5.

51 *Mauclair (1928), pp. 137–43, 'La Messe en ré (Beethoven et Michel-Ange)' links the two artists through the notions of the tragic and the overweening; in *La vie de Beethoven* (Paris, 1929), p. 331, Edouard Herriot sees in both figures 'the same physical and spiritual pain . . . , the same fate', and compares the Ninth Symphony to the Sistine Chapel.

52 Heinrich Heine, *Lutezia* I, 20 April 1841, in *Historisch-kritische Gesamtausgabe*, XIII, ed. Manfred Windfuhr (Hamburg, 1988), p. 125. For another comparison between the 'demon' Liszt and the 'angel' Chopin, cf. Jean-Jacques Eigeldinger, *Chopin vu par ses élèves* (Neuchâtel, 1983), p. 372.

53 If we exclude the *Vie de Mozart* (pp. 178 and 184), a text not by Stendhal, and translated from the German by Schlichtegroll. It compares Mozart and Raphael only on the basis of their shared fame and universality.

54 *Stendhal (1815), p. 377.

55 *Stendhal (1829), pp. 607–8. In his *Vie de Rossini*, Stendhal writes: 'It is due to the combination of these two qualities, the awe-inspiring and the delicately sensual, that Mozart is in a class of his own; Michelangelo is only awe-inspiring, and Correggio is only sensual.'

56 *Stendhal (1815), p. 200.

57 *Stendhal (1829), p. 170.

58 Ibid., pp. 232 and 527.

59 Ibid., p. 296.

60 Ibid., p. 390.

61 Ibid., p. 885.

62 *Stendhal (1815), p. 142, and *Carpani (1812), p. 204.

63 *Stendhal (1829), p. 635.

64 Ibid., p. 885.

65 *Stendhal (1815), p. 388. It should be noted that in the same period E.T.A. Hoffmann compared Beethoven with Shakespeare in his *Kreisleriana*, p. 39, and Hippolyte Taine linked Dante, Shakespeare, Beethoven and Michaelangelo in his *Voyage en Italie* [1865] 4th edn (Paris, 1914) I, p. 217.

66 *Stendhal (1815), p. 74.

67 Ricciotto Canudo, *Le Livre de l'Evolution – L'Homme* (Paris, 1907), pp. 303–4.

68 *Walzel (1917).

69 Alois Riegl, *Spätrömische Kunstindustrie* (Vienna, 1901).

70 Christophe Butler, *Early Modernism, Literature, Music and Painting in Europe* (Oxford, 1994), p. xv.

71 Sabatier (1998), p. 9.

8 Modern Variations on an Ancient Theme: The Music of the Spheres

1 Arnold Schönberg, 'Breslau lecture on *Die glückliche Hand*', 1928, in *Albèra (1995), pp. 203–8 (205).

2 Dahlhaus (1985); Oechslin (1985); Vergo (2005). For a general bibliography, cf. Paul von Naredi-Rainer, *Architektur und Harmonie. Zahl, Mass und Proportion in der abendländichen Baukunst* (Cologne, 1982, new edn 1995).

3 *Galilei (1581), p. 86.

4 Wittkower (1967); Onians (1984); Moyer (2008).

5 Weddigen (1984).

6 Pizzani (1987).

7 Plato, *Timaeus*, 36 d and *The Republic*, 616 d–617.

8 Cicero, *Somnium Scipionis*, 18–19. Cf. Karl Büchner, *Somnium Scipionis. Quellen, Gestalt, Sinn* (Wiesbaden, 1976), pp. 8–11 and 67–9.

9 Vitruvius, *De Architectura*, trans. Claude Perrault, *Les dix livres d'architecture* (2nd edn Paris, 1684; new edn Liège, 1996), book III, ch. 1 and book V, ch. 4. This French translation by Perrault was for many years the standard reference. English trans., *The Ten Books on Architecture*, trans. Morris Hicky Morgan (London, 1914).

10 Isabelle Marchesin, 'Cosmologie et musique au Moyen Âge', in *Moyen Âge entre ordre et désordre*, ed. Laurent Bayle et al. (Paris, 2004), pp. 29–35, 58 and 61ff.

11 *Gaffurio (1492), pp. 30–34.

12 Cornelius Agrippa de Nettesheim, *La philosophie occulte ou magie* [1533] (Paris, 1981–2), I, ch. XXVI.

13 *Zarlino (1573), pp. 7–8 and 16–17.

14 *Kepler (1619), V, ch. 5–8. Cf. P. D. Walker, 'Kepler's Celestial Music', *Journal of the Warburg Institute* (1967), pp. 228–50, and Stephenson (1994).

15 Peter J. Ammann, 'The Musical Theory and Philosophy of Robert Fludd', *Journal of the Warburg Institute* (1967), pp. 198–227.

16 *Kircher (1650). The whole of book X, pp. 364ff., is devoted to this theme, '*Caelestium corporum musica*', '*Musica mundana*', '*De harmonia stellarum*', '*De symfonismo planetarum*', and so on, on the basis of a recurrent metaphor: '*Mundus organo comparatur*'.

17 *Mersenne (1636), pp 103ff. *et passim* often quotes Galileo, and discusses astronomy and music together.

18 Dante Alighieri, *Purgatorio*, XXX, 92, and *Paradiso*, XXVIII, 94 and 118.

19 William Shakespeare, *Merchant of Venice*, V, 1, v. 54–65, and *Twelfth Night*, III, 1.

20 John Milton, *Paradise Lost*, V, 166ff. and 620ff.

21 Mozart wrote a *Serenata dramatica* in the style of Metastasio entitled the *Sogno du Scipione* (KV (Köchel Verzeichnis) 126).

22 Hans Kayser, *Akroasis. die Lehre von der Harmonik der Welt* [1946] (Basel, 1976). For the history of this theme, cf. Charles de Tolnay, 'The Music of the Universe', *Journal of the Walters Art Gallery*, VI (1943), pp. 83–104; Heinrich Hüschen, 'Harmonie', in *Die Musik in Geschichte und Gegenwart* [1956] (Munich, 1989), V, 1588–1614; Fritz Stege, *Musik, Magie, Mystik* (Remagen, 1961), ch. II; Leo Spitzer, *Classical and Christian Ideas of World Harmony: Prolegomena to an Interpretation of the Word 'Stimmung'* (Baltimore, MD, 1963); James Haar, 'Pythagorean Harmony of the Universe', in *Dictionary of the History of Ideas*, V (New York, 1973), IV, pp. 38–42; Mirimonde (1977); Kathi Meyer-Baer, *Music of the Spheres and the Dance of Death*,

Studies in Musical Iconology (Princeton, NJ, 1979); Hans Schavernoch, *Die Harmonie der Sphären. Die Geschichte der Idee des Welteneinklangs und der Seeleneinstimmung* (Freiburg and Munich, 1981); Jean Pépin, 'Harmonie der Sphären', *Reallexikon für Antike und Christentum*, XIII (1986), pp. 593–618; Joscelyn Godwin, *Harmonies of Heaven and Earth* (London, 1987); Joscelyn Godwin, *The Harmony of the Spheres: A Source Book of the Pythagorean Tradition in Music* (Rochester, NY, 1993); Martine Clouzot, 'Les anges musiciens aux XIV–XVe siècles, figuration et idéalisation du cosmos divin', in *Les méthodes de l'interprétation de l'image*, ed. Andrea von Hülsen-Esch and
Jean-Claude Schmitt (Göttingen, 2002), pp. 493–528 (503ff.).

23 The concentric organization of the world can be found as late as Dürer, in a woodcut for the *Schedelsche Weltchronik*, rpt. in *Dürer, Holbein, Grünewald, Meisterzeichnungen der deutschen Renaissance* (Basel, 1997), pp. 96–7.

24 Farago (1992).

25 Philippe Verdier, 'L'iconographie des arts libéraux dans l'art du moyen âge jusqu'à la fin du XVe siècle', in *Arts libéraux et philosophie au moyen âge* (Paris, 1969), pp. 305–55.

26 André Linzeler, *Inventaire du Fonds français de la B.N. Graveurs du XVIe s.* (Paris, 1932), pp. 296–7.

27 See, for example, an anonymous Italian miniature (*c.* 1350, Vienna, Nationalbibliothek, Cod. S.n.2639, fol. 4), or another miniature, by Niccolò da Bologna (*c.* 1375, Milan, Ambrosiana, Ms. B.42, fol. 1).

28 Plato, *The Republic*, VII, 530d.

29 Simone Bergmans, 'Le triptyque des sept arts libéraux des Musées royaux des Beaux-Arts', *Bulletin MRBAB*, XIII, no. 3–4, pp. 169–85. The same symmetry between Music and Astronomy can be found in a Venetian engraving from the sixteenth century representing 'the Children of Mercury', reproduced in Mirimonde (1977), p. 51.

30 Reproduced in Valentin Vermeersch, *Musiques et sons* (Bruges, 1990), p. 38.

31 Mario Giuseppe Genesi, 'Il dittico allegorico astrologico-musicale di Jan Soens nella Pinacoteca del Museo Civico di Piacenza', *RidIM Newsletter*, XVII/2 (1992), pp. 22–30.

32 Pierre Boyancé, 'Les Muses et l'harmonie des sphères', in *Mélanges Félix Grat* (Paris, 1946), I, pp. 3–16; Franz Cumont, *Recherches sur le symbolisme funéraire des Romains* [1942] (Paris, 1966), pp. 258ff.; Marie Thérèse d'Alverny, 'Les Muses et les sphères célestes', in *Classical, Mediaeval and Renaissance Studies in Honor of B. L. Ullman* (Rome, 1964), II, pp. 7–19. Bernardo Buontalenti illustrated this theme in his stage set for the first of the interludes of Bastiano de' Rossi's *La Pellegrina*, cf. James S. Saslow, *The Medici Wedding of 1589* (London and New Haven, CT, 1996), pp. 198–9.

33 See the painting by Jacques Stella, *Minerva with the Muses*, reproduced in Gilles Chomer and Sylvain Laveissière, *Autour de Poussin* (Paris, 1994), no. 24.

34 Albert Pomme de Mirimonde, 'L'Hélicon ou la visite de Minerve aux Muses',

Jaarboek Koninklijk Museum voor Schone Kunsten Antwerpen (Antwerp, 1961), pp. 141–50, and 'Les concerts des Muses chez les maîtres du Nord', *Gazette des Beaux-Arts* (March 1964), pp. 129–58.

35 Reproduced in Tilman Seebass, *Musikdarstellung und Psalterillustration im früheren Mittelalter* (Bern, 1973), II, p. 82.

36 Reproduced in the catalogue of the exhibition *I Farnese. Arte e collezionismo* (Milan, 1995), p. 443 and in George Francis Hill, *A Corpus of Medals of the Renaissance Before Cellini* (London, 1930), nos 340–42 and pl. 55.

37 Reproduced in *RidIM Newsletter*, XVIII/2 (1993), p. 62.

38 Philippe Morel et al., *La chambre des Muses* (Rome, 1995), p. 43.

39 Kristen Lippincott et al., *The Story of Time* (London, 2000), p. 178.

40 Cesare Ripa, *Iconologia* [Padua 1618] (Turin, 1986), II, p. 71: '*Donna giovane à sedere sopra una palla di color celeste*'.

41 Emmanuel Winternitz, *Gaudenzio Ferrari and the Early History of the Violin* (Varallo Sesia, 1967), pp. 11ff.

42 Maria De Angelis, 'Un maestro del Seicento lombardo: Isidoro Bianchi', *Nos monuments d'art et d'histoire*, no. 4 (1989), pp. 446–8.

43 Charles Hope, 'The Ceiling Paintings in the Libreria Marciana', in *Nuovi studi su P. Veronese*, ed. Massimo Gemin (Venice, 1990), p. 297.

44 Reproduced in Mirimonde (1977), p. 108. See also, by the same M. de Vos, the frontispiece *Boni et mali scientia* (1583), reproduced in Friedrich Hollstein, *Dutch and Flemish Etchings, Engravings and Woodcuts, 1450–1700* (Rotterdam, 1996), XLV/25.

45 Bini (2000), pp. 150 and 156.

46 The tutor has been identified by Jaynie Anderson as Nicolo Leonico Tomeo, the translator of Ptolemy, *Giorgione, peintre de la brièveté poétique* (Paris, 1996), p. 145. The case of the frieze in the Casa Marta-Pellizzari at Castelfranco, whose attribution to Giorgione is contested, remains problematic. Terisio Pignatti's interpretation of it as a representation of the liberal and mechanical arts – *Giorgione* (London, 1971), no. 16 – has been refuted by Annalisa Perissa Torrini (*Giorgione* (Paris, 1993), pp. 12–14), Jaynie Anderson (*Giorgione, peintre de la brièveté poétique*, pp. 324–5) and Simona Cohen ('Virtuousness and Wisdom in the Giorgionesque Fresco of Castelfranco', *Gazette des Beaux-arts* (July–August 1996), pp. 1–20). Augusto Gentili accepts this interpretation and proposes another one, in relation to a contemporary poem by Aurelio Augurello: 'The Castelgandolfo Frieze: The Great Conjunction of 1503 / 1504 and the Decline of the Arts', in Sylvia Ferino-Pagden et al., *Giorgione: Myth and Enigma* (Milan, 2004), pp. 124–31. Regardless of its authorship, we are interested here in the fact that the frieze shows numerous attributes of music and astronomy.

47 Gian Casper Bott, *Stilleben*, Braunschweig: Herzog Anton Ulrich-Museum (1996), p. 48.

48   Michèle-Caroline Heck, *Sébastien Stoskopff, 1597–1657, un maître de la nature morte* (Strasbourg, 1997), nos 16 and 28.

49   Cf. *Evaristo Baschenis e la natura morta in Europa* (Bergamo, 1996), pp. 41, 193, 195, 207, 245, 253, 263, 265 and 271. On the harmony of the spheres cf. also Bott (1997), pp. 19ff. and 67.

50   There are many examples of this, particularly in Dutch still-lifes. E. de Jongh, in a commentary on Collier's *Vanitas* (Leiden Museum), in which a terrestrial and a celestial globe are juxtaposed with musical instruments, writes that 'Beyond this obvious antithesis, it remains unclear what Edward Collier intended to express in his painted globes, in particular the celestial globe', *Still-life in the Age of Rembrandt* (Auckland, 1982), p. 201. But why should the symbolism of the music of the spheres be incompatible with that of a *Vanitas*?

51   Alessandro Vezzosi, *Il giardino d'Europa. Pratolino come mondo nella cultura europea* (Florence, 1986).

52   Cf. Buijsen (1994), p. 98.

53   A manuscript held at the *Archives musicales de la Bilbiothèque Cantonale et Universitaire* at Lausanne.

54   See also *Dénéréaz (1926), pp. 39–69.

55   *Boschini (1660), pp. 323 ff and 752ff.

56   Ripa, *Iconologia*, I, pp. 52–3.

57   Cf. John Gage, 'Newton and Painting', in Martin Pollock et al., *Common Denominators in Art and Science* (Aberdeen, 1983), pp. 16–25. Newton also plays an important role because of his theorization of the laws of motion. In a homage to him painted between 1785 and 1795, Januarius Zick represents him next to a sphere, presiding over a concert of the Muses. Cf. Brigitte Reinhardt et al., *Januarius Zick und sein Wirken in Oberschwaben* (Munich, 1993), p. 119.

58   Cumont, *Recherches*, pp. 18–19.

59   Cf. for example Romano Micheli's canon in the *Dialogus annuntiationis* (1625), reproduced in *Cinque secoli di Stampa musicale in Europa* (Naples, 1985), p. 79.

60   *Castel (1740), pp. 165, 299 and 478.

61   *Tartini (1754), pp. 88ff. and 389–93.

62   Francis Webb, *Panharmonicon*, 1814, reproduced in John Gage, *Colour and Culture* (London, 1993), p. 234.

63   Cf. Dieter Bogner, 'Zwei Formthemen. Johannes Itten und Joseph Matthias Hauer', in *Johannes Itten* (Zurich and Vienna, 1988), pp. 72–9.

64   Cf. Friedrich H. Dahlberg, *Blicke eines Tonkünstlers in die Musik der Geister* (Mannheim, 1787), quoted by Bandmann (1960), pp. 134–5.

65   Louis-Claude de Saint-Martin, *L'homme de désir* (1790), in *Oeuvres majeures*, vol. III (Hildesheim, 1980), ch. 46, p. 100.

66   Nicolas Perot, 'Un mythe littéraire. l'harmonie des sphères célestes', in *Discours sur la musique à l'époque de Chateaubriand* (Paris, 2000), pp. 104–13.

67 Alphonse de Lamartine, 'La voix humaine', in *Harmonies poétiques et religieuses*, ed. Jean Guillaume and Claude Pichols [1830] (Paris, 1922), pp. 308–11.

68 Gérard de Nerval, *Aurélia*, II, VI, in *Oeuvres complètes*, ed. Jean Guillaume and Claude Pichols (Paris, 1993), III, p. 740.

69 '*Ce sourd entendait l'infini. Penché sur l'ombre, mystérieux voyant de la musique, attentif aux sphères, cette harmonie zodiacale que Platon affirmait, Beethoven l'a notée*', Victor Hugo, *William Shakespeare* (1864), ed. Bernard Leuillot (Paris, 1973), p. 479. Referring to Palestrina, Hugo writes of the 'muddled stammering of the spheres' in his poem '*Que la musique date du XVIe siècle*' ('That music dates from the sixteenth century') (*Oeuvres poétiques*, I (Paris, 1964), p. 1101), and of the 'musical mystery of the heavens' in 'Usefulness of the Beautiful' ('*Utilité du Beau*') (*Oeuvres complètes*, ed. Jean Massin (Paris, 1969), XII, p. 364).

70 *Berlioz (2001), p. 249 (to Humbert Ferrand, 26 April 1865).

71 Georges Clémenceau, *Claude Monet. Les Nymphéas* (Paris, 1928), p. 1000.

72 Thomas Mann, *Doktor Faustus. Das Leben des deutschen Tonsetzers Adrian Leverkühn, erzählt von einem Freund* [1947] (Stockholm, 1948), pp. 423–4 and 577–8, writes of 'cosmic music, *Symphonia cosmologica*, an orchestral portrait of the universe, a cosmos of sounds, a cosmic music of the spheres'.

73 'Fragmente und Studien' (1799) in *Novalis (1977–88), III, p. 515. See also Ludwig Schrader, *Sinne und Sinnesverknüpfungen. Studien und Materialen zur Vorgeschichte der Synästhesie und zur Bewertung der Sinne in der italienischen, spanischen und französischen Literatur* (Heidelberg, Winter 1969), pp. 190–93.

74 *A. W. Schlegel (1801–2), *Die Kunstlehre*, pp. 217–18.

75 *Schelling (1802–3), p. 983: 'The whole system of music is expressed even in the solar system' ('*Auch im Sonnensystem drückt sich das ganze System der Musik aus*').

76 'this wonderful music, the poetry of the heavens' ('*diese wunderliche Musik die der Himmel heute dichtet*'). Ludwig Tieck, *Franz Sternbalds Wanderungen. Eine altdeutsche Geschichte* (1798), in *L. Tiecks Schriften* (Berlin, 1843), XVI, p. 302.

77 Wilhelm Heinrich Wackenroder and Ludwig Tieck, *Phantasien über Kunst für Freunde der Kunst* (1799), in *Werke und Briefe* (Munich and Vienna, 1984), p. 295: 'Our thirsting imagination hopes one day to encounter a song of the spheres more unearthly and sublime than the art of this world, which is primitive and clumsy by comparison' ('*Die wollustige Phantasie hofft, einst einen noch höheren überirdischen Gesang der Sphären anzutreffen, gegen den alle hiesige Kunst roh und unbeholfen ist*').

78 *Rochlitz (1800), p. 386.

79 *Hoffmann (1814–15), p. 36. See also *Hoffmann (1985), p. 39.

80 *Schopenhauer (1819), §52.

81 Rudolf Steiner, *Theosophie. Einführung in übersinnliche Welterkenntnis und Menschenbestimmung* [1904] (Stuttgart, 1962), p. 88.

82 Cf. Schawelka (1993), pp. 205 and 216.

83   Corinne Heline, *Color and Music in the New Age* (Marina del Rey, CA, 1964), ch. I *et passim*. See also Sophie Duplaix, 'Om / Ohm ou les avatars de la musique des sphères', in *Sons et lumières* (Paris, 2004), pp. 91–101.

84   Robert Delaunay, *Du cubisme à l'art abstrait* (Paris, 1957), p. 178.

85   For example, in 1923 (Philadelphia, Museum of Fine Arts), 1926 (New York, Guggenheim Museum) and 1927 (coll. Norton Simon).

86   *MacDonald-Wright (1924), p. 17, and in David W. Scott, *The Art of S. MacDonald-Wright* (Washington, DC, 1967). See also Will South et al., *Color, Myth and Music: S. MacDonald-Wright and Synchromism* (Raleigh, NC, 2001).

87   The increase, in the years 1910–30, of compositions relating to the cosmos, and based on the circle or the sphere, is striking. See for example Alexander Scriabin, Vladimir Baranov-Rossiné, Louis Survage, Franz Marc, August Macke, Giacomo Balla, Thomas Hart Benton, Jean Crotti, Max Ernst, Oskar Fischinger, and so on. For the cosmos as an inspiration for twentieth-century artists, cf. Jean Clair, ed., *Cosmos: From Goya to De Chirico, Art in the Pursuit of the Infinite* (Venice and Milan, 2000).

88   *Albert Trachsel, 1863–1929* (Geneva, 1985), p. 27.

89   Judita Grigiene, ed., *Mikalojus Konstantinas Čiurlionis* (Vilnius, 1984); *M. K. Čiurlionis, 1875–1911* (Paris, 2001), pp. 168ff.

90   *Johannes Itten, Künstler und Lehrer* (Bern, 1984), p. 62.

91   André Breton, *Signe ascendant* (Paris, 1968), p. 167.

92   Interview by James J. Sweeney (1948), quoted in *André Breton. La beauté convulsive* (Paris, 1991), p. 181.

93   Jean-Christophe Ammann, ed., *Robert Strübin (1897–1965). Musik und Farbe* (Lucerne, 1970), and *Robert Strübon, Musik sehen, Bilder hören* (Basel, 2010).

94   Reproduced in Matthias Winzen et al., *Einerseits der Sterne wegen . . . Der Künstlerblick auf die Planeten* (Baden-Baden, 1999), p. 22.

95   Trinh Xuan Thuan, *La Mélodie secrète* (Paris, 1988).

96   Jean-Marie Guyau, *Les problèmes de l'esthétique contemporaine* (Paris, 1913), p. 192.

97   Marie Jaëll, *L'intelligence et le rythme dans les mouvements artistiques* (Paris, 1904), p. 120.

98   Victor Segalen, *Dans un monde sonore* [1906] (Fontfroide, 1985), p. 39.

99   Santeri Levas, *Sibelius: A Personal Portrait* (London, 1972), p. 39.

100   Henri Louis de la Grange, *G. Mahler* (Paris, 1984), III, p. 684. See also his letter to Mengelberg, in August 1906.

101   *Scriabin (1979), p. 35.

102   *Busoni (1910), p. 57.

103   Wassily Kandinsky, 'Über die Formfrage' (1912), in *Essays über Kunst und Künstler* (Bern, 1955), p. 40. See also Ringbom (1970).

104   *Kandinsky (1913–18), p. 116.

105 An article of 1929 quoted by Laurent Guido, 'Le Dr. Ramain, théoricien du musicalisme', *Mille huit cent quatre-vingt-quinze*, no. 38 (October 2002), pp. 67–100 (78).

106 *Menschen finden ihren Maler. Texte, Bilder und Graphiken von Mopp* (Zurich, 1938), p. 43.

107 *Messiaen (1986), p. 183.

108 Joseph Matthias Hauer, *Vom Wesen des Musikalischen* (Leipzig and Vienna, 1920); see also *L'essence du musical. Du melos à la timbale, technique dodécaphonique*, ed. Alain Fourchotte (Nice, 2000), p. 6.

109 Paul Hindemith, *A Composer's World* (Cambridge, MA, 1952), frequently refers to Boethius and the *musica mundana*. Cf. Florence Malhomme, 'Hindemith et le concept pythagoricien de *l'harmonie du monde*: fondement d'une esthétique', *Ostinato rigore, Revue internationale d'études musicales*, nos 6/7 (1995/6), pp. 135–45.

110 Cf. Jacques Viret, 'Frank Martin et Paul Hindemith. Convergences de deux démarches créatrices', *Revue musicale de Suisse romande* (September 1988), pp. 102–12.

111 Hans Haug, 'Considérations sur l'harmonie naturelle des sons', unpublished lecture, typed manuscript in the *Archives musicales de la BCU*, Lausanne.

112 Quoted by Stege, *Musik, Magie, Mystik*, pp. 164–5.

113 Albert Wellek, 'Das Doppelempfinden in der Geistesgeschichte', *Zeitschrift für Ästhetik*, XXIII (1929), pp. 32–3, and 'Renaissance und Barock-Synästhesie', *DVfLG*, IX (1931), pp. 534–84; Ludwig Schrader, *Sinne und Sinnesverknüpfungen. Studien und Materialen zur Vorgeschichte der Synästhesie und zur Bewertung der Sinne in der italienischen, spanischen und französischen Literatur* (Heidelberg, Winter 1969), ch. VII; and Lawrence E. Marks, *The Unity of the Senses: Interrelations among the Modalities* (London, 1978), p. 248.

114 *D'Udine (1929), p. 71.

115 *Blanc-Gatti (1934), p. 66. See also pp. 141–5.

116 Galeyev (1976).

117 *Klangkunst* (Berlin, 1996), p. 74 (Robert Jacobsen, *Solarharp – wie die Sonne klingen könnte*, 1989) and p. 89 (Bernhard Leitner, *Firmament*, 1996).

118 Henri Stierlin, ed., *L'art de Karl Gerstner* (Paris, 1981), p. 168.

119 Hélène and Nicolas Calas, *Takis. Monographies* (Paris, 1984), p. 211. Lista (2005), p. 189, sees in the works of Takis and Len Lye 'a profound reinterpretation of the music of the spheres'.

120 Cf. Jean Clair, ed., *Cosmos: From Romanticism to the Avant-garde* (Montreal, 1999), p. 283.

121 Maurice Tuchman et al., *The Spiritual in Art: Abstract Painting, 1890–1985* (Los Angeles, CA, 1986); see also the special issue of *Art Journal* (Spring 1987): 'Mysticism and Occultism in Modern Art'.

122 Spitzer, *Classical and Christian Ideas*, p. 138.

9 A Survey of Architecture and Music

1   François René de Chateaubriand, *Mémoires d'Outre-Tombe*, II, ch. 7 (Paris, 1988), I, p. 70.

2   James A. Murray seems to be the first to broach this topic, 'Parallels in Music and Architecture', *Journal of the Royal Architectural Institute of Canada*, XXXIII (1956), pp. 99–102. For more recent studies, cf. Vergo (2005); Vasco Zara, 'Musica e Architettura tra Medio Evo e Età moderna. Storia critica di un' idea', *Acta musicologica*, LXXXVII (2005), pp. 1–27; 'Da Palladio a Wittkower. Questioni di metodo, di indagine e di discipline nello studio dei rapporti tra musica e architettura', in Nicoletta Guidobaldi, ed., *Prospettive di iconografia musicale* (Milan, 2007), pp. 153–90; 'Musique et architecture: théories, composition, théologie (XIIIe–XVIIe siècles)', *Bulletin du centre d'études médiévales d'Auxerre*, no. 11 (2007), pp. 1–9; '"Componere ad quadratum". Metafore letterarie e processi compositivi nell'analogia musica-architettura', in *I Luoghi e la Musica*, ed. Fabrizio Pezzopane (Rome, 2010), pp. 101–16. See also Sabine Rommevaux, Philippe Vendrix and Vasco Zara, 'Proportions. Arts, architecture, musique, mathématiques et sciences', ibid., 12 (2008), http://cem.revues.org/document7302.html – A much shorter version of this chapter was published in *Art + Architecture en Suisse*, no. 3 (2009), pp. 6–12.

3   Philostratus, *Imagines* (London, 1969), pp. 41–5. Another source is Apollodorus, *La Bibliothèque. Un manuel antique de mytholologie*, ed. Paul Schubert (Lausanne, 2003), p. 140.

4   Joshua, 6. Athanasius Kircher considers this episode at length: *Musurgia universalis sive ars magna consoni et dissoni* (Rome, 1650), II, pp. 231–2.

5   Cf. Paul Valéry, 'Histoire d'Amphion' (1932), in *Pièces sur l'art*, in *Oeuvres*, ed. Jean Hytier (Paris, 1960), II, pp. 1277–83.

6   *Wie von Apollos Leier aufgefordet*
    Bewegt, zu Mauern, das Gestein sich her
    Und wie zu Orpheus Zaubertönen eilt
    Ein Wald heran und bildet sich zum Tempel,
    Johann Wolfgang Goethe, *Was wir bringen*, in *Sämtliche Werke* (Frankfurt, 1993), VI, p. 298.

7   Johann Wolfgang von Goethe, *Maximen und Reflexionen*, no. 776, in *Schriften zur Kunst*, 6th edn (Hamburg, 1967), p. 474. In other editions this text has the number 1133. On the shift from Amphion to Orpheus, cf. Herbert von Einem, 'Man denke sich den Orpheus. Goethes Reflexion über die Architektur als verstummte Tonkunst', *Jahrbuch des Wiener Goethe-Vereins*, LXXXI–LXXXIII (1977–9), pp. 91–113. These two heroes are frequently cited together as an example of the powers of music. Cf. for example Jean Benjamin de la Borde, *Essai sur la musique ancienne et moderne* (Paris, 1780), I, p. 27, and III, p. 76.

8 *A. W. Schlegel, *Vorlesungen, Die Kunstlehre* (1801–2), Kritische Ausgabe E. Behler (Paderborn, 1989), p. 317.

9 Paul Valéry, *Eupalinos ou l'architecte* (1923) (Paris, 1944), p. 57.

10 One can find this cliché even in J. A. Murray, 'Parallels in Music and Architecture', who associates the Parthenon with Bach, whereas Beethoven is associated with Roman architecture.

11 Joan Miró, *Ecrits et entretiens*, ed. Margit Rowell (Paris, 1995), p. 163.

12 Daniel Henri Kahnweiler, *Juan Gris. Sa vie, son oeuvre, ses écrits*, 4th edn (Paris, 1946), p. 214.

13 Théophile Gautier, *Voyage en Russie* (Paris, 1867), pp. 327–8.

14 Oswald Spengler, *Der Untergang des Abendlandes. Umrisse einer Morphologie der Weltgeschichte* (Munich, 1921). Spengler also wrote that in the eighteenth century, 'architecture drowns in rococo music'!

15 Paul Valéry, 'Paradoxe sur l'architecte' (1891), in *L'âme et la danse, Eupalinos* (Paris, 1931), pp. 193–8 (196).

16 Interview with A. Varga Balint, in *Ligeti / Kurtag, Contrechamps*, no. 12–13 (1990), p. 180.

17 Wolfgang Pehnt, 'Verstummte Tonkunst, Musik und Architektur in der neueren Architekturgeschichte', in *Vom Klang der Bilder,* ed. K. Von Maur (Munich, pp. 394–9); Gerd Zimmermann, 'Architektur ist gefrorene Musik', in Ingeborg Stein et al., *Raum und Zeit. Beiträge zur Analyse von Musikprozessen* (Iena, 1988), pp. 124–32.

18 Germaine de Staël, *Corinne* (1807), ed. Simone Balayé (Paris, 2000), p. 75. On setting eyes on the cathedral of St Peter's the heroine exclaims that 'The sight of such a monument is like an unceasing yet fixed music.'

19 *Arthur Schopenhauer, *Die Welt als Wille und Vorstellung* (1819) (Darmstadt, 1980), II, §39, p. 582, calls this formula a *Witzwort* (a joke, a quip) and finds the analogy between music and architecture to be superficial. For him, the two arts are poles apart (p. 581). See also I, § 52, p. 357.

20 Charles Blanc-Gatti, *Sons et couleurs* (Neuchâtel, 1958) 2nd edn, pp. 26 and 53; Hugh Honour, *Romanticism* (Harmondsworth, 1979), p. 119.

21 *Schelling (1802–5) (Darmstadt, 1990), p. 220. The § 106–17 have a long section on architecture described as 'concrete music'.

22 Igor Stravinsky, *Chroniques de ma vie* (1935) (Paris, 1962), p. 64.

23 Byron, cited by Erika von Ehrhardt-Siebold, 'Harmony of the Senses in English, German and French Romanticism', PMLA, XLVII (1932), pp. 577–92 (587).

24 Colin Davies, *Hopkins 2* (London, 2001).

25 Moritz Hauptman, *Die Natur der Harmonik und der Metrik. Zur Theorie der Musik* (Leipzig, 1853); Iannis Xenakis, *Musique de l'architecture* (Marseilles, 2006), p. 79.

26 Goethe, *Entretiens avec Eckermann*, 23 March 1829.

27   *Italienische Reise*, September 1787, in *Goethes Werke* (Hamburg, 1967), XI, p. 408. For an analysis of these terms, cf. Takeo Ashizu, 'Die Architektur als verstummte Musik', *Goethe-Jahrbuch* (Goethe-Gesellschaft in Japan), XI (1998), pp. 7–19.

28   Friedrich Weinbrenner, *Architektonisches Lehrbuch, Dritter Theil: Über die höhere Baukunst* (Tübingen, 1819).

29   Giorgio Vasari, 'Bramante da Urbino', in *Le Vite* [1568] (Florence, 1906), IV, p. 164: 'volentieri udiva e diceva improviso in su la lira'.

30   Eva Börsch-Supan, 'Die Bedeutung der Musik im Werke K .F. Schinkels', *Zeitschrift für Kunstgeschichte*, no. 34 (1971), pp. 257–95.

31   This is a much-debated case. Cf. among others Anne-Marie Mathy, 'La consécration de la cathédrale de Florence par le pape Eugène IV', in *Musica e arti figurative*, ed. Giulio Einaudi (Turin, 1968), pp. 87–108; Charles W. Warren, 'Brunelleschi's Dome and Dufay's Motet', *The Musical Quarterly* (January 1973), pp. 92–105; Hans Ryschawy and Rolf W. Stoll, 'Die Bedeutung der Zahl in Dufays Kompositionsart: *Nuper rosarum flores*', *Musik-Konzepte*, no. 60 (April 1988), pp. 3–73; Craig Wright, 'Dufay's *Nuper rosarum flores*, King Solomon's Temple, and the Veneration of the Virgin', *Journal of the American Musicological Society*, XLVII/3 (1994), pp. 395–441; Marvin Trachtenberg, 'Architecture and Music Reunited: A New Reading of Dufay's *Nuper Rosarum Flores* and the Cathedral of Florence', *Renaissance Quarterly*, LIV/3 (2001), pp. 740–75; Vergo (2005), pp. 163–70.

32   Laura Meretti, 'Architectural Spaces for Music: Jacopo Sansovino and Adrian Willaert at St Mark's', *Early Music History*, XXIII (2004), pp. 153–84.

33   Wilton Mason, 'The Architecture of St Mark's Cathedral and the Venetian Polychoral Style: A Clarification', in J. W. Pruett, *Studies in Musicology: Essays in the History, Style and Bibliography of Music* [1969] (Westport, CT, 1976), pp. 163–78; Vergo (2005), pp. 170–77.

34   Girolamo Diruta, *Il Transilvano, Dialogo* [Venice, 1593] (Netherlands, 1983), p. 36.

35   See for example Michael Fowler, 'Reading John Cage's *Variations III* as a Process for Generating Proto-architectural Form', *Leonardo*, XLIII (2012), pp. 35–41.

36   Jehanne Dautrey et al., '*Musique, Architecture*', in *Rue Descartes*, no. 56 (2007). See also Helga de la Motte-Haber, ed., *Klangkunst. Tönende Objekte und klingende Räume* (Laaber, 1999) and Carlotta Darò, *Avant-gardes sonores en architecture* (Paris, 2013).

37   Séverine Bridoux-Michel, 'Architecture et musique: une rencontre utopique?', *Archistorm*, no. 22 (November–December 2006), pp. 54–5.

38   Michael Forsyth, *Buildings for Music: The Architect, the Musician and the Listener from the XVIIth Century to the Present Day* (Cambridge, 1985); Hans Ulrich Glogau, *Der Konzertsaal. Zur Struktur alter und neuer Konzerthäuser* (Hildesheim, 1989); Leo Beranek, *Concert Halls and Opera Houses: Music, Acoustics and Architecture* [1996] (New York, 2004); Daniel E. Commins, 'L'acoustique des salles de concert' (2002), in *Musiques. Une encyclopédie pour le XXIème siècle*, vol. II,

Les savoirs musicaux, ed. Jean-Jacques Nattiez (Paris, 2004), pp. 1149–82; Michel Mauge, ed., *Konzerthäuser* (Mannheim, 2012). See also Ernst Lichtenhahn, 'Musik und Raum. Gesellschaftliche und ästhetische Perspektiven zur Situation um 1800', in *Musik und Raum Vier Kongressbeiträge und ein Seminarbericht,* ed. Marietta Morawska-Büngeler (Mainz, 1989), pp. 8–19; Chantal Bauer et al., 'Musique et architecture', *Monuments historiques,* no. 175 (Paris 1991), pp. 2–104; Sabine von Fischer, 'Mysterien und Messungen. Das Problem der Objektivierung von Klang beim Bauen für Musik', *Art + Architecture en Suisse,* no. 3 (2009), pp. 20–26; and Birgit Schmolke, *Theatres and Concert Halls* (Berlin, 2011).

39   Andrea Petrilli, *Acustica e architettura. Spazio, suono, armonia in Le Corbusier* (Venice, 2001).

40   Jean-Philippe Rameau, *Code de musique pratique* (Paris, 1760). The compass is also mentioned on p. 237.

41   Peter Zumthor, *Penser l'architecture* (2006) (Basel, 2008), pp. 66, 10 and 11.

42   Cesare Cesariano, *Vitruvius de architectura* [Como 1521] (Munich, 1969), p. 77 *et passim.*

43   Le Corbusier, *Le Modulor* [1950] (Boulogne, 1954), p. 76.

44   Franchinus Gaffurius, *The Theory of Music*, trans. W. K. Kreyszig (New Haven, CT, 1993), p. 28.

45   Ibid.

46   Jean-Philippe Rameau, *Lettre à Bernoulli* of 27 April 1750, and *Observations sur notre instinct pour la musique et sur son principe* (1754), in *Musique raisonnée*, texts chosen and presented by C. Kintzler and J.-C. Malgoire (Paris, 1980), pp. 115 and 149.

47   Pierre Boulez et al., *Oeuvre: fragment* (Paris, 2008), p. 46 (on the Guggenheim Museum's ascending spiral).

48   Vergo (2005), pp. 128–9.

49   Cf. Anthony Beaumont, *Busoni the Composer* (Bloomington, IN, 1985), pl. 34.

50   Joseph Matthias Hauer, *L'essence du musical. Du melos à la timbale. Technique dodécaphonique* (Nice, 2000), p. 119.

51   Felix Meyer and Heidy Zimmermann, *Edgar Varèse Komponist, Klangforscher, Visionär* (Basel and Mainz, 2006), pp. 310–12.

52   Eugène Viollet-le-Duc, *Entretiens sur l'architecture* [1858–72] (Brussels, 1977), I, p. 12. See also pp. 19–20, 22, 28 and 134.

53   Luca Pacioli, *De divina proportione* (1509), ch. III.

54   Marie-Pauline Martin, 'Die Allegorien der Musik und der Architektur im *Discours préliminaire* und im Frontispiz der *Encyclopédie*', in *Druckgraphik zwischen Reproduktion und Invention* (Berlin and Munich, 2010), pp. 93–104; Théodora Psychoyou, 'Entre les arts libéraux et les beaux-arts: le *Cabinet des beaux Arts* de Charles Perrault (1690) et la fortune disciplinaire de la musique', in *La musique face au système des arts, ou les vissicitudes de l'imitation au Siècle des Lumières,* ed. M. P. Martin and Ch. Savettieri (Paris, 2013), pp. 29–44; and M. P. Martin, 'Le *Cabinet des*

Beaux-arts de Charles Perrault: le monument d'un moderne', *Revue de l'art*, CXC/4 (2015), pp. 9–18.

55 Marin Mersenne, *Traité de l'harmonie universelle* [1617] (Paris, 2003), p. 338.

56 Plato, *Timaeus*, 35 b–36 b.

57 Aristotle, *De Anima*, III, 2, 426 b.

58 On the influence of Ptolemy, cf. Bruce Stephenson, *The Music of the Heavens: Kepler's Harmonic Astronomy* (Princeton, NJ, 1994), pp. 32ff. and 102ff.

59 Boethius, *De instittUione musica*, I, x. All these figures are mentioned by Cesariano, *Vitruvius*, alongside Orpheus, Apollo and the Muses, and Martianus Capella.

60 Cf. Georg Germann, *Vitruve et le vitruvianisme. Introduction à la théorie architecturale* [1991] (Lausanne, 2016).

61 Peter Legh, *The Music of the Eye; or, Essays on the Vitruvian Analysis of Architecture, or, Essays on the Principles of the Beauty and Perfection of Architecture, as founded on and deduced from Reason and Analogy, and adapted to what may be traced of the Ancient Theory of Taste, in the three first Chapters of Vitruviu*s (London, 1831).

62 Rudolf Wittkower, 'The Problem of Harmonic Proportion in Architecture', in *Architectural Principles in the Age of Humanism* (London, 1967), pp. 101–66.

63 Franco Borsi, 'Note sulle proporzioni musicali nell'architettura del Rinascimento', in *Musica e arti figurative, Quaderni della Rassegna musicale*, no. 4 (Turin, 1968), pp. 85–95.

64 John Onians, 'How to Listen to High Renaissance Art', *Art History*, no. 4 (1984), pp. 411–37.

65 Paul Naredi-Rainer, *Architektur und Harmonie. Zahl, Mass und Proportion in der abendländischen Baukunst* [1982], 5th edn (Cologne, 1995); 'Musiktheorie und Architektur', in *Ideen zu einer Geschichte der Musiktheorie* (Darmstadt, 1985), pp. 149–76; 'Joh. Bernhard Fischer von Erlach und Joseph Fuchs. – Beziehungen zwischen Architektur und Musik', *Jahrbuch des Kunsthistorischen Instituts der Univ. Graz*, XXV (1993), pp. 275–90.

66 George L. Hersey, *Architecture and Geometry in the Age of Baroque* (Chicago, IL, 2000) – particularly ch. II, 'Frozen Music', pp. 22–51.

67 See also Barbara Barthelmes, 'Polyphonie der Proportionen. Zum Verhältnis von Architektur und Musik in der Renaissance', *Musica* (March–April 1985), pp. 129–36, and Anne E. Moyer, 'Music, Mathematics and Aesthetics: The Case of the Visual Arts in the Renaissance', in *Music and Mathematics in Late Medieval and Early Modern Europe,* ed. Philippe Vendrix (Turnhout, 2008), pp. 114–46.

68 '*ritrovare el modo de' murari ecellenti e di grandi artificio degli antichi e le loro proporzioni musicali'*, in Antonio di Tuccio Manetti, *Vita di Brunelleschi*, a cura di Carlachiara Perrone (Rome, 1992), p. 64. See also Leonardo Benevolo, 'Indagine sul S. Spirito di Brunelleschi', *Quaderni dell'Istituto di storia dell'architettura di Roma*, no. 85–90 (1968), pp. 1–52 (17): '*La teoria delle proporzioni armoniche – appresa da Paolo Toscanelli o anche solo dai testi che circolavano allora a Firenze*

– è stata applicata all'architettura solo per quel tanto che serviva a mettere ordine nel sistema tradizionale di quotazione, senza perdere di vista il contatto con la realtà costrutiva.'

69 Leon Battista Alberti, *De re aedificatoria: On the Art of Building in Ten Books*, trans. Joseph Rykwert, Robert Tavernor and Neil Leach (Cambridge, MA, 1988) (Book IX, ch. V). On Alberti's numerical and musical aesthetic, cf. Paul-Henri Michel, 'L'esthétique arithmétique du Quattrocento: une application des médiétés pythagoriciennes à l'esthétique architecturale', in *Mélanges offerts à Henri Hauvette* (Paris, 1934), pp. 181–9, and Paul Naredi-Rainer, 'Musikalische Proportionen, Zahlenästhetik und Zahlensymbolik im architektonischen Werk L. B. Albertis', *Jahrbuch des Kunsthistorischen Instituts der Univ. Graz*, XII (1977), pp. 81–213.

70 Letter of November 1454, published by Corrado Ricci, *Il Tempio malatestiano* (Milan, 1974), p. 587.

71 '*In questa facciata non son compartite le finestre d'eguale distanza . . . ma è una discordia concordante: come ancora avviene nella musica: percioche il Soprano, il Contrabasso, & il Tenore, & il Contralto, che acconcia il tutto, paiono discordi uno dall'altro nelle voci . . . per la bellissima arte del compositore, fanno quella grata armonia all'orecchie*', in Sebastiano Serlio, *Tutte l'opere d'architettura e prospettiva* [Venice, 1619] (Farnborough, 1964), p. 168.

72 Francesco di Giorgio Martini, *Trattati di architettura, ingegneria e arte militare* [*c.* 1470–92] (Milan, 1967), I, pp. 37–8.

73 Jacopo de' Barbari, 'De la ecelentia de pitura', in *Scritti d'arte del Cinquecento*, ed. Paola Barocchi (Milan, 1971), I, p. 67.

74 Philibert de l'Orme, *Le premier tome de l'architecture* (Paris, 1568), fol. 1v and 10v–11r. Philibert de l'Orme explicitly extended the question of acoustics to music, in order that 'speech and voice resonate and be heard . . . something required by Temples and Churches for the preaching that takes place there, and for the psalms and other things sung there.'

75 Gioseffo Zarlino, *Istitutioni harmoniche* (Venice, 1573), p. 8.

76 Vitruvius I, i and v, iii, trans. Claude Perrault [Paris, 1684] (Liège, 1996), pp. 6 and 158.

77 Valéry, *Eupalinos*, p. 39.

78 For examples, cf. 'Fonctions de l'analogie musicale dans les théories picturales', in *Contrepoints*, pp. 19–32.

79 Cesariano, *Vitruvius*, book v, ch. lv.

80 '*Questa bella maniera sì nella musica, come nell'architettura è detta eurithmia . . . Similmente è nella citara . . . come nel cantare . . . come adviene a quei musici . . .*', Daniele Barbaro, *Vitruvio. I dieci libri dell'architettura tradotti e commentati* [1567] (Milan, 1983), p. 53. See also pp. 14, 18–19 and 227–43.

81 'the architect . . . exactly like a musician, [seeks] to make the whole building harmonious and in pleasing proportions': Francesco Colonna, *Hypnerotomachia Poliphili* (Venice, 1499).

82 Cesare Vasoli, 'Il tema musicale e architettonico della "*Harmonia mundi*" da Francesco Giorgio Veneto all'Accademia degli Uranici e a Gioseffo Zarlino', *Musica e storia*, VI, no. 1 (1998), pp. 193–210.

83 Cf. F. Alberto Gallo, 'La musica nel commento a Vitruvio in C. Cesariano (Como, 1521) e G. B. Caporali (Perugia, 1536)', in *Arte e musica in Umbria tra Cinquecento e Seicento* (Perugia, 1981), pp. 89–92.

84 Erik Forssman, *Visible Harmony: Palladio's Villa Foscari at Malcontenta* (Stockholm, 1973). R. Wittkower's analysis ('The Problem of Harmonic Proportion', see note 62, pp. 126ff.) provoked some debate. Cf. Eugenio Battisti, 'Un tentativo di analisi strutturale del Palladio tramite le teorie musicali del Cinquecento e l'impiego di figure rettoriche', *Bollettino del Centro Internazionale di Studi di Architettura A. Palladio*, XV (1973), pp. 211–32; Deborah Howard and Malcolm Longair, 'Harmonic Proportion and Palladio's Quattro Libri', *Journal of the Society of Architectural Historians*, XLI/2 (March 1982), pp. 116–24; and Branko Mitrovic, 'Palladio's Theory of Proportions and the Second Book of the *Quattro libri dell'architecttura*', ibid., XL/3 (1990), pp. 279–92.

85 Sabina Sanchez de Enciso, 'Música y arquitectura en el "De postrema Ezechielis prophetae visione" de J. B. Villalpando', *Cuadernos de Música Iberoamericana*, XV (2008), pp. 7–40.

86 Cf. Ann E. Moyer, *Musica Scientia: Musical Scholarship in the Italian Renaissance* (Ithaca, NY, 1992), and Vergo (2005), ch. IV.

87 Charles Etienne Briseux, *Traité du beau essentiel dans les arts . . . avec un traité des proportions harmoniques* [Paris, 1752] (Geneva, 1974). Cf. Marie-Pauline Martin, 'L'analogie des proportions architecturales et musicales: évolution d'une stratégie', in D. Rabreau and D. Massounie, *Claude Nicolas Ledoux et le livre d'architecture français* (Paris, 2006), pp. 40–47.

88 La Font de Saint-Yenne, 'Remarques sur ce qui est dit de l'Architecture dans l'Esprit des beaux Arts' (1753), in *Oeuvre critique*, ed. E. Jollet (Paris, 2001), pp. 266–74 (270–72). The text is concerned with a polemic against Laugier.

89 Werner Oechslin, 'Musik und Harmonie: Universalien der Architektur. Versuche der Annäherung', *Daidalos*, no. 17 (1985), pp. 59–73.

90 Nicolas Le Camus de Mézières, *Le génie de l'architecture ou l'analogie de cet art avec nos sensations* [Paris, 1780] (Geneva, 1972), p. 11.

91 Denis Diderot, 'L'origine et la nature du Beau' (1752), in *Oeuvres esthétiques*, ed. Paul Vernière (Paris, 1959), p. 419.

92 François Blondel, *Cours d'architecture,* 2nd edn (Paris, 1698), pp. 756–8. On René Ouvrard and his *Architecture harmonique* (Paris, 1679), cf. Philippe Vendrix, 'Proportions harmoniques et proportions architecturales dans la théorie française des XVIIe et XVIIIe siècles', *International Review of the Aesthetics and Sociology of Music*, XX/1 (June 1989), pp. 3–10, and Vasco Zara, 'Dall' *Hypnerotomachia Poliphili* al Tempio di Salomone: modelli architettonico-musicali nell' *Architecture*

harmonique di René Ouvrard, 1679', in *Migration, mutation, métamorphose: la réception des modèles 'cinquecenteschi' dans l'art français du XVIIe siècle,* ed. Sabine Frommel and Flaminia Bardati (Paris, 2009), pp. 131–56. A new edition of Ouvrard's *Architecture harmonique*, presented by Vasca Zara, is in preparation.

93 Andrea Palladio, *I quattro libri dell'architettura* (Venice, 1570), English trans., *The Four Books on Architecture*, trans. Richard Schofield and Robert Tavernor (Cambridge, MA, 1997).

94 Blondel, *Cours d'architecture*, pp. 759–60. For a detailed analysis of this mathematical demonstration, cf. Hersey, *Architecture and Geometry in the Age of Baroque*, pp. 37–41, and Vasco Zara's refutation, 'Suono e carattere della base attica. Itinerari semantici d'una metafora musicale nel linguaggio architettonico francese del Settecento', *Musica e Storia*, XV/2 (2007) (Actes du Colloque "Nuove fonti per l'estetica musicale", Venice, 2006), pp. 443–74.

95 Charles Perrault, *Parallèle des Anciens et des Modernes en ce qui regarde les arts et les sciences* [Paris, 1692], 2nd edn (Geneva, 1971), p. 136. Bernin de Saint-Hilarion has a similar refutation, cf. Maria Luisa Scalvini and Sergio Villari, 'Il manoscritto sulle proporzioni di François Bernin de Saint-Hilarion', *Aesthetica preprint*, no. 42 (1994).

96 On the polemic between Ouvrard and Claude Perrault, cf. Philippe Vendrix, 'L'augustinisme musical en France', *Revue de musicologie*, LXXVIII/2 (1992), pp. 250–54. And on the link between the two debates, Vasco Zara, 'Antichi e Moderni tra Musica e Architettura. All'origine della Querelle des Anciens et des Modernes', *Intersezioni, Rivista di storia delle idee*, XXVI/1 (April 2006), pp. 191–210.

97 Cf. C. Vasoli, 'Il tema musicale e architettonico . . .'.

98 Jean-Philippe Rameau, 'Nouvelles réflexions sur le principe sonore', in *Code de musique pratique*, p. 189.

99 Cf. Stephenson (1994) and Vergo (2005), pp. 57ff. and 179ff.

100 For an interpretation of the frontispiece of the *Templum Musicae*, cf. Peter J. Ammann, 'Musical Theory and Philosophy of Robert Fludd', *Journal of the Warburg Institute*, XXX (1967) pp. 198–227 (205–6). And for the controversy with Kepler, pp. 110ff.

101 *Schlegel (1801–2; *Vorlesungen*), p. 366.

102 Rameau, *Musique raisonnée*, p. 50.

103 Valéry, *Eupalinos*, p. 56.

104 *Fausto Melotti: L'art du contrepoint* (Antibes and Milan, 1992), p. 21.

105 This classical doctrine of the three styles comes from Cicero, *Orator*, 69–74 and 100.

106 Cf. Yves Pauwels, '*Harmonia est discordia concors*: le modèle musical dans l'architecture des temps modernes', in *L'harmonie*, ed. Christophe Charraud (Orléans, 2000), pp. 313–25 (319).

107 Erik Forssman, *Dorisch, Jonisch, Korinthisch. Studien über den Gebrauch der Säulenordnungen in der Architektur des 16.–18. Jh.* (Uppsala, 1961), p. 13; John Onians, *Bearers of Meaning: The Classical Orders in Antiquity, the Middle Ages and the Renaissance* (Princeton, NJ, 1988), pp. 36–40 and pp. 208ff.; see also Ann

E. Moyer, 'Music, Mathematics and Aesthetics: The Case of the Visual Arts in the Renaissance', in *Music and Mathematics in Late Medieval and Early Modern Europe*, ed. Philippe Vendrix (Turnhout, 2008), pp. 114–46.

108 Letter to Chantelou of 24 November 1647, in Nicolas Poussin, *Lettres et propos sur l'art* (Paris, 1964), pp. 123–4. Cf. Jan Bialostocki, 'Das Modusproblem in den bildenden Künsten' (1961), in *Stil und Ikonographie. Studien zur Kunstwissenschaft* (Cologne, 1981), pp. 12–42, Vergo (2005), pp. 64–8 and 199–212, and Vasco Zara, 'Modes musicaux et ordres d'architecture: migration d'un modèle sémantique dans l'œuvre de Nicolas Poussin', *Musique – Images – Instruments, Revue française d'organologie et d'iconographie musicale*, x (2008), pp. 62–79.

109 David J. Buch, 'The Coordination of the Text, Illustration, Music in a xviith-cent. Lute Manuscript: *La Rhétorique des Dieux*', *Imago Musicae*, vi (1989), pp. 39–81 (57 and fig. 9) and Vergo (2005), pp. 212–15.

110 Cf. Vergo (2005), p. 90.

111 Cf. Moyer, 'Music, Mathematics and Aesthetics', pp. 111–46 (126–7).

112 '*In qual maniera le Harmonie si accommodino alle soggette Parole*', and '*ogni cosa sia fatta con proportione*', Gioseffo Zarlino, *Istitutioni Harmoniche* (Venice, 1558) part iv, ch. 32, p. 339.

113 Pierre Caye, 'Eurythmie et *Temperantia*. Du modèle musical au modèle architectural de la *Politeia*', in *Musikè et Areté. La musique et l'éthique de l'Antiquité à l'Âge moderne*, ed. F. Malhomme and A. G. Wersinger (Paris, 2007), pp. 167–74. See also Vergo (2005), pp. 126ff. and 147ff.

114 Adolphe Appia, *Oeuvres complètes* (Lausanne, 1986), ii, pp. 105–10 and 300–327. See also Jörg Zutter, 'La musique rendue visible', in *Adolphe Appia ou le renouveau de l'esthétique théâtrale* (Lausanne, 1992), pp. 109–22.

115 Albert Pfrimmer, *Compte rendu du Ier Congrès du rythme* (Geneva, 1926).

116 Moisei Yakovlevich Ginzburg, *Rhythm in Architecture* (1923); rpt 2016.

117 Yves Pauwels, *L'architecture au temps de la Pléiade* (Paris, 2002), pp. 100–103.

118 *Schelling (1802–3/1990) pp. 234–5 (590–91).

119 Heinrich von Geymüller, *Die Baukunst der Renaissance in Frankreich* (Stuttgart, 1898–1901), pp. 384–93 and 666.

120 *Schopenhauer (1818/1982), ii, p. 527. In a note, ii, p. 581, he nevertheless conceded that time can play a role in painting and sculpture, but he does not mention architecture.

121 Cf. Georg Germann, 'Espace et spatialité', in *Aux origines du patrimoine bâti* (Gollion, 2016), pp. 117–48. On the issue of the spectator's movement, cf. Etienne Gilson, *Matières et formes. Poétiques particulières des arts majeurs* (Paris, 1964), pp. 58–9: '*l'architecture se marche, mais ne marche pas*', whereas '*la symphonie ne se parcourt pas, elle court*'. For other reflections on the comparison between music and architecture, cf. pp. 51 and 72–5.

122 '[Swann] s'en représentait l'étendue, les groupements symétriques, la graphie, la valeur expressive; il avait devant lui cette chose qui n'est plus de la musique pure, qui est du

dessin, de l'architecture, de la pensée, et qui permet de se rappeler la musique', Marcel
Proust, 'Du côté de chez Swann' (1917), À la recherche du temps perdu (Paris, 1963), I,
p. 209. English trans., 'Swann's Way' [vol. 1 of Remembrance of Things Past],
trans. C. K. Scott Moncrieff (New York, 1922).

123 Charles Baudelaire, 'Richard Wagner et Tannhäuser à Paris' (1861), in Oeuvres
complètes (Paris, 1976), II, pp. 784–5.

124 Spengler, Der Untergang des Abendlandes, p. 365.

125 Peter Zumthor, Atmospheres: Architectural Environments (Basel, 2006),
pp. 41 and 29.

126 Thüring Bräm, ed., Musik und Raum (Basel, 1986); Jean-Marc Chouvel and Makis
Solomos, ed., L'espace: Musique / Philosophie (Paris, 1998).

127 Chevalier de Chastellux, 'Idéal', in Supplément à l'Encyclopédie ou dictionnaire
raisonné des sciences, arts et métiers, III [Amsterdam, 1777] (Stuttgart, 1967),
pp. 516–17; Michel Paul Guy de Chabanon, Observations sur la musique et
principalement sur la métaphysique de l'art [Paris, 1779] (Geneva, 1969), p. 167.

128 *Schopenhauer (1818), I, p. 368 and II, pp. 574–6.

129 Frantisek Kupka, Creation in the Plastic Arts (Liverpool, 2002). Clark V. Poling,
Kandinsky's Teaching at the Bauhaus (1986), and Punkt und Linie zu Fläche [1926]
(Bern, 1973), p. 14.

130 Ben Nicholson, 'Notes on "Abstract" Art', in Herbert Read, Ben Nicholson: Paintings,
Reliefs, Drawings, 2nd edn (London, 1955), p. 27.

131 Le Corbusier, Modulor, p. 29.

132 Patrick Moser and Erling Mandelmann, Le photographe, le musicien et l'architecte
(Vevey, 2010).

133 The work was a Sonata for solo violin, and the typography was composed with the
help of the Modulor.

134 Peter Bienz, 'Vom "poetischen Schock" zum "akustischen Wunder"', Georges-Bloch-
Jahrbuch, 5 (1998), pp. 201–10.

135 Le Corbusier, Modulor 2 (La parole est aux usagers) (Boulogne, 1955), pp. 266, 300,
334.

136 Le Corbusier, Les carnets de la recherche patiente, no. 2 (Zurich, 1957), p. 47.

137 Le Corbusier, Chapelle Notre Dame du Haut à Ronchamp (Paris, 1957), p. 27. See also
Le Corbusier ou la synthèse des arts (Geneva, 2006), and Peter Bienz, Le Corbusier
und die Musik (Braunschweig and Wiesbaden, 1999).

138 Le Corbusier, Vers une architecture (Paris, 1923), p. 175. In order to challenge how
architecture is reduced to a purely utilitarian function, Le Corbusier also referred to
painting and poetry. On the history of this debate, cf. Claire J. Farago, Leonardo da
Vinci's Paragone: A Critical Interpretation with a New Edition of the Text in the Codex
Urbinas (Leiden, 1992).

139 *Schelling (1990), pp. 219–24 (575–80).

140 Le Corbusier, Modulor, pp. 16, 131 and 29.

141   Le Corbusier, *Précisions sur l'état présent de l'architecture* [Paris, 1930] (Paris, 1994), p. 12.

142   Iannis Xenakis, 'Préface', in *Le Corbusier, Le couvent de la Tourette*, ed. S. Ferro et al. (Marseilles, 1987), p. 5, rpt. in *Musique de l'architecture*, p. 120. A conference on 'Music and Architecture' was organized at Sainte Marie de La Tourette in October 2008.

143   Le Corbusier, Xenakis, Varèse et al., *Le poème électronique* (Paris, 1958). See also Karen Michels, 'Le Corbusier: Poème Electronique. Die Synthese der Künste im Philips Pavillon der Weltaustellung Brüssel 1958', *Idea, Jhb. der Hamburger Kunsthalle*, IV (1985), pp. 147–63; Bart Lootsma, 'Poème électronique: Le Corbusier, Xenakis, Varèse', in *Le Corbusier, Synthèse des arts, Aspekte des Spätwerks* (Karlsruhe, 1986), pp. 111–47; Gisela Baurmann and Georg Weckwerth, 'Klang und Baukunst', in *Klangkunst* (Berlin and Munich, 1996), pp. 226–9. On the origins of this project: Bienz, 'Le Poème électronique', pp. 97ff., and Séverine Bridoux-Michel, 'Musique, architecture, un projet multimédia: le Pavillon Philips de l'Exposition internationale de 1958', in Roberto Barbanti et al., *Musiques, arts, technologies. Pour une approche critique* (Paris, 2004), pp. 91–103, and 'E. Varèse et Le Corbusier . . . à la conquête des temps modernes', in Timothée Horodyski and Philippe Lalitte, *Edgar Varèse. Du son organisé aux arts audio* (Paris, 2008), pp. 279–92.

144   Iannis Xenakis, 'Notes sur un "geste électronique"' (1958), in *Musique de l'architecture*, pp. 197–202.

145   '*eine abstrakte malerische phantastisch-musikalische Dichtung mit Chören, eine Komposition für alle drei Künste zusammen, wofür die Baukunst ein eigenes Gebäude aufführen sollte*', Philipp Otto Runge, letter to his brother 22 February 1803, in *Hinterlassene Schriften* (Göttingen, 1965), II, p. 20.

10 *Magister Dixit*, or the History of a Misunderstanding

1   Aristotle himself does not seem to have mentioned how many feet his spiders had. Only Pliny (*Natural History*, XI) sometimes gives them six. On this subject, cf. Steier, 'Spinnentiere', in *Paulys Real-Encyclopädie der klassischen Altertumswissenschaft* (Stuttgart, 1929), t. 27, col. 1786–1812 (1787).

2   Charles Perrault, *Parallèle des anciens et des modernes* (Paris, 1688), p. 64.

3   The great *Augustinus-Lexikon*, ed. Cornelius Mayer (Basel, 1986–94), II, pp. 433–41, does not mention the term; the reader goes straight from *Arbor* to *Archium*. Nor does the word figure in David Lenfant's *Concordantiae Augustinianae sive collectio sententiarum quae sparsim reperiuntur* (Paris, 1666), where *aedificare* and its cognates are taken in a purely theological sense. Architecture is also absent from the encyclopaedia edited by Allen D. Fitzgerald, *Augustine through the Ages* (Grand Rapids, MI, 1999).

4   Tanja Ledoux, 'Geometria e Musica: Sant'Agostino e una personificazione tardo medievale', *Prospettiva*, no. 45 (April 1986), pp. 75–8.

5   Dominique Iogna-Prat, *La Maison Dieu. Une histoire monumentale de l'église au moyen age* (Paris, 2006), p. 36.

6   Martianus Capella, *De nuptiis philologiae et mercurii*, IX, 891. Cf. Ilsetraut Hadot, who shows that for Augustine, architecture could not be counted among the *disciplinae*, in *Arts libéraux et philosophie dans la pensée antique: contribution à l'histoire de l'éducation et de la culture dans l'antiquité* (Paris, 2005), pp. 176, 407 and 474.

7   Gabriele Frings, 'Dosso Dossi's Allegorie der Musik und die Tradition des *inventor musicae* im Mittelalter und Renaissance', *Imago musicae*, XI/XII (1992–5), pp. 156–203 (171–2).

8   Philippe Vendrix, 'L'augustinisme musical en France au XVIIe siècle', *Revue de musicologie*, LXXVIII (1992), pp. 237–55.

9   Otto von Simson, *The Gothic Cathedral: Origins of Gothic Architecture and the Medieval Concept of Order* (New York, 1956). The work was reprinted in 1962, and the German translation had three reprints. It consequently enjoyed a wide circulation. For a critique of Simson, cf. Vergo (2005) ch. III: 'Gothic Architecture and Polyphony'.

10 Augustine, *De ordine*, II, 40–42.

11 Augustine, *De libero arbitrio*, II, XVI, 42.

12 Augustine, *De musica*, VI, XIII, 38.

13 Herbert von Einem, 'Man denke sich den Orpheus. Goethes Reflexion über die Architektur als vestummte Tonkunst', *Jahrbuch des Wiener Goethe-Vereins*, LXXXI–LXXXIII (1977–9), pp. 91–113 (97–8).

14 Georg Germann, *Einführung in die Geschichte der Architekturtheorie* (Darmstadt, 1980), p. 31.

15 Karen Michels, 'Le Corbusier: Poème Electronique. Die Synthese der Künste im Philips Pavillon der Weltaustellung Brüssel 1958', *Idea, Jhb. der Hamburger Kunsthalle*, IV (1985), pp. 147–63 (162, note 1).

16 Ledoux, 'Geometria e Musica', p. 76.

17 Ulrike Steinhauser, 'Musik und Architektur', in *MGG: Die Musik in Geschichte und Gegenwart. Allgemeine Enzyklopädie der Musik* (Kassel, 1997), VI, col. 729–45 (730).

18 Vasco Zara, 'Musica e Architettura tra Medio Evo e Età Moderna. Storia Critica di un' idea', *Acta musicologica*, LXXXXVII (2006), p. 19, and 'Musique et Architecture: théories, composition, théologie (XIIIe–XVIIe siècles)', *Bulletin du centre d'études médiévales d'Auxerre* [online], XI (2007), p. 1, http://cem.revues.org/index1178.html

19 Wilhelm Perpeet, *Aesthetik im Mittelalter* (Freiburg, 1977), p. 40.

20 Naredi-Rainer (1985), pp. 149–76 (172).

21 Ibid., p. 37.

11 The Paradox of Music with Sculpture

1 'In den entgegengesetzten Extremen von Geist und Materie . . . die Plastik durch Körper, die Poesie durch Gedanken darstellt', *Schlegel [1802] (Paderborn, 1989), p. 273.

2 Germaine de Staël, De l'Allemagne [1813] (Paris, 1959), III, p. 360.

3 Vincent van Gogh, August 1888, letter 528, in Correspondance générale (Paris, 1990), III, p. 270.

4 Paul Valéry, Eupalinos ou l'architecte [1923] (Paris, 1944), p. 57.

5 'Innere Vergeistigung des Menschen' (Ernst Theodor Amadeus Hoffmann, 'Alte und neue Kirchenmusik') (1814), in Sämtliche Werke (Frankfurt, 1993), II, pp. 503–31 (505 and 506).

6 *Hegel (1976), III, p. 140.

7 *Carus (1835), pp. 81–3.

8 Heinrich Heine, 'Chronicle of 20 April 1841', in Lutèzia (Paris, 1892), pp. 185–6.

9 Eugène Delacroix, 'Des variations du Beau' (1857), in Écrits sur l'art (Paris, 1988), pp. 33–49, 43.

10 *Wyzewa (1895), pp. 16–19.

11 Oswald Spengler, Der Untergang des Abendlandes. Umrisse einer Morphologie der Weltgeschichte (Munich, 1921), vol. I, ch. IV, paragraphs 16, 15 and 4. English trans., Oswald Spengler, The Decline of the West, ed. Arthur Helps and Helmut Werner, trans. Charles F. Atkinson (New York, 1991).

12 *Schelling (1990), ch. II, D, 1, c) a). English trans., The Philosophy of Art, trans. Douglas W. Stott (Minneapolis, MN, 1989).

13 Anton Hanak, 'Aber lässt sich Musik versteinern?', quoted in Die Botschaft der Musik. 1000 Jahre Musik in Österreich, exh. cat. (Vienna and Milan, 1996), p. 273.

14 Charles Baudelaire, 'Salon de 1846', ch. XVI, 'Pourquoi la sculpture est ennuyeuse', and 'Salon de 1845', in Oeuvres complètes, ed. Claude Pichois (Paris, 1976), II, pp. 487–9 and 376.

15 Auguste Rodin, L'art, conversations selected by Paul Gsell [1911] (Paris, 1967), p. 126.

16 Alessandra Comini, The Changing Image of Beethoven: A Study in Mythmaking (New York, 1987).

17 Ibid., p. 189.

18 Stella Wega Mathieu, Max Klinger: Leben und Werk (Frankfurt, 1976), p. 96.

19 Claude Lapaire, Auguste de Niederhäusern-Rodo, 1863–1913, catalogue raisonné (Bern, 2001), nos 221 and 228.

20 Antoine Bourdelle, Cours et leçons à l'Académie de la Grande Chaumière (Paris, 2007), II, p. 29.

21 See Eleonora M. Beck, 'Revisiting Dufay's Saint-Anthony Mass and its Connection to Donatello's Altar of Saint Anthony of Padua', Music in Art, XXVI/1–2 (2001), pp. 5–19.

22 David Bindman and Malcolm Baker, Roubiliac and the Seventeenth-century Monument (New Haven, CT, 1995), pp. 65–6, 80 and 332–6.

23 Bouillon (1986), pp. 11ff.

24 See Mathieu, *Max Klinger*, p. 70. See also Helmut Loos, 'Max Klinger und das Bild des Komponisten', *Imago musicae*, XIII (1996), pp. 165–88.

25 Bruno Gaudichon, 'Une oeuvre manifeste du classicisme Art Déco, le monument à Claude Debussy', in *Joël et Jean Martel, sculpteurs, 1896–1966* (Paris, 1996), pp. 159–73.

26 Josef Danhauser also sculpted the bust placed imposingly on the piano, in his painting representing people enthralled by Liszt's playing (1840, Berlin).

27 *Danton Jeune. Caricatures et portraits de la société romantique*, exh. cat. (Paris, 1989), pp. 102–16.

28 Lapaire, *Auguste de Niederhäusern-Rodo*, nos 274 and 275.

29 Peter Meech, 'The Frog and the Star, the Role of Music in the Dramatic and Visual Works of Ernst Barlach', in *Literature and the Plastic Arts, 1880–1930*, ed. Ian Higgins (Edinburgh, 1973), pp. 24–34.

30 Johannes Langner, 'Figur und Saiteninstrument bei Picasso. Ein Bildthema im Kubismus', *Pantheon*, XL (1982), pp. 98–113.

31 Quoted by Alexandre Liberman, *Maîtres et ateliers* (Paris, 1989), p. 168.

32 Gérard Nicollet, 'Bernard et François Baschet', in *Les chercheurs de sons. Instruments inventés, machines musicales, sculptures et installations* (Paris, 2004), pp. 18–23.

33 This is Laurent Garcin's expression, *Traité du mélodrame* (Paris, 1772), p. 3.

34 See *Qu'est-ce que le musicalisme?*, exh. cat. (Paris, n.d.), pp. 120 and 137.

35 Hans Urs von Balthasar et al., *Albert Schilling* (Zurich, 1966), nos 55–6 and 96.

36 Michael Baumgartner, *Walter Linck, das plastische Werk* (Bern, 1994).

37 See Gabriele Frings, 'Dosso Dossis Allegorie der Musik und die Tradition des *inventor musicae* im Mittelalter und Renaissance', *Imago Musicae*, XI/XII (1992–5), pp. 156–203.

38 Pomponius Gauricus, *De sculptura* (1504), ed. André Chastel and Robert Klein (Geneva, 1969), paragraph 8, pp. 98–101.

39 Marcel Joray, *Soto* (Neuchâtel, 1984), p. 40.

40 Quoted by Marc Collet, 'Le domaine musical de Soto', in *Jesus Rafael Soto*, exh. cat. (Paris, 1997), pp. 33–8, quoted pp. 35–6.

41 *Fausto Melotti. L'art du contrepoint*, exh. cat. (Antibes and Milan, 1992), p. 21. See also Paolo Repetto, 'L'acrobata invisibile. Melotti e la musica', in *Visioni musicali. Rapporti tra musica e arti visive nel Novecento*, ed. Francesco Tedeschii and Paolo Bolpagni (Milan, 2009), pp. 135–40.

42 Ibid., pp. 105, 10 and 107.

43 Germano Celant, *Melotti. Catalogo generale* [1944] (Milan, n.d.).

44 Xavier Deryng and Anna Czamocka, *Biegas et la musique*, exh. cat. (Krakow, 2006).

45 Edith Balas's study, 'Brancusi and Bartok, a Parallel', *Imago musicae*, VI (1989), pp. 165–82, attempts to ground the sculpture–music comparison in objective elements, both biographical and structural.

46   See Von Maur (1985), pp. 452–64, and Fink (1988).

47   Claude Lapaire, *Statues de chair, sculptures de James Pradier, 1790–1852*, exh. cat. (Paris, 1985), pp. 345–46.

48   *Les Saint-Marceaux. Une famille d'artistes en 1900*, exh. cat. (Paris, 1992), pp. 62–90.

49   Wolff (1984), pp. 81–90.

50   Auguste de Lapaire, *Niederhäusern-Rodo*, pp. 207–9.

51   Joray, *Soto*, p. 36.

52   Jennifer Gonzales et al., *Christian Marclay* (New York, 2005).

53   See Bosseur (1992), p. 15.

54   Jean-Marc Chouvel and Laurent Golon, 'Le moteur du temps. Dialogue électroacoustique avec les sculptures sonores', in *Musique et arts plastiques, analogies et interférences*, ed. Michèle Barbe (Paris, 2006), pp. 241–7.

55   *Takis*, exh. cat. (Paris, 1993). See also Jewanski and Duchting (2009), pp. 362–4.

56   Jacques Remus, 'La sculpture sonore, pratique artistique et recherche de définition', in *Musiques, arts, technologie*, ed. Roberto Barbanti et al. (Paris, 2004), pp. 61–77.

57   Marcel Duchamp, *La boîte verte* [The Green Box] (1934), in *Duchamp du signe, écrits* (Paris, 1975), p. 47.

58   See *Klangskulpturen, Augenmusik. Grenzgänge zwischen Musik und Plastik im 20. Jh.*, exh. cat. (Koblenz, 1995); *Klangkunst* (Berlin, 1996); de la Motte-Haber (1999); Ulrich Tadday, ed., *Klangkunst* (Munich, 2008). See also Thüring Bräm et al., *Musik und Raum* (Basel, 1986).

59   Peter Becker and Peter Rautmann, 'Kann man eine Skulptur hören? Synesthetische Konzepte in der Musik der Gegenwart am Beispiel John Cage', in F. Schneider (2000), pp. 115–27.

60   Oscar Wiggli, *Partition forgée. Sculptures et compositions musicales* (Friburg, 1995).

61   *Oscar Wiggli, Corps-espace-son*, exh. cat. (Bern, 2007).

62   Hans Christoph von Tavel et al., *Arethusa* (Bern, 1986).

Coda

1   *Rousseau (1755), and *Dictionnaire de musique,* in *Oeuvres complètes*, v (Paris, 1995), p. 860.

2   Pierre Boulez, '. . . Auprès et au loin' (1954), in *Relevés d'apprenti* (Paris, 1966), p. 186.

3   *Premier Manifeste du surréalisme* (1924) [First Surrealist Manifesto], in *Breton (1988), p. 324.

4   Thomas von Hartmann, 'Über Anarchie in der Musik', in *Kandinsky and Marc (1912), pp. 88–94.

5   Kandinsky, 'Über die Formfrage', ibid., pp. 132–82 (147), and letter to Schönberg of 22 August 1912, *Albèra (1995), p. 174.

6   Conio (1990), p. 108.

7   Letter to Schönberg of 18 January 1911, in *Albèra (1995), pp. 135–6 and *Kandinsky (1911), p. 109, in which the principle of 'anti-logic' is associated with that of contrast or opposition (*Gegensatz*).

8   Lista (2001), p. 184.

9   Lista (1989), pp. 49 (pl. 24) and 146.

10 *Kandinsky (1911), pp. 118–19.

11 Gudrun Leffin, *Bildtitel und Bildlegenden bei Max Ernst* (Bern, 1988).

12 Letter to Mellerio, 21 July 1898, in *Redon (1923), pp. 30–32, and *Redon (1961), pp. 26–7. Cf. Douglas Druick et al., *O. Redon Prince of Dreams* (New York, 1994), pp. 263–6.

13 Arnold Schönberg, 'Das Verhältnis zum Text', in *Kandinsky and Marc (1912), pp. 60–75.

14 Philippe Beaussant, *La malscène* (Paris, 2005).

15 Cf. Lista (2006), p. 217.

16 See the musicologist Carl Dahlhaus's justified criticism of the commonplace assimilation of dissonance to abstraction in Dahlhaus, 1984.

17 '*Wer kann wissen, ob nicht der Genius Menschheit selbst zu einem grossen Kunstwerk verarbeitet und ordnet, worin auch Dissonanzen ihre Stelle finden müssen?*', *Schlegel (1801–2), p. 22.

18 *Kandinsky (1911), p. 49.

19 '*Die Ausdrücke Konsonanz und Dissonanz, die einen Gegensatz bezeichnen, sind falsch*', *Schönberg (1911), p. 18.

20 Balilla Pratella, *Manifeste des musiciens futuristes* (1911) [Manifesto of Futurist Musicians], in *Lista (1973), p. 309.

21 Etienne Pivert de Senancourt, *Obermann* [1804] (Paris, 1931), I, p. 147.

22 Marcel Proust, 'Noms de pays: le nom', in 'Du côté de chez Swann' (1917), *À la recherche du temps perdu*, ed. Pierre Clarac and André Ferré (Paris, 1954), I, pp. 383–427.

23 *Kandinsky (1911), pp. 108–9.

24 '. . . *dass scheinbares Divergieren an der Oberfläche nötig sein kann wegen eines Parallelgehens auf einer höheren Ebene*', Schönberg, 'Das Verhältnis zum Text', p. 65.

25 '*Schönberg geht von dem Prinzip aus, dass die Begriffe Konsonanz und Dissonanz überhaupt nicht existieren. Eine sogenannte Dissonanz ist nur eine weiter auseinanderliegende Konsonanz*', letter of 14 January 1911, in *Briefwechsel* (Cologne, 1964), p. 36.

26 Letter to Schönberg, 18 January 1911, *Albèra (1995), p. 135.

BIBLIOGRAPHY

Primary Sources

Albèra, Philippe, ed., *Schönberg – Busoni, Schönberg – Kandinsky. Correspondances, textes* (Geneva, 1995)

Alberti, Leon Battista, *De re aedificatoria: On the Art of Building in Ten Books*, trans. Joseph Rykwert, Robert Tavernor and Neil Leach (Cambridge, MA, 1988)

—, *On the Art of Building in Ten Books*, trans. Joseph Rykwert, Neil Leach and Robert Tavernor (Cambridge, MA, 1991)

André, Yves-Marie, *Discours VI*, in *Essai sur le Beau, nouvelle édition augmentée de six discours* (Paris, 1763)

Anschütz, Georg, ed., *Farbe-Ton-Forschungen*, I (Leipzig, 1927)

—, *Farbe-Ton-Forschungen*, III (Bericht über den II. Kongress, 1930), Hamburg, Psychologisch-ästhetische Forschungsgesellschaft, 1931

Apel, Johann August, 'Musik und Poesie', *Die allgemeine musikalische Zeitung* (1806)

Apollinaire, Guillaume, 'Du sujet dans la peinture moderne', *Soirées de Paris*, no. 1 (February 1912), in *Les peintres cubistes* [1913] (Geneva, 1950), pp. 13–16

—, 'L'esprit nouveau et les poètes' (1917), in *Oeuvres en prose complètes*, ed. P. Caizergues and M. Décaudin (Paris, 1991), II, pp. 943–54

Appia, Adolphe, *Oeuvres complètes* (Lausanne, 1987–92), 4 vols

—, *La musique et la mise en scène* [1892–97] (Bern, 1963)

Argelander, Annelies, *Das Farbenhören und der synästhetische Faktor der Wahrnehmung* (Jena, 1927)

Aristotle, *De sensu*, 439 b, trans J. I. Beare, *On Sense and the Sensible*, in *The Works of Aristotle*, vol. III, ed. W. D. Ross (London, 1931)

Artaud, Antonin, 'Letters on Language, second letter to J. P. Paris, September 28, 1932', in *The Theater and Its Double*, trans. Mary Caroline Richards (New York, 1958)

Bahr, Hermann, 'Colour Music', *Die Zeit*, IV/45 (1895), in Wunberg (1981), pp. 232–4

Balzac, Honoré de, *Seraphita* [1835], in *La Comédie humaine*, ed. Rolland Chollet (Lausanne, 1959), IX, pp. 147–298

—, *Gambara* [1837], ibid., X, pp. 479–545

Barocchi, Paola, ed., *Trattati d'arte del Cinquecento* (Bari, 1960–62), 3 vols

Baudelaire, Charles, *Salon de 1845*, in *Oeuvres complètes*, ed. Y.-G. Le Dantec (Paris, 1954), pp. 557–604

—, *Salon de 1846*, ibid., pp. 605–80

—, *Salon de 1859*, ibid., pp. 761–833

—, Lettre à Wagner, 17 November 1860, in *Oeuvres complètes*, II, ed. Claude Pichois, (Paris, 1976), pp. 1452–3

—, 'Richard Wagner et Tannhäuser' [1861], ibid., pp. 779–815

—, *His Prose and Poetry*, ed. T. R. Smith (New York, 1919)

—, *The Painter of Modern Life and Other Essays*, trans. Jonathan Mayne (New York, 1964)

Becker, Julius, 'Ideen über Malerei und Musik', *Neue Zeitschrift für Musik* (21 October 1840), pp. 129–31, and 24 October 1840, pp. 133–4

Bellia, Angela, *Scene musicali della ceramica attica in Sicilia (VI–IV BC)* (Roma, 2010)

Bellori, Giovan Pietro, *Le vite de' pittori, scultori e architetti moderni* [1672] (Turin, 1976)

Belmont, Ira Jean, *The Modern Dilemma in Art: The Reflections of a Color-Music Painter* (New York, 1944)

Berlioz, Hector, *A travers chants. Études musicales, boutades et critiques* [1862] (Paris, 1886, reissued, Farnborough, 1970)

—, *Correspondance générale*, VII (Paris, 2001)

Bernard, Émile, *Propos sur l'art* (Paris, 1994)

Besant, Annie and Charles Webster Leadbeater, 'Les formes construites par la musique', in *Thought-forms* (1905), trans. *Les formes-pensées* (Paris, 1925)

Binet, Afred, 'L'audition colorée', *Revue des deux mondes* (1 October 1892), pp. 586–614

Blanc-Gatti, Charles, *Sons et couleurs* [Paris, 1934], new expanded edn (Neuchâtel, 1958)

Boccioni, Umberto, 'La peinture des sons, des bruits et des odeurs', in *Dynamisme plastique* [1914], ed. G. Lista (Lausanne, 1973), pp. 103–7

Borghini, Vincenzo, 'Testimonianze sulla pittura e sulla scultura. Pittura, poesia e musica' [1564], in Paola Barocchi, *Pittura e scultura nel Cinquecento* (Livorno, 1998), pp. 116–22

Boschini, Marco, *La carta del navegar pitoresco* [1660], ed. Anna Pallucchini (Venice and Rome, 1966)

Boulez, Pierre, *Penser la musique aujourd'hui* (Paris, 1963)

—, *Relevés d'apprenti* (Paris, 1966)

—, *Le pays fertile. Paul Klee* (Paris, 1989)

—, 'Fragment: entre l'inachevé et le fini', in *Oeuvre; fragment* (Paris, 2008), pp. 9–16

Bourgogne, Gustave, 'La peinture musicale et son application aux *symphonies* de Beethoven', in *Le Courrier musical et théâtral*, 15 May, 15 June and 15 December 1932, 1 February 1933 and 15 December 1934

—, *La peinture musicale* (Paris, 1934)

Brand, Hans Bartolo, *Der Akkord- und Quintelzirkel in Farben und Tönen. Ein einfaches Gesetz der Farbenharmonie* (Munich, 1914)

Brès, 'Études de la nature appliquées aux arts dépendant du dessin', *Journal des artistes et des amateurs*, II (13 July 1828), pp. 17–22, 20 July, pp. 37–40 and 27 July, pp. 53–6

Breton, André, *Manifestos of Surrealism*, trans. Richard Seaver and Helen R. Lane (Ann Arbor, MI, 1969)

—, *What Is Surrealism?: Selected Writings*, ed. Franklin Rosemont (New York, 1978)

—, 'Surrealist Comet' (1947), in *Free Rein*, trans. Michel Parmentier and Jacqueline d'Amboise (Lincoln, NE, 1995)

—, *Oeuvres complètes* (Paris, 1988 and 1992)

Busoni, Ferruccio, 'Le royaume de la musique. Postface à la *Nouvelle esthétique*' (1910), in *L'esthétique musicale* (Paris, 1990)

Canudo, Ricciotto, 'Essai sur la musique comme religion de l'avenir', *La Renaissance contemporaine*, nos 22–3 (1911–12)

—, 'La convergence musicale de tous les arts', *Le Courrier musical* (15 April 1921), pp. 123–4

—, *Manifeste des Sept Arts* [1923] (Paris, 1995)

—, *L'usine aux images* [1927], ed. Jean-Paul Morel (Paris, 1995)

Carpani, Giuseppe, *Le Haydine, ovvero Lettere su la vita e le opere del celebre Maestro Giuseppe Haydn* (Milan, 1812; Padua, 1823; reprint Bologna, 1969)

Carrà, Carlo, *La peinture des sons, des bruits et odeurs* (1913), in *Lista (1973), pp. 182–6

Carus, Carl Gustav, *Briefe über die Landschaftsmalerei* [1835] (Heidelberg, 1972), pp. 81–3

Castel, Louis-Bertrand, 'Clavecin pour les yeux, avec l'art de peindre les sons, et toutes sortes de pièces de musique', *Mercure de France*, IX (November 1725), pp. 2552–77

—, *L'optique des couleurs* (Paris, 1740)

—, *Esprit, saillies et singularités* (Amsterdam, 1763)

Champfleury, *Grandes figures d'hier et d'aujourd'hui* [Paris, 1861] (Geneva, 1968)

Coleridge, Samuel Taylor, 'On the Principles of Genial Criticism Concerning the Fine Arts' (1814), in *Biographia Leteraria* (1817), II (Oxford, 1907), pp. 219–46

—, 'On Poesy or Art', ibid., pp. 253–63

Condillac, Etienne Bonnot de, *Essay on the Origin of Human Knowledge*, trans. and ed. Hans Aarsleff (Cambridge, MA, 2001)

Constable, John, *Discourses*, ed. R. Beckett (Suffolk Records Society, 1970)

Corradini, Bruno, *Musica cromatica* (1912), in Corra[dini], Bruno and Ginna, Arnaldo, *Manifesti futuristi e scritti teorici*, ed. Mario Verdone (Ravenna, 1984), pp. 155ff., trad. *Cinéma abstrait – Musique chromatique*, in *Lista (1973), pp. 293–7

Darwin, Erasmus, *The Botanic Garden. Part II Containing the Loves of the Plants* (1791), Lichfield: Jackson [1799], 4th edn (Oxford, 1991)

Dauven, Jean, *La gamme mystique de R. Wagner, suivi de Couleur et musique* (Paris, 1961)

Debussy, Claude, *Monsieur Croche et autres écrits*, ed. F. Lesure (Paris, 1971)

De Gourmont, Rémy, 'De Baju à René Ghil', in *Promenades littéraires*, IV (Paris, 1920), pp. 44–57

Delacroix, Eugène, *Oeuvres littéraires* (Paris, 1923)

—, *Journal*, ed. André Joubin (Paris, 1932), 3 vols

—, *Dictionnaire des Beaux-Arts*, ed. Anne Larue (Paris, 1996)

De La Moussaye, Gustave, 'Les couleurs et les sons', *L'Artiste* (15 January 1853), pp. 189–90

—, 'Harmonie des sensations', ibid. (1 September 1853), pp. 33–4

Delaunay, Robert, *Du cubisme à l'art abstrait*, ed. Pierre Francastel (Paris, 1957)

Dénéréaz, Alexandre, *Rythmes humains et rythmes cosmiques* (Geneva, 1926)

—, *La gamme, le problème cosmique. Considérations sur la gamme naturelle* (Zurich, n. d.)

Dénéréaz, Alexandre, and Lucien Bourguès, *La musique et la vie intérieure, Essai d'une histoire psychologique de l'art musical* (Paris, 1921)

Denis, Maurice, *Le ciel et l'Arcadie*, ed. J. P. Bouillon (Paris, 1993)

De Piles, Roger, *L'idée du peintre parfait* [1699] (Paris, 1993)

—, *Cours de peinture par principes* [1708] (Nîmes, 1990)

De Rochas, A., 'La notation des couleurs', *La Nature: Revue des sciences illustrées* (1891), pp. 186–7

Deschanel, Paul, *Physiologie des écrivains et des artistes ou essai de critique naturelle* (Paris, 1864)

De Staël, Germaine, *De l'Allemagne* [1813] (Paris, 1959)

Diderot, Denis, *Lettre sur les aveugles à l'usage de ceux qui voient* [1749], in *Oeuvres philosophiques* (Paris, 1964)

—, *Lettre sur les sourds et muets* [1751], ed. P. H. Meyer (Geneva, 1965), *Letter on the Deaf and Dumb*, in *Diderot's Early Philosophical Works*, trans. and ed. Margaret Jourdain (Chicago, IL, and London, 1916)

—, *Lettre à Mademoiselle De la Chaux* [1751], in *Correspondance*, I (Paris, 1955), pp. 117–30

—, *Recherches philosophiques sur l'origine et la nature du beau* [1752], in *Oeuvres esthétiques* (Paris, 1959)

—, 'Clavecin oculaire' [1753] de *L'Encyclopédie*, in *Oeuvres complètes*, ed. Roger Lewinter, XV (Paris, 1973), p. 191

—, *Essais sur la peinture* [1766], ibid., pp. 657–740

D'Udine, Jean [Albert Cozanet], *De la corrélation des sons et des couleurs* (Paris, 1897)

—, *Lettres paradoxales sur la musique* (Paris, 1900)

—, *L'orchestration des couleurs* (Paris, 1903)

—, *L'art et le geste* (Paris, 1910)

—, *Qu'est-ce que la musique?* (Paris, 1925)

—, *Qu'est-ce que la peinture et les autres arts plastiques?* (Paris, 1929)

Dujardin, Edouard, 'Le mouvement symboliste et la musique', *Mercure de France* (March–April 1908), pp. 5–24

Dukas, Paul, *Écrits sur la musique* (Paris, 1948)

Duret, Théodore, 'James Whistler' [1881], in *Critique d'avant-garde*, ed. Denys Riout (Paris, 1998), pp. 118–23

Eisenstein, Sergei, 'Synchronisation of Senses', in *The Film Sense* (New York, 1947), pp. 67–109

—, 'Color and Meaning', ibid., pp. 111–53

Endell, August, 'Formen Schönheit und dekorative Kunst', *Dekorative Kunst*, I/1 (1898), p. 75

Engel, Johann Jakob, *Über die musikalische Malerei* (Berlin, 1780)

Euler, Leonard, 'Réflexions sur l'analogie entre les couleurs et les sons', in *Lettres à une princesse d'Allemagne sur divers sujets de physique et de philosophie* [1760–62] (Lausanne, 2003) (letters XXXI, 27 July 1760, and CXXXIV, 6 June 1761)

Favre, Louis, *La musique des couleurs et les musiques de l'avenir* (Paris, 1900)

—, *La musique des couleurs et le cinéma* (Paris, 1927)

Félibien, André, *Conférences de l'Académie royale de peinture et de sculpture pendant l'année 1667* [Paris, 1669] (Portland, OR, 1972)

—, *L'idée du peintre parfait* [1707] (Geneva, 1970)

Fénéon, Félix, *Oeuvres plus que complètes* (Geneva, 1970)

Fernow, Ludwig, *Römische Studien* (Zurich, 1806)

Feuillie, Nicolas, ed., *Fluxus dixit: Une anthologie* (Dijon, 2002)

Flournoy, Théodore, *Des phénomènes de synopsie (audition colorée)* (Paris, 1893)

Gaffurio [Gaffurius], Franchino, *Practica musicae* [Milan, 1496] (Farnborough, 1967)

—, *De Harmonia Musicorum Instrumentorum Opus* (Milan 1518), trans. Walter Kurt Kreyszig, *The Theory of Music* (New Haven, CT, 1993)

Galilei, Vincenzo, *Della musica antica e moderna* (Florence, 1581)

Galton, Francis, 'Colour Associations', in *Inquiries into Human Faculty and its Development* (London 1883; New York, 1907), pp. 145ff.

Garnier, Pierre, 'Manifesto for a New Poetry Visual And Phonic' (1962)

Gauguin, Paul, *Avant et après* (Paris, 1923; Taravao, 1989)

—, *Lettres à sa femme et à ses amis*, ed. M. Malingue (Paris, 1946)

—, *Lettres à Daniel de Monfreid* (Paris, 1950)

—, *Racontars de rapin* (Paris, 1951)

—, *Oviri. Écrits d'un sauvage* (Paris, 1974)

—, *Correspondance*, ed. Victor Merlhès (Paris, 1984)

—, *Lettres à André Fontainas* (Paris, 1994)

Genette, Gérard, *Mimologics*, trans. Thaïs E. Morgan, Foreword by Gerald Prince (Lincoln, NE, 1995)

Gérôme-Maësse, 'L'audition colorée', *Les tendances nouvelles*, no. 33 (November 1907), pp. 655–63

Gerstner, Karl, *Korrespondenzen. Über Übereinstimmung und Nichtübereinstimmung von Tonen, Farben und Formen* (Basel [Typescript], 1985)

—, *Les formes des couleurs* (Paris, 1986)

Ghil, René, *Traité du verbe* (Paris, 1885), ed. Tiziana Goruppi, *Traité du verbe, états successifs* (Paris, 1978)

—, *En méthode à l'oeuvre* (Paris, 1904)

—, *De la poésie scientifique* (Paris, 1909)

Ginzburg, Moisei Yakovlevich, *Rhythm in Architecture* [1923] (London, 2016)

Giustiniani, Vincenzo, *Discours sur la musique* (1628)

Goethe, Johann Wolfgang von, 'Einleitung in die Propyläen' (1798), in *Werke*, Hamburger
Ausgabe XII: *Schriften zur Kunst* (Hamburg, 1967), pp. 38–55
—, *Farbenlehre, Didaktischer Teil*, V, 'Verhältnis zur Tonlehre' (Munich, 1970), p. 164
Greenberg, Clement, 'Towards a Newer Laocoon' (1940), in *Collected Essays and Criticism*,
rd. I, ed. John O'Brian (Chicago, IL, 1986), pp. 23–38
—, 'Modernist Painting' (1960), ibid., vol. IV, ed. John O'Brian (Chicago, IL, 1993),
pp. 85–93
—, 'Intermedia', *Arts Magazine* (October 1981), pp. 92–3
Grétry, André-Ernest, 'Analogie des couleurs avec les sons', in *Mémoires ou Essais sur
la musique* [1789] (Paris, 1796), III, pp. 234–9
Grimm, Jacob Ludwig, *On the Origin of Language* [1851], trans. Raymond A. Wiley
(Leiden, 1984)
Hanslick, Eduard, *Vom musikalischen Schönen* [Leipzig, 1854] (Darmstadt, 1965), French
trans., *Du beau dans la musique* (Paris, 1986)
Hauer, Joseph Matthias, *Vom Wesen des Musikalischen* (1920), French trans., *L'essence du
musical* (Nice, 2000)
Hausmann, Raoul, 'Optophonétique' (1922), in *R. Hausmann* (Saint-Etienne, 1994), p. 241
Hegel, Georg Wilhelm Friedrich, *Vorlesungen über die Ästhetik* [1836–45] (Frankfurt, 1976)
Heine, Heinrich, *Pariser Berichte 1840–1848*, in *Werke, Säkularausgabe*, X (Berlin, 1979)
Heinse, Wilhelm, *Ardinghello und die glücklichen Inseln* [1787] (Stuttgart, 1975)
Heline, Corinne, *Color and Music in the New Age* [1964] (Halle, 1985)
Henry, Charles, 'Introduction à une esthétique scientifique', *Revue contemporaine*
(August 1885), pp. 441–69
Herder, Johann Gottfried, *Über den Ursprung der Sprache* (1770), in *Werke*, ed. Wolfgang
Pross, II (Munich, 1987), pp. 251–357. 'Treatise on the Origin of Language', in
Philosophical Writings, trans. Michael N. Forster (Cambridge, 2002)
—, *Kalligone*. II. *Von Kunst und Kunstrichterei* (1800), in *Sämtliche Werke*, ed. B. Suphan,
XXII (Berlin, 1880)
Hess, Walter, *Das Problem der Farbe in den Selbstzeugnissen der Maler* (Mittenwald, 1981)
Higgins, Dick, *Horizons: The Poetics and Theory of Intermedia* (Carbondale, IL, 1984)
Hoffmann, Ernst Theodor Amadeus, *Kreisleriana* (1814–15), in *Dichtungen und Schriften*,
I (Weimar, 1924), French trans. Albert Béguin (Paris, 1931)
—, *Écrits sur la musique* (Lausanne, 1985)
Huysmans, Joris K., *À rebours* (1884), in *Oeuvres complètes* (Paris, 1929)
Itten, Johannes, *Werke und Schriften*, ed. W. Rotzler (Zurich, 1978)
Ivanov, Viatcheslav, 'Le théâtre de l'avenir' [1906], in Claudine Amiard-Chevrel,
Les symbolistes russes et le théâtre (Lausanne, 1994), pp. 208–19
—, 'Ciurlionis und das Problem der Synthese der Künste' [1914], in R. Stanislawski et al.,
Europa Europa (Bonn, 1994), III, pp. 83–5
Janin, Louise, *La musicalité picturale* (1933), new edn in Schidlower (1990), pp. 25–34
Junker, C. L., *Betrachtungen über Malerey, Ton- und Bildhauerkunst* (Basel, 1778)

Kandinsky, Wassily, *Über das Geistige in der Kunst* [Munich, 1911] (Bern, 1973),
  French trans., *Du spirituel dans l'art* (Paris, 1969)
—, 'Über Bühnenkomposition' (1912), in *Essays über Kunst und Künstle* (Bern, 1973),
  pp. 49–61
—, *Rückblicke* (1913–18), trad. *Regards sur le passé et autres textes*, ed. J. P. Bouillon
  (Paris, 1974)
—, 'De la méthode de travail sur l'art synthétique' (Conférence à l'Académie russe des
  Sciences artistiques, 1921), in Christian Derouet and Jessica Boissel, *Kandinsky,
  oeuvres* (Paris, 1984), pp. 158–9
—, 'Über die abstrakte Bühnensynthese' (1923), in *Essays*, pp. 79–83
—, *Punkt – Linie – Fläche* [1926] (Bern, 1955), trad. *Point – ligne – plan*, in *Écrits complets*,
  II, ed. Philippe Sers (1970), pp. 51–189. [*Point, Line and Plane* (1926), Dover
  Publications, rpt of New York, 1947]
—, 'Konkrete Kunst' (1938), in *Essays*, pp. 217–21
—, *La synthèse des arts, Écrits complets*, III (Paris, 1975)
—, correspondance avec Schönberg, in *Albèra (1995)
Kandinsky, Wassily, and Franz Marc, *Der Blaue Reiter* [1912] (Munich, 1965)
Kaprow, Alan, 'Notes sur la création d'un art total' [1958], in *L'art et la vie confondus*,
  ed. Jeff Kelley, trans. Jacques Donguy (Paris, 1996), pp. 38–42
Kastner, Frédéric, *Les flammes chantantes: Théorie des vibrations et considérations sur
  l'électricité* [1875] (Paris, 1976)
Kepler, Johannes, *Harmonice mundi* [1619], trad. Max Caspar, *Welt-Harmonik*
  (Munich, 1990)
Khlebnikov, Velimir, *Collected Works of Velimir Khlebnikov: Selected Poems*,
  ed. Ronald Vroom, trans. Paul Schmidt (Cambridge, MA, 1997)
Kircher, Athanasius, *Ars magna Lucis et Umbrae* (Rome, 1646)
—, *Musurgia universalis* [1650] (Hildesheim, 1970)
Klausz, Ernest, 'L'art total', in Schidlower (1990), pp. 53–6
Klee, Paul, *Das bildnerische Denken*, ed. Jürg Spiller (Basel, 1964)
—, *Schriften. Rezensionen und Aufsätze*, ed. Christian Geelhaar (Cologne, 1976)
—, *Briefe an die Familie 1893–1940*, ed. Felix Klee (Cologne, 1979)
—, *Tagebücher 1989–1918* (Cologne, 1988)
Klinger, Max, *Malerei und Zeichnung* [1891], in Manfred Boetzkes et al., *Max Klinger:
  Wege zum Gesamtkunstwerk* (Mainz, 1984)
Kupka, Frantisek, *La création dans les arts plastiques* [1913] (Paris, 1989), trans. *Creation
  in the Plastic Arts* (Liverpool, 2002)
Laforgue, Jules, 'L'impressionnisme' [1883], in *Mélanges posthumes*, new edn in *Textes de
  critique d'art*, ed. Mireille Dottin (Lille, 1988), pp. 167–75
Laszlo, Alexander, *Farblicht Musik* (Leipzig, 1925)
—, 'Die Farblichtmusik und ihre Forschungsgebiete. Ein Vortrag für Universitäten, Colleges
  und musikalische Hochschulen' (1939), in Jewanski and Sidler (2006), pp. 276–337

Lavignac, Albert, *La musique et les musiciens* [1895] (Paris, 1896)

Lechalas Georges, 'Les comparaisons entre la musique et la peinture', *Revue philosophique de la France et de l'étranger*, xx (July–December 1885), pp. 136–59

Leitner, Bernhard, *Sound, Space* (Ostfildern, 1998)

Leonardo da Vinci, *Il paragone delle arti*, ed. Claudio Scarpati (Milan, 1993)

Lessing, Gotthold Ephraim, *Laokoon* [1766] (Stuttgart, 1964)

Lista, Giovanni, ed., *Futurisme. Manifestes – Proclamations – Documents* (Lausanne, 1973)

Liszt, Franz, Avant-propos de *L'Album d'un voyageur* (Vienne, n.d.)

—, *Gesammelte Schriften* [Wiesbaden, 1882] (New York, 1978), 6 vols

—, *Lettres d'un bachelier ès musique* (Geneva, 1991)

—, *Artiste et société*, ed. Rémy Stricker (Paris, 1995)

Lomazzo, Gian Paolo, *Idea del Tempio della Pittura* (1590), in *Scritti sulle arti*, ed. R. P. Ciardi (Florence, 1974)

—, *Trattato dell'arte della pittura, scultura et architettura* (1584), in *Scritti sulle arti*, ed. R. P. Ciardi (Florence, 1974), vol. II

MacDonald-Wright, Stanton, *A Treatise on Color* (Los Angeles, CA, 1924)

Magnard, Albéric, 'La synthèse des arts', *Revue de Paris*, I (15 September 1894), pp. 424–42

Magnin, Emile, *L'art et l'hypnose. Interprétation plastique d'oeuvres littéraires et musicales*, Geneva (Paris, n.d.)

Mallarmé, Stéphane, *Oeuvres complètes* (Paris, 1956)

Marinetti, Filippo Tommaso, *Destruction of Syntax – Imagination without Strings – Words-in-freedom: Futurist Manifesto* [May 1913], in *Documents of 20th Century Art: Futurist Manifestos*, ed. Umbro Apollonio, trans. Robert Brain, R. W. Flint, J. C. Higgitt and Caroline Tisdall (New York, 1973)

Martinet, Louis, 'Les peintres et les musiciens', *Le Courrier artistique* (15 September 1861)

Matisse, Henri, *Écrits et propos sur l'art* (Paris, 1972)

Mauclair, Camille, 'La peinture musicienne et la fusion des arts', *La Revue Bleue*, no. 10 (6 September 1902), pp. 297–303

—, 'L'identité et la fusion des arts', in *Idées vivantes* (Paris, 1904), pp. 197–309

—, 'La Messe en ré (Beethoven et Michel-Ange)', in *La religion de la musique* (Paris, 1928)

Mendelssohn, Moses, 'Über die Empfindungen' [1755], *Brief*, 11, in *Gesammelte Schriften*, I (Stuttgart, 1971), pp. 86–7

Ménestrier, Claude François, *Des représentations en musique ancienne et moderne* [Paris, 1681] (Geneva, 1972)

Merleau-Ponty, Maurice, *Phenomenology of perception* [1945], trans. Colin Smith (London and New York, 1962)

Mersenne, Marin, *Harmonie universelle contenant la théorie et la pratique de la musique* [1636], ed. François Lesure (Paris, 1975)

Messiaen, Olivier, *Musique et couleur*, new interviews with Claude Samuel (Paris, 1986)

—, *Traité du rythme* (Paris, 1994)

Miró, Joan, *Écrits et entretiens*, ed. Margit Rowell (Paris, 1995)

Mondrian, Piet, 'Le Jazz et le néo-plasticisme' [1927], *Macula*, no. 1 (1976), pp. 77–87

Moreau, Gustave, *L'assembleur de rêves: Écrits complets* (Fontfroide, 1984)

Morellet, André, 'De l'expression en musique et de l'imitation dans les arts', in *Mélanges de littérature et de philosophie du XVIIIe siècle*, IV (Paris, 1818), pp. 366–413

Morice, Charles, *Demain: Questions d'esthétique* (Paris, 1888)

—, *La littérature de tout à l'heure* (Paris, 1889)

Morse, Samuel F. B., *Lectures on the Affinities of Painting with the Other Arts* [1826], (Columbia, MO, and London, 1983)

Myers, Charles S., 'Two Cases of Synaesthesia', *British Journal of Psychology*, VII (1915), pp. 112–17

Nerval, Gérard de, *Aurélia* [1853], in *Oeuvres complètes*, III (Paris, 1993), pp. 359–414

Neuhaus, Max, *Evocare l'udibile / évoquer l'auditif* (Milan, 1995)

Nono, Luigi, *Écrits* (Paris, 1993)

Nouveau, Henri, 'Notes', *Revue musicale*, no. 246 (1960), new edn in *Henri Nouveau / Henrik Neugeboren 1901–1959. Au-delà de l'abstraction* (Paris, 2002), pp. 77–80

Novalis, *Schriften*, ed. Paul Kluckhohn and Richard Samuel (Darmstadt, 1977–88)

Palladio, Andrea, *I quattro libri dell'architettura* (Venice, 1570), trans. Richard Schofield and Robert Tavernor, *The Four Books on Architecture* (Cambridge, MA, 1997)

Pater, Walter, 'The School of Giorgione', in *The Renaissance* [1877], introduction by Arthur Symons (New York, 1919)

Philostratus the Elder, *Imagines*, trans. Arthur Fairbanks (London, 1931)

Plotinus, *An Essay on the Beautiful*, trans. Thomas Taylor (London, 1917)

Poling, Clark V., *Kandinsky's Teaching at the Bauhaus* (New York, 1986)

Poncelet, Polycarpe, *Chimie du goût et de l'odorat pour composer facilement et à peu de frais les liqueurs à boire et les eaux de senteurs* [Paris, 1755] (Paris, 1993)

Poussin, Nicolas, *Lettres*, ed. Anthony Blunt (Paris, 1964)

Prampolini, Enrico, 'La cromofonia e il valore degli spostamenti atmosferici' [1913], in *Prampolini: dal Futurismo all'informale* (Rome, 1992), pp. 74–6

—, 'L'atmosfera scenica futurista', *Noi* (Rome, 1924), reprinted in *Enrico Prampolini* (Modena, 1986)

Proust, Marcel, 'Du côté de chez Swann' [1917], trans. C. K. Scott Moncrieff (New York, 1922)

Quatremère de Quincy, Antoine Chrysostome, *Essai sur la nature, le but et les moyens de l'imitation dans les Beaux-Arts* [Paris, 1823] (Brussels, 1980). English trans., *An Essay on the Nature, the End, and the Means of Imitation in the Fine Arts* (London, 1837)

Rainer, Oskar, *Musikalische Graphik: Studien und Versuche über die Wechselbeziehungen zwischen Ton- und Farbharmonien* (Wien, 1925)

Redon, Odilon, *À soi-même* (Paris, 1961)

—, *Critiques d'art* (Perigueux, 1987)

—, *Lettres d'Odilon Redon, 1878–1916* (Paris and Brussels, 1923)

Reynolds, Joshua, *Discourses on Art*, ed. Robert R. Wark (New Haven, CT, 1975)

Richardson, Jonathan, *An Essay on the Theory of Painting* [1715] (London, 1725), reprinted and ed. R. Woodfield (Menston, 1971)

Rimbaud, Arthur, *Oeuvres complètes* (Paris, 1972)

Rimington, Wallace, *A New Art, Colour-music* (1895), in Klein (1936), pp. 256–73

Rochlitz, Johann Friedrich, 'Raphael und Mozart, eine Paralelle', *Die allgemeine musikalische Zeitung* (Leipzig, 1799–1801), pp. 641–53

—, 'Musikalische Aufsätze von Joseph Berglinger' [1800], in *Für Freunde der Tonkunst* (Leipzig, 1830), III, pp. 382–95

Rodin, Auguste, *L'Art: Entretiens réunis par Paul Gsell* [1911] (Paris, 1967)

Rossigneux, Charles, 'Essai sur l'audition colorée et sa valeur en esthétique', *Journal de psychologie normale et pathologique* (1905), pp. 193–215

Rothschild, Judith, 'On the Use of a Color-music Analogy and on a Change in Paintings', *Leonardo*, III/3 (1970), pp. 275–83

Rousseau, Jean-Jacques, 'Fausse analogie entre les couleurs et les sons', in *Essai sur l'origine des langues* [1755] (Paris, 1974), pp. 159–63

Rovel, Henri, 'Les lois d'harmonie de la peinture et de la musique sont les mêmes', *Les Tendances nouvelles*, no. 35, March 1908, new edn (New York, 1980)

Runge, Philipp Otto, 'Gespräche über Analogie der Farben und Töne', in *Hinterlassene Schriften* [Hamburg, 1840] (Göttingen, 1965), pp. 168–70

Ruskin, John, 'The Musical or Harmonic Element in Every Art', in *Aratra Pentelici: Six Lectures on the Elements of Sculpture* [1870], in *Works*, vol. XX (London, 1905), pp. 207–19

Russolo, Luigi, *L'art des bruits* [1913], preface by Giovanni Lista (Lausanne, 1975)

—, *L'arte dei rumori* (Milan, 1916)

Saint-Yves d'Alveydre, *L'archéomètre musical* (Paris, 1911)

Sand, George, *Impressions et souvenirs* (Paris, 1873)

Satie, Eric, *Écrits*, ed. Ornella Volta (Paris, 1977)

Schelling, Friedrich Willhelm Joseph, *Philosophie der Kunst* [1802–3] (Darmstadt, 1990)

—, trans., *The Philosophy of Art*, trans. Douglas W. Stott (Minneapolis, MN, 1989)

Schiller, Friedrich, *Über die ästhetische Erziehung des Menschen* [1795] (Stuttgart and Berlin, 1904)

Schlegel, August Wilhelm, 'Betrachtungen über die Metrik' (1800), in *Sämtliche Werke*, ed. Eduard Böcking, VII (Leipzig, 1846), pp. 155–96

—, *Die Kunstlehre* (1801–2), in *Kritische Schriften und Briefe*, ed. E. Lohner, vol. II (Stuttgart, 1963)

—, *Vorlesungen, Die Kunstlehre* (1801–2), Kritische Ausgabe E. Behler (Paderborn, 1989)

Schlegel, Friedrich, 'On the Language and Wisdom of the Indians,' in *The Aesthetic and Miscellaneous Works of Friedrich von Schlegel*, trans. E. Millington (London, 1808), ch. V: 'On the Origin of Language'

—, *On the Language and Philosophy of the Indians* (1808), ch. V: 'On the Origin of Language'

Schlemmer, Oskar, 'Abstraction in Dance and Costume' (1928), in *Oskar Schlemmer Man: Teaching Notes from the Bauhaus*, ed. Heimo Kuchling, trans. Janet Seligman (London, 1971)

—, *Briefe und Tagebücher* (Stuttgart, 1977)

Schönberg, Arnold, *Harmonielehre* [1911] (Wien, 1922)

—, *Style and Idea* (1975), French trans. *Le style et l'idée* (Paris, 1977) new edn (1994)

—, correspondance avec Kandinsky, in *Albèra (1995)

Schopenhauer, Arthur, *Über das Sehen und die Farben* [1816], French trans., *Textes sur la vue et les couleurs* (Paris, 1986)

—, *Die Welt als Wille und Vorstellung* [1818] (Darmstadt, 1982)

Schreyer, Lothar, 'Die neue Kunst', *Sturm-Bücher*, xv (1919), rpt. Kraus (Nendeln, 1974)

Schumann, Robert, *Schriften über Musik und Musiker* (Leipzig, 1854)

—, 'Aus Meister Raros, Florestans und Eusebius Denk- und Dicht-Büchlein', *Gesammelte Schriften über Musik und Musiker* (Leipzig, 1891), I, pp. 25–38

—, Edouard, *Histoire du drame musical* (Paris, 1876)

Schuré, Edouard, *Histoire du drame musical* (Paris, 1876)

—, *R. Wagner; son oeuvre et son idée* (Paris, 1904)

Schwitters, Kurt, 'Vermischung von Kunstgattungen', in *Manifeste und kritische Prosa* (Cologne, 1981), p. 371

Scriabin, Alexandre, *Notes et réflexions*, French trans. Marina Scriabine (Paris, 1979)

Sebba, Rachel, 'Structural Correspondence between Music and Color', *Color Research and Application*, xvi/2 (April 1991), pp. 81–8

Segalen, Victor, 'Les synesthésies et l'école symboliste', *Mercure de France* (April 1902), new edn (Paris, 1981)

— *Oeuvres complètes* (Paris, 1995)

Sérusier, Paul, *ABC de la peinture*, suivi d'une étude sur la vie et l'oeuvre de P. Sérusier par Maurice Denis [1921] (Paris, 1942)

Severini, Gino, *Du cubisme au classicisme* (Paris, 1921)

Sidenius, W. Christian, 'Lumia Kinetic Art with Music: My Theatre of Light', *Leonardo*, xv (1982), pp. 188–92

Signac, Paul, *D'Eugène Delacroix au néo-impressionnisme* (1899), ed. Françoise Cachin (Paris, 1964)

Slawson, Wayne, *Sound Color* (Berkeley, CA, 1985)

Smith, Adam, *De la nature de l'imitation*, in *Essais esthétiques et autres textes*, ed. Patrick Thierry (Paris, 1997), pp. 65–79

Souriau, Paul, 'Le symbolisme des couleurs', *Revue de Paris* (15 April 1895), pp. 849–70

—, *L'imagination de l'artiste* (Paris, 1901)

Spengler, Oswald, *Der Untergang des Abendlandes* (1918–22), English trans., *The Decline of the West*, ed. Arthur Helps and Helmut Werner, trans. Charles F. Atkinson, Preface H. Stuart Hughes (New York and Oxford, 1991)

Steiner, Rudolph, *Eurythmie curative* [1921], Saint-Prex: Formation professionnelle eurythmique, 1979. English trans., *Curative Eurythmy*, trans. Kristina Krohn and Dr Anthony Degenaar (London, 1983)

Stendhal [Louis-Alexandre-César Bombet], *Lettres écrites de Vienne en Autriche sur le célèbre compositeur J. Haydn, suivies d'une vie de Mozart et de considérations sur Métastase et l'état de la musique en France et en Italie* [1814], in Stendhal, *L'âme et la musique*, ed. Suzel Esquier (Paris, 1999)

—, *Vies de Haydn, de Mozart et de Métastase* [1815] (Paris, 1914)

—, *Vie de Rossini* [1824], ed. Pierre Brunel (Paris, 1987)

—, 'Promenades dans Rome', in *Voyages en Italie* [1829] (Paris, 1973)

Stifter, Adalbert, 'Die Sonnenfinsternis am 8. Juli 1842', in *Gesammelte Werke in sechs Bänden* (Wiesbaden, 1959), VI, pp. 584–95

Stockhausen, Karlheinz, 'Musik und Graphik', *Darmstädter Beiträge zur neuen Musik*, III/3 (1960), pp. 5–25

Stoltenberg, Hans Lorenz, *Reine Farbkunst in Raum und Zeit und ihr Verhältnis zur Tonkunst* (Leipzig, 1920), new expanded edn (Berlin, 1937)

Stravinsky, Igor, *Poétique musicale* (Paris, 1945), new edn (Paris, 1952)

Suarez de Mendoza, Ferdinand, *L'audition colorée: Étude sur les fausses sensations* (Paris, 1890)

Survage, Léopold, 'Le rythme coloré', *Soirées de Paris* [1914], et 'La couleur, le mouvement, le rythme' [1914], in *Écrits sur la peinture*, ed. Hélène Seyrès (Paris, 1992), pp. 21–7

Tartini, Giuseppe, *Trattato di musica secondo la vera scienza* [1754] (Düsseldorf, 1966)

Teige, Karel, 'Manifest Poetismus' [1928], in *Liquidierung der 'Kunst': Analysen, Manifeste*, ed. Paul Kruntrorad (Frankfurt, 1968), pp. 70–111

Tieck, Ludwig, *Franz Sternbalds Wanderungen* [1798], in *Frühromantische Erzählungen*, VI, ed. Paul Kluckhohn (Leipzig, 1933)

—, and Wilhelm-Heinrich Wackenroder, 'Die Farben', in *Phantasien über die Kunst* [1799] (Berlin-Stuttgart, 1886), pp. 42–6

Töpffer, Rodolphe, *Réflexions et menus propos d'un peintre genevois* [1848] (Lausanne, 1928)

Tritten, Gottfried, 'Umsetzung akustischer Elemente in Bildformen', in *Malen. Handbuch der bildnerischen Erziehung* (Bern, 1985), pp. 220–26

Valensi, Henry, 'La couleur et les formes', in *L'année 1913*, ed. L. Brion-Guerry (Paris, 1973), III, p. 176

—, 'L'allègement progressif de la matière à travers l'évolution de l'art', *Journal de psychologie normale et pathologique* (15 January–15 February 1934), pp. 160–70

—, *Le musicalisme* (Paris, 1936), new edn in Schidlower (1990), pp. 35–52

Valensi, Henry, et al., *Manifeste du groupe des peintres 'Les artistes musicalistes'*, *Comoedia* (17 April 1932)

Van Gogh, Vincent, *Correspondance générale* (Paris, 1990), 3 vols

Vasari, Giorgio, *Le vite*, ed. Gaetano Milanesi (Florence, 1906)

—, *Vasari on Technique*, trans. Louisa S. Maclehose, ed. G. Baldwin Brown (London, 1907)

Verhaeren, Emile, *Écrits sur l'art* (Brussels, 1997)

Veronesi, Luigi, *Proposta per una ricerca sui rapporti fra suono e colore* (Milan, 1977)

Vian, Boris, *L'écume des jours* [1946], in *Oeuvres*, ɪɪ (Paris, 1999)

Viardot, Louis, 'Ut pictura musica', *Gazette des Beaux-Arts* (January 1859), pp. 19–29

Vico, Giambattista, *The New Science* [1725], trans. Thomas Bergin and Max Fisch (New York, 1948)

Vignier, Charles, 'Note d'esthétique. La suggestion en art', *Revue contemporaine littéraire, politique et philosophique*, ɪɪɪ/4 (25 December 1885), pp. 464–76

Villoteau, Guillaume André, *Recherches sur l'analogie de la musique avec les arts qui ont pour objet l'imitation* [Paris, 1807] (Geneva, 1970)

Vitruvius, *The Ten Books on Architecture*, trans. Morris Hicky Morgan (London, 1914)

Voltaire, 'Du rapport des 7 couleurs primitives avec les 7 tons de la musique', ch. xɪv des *Eléments de la physique de Newton* [1738], in *Works*, xv (Oxford, 1992), pp. 386–95

Von Schwind, Moritz, *Briefe*, ed. Otto Stoessl (Leipzig, n.d. [1924])

Wagner, Richard, *Das Kunstwerk der Zukunft* [1849], in *Gesammelte Schriften und Dichtungen*, ɪɪɪ [Leipzig, 1887] (Moers, 1976)

—, *Oper und Drama* [1851], trad. *Opéra et drame* (Paris, 1982), trans. W. Ashton Ellis, *Opera and Drama* (Lincoln, ɴᴇ, 1995)

—, *Quatre poèmes d'opéras,* précédés d'une *Lettre sur la musique* (Paris, 1861)

— *Revue wagnérienne* [1885–8] (Geneva, 1968)

Walzel, Oskar, *Wechselseitige Erhellung der Künste* (Berlin, 1917)

Webern, Anton, *Weg zur neuen Musik* (Wien, 1960), French trans., *Chemin vers la nouvelle musique* (Paris, 1980)

Weder, Jakob, *Die Wahrheit der Farbe* (2006)

Wells, Alan, 'Music and Visual Color: A Proposed Correlation', *Leonardo*, xɪɪɪ/2 (Spring 1980), pp. 101–7

Whistler, James McNeil, *The Gentle Art of Making Enemies* [1890] (New York, 1967)

Wyzewa, Théodore de, *Nos maîtres* (Paris, 1895)

—, *Beethoven et Wagner, essais d'histoire et de critique musicale* (Paris, 1898)

X., 'De la peinture et de la musique', *Journal des artistes* (14 September 1828), pp. 165–8; (21 September 1828), pp. 180–82

Xenakis, Iannis, *Musique, architecture* [1971] (Paris, 1976)

Zarlino, Gioseffo, *Istitutioni harmoniche* [Venezia, 1573] (Ridgewood, ɴᴊ, 1966)

Secondary Sources

Abel, Angelika, *Die zwölften Technik Weberns und Goethes Methodik der Farbenlehre. Zur Kompositionstheorie und Aesthetik der neuen Wiener Schule* (Wiesbaden, 1982)

Abromont, Claude, 'A propos de *Farben*: invention et figuration dans la pensée musicale de Schoenberg', *Analyse musicale* (1986), pp. 46–9

Adler, Hans, and Ulricke Zeuch, ed., *Synästhesie. Interferenz – Transfer – Synthese der Sinne* (Würzbug/Königshausen, 2002)

Adorno, Theodor W., *Versuch über Wagner* [1952] (Frankfurt, 1974), pp. 66–79

—, 'Wagners Aktualität' [1965], in *Gesammelte Schriften*, XVI (Frankfurt, 1978), pp. 543–64

—, 'Die Kunst und die Künste', in *Ohne Leitbild. Parva Aesthetica* (Frankfurt, 1967), pp. 168–92, trans. 'L'art et les arts', in Lauxerois and Szendy (1997), pp. 25–52

—, *Über einige Relationen zwischen Musik und Malerei* [1965], in *Musikalische Schriften (Gesammelte Schriften, XVI)* (Frankfurt, 1978), pp. 628–42

Aichele, Kathryn Porter, 'Paul Klee's Operatic Themes and Variations', *Art Bulletin* (September 1986), pp. 450–66

Albèra, Philippe, '*Klänge, Farben, Klangfarben*: Schoenberg vs Kandinsky', in *Points de vue,* ed. Danielle Chaperon and Philippe Kaenel (Paris, 2003), pp. 313–32

Allard, Joseph C., 'Mechanism, Music and Painting in 17th Cent. France', *Journal of Aesthetics and Art Criticism*, XL/3 (Spring 1982), pp. 269–79

Ammann, Jean-Christophe et al., *Robert Strübin. Musik sehen, Bilder hören* (Basel, 2010)

Annibaldi, Claudio, 'La musica e le arti figurative nel pensiero artistico moderno', in *Musica e arti figurative* (Turin, 1968), p. 25

Aparicio, Octavio, *La musica en la pintura* (Madrid, 1975)

Arnaldo, Javier, ed., *Analogias musicales: Kandinsky y sus contemporaneos* (Madrid, 2003)

—, ed., '*El mundo suena'. El modelo musical de la pintura abstracta* (Madrid, 2004)

Babbitt, Irving, *The New Laokoon: An Essay in the Confusion of the Arts* (London, 1910)

Bablet, Denis, 'La plastique scénique', in L. Brion-Gerry (dir.), *L'année 1913* (Paris, 1971), I, pp. 789–815

—, ed., *L'oeuvre d'art totale* (Paris, 1995)

Bandmann, Günter, *Melancholie und Musik, ikonographische Studien* (Cologne, 1960)

Barbanti, Roberto, et al., *Musiques, arts, technologie, pour une approche critique* (Paris, 2004), pp. 91–103

Barbe, Michèle, ed., *Musique et arts ploastiques: analogies et interférences* (Paris, 2005)

Barbier, Muriel, et al., *Un air de Renaissance. La musique au XVIe s.* (Château d'Ecouen, 2013)

Barilier, Etienne, 'Segalen, Gauguin, Debussy', *Cahiers de l'Herne* (1998), pp. 111–16

Barthelmes, Barbara, 'Polyphonie der Proportionen. Zum Verhältnis von Architektur und Musik in der Renaissance', *Musica* (March–April 1985), pp. 129–36

Bauer, Chantal, et al., *Musique et architecture*, in *Monuments historiques*, no. 175 (1991), pp. 2–104

Bauschatz, Paul, 'Paul Klee's Anna Wenne and the Work of Art', *Art History*, XIX/1 (March 1996), pp. 74–101

Bayer, Francis, *De Schönberg à Cage. Essai sur la notion d'espace sonore dans la musique contemporaine* (Paris, 1981)

Beatrice, Luca, *Sound and Vision* (Bologna, 2006)

Beattie, Louise A., *Color and Sound Interrelated* (Ann Arbor, MI, 1999)

Bedriono, Emile, *Proust, Wagner et la coïncidence des arts* (Paris, 1984)

Bellas, Jacqueline, 'Franz Liszt, le grand transpositeur', in *Transpositions*, Actes du colloque de l'Université de Toulouse-Le Mirail (Toulouse, 1986), pp. 223–33

Belli, Gabriella, and Guzzo Vaccarino, *La danza delle Avanguardie. Dipinti, scene e costumi da Degas a Picasso, da Matisse a Keith Haring* (Rovereto, 2005)

Bentgens, Wilfried Johannes, *An der Grenze des Fruchtlandes. Musik und Malerei im Vorfeld der Moderne* (Zülpich, 1997)

Bentivoglio, Mirella, ed., *Ascoltare l'immagine. L'esperienza del suono negli artisti della visualità* (Seravezza, 1996)

Bernard, Jonathan W., 'Messiaen's Synesthesia: The Correspondence between Color and Sound Structure in His Music', *Music Perception*, IV/1 (autumn 1986), pp. 41–68

Bernard, Suzanne, 'La palette de Rimbaud', *C.A.I.E.F*, no. 12 (June 1960), pp. 105–13

Bertling Biaggini, Claudia, *Giorgione pictor et musicus amatus – Vom Klang der Bilder. Eine musikalische Kompositionsästhetik in der Malerei gegen die Aporie der Norm um 1500* (Hildesheim, 2011)

Bienz, Peter, *Le Corbusier und die Musik* (Braunschweig and Wiesbaden, 1998)

Billeter, Jean-François, 'Un art musical', in *L'art chinois de l'écriture* (Geneva, 1989)

Bini, Annalisa, et al., *Colori della Musica. Dipinti, strumenti e concerti tra Cinquecento e Seicento* (Milan, 2000)

Bisanz, Rudolf M., 'The Romantic Synthesis of the Arts. XIXth Cent. German Theories on a Universal Art', *Konsthistorik Tidskrift*, XLIV (1975), pp. 38–46

Bisanz-Prakken, Marian, *G. Klimt: der Beethovenfries. Geschichte, Funktion und Bedeutung* (Salzburg, 1977)

—, 'The Beethoven Exhibition of the Secession and the Younger Viennese Tradition of the Gesamtkunstwerk', in *Focus on Vienna 1900,* ed. Erika Nielsen (Munich, 1982), pp. 140–49

Bischloo, A. W., et al., *Die bemalten Orgelflügel in Europa. Inventar* (Rotterdam, 2001)

Böckmann, Paul, 'Das Laokoonproblem und seine Auflösung in der Romantik', in *Bildende Kunst und Literatur. Beiträge zum Problem ihrer Wechselbeziehungen im 19. Jh.,* ed. Wolfdietrich Rasch (Frankfurt, 1971), pp. 59–78

Body, Veruschka, and Peter Weibel, ed., *Clip, Klapp. Bum. Von der visuellen Musik zum Musikvideo* (Cologne, 1987)

Boehm, Gottfried, et al., *Canto d'amore. Klassizistische Moderne in Musik und bildender Kunst 1914–1935* (Basel, 1996); French trans., *Modernité et classicisme dans la musique et les beaux-arts entre 1914 et 1935*

Boehmer, Konrad, ed., *Schönberg and Kandinsky. An Historic Encounter* (Amsterdam, 1997)

Bogner, Dieter, 'Musik und bildende Kunst in Wien', in Von Maur (1985), pp. 346–53

Böhme, Gernot, 'Über Synästhesien', *Daidalos* (September 1991), pp. 26–36

Bolpagni, Paolo, *Il rapporto tra suono e colore. Una ricognizione storica*, in 'Brescia Musica. Bimestrale di informazio ne e cultura musicale del l'Associazione Filarmonica

"Isidoro Capitanio"', XVIII/8 (February 2004), p. 16; XVIII, no 89 (April 2004), pp. 16–17; XVIII/90 (June 2004), p. 16; XVIII/91 (October 2004), p. 20; XVIII/92 (December 2004), p. 20.

—, *Partitura musicale come oggetto artistico*, in 'Titolo. Rivista scientifico-culturale d'arte contem po ranea', XVII/50 (Perugia, 2006), pp. 22–5

—, *Suono e arti visive. Un tema al centro della cultura contemporanea l'Associazione Filarmonica 'Isidoro Cap tanio'*, XX/101 (October 2006), pp. 16–17

—, *Klee e la musica*, in AA.VV., *Paul Klee. Teatro magico* (catalogo della mostra tenuta dal 26 gen na io al 13 maggio 2007 a Milano)

—, *'Ut musica pictura'. Per una storia del rapporto tra suono e colore nel XIX secolo, da Goethe a Henry*, in A. Valvo and R. Gazich, ed., *Analecta Brixiana II. Contributi dell'Istituto di Fi_lo logia e storia dell'Università Cattolica del Sacro Cuore*, Vita e Pensiero (Milan, 2007), pp. 35–58.

—, *La 'pittura della musica' di Alzek Misheff. Problemi di definizione statutaria* (October 2007), www.alzekmisheff.com/ITA/mpvideos.html

—, *L'elemento verbale nelle partiture della Nuova Musica tra concettualità e iconismo*, in 'De Musica', XII/21 (May 2008), http://users.unimi.it

—, *La ricerca verbovisuale negli anni cinquanta-settanta, dalla poesia sonora alla Nuova Musica ranea'*, XIX/5 (Perugia, 2008)

—, and Francesco Tedeschi, ed., *Visioni musicali. Rapporti tra musica e arti visive nel Novecento* (Milan, 2009)

Bolpagni, Paolo, Di Brino, Andreina, Savettieri, Chiara, *Ritmi visivi. Luigi Veronesi nell'astrattismo europeo* (Lucca, 2011)

Bonito Oliva, Achille, et al., *Ubi Fluxus, ibi Motus* (Venice/Milan, 1990)

Bonnefoit, Régine, 'Paul Klee und die Kunst des Sichtbarmachens von Musik', *Archiv für Musikwissenschaft*, LXV (2008), book 2, pp. 121–51

Booth, Shem, *Synaesthesia and the Unification of Art: Past, Present, Future*, http://shembooth.com

Bordwell, David, 'The Musical Analogy', *Yale French Studies*, LX (1980), pp. 141–56

Börsch-Supan, Eva, 'Die Bedeutung der Musik im Werke K. F. Schinkels', *Zeitschrift für Kunstgeschichte*, 34 (1971), pp. 257–95

Bosseur, Jean-Yves, 'L'oeil de l'écriture musicale', in *L'oeil musicien, les écritures et les images de la musique* (Charleroi, 1985), pp. 33–53

—, *Musique, passion d'artistes* (Geneva, 1991)

—, *Le sonore et le visuel: intersection musique / arts plastiques aujourd'hui* (Paris, 1992)

—, *Musique et arts plastiques. Interactions au XXe siècle* (Paris, 1998)

—, *Musique et Beaux-Arts. De l'Antiquité au XIXe siècle* (Paris, 1999)

Bott, Gian Casper, *Der Klang im Bild. Evaristo Baschenis und die Erfindung des Musikstillebens* (Berlin, 1997)

Boudinet, Gilles, *Des arts et des idées au XXe siècle. Musique, peinture, philosophie et sciences humaines: fragments croisés* (Paris, 1998)

Bouillon, Jean-Paul, *Klimt: Beethoven* (Geneva, 1986)

—, 'Arabesques', in *Paradis perdus: L'Europe symboliste*, exh. cat. Montréal, Musée des Beaux-Arts (Paris, 1995), pp. 376–83

Boydell, Barra, *Music and Paintings in the National Gallery of Ireland* (Dublin, 1985)

Brachert, Thomas, 'A Musical Canon of Proportion in Leonardo da Vinci's *Last Supper*', *Art Bulletin*, LIII (1971), pp. 461–6

Brachmann, Jan, *'Ins Ungewisse hinauf . . .' J. Brahms und M. Klinger im Zwiespalt von Kunst und Kommunikation* (Kassel, 1999)

Bräm, Thuring, et al., *Musik und Raum: eine Sammlung von Beiträgen aus historischer und künstlerischer Sicht zur Bedeutung des Begriffs 'Raum' als Klangträger für die Musik* (Basel, 1986)

Brenez, Nicole, and Miles McKane (dir.), *Poétique de la couleur. Une histoire du cinéma expérimental. Anthologie* (Paris, 1995)

Brenneman, David A., 'Intended by Nature for a Musician: Thomas Gainsborough Musician and the Musical Analogy for Painting in England in the 1770s and '80s', in *Seeing and Beyond: Essays in Honor of K. Champa*, ed. Deborah J. Johnson and David Ogawa (New York, 2005), pp. 21–41

Bridoux-Michel, Séverine, 'Musique, architecture, un projet multimédia: le Pavillon Philips de l'Exposition internationale de 1958', in Barbanti (2004), pp. 91–103

Brock, Maurice, '"Ut pictura musica" – Comment l'image fait-elle voir la musique?', *Imago Musicae*, XVI/XVII (1999–2000), pp. 61–79

Brougher, Kerry, et al., *Visual Music: Synaesthesia in Art and Music since 1900* (exposition Los Angeles and Washington; London, 2005)

Brown, Calvin S., 'The Color Symphony before and after Gautier', *Comparative Literature*, V/4 (1953), pp. 289–309

Brüderlin, Markus, 'Kandinsky und Schönberg – Korrespondenzen und Geistesverwandschaften', in *Farben – Klänge* (Basel, 1998), pp. 11–15

Brugnolo, Katia, 'Ut pictura musica: consonanza et harmonia nelle arti sorelle', in *Harmonia, Strumenti musicali nell'arte figurativa vicentina* (Bassano del Grappa, 1993), pp. 13–16

Brumana, Biancamaria, and Galliano Ciliberti, ed., *Musica e immagine. Tra iconografia e mondo dell'opera, Studi in onore di Massimo Bogianchino* (Florence, 1993)

Brunet, François, *Th. Gautier et la musique* (Paris, 2006)

Budde, Elmar, 'Musik – Klang – Farbe. Zum Problem der Synästhesie in den frühen Kompositionen Ligetis', in Otto Kolleritsch, *G. LIgeti. Personalstil – Avantgardismus – Popularität* (Wien, 1987), pp. 44–59

—, '*Ut musica pictura – ut pictura musica*. Musik und Bild. Ein Rückblick nach vorn zu A. Schönberg', in *Der Maler Arnold Schönberg*, Bericht zum Symposium (Wien, 2003), pp. 8–16

Budde, Rainer, ed., *Die Welt als grosse Sinfonie. M. K. Ciurlionis (1875–1911)* (Cologne, 1998)

Buettner, Stewart, 'Catalonia and the Early Musical Subjects of Braque and Picasso',
    Art History, XIX/1 (March 1996), pp. 102–27
Buijsen, Edwin, et al., *Music and Painting in the Golden Age* (The Hague, 1994)
Busch, Günter, 'Synästhesie und Imagination. Zu Delacroix's kunsttheoretischen
    Äusserungen', in H. Koopmann, *Beiträge zur Theorie der Künste im 19. Jh.*
    (Frankfurt, 1971), I, pp. 240–55
Butler, Christophe, *Early Modernism, Literature, Music and Painting in Europe* (Oxford, 1994)
Caduff, Corina, 'Phantom Farbenklavier. Die Farbe-Ton-Beziehung im 18. Jh: von
    Analogie zur Differenz', in *Die Literarisierung von Musik und bildender Kunst um
    1800* (Munich, 2003), pp. 83–115
Campbell, Roy, trans., *Poems of Baudelaire* (New York, 1952)
Cassidy, Donna M., *The Painted Music of America in the Works of A. Dove, J. Martin
    and J. Stella: An Aspect of Culture Nationalism* (Ann Arbor, MI, 1988)
—, *Painting the Musical City: Jazz and Cultural Identity in American Art, 1910–1940*
    (Washington, DC, 1997)
Caswell, Augustin B., 'The Pythagoreanism of Arcimboldo', *Journal of Aesthetics and Art
    Criticism*, XXXIX/2 (Winter 1980), pp. 155–61
Cavallaro, Dani, 'Interplay of Music and the Visual Arts', in *Synesthesia and the Arts*
    (London, 2013), pp. 52–71
Champa, Kermit S., 'P. Mondrian's *Broadway Boogie Woogie*', *Arts Magazine*, no. 54/5
    (1979–80), pp. 150–53
—, 'Concert Music: The Master Model for Radical Painting in France, 1830–90', *Imago
    Musicae*, XVI/XVII (1999–2000), pp. 207–21
Chapeaurouge, Donat de, *Das Auge ist ein Herr, das Ohr ein Knecht* (Wiesbaden, 1983)
Chion, Michel, *L'audio-vision. Son et image au cinéma* [1990] (Paris, 2002)
Chouillet-Roche, Anne-Marie, 'Le clavecin oculaire du Père Castel', *XVIIIème siècle*, VIII
    (1976), pp. 141–66
Chouvel, Jean-Marc, and Makis Solomos, ed., *L'espace: Musique / Philosophie* (Paris, 1998)
Ciliberti, Galliano, '"Le passioni degli dei": musica e pittura tra Gluck e David', in *Musica e
    immagine tra iconografia e mondo dell'opera, Studi in onore di Massimo Bogianckino*
    (Florence, 1993), pp. 177–95
Clouzot, Martine, et al., *Moyen âge entre ordre et désordre* (Paris, 2004)
Cogan, Robert, *New Images of Musical Sound* (Cambridge, MA, 1984)
Cohen, Huguette, 'The Intent of the Digression on Father Castel and Father Porée in
    Diderot's *Lettre sur les sourds et muets*', *Studies on Voltaire and the XVIIIth Century*,
    no. 201 (1982), pp. 163–83
Collet, Marc, 'Le domaine musical de Soto', in *Jesus Rafael Soto* (Paris, 1977), pp. 35–8
Collopy, Fred, 'Color, Form and Motion: Dimensions of a Musical Art of Light', *Leonardo*,
    XXXIII/5 (2009), pp. 355–60
Conio, Gérard, 'Les sonorités de Kandinsky et la synthèse des arts', in *L'avant-garde russe
    et la synthèse des arts* (Lausanne, 1990), pp. 106–12

Cropper, Elisabeth, 'The Harmony of Color and Sound', in *The Ideal of Painting: Pietro Testa's Düsseldorf Notebook* (New Haven, CT, 1984), pp. 137–46

Cytowic, Richard E., *Synesthesia: A Union of the Senses* (New York/Berlin, 1989; Cambridge, MA, 2002)

—, *The Man who Tasted Shapes* [1993] (New York, 1995)

Da Costa Meyer, Esther, and Fred Wasserman, ed., *Schoenberg, Kandinsky and the Blue Rider* (New York, 2003)

Dahlhaus, Carl, *Die Idee der absoluten Musik* (Kassel, 1978), French trans., *L'idée de la musique absolue. Une esthétique de la musique romantique* (Geneva, 1997)

—, 'La construction du disharmonique. A propos des théories artistiques de Schönberg et de Kandinsky', *Contrechamps*, no. 2 (1984), pp. 137–42

—, 'Musik und Zahl. Zur Geschichtlichkeit eines metaphysischen Prinzips', *Daidalos*, no. 17 (15 September 1985), pp. 18–25

Darò, Carlotta, *Avant-gardes sonores en architecture* (Dijon, 2013)

Dassas, Frédéric, et al., *L'invention du sentiment. Aux sources du romantisme* (Paris, 2002)

Dassas Frédéric, and Jobert Barthélémy, ed., *De la rhétorique des passions à l'expression du sentiment*, actes du colloque de 2002 (Paris, 2003)

Dautrey, Jehanne, et al., *Musique, architecture*, in *Rue Descartes*, no. 56 (2007)

Davies, Hugh M., et al., *Blurring the Bounaries: Installation Art, 1969–1996* (San Diego, CA, 1997)

De Caro, Roberto, 'L'alchimia del violonista. Interpretazione musicale e mediazione demiurgica nell'opera di Klee', in *P. Klee. Figure e metamorfosi,* ed. Marilena Pasquali (Milan, 2000), pp. 97 ff

Décultot, Elisabeth, 'Das frühromantische Thema der "musikalischen Landschaft" bei Ph.O. Runge und L. Tieck', *Athenäum. Jahrbuch für Romantik*, V (1995), pp. 213–34

Delage, Robert, 'Un fou de musique', in *Jacques-Emile Blanche peintre (1861–1942)* (Rouen, 1997), pp. 39–48

De la Motte-Haber, Helga, *Handbuch der Musikpsychologie* (Laaber, 1985)

—, 'Visuelle Eindrücke beim Musikhören: Synästhesien', in *Handbuch der Musikpsychologie* (Laaber, 1985), pp. 307–28

—, *Musik und bildende Kunst* (Laaber, 1990)

—, *Klangkunst: tönende Objekte und klingende Räume* (Laaber, 1999)

Denizeau, Gérard, *Musique and arts* (Paris, 1995)

—, ed., *Le visuel et le sonore. Peinture et musique au XXe siècle. Pour une approche épistémologique* (Paris, 1998)

Deuchler, Florenz, *Stichjahr 1912. Künste und Musik der frühen Moderne im Urteil ihrer Protagonisten* (Regensburg, 2003)

Disertori, Benvenuto, *La musica nei quadri antichi* (Trento, 1978)

Dixon, Laurinda S., 'Art and Music at the Salon de la Rose+Croix', in *The Documented Image: Visions in Art History,* ed. Gabriel Weisberg (Syracuse, NY, 1987), pp. 165–86

Dorfles, Gillo, 'Interferenze tra musica e pittura e la nuova notazione musicale', *Quaderni della Rassegna musicale*, IV (1968), pp. 7–24

Dorra, Henri, 'Le "Texte Wagner" de Gauguin', *Bulletin de la Société d'Histoire de l'Art français* (1984), pp. 281–8

Duborgel, Bruno (dir.), *Figures du graphein. Arts plastiques, littérature, musique* (Saint-Etienne, 2000)

Düchting, Hajo, 'Brennpunkt Bauhaus Bühne. Synästhetik am Bauhaus', in *Farbe am Bauhaus. Synthese und Synästhesie* (Berlin, 1996), pp. 145–60

—, *Paul Klee, Malerei und Musik* (Munich, 1997; 2001)

—, 'Synästhetische Vorstellungen am Bauhaus', in Adler (2002), pp. 249–57

Dufrenne, Mikel, *L'oeil et l'oreille: essai* (Montréal, 1987)

Duplaix, Sophie, et al., *Sons and lumières. Une histoire du son dans l'art du xxe siècle* (Paris, 2004)

Eberhart, Marlene, 'Sensing, Time and the Aural Imagination in Titian's Venus with Organist and Dog', *Artibus et Historiae*, no. 65 (2012), pp. 79–95

Eigeldinger, Jean-Jacques, 'Debussy et l'idée d'arabesque musicale', in *L'oeuvre de Claude Debussy*. Actes du colloque international, *Cahiers Debussy*, no. 12–13 (1988–9), pp. 5–14

—, 'Anch'io son pittore ou Liszt compositeur de *Sposalizio* et *Penseroso*', in Junod (1996), pp. 49–74

—, 'J'ai des tête-à-tête à perte de vue avec Chopin . . .' (Delacroix, Nohant, Summer 1842), in *Points de vue*, ed. Danielle Chaperon and Philippe Kaenel (Paris, 2003), pp. 297–312

Elkoshi, Rivka, 'Is Music "Colorful"? A Study of the Effects of Age and Musical Literacy on Children's Notational Color Expressions', *International Journal of Education and the Arts*, V/2 (10 September 2004), pp. 1–18

Eller-Rüter, Ulrika-Maria, *Kandinsky. Bühnenkomposition und Dichtung als Realisation seines Synthese-Konzepts* (Hildesheim, 1990)

Ember, Ildiko, *La musique dans la peinture* (Budapest, 1984)

Emrich, Hinderk M., et al., *Welche Farbe hat der Montag ? Synästhesie: das Leben mit verknüpften Sinnen* (Stuttgart/Leipzig, 2002)

Escal, Françoise, 'Composer: peinture, musique', *Critique*, no. 515 (April 1990), pp. 265–78

Etiemble, René, *Le Sonnet des voyelles, de l'audition colorée à la vision érotique* (Paris, 1968)

Evers, Frans, 'The Schönberg-Kandinsky Symposium', in *Schönberg and Kandinsky: An Historic Encounter*, ed. Konrad Boehmer (The Hague, 1997)

Fallay d'Este, Lauriane, *Le paragone. Le parallèle des arts* (Paris, 1992).

Farago, Claire J., *Leonardo da Vinci's Paragone. A Critical Interpretation with a New Edition of the Text in the Codex Urbinas* (Leiden, 1992)

Fauchereau, Serge, 'M. K. Ciurlionis. El nacimiento de una abstraccion simbolista y musical', in *El arte abstracto. Los dominios de lo invisible* (Madrid, 2005), pp. 79–99

Fauquet, Joël-Marie, ed., *Musiques, signes, images. Liber amicorum François Lesure* (Geneva, 1988)

Fauser, Annegret, and Manuela Schwartz, ed., *Von Wagner zum Wagnerisme* (Leipzig, 1999), pp. 535–46

Favre, Gladys C., 'Vom Orphismus zum Musicalismus', in Von Maur (1985), pp. 360–65

Ferrara, Laurence, 'Schopenhauer on Music as the Embodiment of the Will', in *Schopenhauer, Philosophy and the Arts*, ed. Dale Jacquette (Cambridge, 1996), pp. 183–99

Fink, Monica, *Musik nach Bildern* (Innsbruck, 1988)

—, 'Musik in Ateliers. Privates Musizieren bildender Künstler', in *Musica privata, Festschrift W. Salmen*, no. 65 (Innsbruck, 1991), pp. 129–39

—, 'Farbe – Klänge und Klang-Farben im Werk von O. Messiaen', in Kalisch (2004), pp. 148–56

Fischer, Pieter, 'Music in Painting of the Low Countries in the xvith and xvii Cent.', *Sonorum Speculum*, no. 50/51 (1972), pp. 1–128

Flamand, Elie-Charles, *Première rétrospective des Salons musicalistes, 1932–1960* (Paris, 1973)

Forneris, Jean, et al., *La musique et la peinture, 1600–1900, Trois siècles d'iconographie musicale, Oeuvres des collections publiques françaises* (Nice, 1991)

Forsyth, Michael, *Buildings for Music: The Architect, the Musician and the Listener from the xviith Cent. to the Present Day* (Cambridge, 1985), French trans., *Architecture et musique: l'architecte, le musicien et l'auditeur du xviie s. à nos jours* (Brussels, 1988)

Franssen, Maarten, 'The Ocular Harpsichord of Louis-Bertrand Castel: The Science and Aesthetics of an Eighteenth-century Cause Célèbre', *Tractrix: Yearbook for the History of Science, Medicine, Technology and Mathematics*, iii (1991), pp. 15–77

Frings, Gabriele, 'Dosso Dossis Allegorie der Musik und die Tradition des *inventor musicae* im Mittelalter und Renaissance', *Imago Musicae*, xi/xii (1992–5), pp. 156–203

—, 'The Allegory of Musical Inspiration by Nicolò Frangipane: New Evidence in Musical Iconography in xvith Cent. Northern Italian Painting', *Artibus et Historiae*, no. 28 (1993), pp. 141–60

—, *Giorgiones Ländliches Konzert. Darstellung der Musik in der venezianischen Malerei der Renaissane* (Berlin, 1999)

Fromrich, Yane, *Musique et caricature en France au 19ème siècle* (Geneva, 1973)

Gage, John, 'The Sound of Colour', in *Colour and Culture* (London, 1993), pp. 227–46

—, 'Synesthesia', in *Encyclopedia of Aesthetics*, ed. Michael Kelly (Oxford, 1998), iv, pp. 348–51

—, 'Making Sense of Colour – The Synaesthetic Dimension', ch. 21 of *Colour and Meaning: Art, Science and Symbolism* (London, 1999)

Galard, Jean, et al. *L'oeuvre d'art totale* (Paris, 2003)

Galeyev, Bulat M., 'Music-kinetic Art Medium: On the Work of the Group Prometei (skb) in Kazan, ussr', *Leonardo*, ix/3 (1976), pp. 177–82

—, 'Kinetic Art: Third Conference on "Light and Music", Kazan 1975', *Leonardo*, ix (1976), pp. 238–9

—, 'The Fire of Prometheus: Music-kinetic Art Experiments in the USSR' and 'At the Sources of the Idea of "Seeing Music" in Russia', *Leonardo*, XXL/4 (1988), pp. 383–91 and 392–6

—, 'Farblichtmusik im System der Künste', in R. Stanislawski et al., *Europa Europa. Das Jahrhundert der Avantgarde in Mittel- und Osteuropa* (Bonn, 1994), pp. 118–21

Gamper, Michael, '". . . in einer fremden, unübersetzbaren Sprache . . ." Das Reden über Malerei und Musik bei Wackenroder und Tieck', in *Farbige Träume aus den durchsichtigen Gedanken*, Romantik-Symposium 1994 in Mariastein (Solothurn, 1996), pp. 22–38

Garner, W., 'The Relationship between Color and Music', *Leonardo*, XI/3 (1978), pp. 225–6

Gaullier, Joëlle, ed., *Le mélange des arts* (Lille, 2003)

Gavrilovich, Donatella, 'Un caleidoscopo sonoro, ovvero la sintesi delle arti in Russia', *Ricerche di storia dell'arte*, no. 25 (1985), pp. 17–28

Gay, Peter, 'The Art of Listening', in *The Bourgeois Experience*, vol. IV: *The Naked Heart* (New York, 1995), pp. 11–35

Gayraud, Régis, 'Ilia Zdanevitch: "Toutisme" et synthèse des arts', in *L'avant-garde russe et la synthèse des arts,* ed. Gérard Conio (Lausanne, 1990), pp. 113–18

Genevois, Hugues, and Yann Orlarey, ed., *Le son et l'espace* (Lyons, 1998)

Gerlach, Reinhard, *Musik und Jugenstil der Wiener Schule, 1900–1908* (Laaber, 1985)

Ghyka, Matila, *Essai sur le rythme* (Paris, 1938)

Godwin, Joscelyn, *Harmonies of Heaven and Earth* (London, 1987)

Goebels, Franzpeter, ed., *Musikalische Graphik – graphische Musik* (Hagen, 1972)

Goldberg, Roselee, *Performance Art: From Futurism to the Present* (London, 1979)

—, *Performances: L'art en action* (Paris, 1999)

Goldfarb, Hilliard T., *Splendore a Venezia. Art et Musique de la Renaissance au Baroque dans la Sérénissime* (Montréal, 2013)

Göltl, Reinhard, *Franz Schubert und Moritz von Schwind. Freundschaft in Biedermeier,* (Munich, 1989)

Gombrich, Ernst H., *Art and Illusion* (London, 1959)

—, 'Some Musical Analogies', in *The Sense of Order: A Study in the Psychology of Decorative Art* (London, 1979), pp. 285–305

Gottdang, *Vorbild Musik. Die Geschichte einer Idee in der Malerei im deutschsprachigen Raum 1780–1915* (Munich, 2004)

Grivel, Delphine, *Maurice Denis et la musique* (Paris, 2011)

Gröger, Sibylle, 'Max Slevogt und die *Zauberflöte* von W. A. Mozart', in *Anschauung und Deutung,* Willy Kurth no. 80 (Geburtstag, Berlin, 1964), pp. 69–76

Grueneisen, Peter, et al., *Soundspace: Architecture for Sound and Vision* (Basel, 2003)

Gruhn, Wilfred, 'Begegnung der Künste: Kandinsky und Schönberg. Von der Hinfälligkeit des Schönen und der Harmonie der Dissonanz', *Musikpädagogische Forschung*, X (1990), pp. 61–80

Guido, Laurent, *L'âge du rythme. Cinéma, musicalité et culture du corps dans les théories françaises des années 1910–1930* (Lausanne, 2006)

Guidobaldi, Nicoletta, ed., *Prospettive di iconografia musicale* (Milan, 2007)

Günther, Hans, ed., *Gesamtkunstwerk zwischen Synästhesie und Mythos* (Bielefeld, 1994)

Hadermann, Paul, 'Musique et espace chez Kandinsky. A propos du *Spirituel dans l'art*', in *Musique et société. Hommages à Robert Wangermée*, ed. Henri Vanhulst and Malou Haine (Brussels, 1988), pp. 143–72

—, *Synästhesie: Stand der Forschung und Begriffbestimmung*, in *Literatur und bildende Kunst. Ein Handbuch zur Theorie und Praxis eines komparatistischen Grenzgebietes*, ed. Ulrich Weisstein (Berlin, 1992), pp. 54–73

—, 'Die Musikalisierung der Malerei im 19. Jh.', in *Welttheater. Die Künste im 19. Jh.*, ed. Peter Andraschke and Edelgard Spaude (Freiburg, 1992), pp. 153–74

—, 'Tendances musicales dans la littérature et la peinture du XIXe siècle', in *Célébration du centenaire de l'Institut des Hautes Études de Belgique* (Brussels, 1994), pp. 53–66

Hadler, Mona, 'Jazz and the Visual Arts', *Arts Magazine* (June 1983), pp. 91–101

Haftmann, Werner, 'Formidentitäten zwischen Musik und moderner Malerei', in *Aspekte der Modernität,* ed. Hans Steffen (Göttingen, 1965)

—, 'Über die Funktion des Musikalischen in der Malerei des 20. Jh.', in *Hommage à Schönberg. Der Blaue Reiter und das Musikalische in der Malerei der Zeit* (Berlin, 1974), pp. 8–41

Hagstrum, Jean H., *The Sister Arts: The Tradition of Literary Pictorialism and English Poetry from Dryden to Gray* (Chicago, IL, 1958)

Hahl-Koch, Jelena, ed., *A. Schönberg, W. Kandinsky. Briefe und Dokumente einer aussergewöhnlichen Begegnung* (Salzburg and Wien, 1980)

—, 'Kandinsky et Schoenberg', *Contrechamps*, no. 2 (April 1984)

—, 'Kandinsky, Schönberg and their Parallel Experiments', in *Schönberg and Kandinsky: An Historic Encounter,* ed. Konrad Boehmer (The Hague, 1997), pp. 75–87

Hammerstein, Reinhold, 'Musik und bildende Kunst. Zur Theorie und Geschichte ihrer Beziehungen', *Imago Musicae*, I (1984), pp. 1–28, new edn in *Schriften 2: Musik und Bild* (Tutzing, 2000), pp. 1–40

Hammond, Frederick, 'Poussin et les modes: le point de vue d'un musicien', in Olivier Bonfait et al., *Poussin et Rome*, Actes du colloque à l'Académie de France à Rome et à la Bibliothèque Hertziana (Rome, 1994), pp. 75–91

Hapkemeyer, Andreas, 'Moholy-Nagy, Hirschfeld-Mack und die Lichtkunst des 20 Jh.', in *Ludwig Hirschfeld-Mack, Bauhäusler und Visionär* (Ostfildern, 2000), pp. 130–35

Harrell, Anne L., 'Visual Music: The Music Analogy in American Modernist Art Criticism and Synchromist Color Theory', PhD, University of Delaware (2000)

Harrison, John, *Synaesthesia: The Strangest Thing* (Oxford, 2001)

Harwell Celenza, Anna, 'Paysages sonores. Images de la musique populaire à Rome au XVIIe siècle', in *Les bas-fonds du baroque. Rome du vice et e la misère* (Paris, 2015), pp. 93–101

Hausheer, Cecilia, *Visueller Sound. Musik zwischen Avantgarde und Populärkultur* (Lucerne, 1994)

Haward, Lawrence, et al., *Music in Painting* (London, 1945)

Heidrich, Jürgen, '"Zwischen Pergolese und Correggio, welche Familien Aehnlichkeit!" – Zur Verbindung von Musik und Malerei im kunsttheoretischen Schrifttum des 18. Jahrhunderts', in *Johann Dominicus Fiorillo. Kunstgeschichte und die romantische Bewegung um 1800* , ed. Antje Middeldorf Kosegarten (Göttingen, 1997)

Heiland, Suzanne, et al., *Musik im Bild: Malerei, Graphik und Plastik aus fünf Jahrhunderten* (Leipzig, 1981)

Hersey, George L., 'Frozen Music', in *Architecture and Geometry in the Age of the Baroque* (Chicago, IL, 2000), pp. 22–51

Hofmann, Werner, 'Beziehungen zwischen Malerei und Musik', in *Schoenberg – Webern – Berg. Bilder – Partituren – Dokumente* (Wien, 1969)

—, 'La disonancia integrada: Kandinsky y Schönberg', in Arnaldo (2004), pp. 11–35

Horsley, Jessica, *Der Almanach des* Blauen Reiters *als gesamtkunstwerk. Eine interdisziplinäre Untersuchung* (Frankfurt, 2006)

House, John, 'Fantin-Latour in 1864; Wagnerism and Realism', in Peter Andraschke et al., *Welttheater. Die Künste im 19. Jh.* (Freiburg, 1992), pp. 248–53

Howat, Roy, *Debussy in Proportion: A Musical Analysis* (Cambridge, 1983)

Hüneke, Andreas, 'Blau klingt wie eine Orgel. Der Blaue Reiter und die Musik', *Bildende Kunst*, no. 2 (1984), pp. 255–7

—, 'Musik am Bauhaus', in W. Rathert et al., *Musikkultur in der Weimarer Republik* (Mainz, 2001), pp. 189–97

Imiela, Hans Jürgen, and Roland Berthold, ed., *Slevokt und Mozart* (Mainz, 1991)

Jacobs, Helmut C., 'Musik, Bild, Text – Stendhals literarische Visualisierung von Musik', in *Stendhal, Image et texte* (Tübingen, 1994), pp. 145–57

Jang, Werner, ed., *Musik und Kunst. Erfahrung – Deutung – Darstellung* (Mannheim, 2000)

Jewanski, Jörg, 'Farbe-Ton-Beziehung', in *Musik in Geschichte und Gegenwart*, 2nd edn (Kassel, 1995), III, col. 345–71

—, 'Die Farblichtmusik Alexander Laszlos', *Zeitschrift für Kunstgeschichte*, LX (1997), pp. 12–43

—, *Ist* C *= rot ? Eine Kultur-und Wissenschaftsgeschichte zum Problem der wechselseitigen Beziehung zwischen Ton und Farbe von Aristoteles bis Goethe* (Berlin, 1999) [Berliner Musik Studien XVII]

—, 'Die neue Synthese des Geistes. Zur Synästhesie-euphorie der Jahre 1925 bis 1933', in Adler and Ulricke (2002), pp. 239–48

—, 'Farbige Töne: Synästhesie und Musik', *Zeitschrift für Semiotik*, XXIV/1 (2002), pp. 39–50

—, and Natalia Sidler, ed., *Farbe – Licht – Musik. Synästhesie und Farblichtmusik* (Bern, 2006)

Jewanski, Jörg, and Hajo Düchting, *Musik und bildende Kunst im 20. Jh.*
(Kassel, 2009)

Johnson, Ray, 'Whistler's Musical Modes', *Arts Magazine* (April 1981), pp. 164–76

Jones, Tom Douglas, *The Art of Light and Color, Featuring Mobile Color Expression, Lumia, KineticLight – with Instructions for the Creation of Dramatic Color and Light Instruments* (New York, 1972)

Jullian, René, 'Delacroix et la musique du tableau', *Gazette des Beaux-Arts* (March 1976), pp. 81–8

Jumeau-Lafond, Jean-David, 'Guillaume Lekeu et Carlos Schwabe: une haute confraternité artistique', *Revue de Musicologie*, LXXIV/1 (1988), pp. 53–68

Jung-Kaiser, Ute, *Kunstwege zu Mozart. Bildnerische Deutungen vom Rokoko bis heute* (Bern, 2003)

Junod, Philippe, *La musique vue par les peintres* (Lausanne, 1988)

—, *Nouveaux contrepoints, sur lal fraternité des arts* (Gollion, 2017)

—, and Sylvie Wuhrmann, ed., *De l'archet au pinceau. Rencontres entre musique et arts visuels en Suisse romande* (Lausanne, 1996)

Kagan, Andrew, 'Paul Klee's *Ad Parnassum*: The Theory and Practice of 18th Cent. Polyphony as Models for Klee's Art', *Arts Magazine* (September 1977), pp. 90–104

—, 'Ut pictura Musica, I: to 1860', *Arts Magazine* (May 1986), pp. 86–91

—, *P. Klee: Art and Music* (Ithaca, NY, and London, 1983)

Kalisch, Volker, ed., *Synästhesie in der Musik – Musik in der Synästhesie* (Essen, 2004)

Karwoski, Theodore F., and Henry S. Odbert, *Color-Music* (Columbus, SC, 1938)

Kearns, James, *Symbolist Landscapes: The Place of Painting in the Poetry and Criticism of Mallarmé and his Circle* (London, 1989)

Kemp, Martin, 'Ingres, Delacroix and Paganini. Exposition and Improvisation in the Native Process', *L'Arte*, new series, III (1970), pp. 49–65

Kersten, Ursula, *Max Klinger und die Musik* (Frankfurt, 1993)

Kienscherf, Barbara, *Das Auge hört mit. Die Idee der Farblichtmusik und ihre Problematik* (Frankfurt, 1996)

Kintzler, Catherine, ed., *Peinture et musique: penser la vision, penser l'audition* (Villeneuve-d'Ascq, 2002)

Klein, Adrian Bernard, *Colour Music: The Art of Light* (London, 1926; 1936)

Kneisel, Christian, et al., *Klangkunst* (Berlin and Munich, 1996)

Kochno, Boris, *Diaghilev et les Ballets russes* (Paris, 1973)

Kostelanetz, Richard, *John Cage* (Cologne, 1973)

Kostenevitch, Herbert, '*La danse* and *La musique* by Henri Matisse. A New Interpretation', *Apollo* (December 1974), pp. 504–13

Kristeller, Paul O., 'The Modern System of the Arts: A Study in the History of Aesthetics', *Journal of the History of Ideas*, XII (1951), pp. 496–527 and XIII (1952), pp. 17–46, French trans., *Le système moderne des arts: étude d'histoire de l'esthétique* (Nîmes, 1999)

Krones, Hartmut, 'Farbe – Klang – Traum. Doppel-und Dreieckbeziehungen durch Jahrhunderte', in *Der Maler Arnold Schönberg*, Bericht zum Symposium (Wien, 2003), pp. 17–33

Kropfinger, Klaus, *Über Musik im Bild. Schriften zu Analyse, Ästhetik und Rezeption in Musik und bildende Kunst* (Cologne, 1995)

Kubisch, Kristina, 'Grenzgänge. Über klingende Räume und räumliche Klänge in Positionen', *Beiträge zur neuen Musik*, v (1990), pp. 8–10

Lang, Paul (dir.), *Richard Wagner: Visions d'artistes* (Geneva, 2005)

Lauxerois, Jean and Szendy, Peter, ed., *De la différence des arts* (Paris, 1997)

Lebenstejn, Jean-Claude, 'Reliefs (Klee et l'esthétique de Boulez)', *Critique*, no. 515 (April 1990), pp. 251–64

Le Coat, Gérard, *The Rhetoric of the Arts, 1550–1650* (Bern, 1975)

Lederer, Joseph-Horst, 'Die Funktion der Luce-Stimme in Skrijabins op. 60', in *A. Skrijabin, Studien zur Wertungsforschung xiii*, ed. Otto Kolleritsch (Graz, 1980), pp. 128–41

Leggio, James, 'Kandinsky, Schoenberg and the Music of the Spheres', in *Music and Modern Art* (New York, 2002), pp. 97–127

Lehmann, A. George, *Symbolist Aesthetic in France, 1885–1895* (Oxford, 1968)

Lemoine, Serge, et al., *Aux origines de l'abstraction, 1800–1914* (Paris, 2003)

Léonard, Anne, 'Picturing Listening in the Late Nineteenth Century', *Art Bulletin* (June 2007), pp. 266–86

Leppert, Richard D., *The Theme of Music in Flemish Paintings of the xviith Cent.* (Munich and Salzburg, 1977), 2 vols

—, 'Concert in a House – Musical Iconography and Musical Thought', *Early Music*, vii (1979), pp. 3–17

—, *Music and Image: Domesticity, Ideology and Socio-cultural Formation in xviiith Cent. England* (Cambridge, 1988)

—, *The Sight of Sound: Music Representation in the History of the Body* (Berkeley, ca, 1993)

Leroi-Gourhan, André, *Gesture and Speech* (1964), trans. Anna Bostock Berger (Cambridge, ma, 1993)

Levi, Lionello, 'L'Arcimboldo musicista', in Benno Geiger, *I dipinti ghiribizzosi di Giuseppe Arcimboldo* (Florence, 1954), pp. 89–94

Lévi-Strauss, Claude, *Regarder, écouter, lire* (Paris, 1993)

Levin, Gail, 'Die Musik in der frühen amerikanischen Abstraktion', in Von Maur (1985), pp. 368–73

Liess, Andreas, 'Cl. Debussy und der Art nouveau: ein Entwurf', *Studi musicali*, iv (1975), pp. 245–76, and v (1976), pp. 143–234

Lingner, Michael, 'Der Ursprung des Gesamtkunstwerkes aus der Unmöglichkeit "Absoluter Kunst". Zur rezeptionsästhetischen Typologisierung von Ph. O. Runges Universalkunstwerk und R. Wagners Totalkunstwerk', in *Der Hang zum Gesamtkunstwerk* (Zurich, 1983), pp. 52–69

Lista, Giovanni, *La scène futuriste* (Paris, 1989)

—, 'Les complexes plastiques', in *Le futurisme. Création et avant-garde* (Paris, 2001), pp. 179–89

Lista, Marcella, 'Les "Compositions scéniques" de Kandinsky. La quête moderne du *Gesamtkunstwerk*', *Cahiers du Musée national d'art moderne*, no. 63 (1998), pp. 39–57

—, 'Prométhée électrique', *Pyrotechnies. Une histoire du cinéma incendiaire, 1895*, no. 39 (February 2003), pp. 3–43

—, 'Le rêve de Prométhée: art total et environnements synesthésiques aux origines de l'abstraction', in Lemoine (2003), pp. 214–29

—, 'Empreintes sonores et métaphores tactiles. Optophonétique, film et vidéo', in *Sons et lumières* (Paris, 2004), pp. 63–76

—, 'Dimension acoustique et art cinétique. De la musique des couleurs au bruit', in *L'oeil moteur. Art optique et cinétique 1958–1975* (Strasbourg, 2005), pp. 182–9

—, *L'oeuvre d'art totale à la naissance des avant-gardes, 1908–1914* (Paris, 2006)

—, et al., *Paul Klee: Polyphonies* (Paris, 2011)

Livermore, Ann L., 'Turner and Music', *Music and Letters*, xxxviii (1957), pp. 170–79

Lockspeiser, Edward, *Music and Painting: A Study of Comparative Ideas from Turner to Schoenberg* (New York, 1973)

Loef, Carl, *Farbe, Musik, Form* (Göttingen, 1974)

—, 'Die Bedeutung der Musik-Oktave im optisch-visuellen Bereich der Farbe', in *Farbe und Farben* (Zurich, 1980), pp. 227–36

Loers, Veit, et al., *Okkultismus und Avant-garde. Von Munch bis Mondrian, 1900–1915*, (Frankfurt, 1995)

Lombardi, Daniele, *Scrittura e suono. La notazione nella musica contemporanea* (Rome, 1980)

—, *Augenmusik = musica per gli occhi* (Florence, 2001)

Lussac, Olivier, 'Peindre par les noms, peindre par les sons', *Musica* (October–November 1998), pp. 40–42

—, *Happening and fluxus. Polyexpressivité et pratique concrète des arts* (Paris, 2004)

Mahling, Friedrich, 'Das Problem der Audition colorée', in *Farbe-Ton-Forschungen*, i, ed. Georg Anschütz (Leipzig, 1927), pp. 297–432

Majer, Carlo, et al., *Musica e pittura* (Milan, 1988)

Malengreau, Thérèse, 'L'arabesque Art nouveau. Correspondances musicales d'un phénomène plastique', *Bulletin de la Classe des Arts, Académie Royale de Belgique*, xx (2009), pp. 37–60

Malmanger, Magne, 'Musikalische Analogien und musikalische Metaphorik in Kritik und Kunsttheorie', in *Welttheater. Die Künste im 19. Jh.*, ed. Peter Andraschke and Edelgard Spaude (Freiburg, 1992), pp. 174–89

Mandeles, Chad, 'Jackson Pollock and Jazz: Structural Parallels', *Arts Magazine* (October 1981), pp. 139–41

Marchesin, Isabelle, *L'image organum. La représentastion de la musique dans les psautiers médiévaux, 800–1200* (Turnhout, 2000)

Marks, Lawrence E., *The Unity of the Senses: Interrelations among the Modalities* (London, 1978)

Marti, Andreas, et al., *Paul Klee: Melodie und Rhythmus* (Bern, 2006)

Martin, Marie-Pauline, et al., 'L'analogie des proportions architecturales et musicales: évolution d'une stratégie', in *Claude Nicolas Ledoux et le livre d'architecture* (Paris, 2006), pp. 40–47

—, 'Die Allegorien der Musik und der Architektur im *Discours préliminaire* und im Frontispiz der *Encyclopédie*', in *Druckgraphik zwischen Reproduktion und Invention* (Berlin and Munich, 2010), pp. 93–104

—, *La musique face au système des arts, ou Les vicissitudes de l'imitation au siècle des Lumières* (Paris, 2013)

Martino, Victoria, 'Kandinsky, Schönberg und das Gesamtkunstwerk', in *Okkultismus und Avant-garde* (Frankfurt, 1995)

—, 'Arnold Schönberg und die Farbe', in *Der Maler Arnold Schönberg*, Bericht zum Symposium (Wien, 2003), pp. 89–94

Martinotti, Sergio, 'Il dialogo tra le arti (appunti e ricerche)', *Rassegna dell'Istruzione Artistica*, III (1968), pp. 50–64

—, 'Musica e immagine: incontro di due arti', in *Musica e arti figurative* (Turin, 1968), pp. 61–83

Mason, Wilton, 'Father Castel and His Color Clavecin', *Journal of Aesthetics and Art Criticism*, XVII (1958), pp. 103–16

Matile, Heinz, *Die Farbenlehre Ph.O. Runges. Ein Beitrag zur Geschichte der Künstlerfarbenlehre* (Munich, 1979)

Mattis, Olivia, 'Scriabin to Gershwin: Color Music from a Musical Perspective', in Brougher (2005), pp. 210–27

Mendelsohn, Leatrice, *Paragoni. Benedetto Varchi's due Lezioni and Cinquecento Art Theory* (Ann Arbor, MI, 1982)

Merlin, Christian, 'La place de Wagner dans l'utopie d'oeuvre d'art totale selon Kandinsky', in *R. Wagner. Points de départ et aboutissements* (Amiens, 2002), pp. 179–88

Merot, Alain, 'Les modes ou le pardoxe du peintre', in *Nicolas Poussin* (Paris, 1994)

Metken, Günter, 'Debussy und die Künstler Fin de siècle', in Von Maur (1985), pp. 336–9

—, *Laut-Malereien, Grenzgänge zwischen Kunst und Musik* (Frankfurt, 1995)

—, 'Une musique pour l'oeil. R. Wagner et la peinture symboliste', in *Paradis perdu*, Montréal, Musée des Beaux-Arts (Paris, 1995), pp. 116–23

Metzger, Christoph, 'Die künstlerische Bach-Rezeption bei Paul Klee und Lyonel Feininger', in *Musikwissenschaft zwischen Kunst, Ästhetik und Experiment, Festschrift Helga de la Motte-Haber*, ed. R. Kopiez (Würzburg, 1998), pp. 371–85

Metzger, Heinz-Klaus, 'Schönberg und Kandinsky. Ein Beitrag zum Verhältnis von Musik und Malerei' (1963), in *Literatur zu Noten* (Frankfurt, 1980), pp. 181–207

Meyer, Christian, et al., *Schönberg, Kandinsky, Blauer Reiter und die Russische Avantgarde* (Wien, 2000)

Meyer, Felix, and Heidi Zimmermann, *Edgar Varèse. Komponist, Klangforscher, Visionär* (Mainz, 2006)

Meyer-Baer, Kathi, *Music of the Spheres and the Dance of Death, Studies in Musical Iconology* (Princeton, NJ, 1979)

Micheli, G. A., *La sincromia. L'analogia suono-colore e la fine della pittura* (Lucca, 1963)

Mies, Paul, 'Malerei und Musik bei L. Feininger', *Zeitschrift für Aesthetik und allgemeine Kunstwissenschaft*, XXI/1 (1976), pp. 123–9

Mirimonde, Albert Pomme de, *Sainte Cécile: métamorphose d'un thème musical* (Geneva, 1974)

—, *L'iconographie musicale sous les rois Bourbons. La musique dans les arts plastiques (XVIIe–XVIIIe siècles)* (Paris, 1975)

—, *Astrologie et musique* (Geneva, 1977)

Missler, Eva, 'Die Farbenmusik des Louis-Bertrand Castel', *Musica*, XLIII/4 (1989), pp. 331–3

Moe, Henrik Ole, et al., *Klee et la musique* (Paris, 1985)

Montagu, Jennifer, 'The Theory of Musical Modes in the Academie Royale de Peinture et de Sculpture', *Journal of the Warburg and Courtauld Institutes*, LXV (1992), pp. 233–48

Morawska-Büngeler, Marietta, ed., 'Ecouter par les yeux. Quelques réflexions autour d'une exposition', *Harmoniques*, no. 3 (March 1988), pp. 178–210

—, *Musik und Raum. Vier Kongressbeiträge und ein Seminarbericht* (Mainz, 1989)

Moritz, William, 'Towards a Visual Music', *Cantrills Filmnotes*, no. 47–8 (August 1985), pp. 35–42

—, 'Abstract Film and Color Music', in *The Spiritual in Art: Abstract Painting, 1890–1985*, ed. Maurice Tuchman (Los Angeles, CA, 1986), pp. 297–311

—, 'Der Traum von der Farbmusik', in *Clip, Klapp, Bum*, ed. Peter Weibel (Cologne, 1987), pp. 17–51

Mortier, Roland, and Hervé Hasquin, ed., *Autour du Père Castel et du clavecin oculaire* (Études sur le XVIIIe siècle XXIII (Brussels, 1995)

Morton, Marsha L., and Peter L. Schmunk, ed., *Music and Painting in the Nineteenth Century* (New York, 2000)

Moyer, Ann E., *Musica Scientia: Musical Scholarship in the Italian Renaissance* (Ithaca, NY, 1992)

—, 'Music, Mathematics and Aesthetics: The Case of the Visual Arts in the Renaissance', in *Music and Mathematics in Late Medieval and Early Modern Europe*, ed. Philippe Vendrix (Turnhout, 2008), pp. 111–46

Mras, George P., 'Ut pictura musica: A Study of Delacroix's *Paragone*', *Art Bulletin* (September 1963), pp. 266–71

—, 'The Paragone', in *Eugène Delacroix's Theory of Art* (Princeton, NJ, 1966), pp. 33–45

Munro, Thomas, *The Arts and their Interrelations* (New York, 1949)

Murasov, Jurij, "'Das Auge des Gehöres". Gesamtkunstwerk und Schriftlichkeit. Zu Richard Wagners *Oper und Drama*', in Günther (1994), pp. 29–53

Naredi-Rainer, Paul, 'Musiktheorie und Architektur', in *Ideen zu einer Geschichte der Musiktheorie* (Darmstadt, 1985), pp. 149–76

—, *Architektur und Harmonie. Zahl, Mass und Proportioin in der abendländischen Baukunst* [1992] (Cologne, 1995)

—, 'Max Klingers *Beethoven* und die Musik Gustav Mahlers', *Musicologica Austriaca*, XVIII (1999), pp. 205–17

Nectoux, Jean-Michel, 'Musique et beaux-arts. Le salon de Marguerite de Saint-Marceaux', in *Une famille d'artistes en 1900* (Paris, 1992), pp. 62–90

—, 'Musique: les liens tissés', in *Paris-Bruxelles* (Paris, 1997), pp. 272–304

—, *Mallarmé. Un clair regard dans les ténèbres: peinture, musique, poésie* (Paris, 1998)

—, '*Nocturne en bleu et or*'. *Debussy, la musique et les arts* (Paris, 2005)

Nectoux, Jean-Michel and Jürg, ed., *Art Nouveau, Jugenstil und Musik*, W. Schuh zum 80 Geburtstag (Zürich, 1980)

Nectoux, Jean-Michel, et al., *1913: Le Théâtre des Champs Elysées* (Paris, 1987)

—, *Debussy, la musique et les arts* (Paris, 2012)

Nelson, Thomas K., 'Klinger's *Brahmsphantasie* and and the Cultural Politics of Absolute Music', *Art History*, XIX/1 (March 1996), pp. 26–43

Nigro Covre, Jolanda, *La 'sintesi delle arti'. Fonti per la cultura tedesca del primo '900* (Rome, 1985)

—, *Riferimenti musicali nelle arti figurative tra simbolismo e prime avanguardie – da Wagner a Bach* (Rome, 1993)

Norris, Lisa A., 'The Early Writings of Camille Mauclair: Toward an Understanding of Wagnerism and French Art, 1885–1900', PhD, Brown University, 1993

Oechslin, Werner, 'Musik und Harmonie: Universalien der Architektur. Versuche der Annäherung', *Daidalos*, 17 (1985), pp. 59–73

Onians, John, 'How to Listen to High Renaissance Art', *Art History*, no. 4 (1984), pp. 411–37

Paetzold, Heinz, 'Synästhesie', in *Ästhetische Grundbegriffe*, V (Stuttgart and Weimar, 2003), pp. 840–68

Palisca, Claude V., 'Ut oratoria musica: The Rhetorical Basis of Musical Mannerism', in F. W. Robinson et al., *The Meaning of Mannerism*, (Hanover, NH, 1972), pp. 37–65

Panofsky, Erwin, *Galileo as a Critic of the Arts* (The Hague, 1954), French trans., *Galilée critique d'art*, ed. Nathalie Heinich (Paris, 1992)

Parrat, Jacques, *Les relations entre la peinture et la musique dans l'art centemporain* (Nice, 1993)

Parret, Herman, 'A propos d'une inversion: l'espace musical et le temps pictural', *Analyse musicale*, 3rd term (1986), pp. 25–31

Passuth, Krisztina, 'Les jeux de lumière', in *Electra* (Paris, 1983), pp. 174–87

Peacock, Kenneth, 'Synaesthetic Perception: A. Scriabin's Color Hearing', *Music Perception*, III/2 (1985), pp. 483–505

—, 'Instruments to Perform Color-music: Two Centuries of Technological
Experimentation', *Leonardo*, XXI/4 (1988), pp. 397–406

Perer, M. L., 'Musica e arti figurative nel Rinascimento', *Humanitas*, VI (1951)

Perrier, Danielle, *Klangskulpturen, Augenmusik. Grenzgänge zwischen Musik und
Plastik im 20. Jh.* (Koblenz, n.d., 1995)

Peternak, Miklos, 'Licht und Klang aus Ungarn. Bermerkungen zur Geschichte
der Intermedia in den zwanziger Jahren', in *Wechselwirkungen. Ungarische
Avantgarde in der Weimarer Republik*, ed. Hubertus Gassner (Marburg, 1986),
pp. 456–70

Petrilli, Andrea, *Acustica e architettura. Spazio, suono, armonia in Le Corbusier*
(Venice, 2001)

Phillips, Tom, *Music in Art* (Munich, 1997)

Piana, Giovanni, *Mondrian e la musica* (Milan, 1995)

Pierini, Marco, *Good Vibrations. Le arti visive e il rock* (Florence, 2006)

Pierre, Arnauld, 'Picabia, danse et musique: une clé pour *Udnie*', *Cahiers du Musée
national d'art moderne*, no. 75 (2001), pp. 58–81

—, 'La musique des gestes. Sens du mouvement et images motrices dans les débuts
de l'abstraction', in Lemoine (2003), pp. 84–101

—, 'La "musique des couleurs" au cinéma. *Chromophonie* de Charles Blanc-Gatti',
Les Cahiers du MNAM, no. 94 (Winter 2005/6), pp. 53–71

Pirina, Caterina, 'Michelangelo and the Music and Mathematic of his Time', *Art Bulletin*
(September 1985), pp. 368–82

Pizzani, Ubaldo, 'Plinio, Boezio e la teoria pitagorica dell'armonia delle sfere', in *Pline
l'Ancien témoin de son temps* (Nantes, 1987), pp. 185–99

Plassard, Didier, 'Ni théâtre, ni cinéma: les jeux de lumière colorée au Bauhaus', in *Théâtre
et cinéma années vingt* (Lausanne, 1990), pp. 25–38

—, 'Approches de l'art monumental. Kandinsky et la synthèse des arts', in *L'oeuvre d'art
totale* (Paris, 1995), pp. 111–28

Pointon, Marcia, and Paul Binski, 'Image: Music: Text', *Art History*, XIX/1 (March 1996)

Polheim, Karl Konrad, *Die romantische Einheit der Künste*, in W. Rasch, *Bildende Kunst
und Literatur* (Frankfurt, 1970), II, pp. 157–78

Poling, Clark V., 'Synaesthesia and the Inner Effect of Color', in *Kandinsky's Teaching at
the Bauhaus, Color Theory and Analytical Drawing* (New York, 1982), pp. 48ff

Preiss, Pavel, 'Farbe und Klang in der Theorie und Praxis des Manierismus', in *Mannerism
and Music of the XVIth and XVIIth Centuries, Colloquium Musica Bohemica et
Europaea*, ed. R. Pecman (Brno, 1970), pp. 163–70

Pukl, Oldrich and Spielman, Peter, 'Kubismus und Musik', in *Hommage à Picasso.
Kubismus und Musik* (Bochum, 1981)

Puttfarken, Thomas, 'The Modes in Poussin's and Félibien's Theory of Art', in *Roger
de Piles' Theory of Art* (New Haven, CT, 1985), pp. 29–37

Pütz, Andreas, *Von Wagner zu Skrjabin* (Kassel, 1995)

Ramos, Julie, *Nostalgie de l'unité. Peinture et musique dans la peinture de P. O. Runge et C. D. Friedrich* (Rennes, 2008)

Ratcliff, Carter, 'Looking at Sound', *Art in America*, no. 68 (March 1980), pp. 87–95

Rathbone, Eliza, 'The Role of Music in the Development of Mark Tobey's Abstract Style', *Arts* (December 1983), pp. 94–100

Rauhut, Franz, 'Die Idee der Einheit oder Verwandtschaft und der Vereinigung oder Verschmelzung der Künste', *Wissenschaftliche Zeitschrift der Karl-Marx-Universität Leipzig*, VI (1956–7), pp. 553–75

Reck, Ulrich, 'Der Streit der Kunstgattungen im Kontext der Entwicklung neuer Medientechnologien', *Kunstforum International*, CXV (September/October 1991), pp. 81–98

Reeder, Roberta, 'Gesamtkunstwerk and Technology in the USSR', in Günther (1994) pp. 201–39

Reibel, Emmanuel, 'De l'oeil à l'oreille: Romantisme et paysage', in *Comment la musique est devenue 'romantique'. De Rousseau à Berlioz* (Paris, 2013)

—, 'Ut pictura musica: la métamorphose "romantique" d'une ancienne métaphore', in Martin (2013), pp. 161–70

Reifenscheid, Beate, *Die innere Notwendigkeit. Gedanke zur Musik, Malerei und Bühne bei Schönberg, Kandinsky und anderen* (Koblenz, 2000)

Revault d'Allonnes, Olivier, 'La correspondance des arts selon Eugène Delacroix', *Harmoniques*, 5 (Paris, 1989), pp. 72–87

Révész, Géza, 'Ton und Farbe', in *Einführung in die Musikpsychologie* (Bern, 1946), ch. VI, pp. 146–58

Ricci, Giancarlo, 'Il suono dei colori. Anamorfosi tra il guardare e il sentire', *D'Ars. Periodico d'arte contemporanea*, no. 96 (July 1981), pp. 86–93

Riccò, Dina, 'Sinestesie della Musica: Interscambi fra immaginazione Sonora e rappresentazione visiva', *Hortus Musicus*, XIV (April–June 2003), pp. 24–9, http://home.comcast.net/-sean.day/Ricco2003.pdf, accessed 16 March 2009

Riley, Charles A. II, 'Color in Music', in *Color Codes: Modern Theories of Color in Philosophy, Painting and Architecture, Literature and Psychology* (Hanover, NH, 1995), pp. 273–97

Ringbom, Sixten, 'Art in the Epoch of the Great Spiritual: Occult Elements in the Early Theory of Abstract Painting', *Journal of the Warburg Institute*, XXXIX (1966), pp. 386–418

—, 'The Sounding Cosmos: A Study in the Spiritualism of Kandinsky and the Genesis of Abstract Painting', *Acta Academiae Aboensis*, Ser. A, XXXVIII/2 (1970)

Risatti, Howard, 'Music and the Development of Abstraction in America: The Decade Surrounding the Armory Show', *Art Journal*, XXXIX (Autumn 1979), pp. 8–13

Rodoni, Laureto, *Tra futurismo e cultura mitteleuropea: l'incontro di Boccioni e Busoni a Pallanza* (Verbania, 1998)

Rookmaaker, Henderik R., *Synthetist Art Theories: Genesis and Nature of the Ideas on Art of Gauguin and His Circle* (Amsterdam, 1959)

Rosen, Charles, and Henri Zerner, 'L'union des arts, un idéal romantique ?', in Dassas (2002), pp. 40–42

Rösing, Helmut, 'Musik und bildende Kunst. Über Gemeinsamkeiten und Unterschiede beider Medien', *International Review of the Aesthetics and Sociology of Music*, II (1971), pp. 65–76

—, 'Synästhesie', in MGG, IX (1998), col. 168–85

Rousseau, Pascal, 'Cherchons à voir. R. Delaunay, l'oeil primitif et l'esthétique de la lumière', *Cahiers du MNAM*, no. 61 (Autumn 1997), pp. 21–47

—, 'Confusion des sens. Le débat évolutionniste sur la synesthésie dans les débuts de l'abstraction en France', ibid., no. 74 (Winter 2000–2001), pp. 5–33

—, '*The Art of Light*. Couleurs, sons et technologies de la lumière dans l'art des synchromistes', in Eric de Chassey (dir.), *Made in USA: L'art américain, 1908–1947* (Bordeaux, Rennes, Montpellier, 2001), pp. 69–81

—, 'Un langage universel. L'esthétique scientifique aux origines de l'abstraction', in Lemoine (2003), pp. 18–33

—, '"Arabesques". Le formalisme musical dans les débuts de l'abstraction', ibid., pp. 230–45

—, 'Synesthésie et conscience cosmique dans la *Color Music*', in *Sons and lumières* (Paris, 2004), pp. 29–38

—, '"Optofonias". La transcripcion grafica del sonido en los primeros tiempos de la abstraccion', in Arnaldo (2004), pp. 103–26

—, 'Musica coloreada. Luces y sonidos en los inicios de la abstraccion', in *El arte abstracto. Los dominios de lo invisible* (Madrid, 2005), pp. 53–77

—, 'Le spectacle des sens. La synesthésie sur la scène symboliste du Théâtre d'Art', in Isabelle Moindrot (dir.), *Le spectaculaire dans les arts de la scène, du Romantisme à la Belle époque* (Paris, 2006), pp. 157–63

Rufer, Josef, 'Schönberg als Maler – Grenzen und Konvergenzen der Künste', in *Aspekte der neuen Musik*, ed. Wolfgang Burde (Kassel, 1968), pp. 50–57

—, 'Schönberg – Kandinsky. Zur Funktion der Farbe in Musik und Malerei', in *Hommage à Schönberg. Der Blaue Reiter und das Musikalische in der Malerei der Zeit* (Berlin, 1974), pp. 69–75

Rummenhöller, Peter, 'Romantik und Gesamtkunstwerk', in *Beiträge zur Geschichte der Musikanschauung im 19. Jh.*, ed. Walter Salmen (Regensburg, 1965), pp. 161–70

Sabatier, François, *Les miroirs de la musique. La musique et ses correspondances avec la littérature et les beaux-arts* (Paris, 1995–8), 2 vols

Salio, Maria Paola, *Quando la musica incontra la pittura* (Genova, 2010)

Salmen, Walter, *Haus und Kammermusik. Privates Musizieren im gesellschaftlichen Wandel zwischen 1600 und 1900* (Leipzig, 1969) [*Musikgeschichte in Bildern* IV, 3]

—, *Musiker im Porträt* (Munich, 1982–4), 5 vols

—, 'Raphael und die Musik', in *Der Aquädukt* (Munich, 1988), pp. 364–71

—, 'Liszt und Wagner in ihren Beziehungen zur bildenden Kunst', *Liszt-Studien*, III (1986), pp. 152–61

Schaeffner, André, 'Corrispondenze baudelairiane', in *Musica e arti figurative, Quaderni della rassegna musicale*, IV (1968), pp. 97ff

Schawelka, Karl, *Quasi una musica. Untersuchungen zum Ideal des 'Musikalischen' in der Malerei ab 1800* (Munich, 1993)

—, 'Klimts Beethovenfries und das Ideal des "Musikalischen"', in *Die Wiener Jahrhundertwende*, ed. Jürgen Nautz and Richard Vahrenkamp (Wien, 1993), pp. 559–75

—, 'J. Itten und die Musik', in Christa Licztenstern et al., *Johannes Itten und die Moderne. Beiträge eines wissenschafzlichen Symposiums* (Ostlildern, 2003), pp. 157–77

Schidlower, Daniel, *Qu'est-ce que le musicalisme?* (Paris, 1990)

Schmierer, Elisabeth, et al., *Töne, Farben, Formen. Über Musik und die bildenden Künste* (Laaber, 1995)

Schmunk, Peter, 'Van Gogh in Nuenen and Paris: The Origins of a Musical Paradigm for Painting', in Morton (2000), pp. 177–207

Schneider, Albrecht, 'Musik sehen – Musik hören. Über die Konkurrenz und Komplementarität von Auge und Ohr', in *Theorie der Musik* (Laaber, 1995), pp. 123–50

Schneider, Angela, 'Zum Musikalischen im Werk Paul Klees', in *Hommage à Schönberg. Der Blaue Reiter und das Musikalische in der Malerei der Zeit* (Berlin, 1974), pp. 80–91

Schneider, Frank, ed., *Im Spiel der Wellen. Musik nach Bildern* (Munich, 2000)

Schneider, Max F., *A. Böcklin, ein Maler aus dem Geiste der Musik* (Basel, 1943)

Schönjahn, Claudia, 'Auf der Suche nach dem Generalbass', in *Adolf Hölzel, Wegbereiter der Abstraktion* (Stuttgart, 1999), pp. 97–104

Schrader, Ludwig, *Sinne und Sinnesverknüpfungen. Studien und Materialen zur Vorgeschichte der Synästhesie und zur Bewertung der Sinne in der italienischen, spanischen und französischen Literatur* (Heidelberg, 1969)

Schueller, Herbert, 'Correspondences between Music and the Sister Arts According to 18th Century Theory', *Journal of Aesthetics and Art Criticism*, XI (June 1953), pp. 334–59

Schwab Heinrich W., *Konzert. Öffentliche Musikdarbietung vom 17. bis 19. Jahrhundert* (Leipzig, 1971) [*Musikgeschichte in Bildern*, IV/2]

Seba, Rachel, 'Structural Correspondence between Music and Color', *Color Research and Application*, XVI/2 (April 1991), pp. 81–8

Selz, Peter, 'Schoenberg and the Visual Arts' (1974), in *Beyond the Mainstream: Essays on Modern Contemporary Art* (Cambridge, 1997), pp. 55–68

Sequeira de Freitas, Alexandre, *Rencontre des arts. Correspondances entre œuvres sonores et visuelles au XXe siècle. Musique – Peinture – Opéra - Cinéma* (Paris, 2015)

Shaw-Miller, Simon, 'Concerts of Everyday Living: Cage, Fluxus and Barthes, Interdisciplinary and Inter-media Events', *Art History*, XIX/1 (March 1996), pp. 1–25

—, *Visible Deeds of Music: Art and Music from Wagner to Cage* (New Haven, CT, 2002)

Siegel, Linda, 'Synaesthesia and the Paintings of C. D. Friedrich', *Art Journal*, XXXIII (1974), pp. 196–204

Simson, Otto von, *Die gotische Kathedrale. Beiträge zu ihre Entstehung und Bedeutung* (Darmstadt, 1968)

Smith, Andrew James Thomas, 'Les Vingt and the Belgian Avant-garde: A Discussion of the Music Staged under the Auspices of Les Vingt; Its Aesthetic Relationship to Music, Art and Literature in Belgium and France', Ph.D. University of Hartford, CT (2003)

Souriau, Etienne, *La correspondance des arts. Eléments d'esthétique comparée* (Paris, 1947)

—, 'Mozart et Ingres', *Revue musicale* (Paris, 1956), pp. 177–83

—, *H. Valensi et le musicalisme* (Lyons, 1963)

Spear, Richard E., 'Domenichino and Music', in *Domenichino* (New Haven, CT, 1982), pp. 40–46

Spielmann, Heinz, *Oskar Kokoschka und die Musik* (Schleswig, 1996)

Staehelin, Martin, 'Mozart und Raphael. Zum Mozart-Bild des 19. Jh.', *Schweizerische Musikzeitung*, no. 117 (1977), pp. 322–30

Staiti, Nicos, *Le metamorfosi di S. Cecilia. L'imagine et la musica* (Innsbruck, 2002)

Staley, Allen, 'The Condition of Music', *Art News Annual* (1967), pp. 80–87

Stanislawski, Ryszard / Brockhaus, Christoph, ed., 'Synthese der Künste und Entmaterialisierung', in *Europa Europa. Das Jahrhundert der Avant-garde in Mittel- und Osteuropa* (Bonn, 1994), vol. III, pp. 80–121

Stasny, Peter, 'Die Farbenlichtspiele', in *Ludwig Hirschfeld-Mack, Bauhäusler und Visionär* (Ostfildern, 2000), pp. 94–112

Stechow, Wolfgang, 'Problems of Structure in Some Relations between Visual Arts and Music', *Journal of Aesthetics and Art Criticism*, XI/4 (June 1953), pp. 324–33

Steglich, Rudolf, 'Über die Wesensgemeinschaft von Musik und BildKunst', in Heinrich Besseler, ed., *Musik und Bild* (Kassel, 1938), pp. 23–34

Steiert, Thomas, *Das Kunstwerk in seinem Verhältnis zu den Künsten. Beziehungen zwischen Musik und Malerei* (Frankfurt, 1995)

Stein, Susan Alyson, 'Kandinsky and Abstract Stage Composition: Practice and Theory', *Art Journal*, XLIII/1 (1983), pp. 61–6

Steinbeck, Wolfram, 'Musik nach Bildern. Zu Franz Liszts *Hunnenschlacht*', in Schmierer (1995), pp. 16–38

—, 'Musik über Musik. Vom romantischen Sprachproblem der Instrumentalmusik zu Liszts Symphonischer Dichtung *Orpheus*', *Schweizer Jahrbuch für Musikwissenschaft*, N. F., S.15 (1995), pp. 163–81

Steinhauser, Ulrike, 'Musik und Architektur', in MGG (1997), VI, col. 729–45

Stelzer, Otto, *Vorgeschichte der abstrakten Kunst* (Munich, 1964)

Stenzl, Jürg, ed., *Art nouveau, Jugenstil und Musik* (Zürich, 1980)

Stephenson, Bruce, *The Music of the Heavens: Kepler's Harmonic Astronomy* (Princeton, NJ, 1994)

Storch, Wolfgang, ed., *Les symbolistes et R. Wagner* (Berlin, 1991)

Storck, Karl, *Musik und Musiker in Karikature und Satire* [1910] (Laaber, 1998)

Stuckenschmidt, Hans Heinz, *Musik am Bauhaus* (Berlin, 1978)

Sündemann, Hans, 'Musikalische Graphik. Bezüge zwischen Klang, Farbe und Gebärde', *Alte und moderne Kunst*, no. 74, pp. 40–43

Surrans, Alain, *Le regard du musicien* (Paris, 1993)

Sutton, Emma, *Aubrey Beardsley and British Wagnerism in the 1890s* (Oxford, 2002)

Szeemann, Harald, et al., *Der Hang zum Gesamtkunstwerk* (Zurich, 1983)

Szendy, Peter, 'Toucher à soi. (C. ou le clavecin des sens)', *Cahiers du Musée national d'art moderne*, no. 74 (Winter 2000/2001), pp. 35–57

Tammen, Björn R., *Musik im Bild im Chorraum mittelalterlicher Kirchen 1110–1500* (Berlin, 2000)

Teyssèdre, Bernard, 'Peinture et musique: la notion d'harmonie des couleurs au XVIIIe siècle français', in *Stil und Überlieferung in der Kunst des Abendlandes*, Akten des 21. Int. Kongresses für Kunstgeschichte (Berlin, 1967), pp. 206–14

Thierry, Solange, et al., *Frédéric Chopin. La note bleue* (Paris, 2010)

Tintori, Giampietro, *Vedere la Musica* (Bergamo, 1985)

Toffolo, Stefano, *Strumenti musicali a Venezia nella storia e nell'arte dal XIV al XVIII secolo* (Cremona, 1995)

—, *Note in arte. La 'Musica' nell'arte veneta da Paolo Veneziano al Tiepolo* (Padua, 2011)

Tognon, Paola, *Musicaxocchi / Augenmusik / eye-music* (Cinisello Balsamo, 2002)

Tornitore, Tonino, 'Giuseppe Arcimboldi e il suo presunto clavicembalo oculare', *Revue des études italiennes*, XXXI (1985), pp. 58–77

—, *Storia delle sinestesie. Le origini dell'audizione colorata* (Genova, 1986)

—, 'Music for the Eyes', in *The Arcimboldo Effect* (Venice and Milan, 1987), pp. 345–57

Touchefeu, Yves, 'Ut musica pictura? J. J. Rousseau et le clavecin oculaire du Père Castel', XIIe *Entretiens de la Garenne Lemot* (Rennes, 2009), pp. 183–92

Troy, Nancy J., 'Theo van Doesburg: From Music into Space', *Arts Magazine* (February 1982), pp. 92–101

Tuchman, Maurice, et al., *The Spiritual in Art: Abstract Painting, 1890–1985* (Los Angeles, CA, 1986)

Utz, Peter, *Das Auge und das Ohr im Text. Literarische Sinneswahrnehmung in der Goethezeit* (Munich, 1990)

Vallier, Dora, 'La rencontre Kandinsky-Schönberg', *Contrechamps*, no. 2 (April 1984), pp. 143–53, new edn (Caen, 1987)

Van der Hoeven, Roland, 'De la musique des sphères aux coulisses de l'opéra', in *Splendeurs de l'idéal: Rops, Khnopff, Delville et leur temps* (Liège, 1997), pp. 239–69

Vaughan, Gerard, 'Maurice Denis and the Sense of Music', *Oxford Art Journal*, VII/1 (1984), pp. 38–48

Verdi, Luigi, *Kandinskij e Skrjabin. Realtà e utopia nella Russia pre-rivoluzionaria* (Lucca, 1996), ch. II: 'Suoni e colori'

Verdi, Richard, 'Musical Influences on the Art of P. Klee', *Chicago Museum Studies* (1968), no. 3, pp. 81–107

Vergo, Peter, 'Music and Abstract Painting: Kandinsky, Goethe and Schönberg', in *Towards a New Art: Essays on the Background to Abstract Art* (London, 1980), pp. 41–63

—, 'The Origins of Expressionism and the Notion of Gesamtkunstwerk', in *Expressionism Reassessed,* ed. S. Behr, D. Fanning and D. Jarman (Manchester, 1993), pp. 11–19

—, 'Music and the Visual Arts', in Kurt Hartley et al., *The Romantic Spirit in German Art, 1790–1990* (London, 1994), pp. 131–7

—, 'Kandinsky and Music', *Experiment (A Journal of Russian Culture)*, IX (2003), pp. 49–56

—, *That Divine Order: Music and the Visual Arts from Antiquity to the XVIIIth Cent.* (London, 2005)

—, *The Music of Painting: Music, Modernism, and the Visual Arts from the Romantics to John Cage* (London, 2010)

Vermeersch, Valentin, *Musiques et sons* (Bruges, 1990)

Von der Weid, Jean-Noël, *Le flux et le fixe. Peinture et musique* (Paris, 2012)

Von Fischer, Kurt, 'Debussy und das Klima des Art Nouveau. Bemerkungen zur Ästhetik Debussys und J. M. Whistlers', in *Art Nouveau, Jugenstil und Musik* (Zurich, 1980), pp. 31–46

Von Maur, Karin, 'Mondrian et la musique', in *L'atelier de Mondrian*, ed. Yves Alain Bois, (Paris, 1982), pp. 94–103

—, ed., *Vom Klang der Bilder* (Stuttgart/Munich, 1985)

—, 'Feininger und die Kunst der Fuge', in *L. Feininger. Von Gelmeroda nach Manhattan*, ed. Roland März (Berlin, 1988), pp. 272–84

—, *Vom Klang der Bilder* (Munich, 1999)

—, 'A. Schönberg oder die Vereinigung von Musik und Malerei', in *Die Visionen von A. Schönberg. Jahre der Malerei* (Frankfurt, 2002), pp. 21–35

Von Simson, Otto, 'Musik und Architektur', in Anil de Silva et al., *Mensch und Musik im Spiegel der Kunst* (Lucerne, 1973), pp. 35–7

Vossler, Karl, 'Über gegenseitige Erhellung der Künste' [1935], in *Aus der romanischen Welt* (Leipzig, 1940), II, pp. 50–65

Wais, Kurt, 'Symbiose der Künste', in *Forschungsgrundlagen zur Wechselberührung zwischen Dichtung, Bild- und Tonkunst* (Stuttgart, 1936), English trans., 'The Symbiosis of the Arts', *Yearbook of Comparative and General Literature*, XXXI (1982), pp. 79–95

Walzel, Oskar, *Wechselseitige Erhellung der Künste* (Berlin, 1917)

Wangermée, Robert, 'Affinités et convergences dans la musique et la peinture du XXe siècle', in *Capriccio. Musique et art au XXe s.* (Brussels, 1986)

Warszawski, Jean-Marc, 'Le clavecin pour les yeux du Père Castel', in Michel Costantini (dir.), *La couleur réfléchie* (Paris, 2000)

Weber, Gregor, 'Zusammenklang von Tönen, Farben und Herzen: Thema und Variationen niederländischer Musikikonographie', *Kunsthistorisches Jahrbuch Graz*, XXV (1993), pp. 137–52

Weddigen, Erasmus, 'Jacopo Tintoretto und die Musik', *Artibus et Historiae*, no. 10 (1984), pp. 67–119

Weibel, Peter, et al., *Clip, Klapp, Bum. Von der visuellen Musik zum Musikvideo* (Cologne, 1987)

Weidner, Karl-Heinz, *Bild und Musik. Vier Untersuchungen über semantische Beziehungen zwischen darstellender Kunst und Musik* (Bern, 1994)

Wellek, Albert, 'Die Farbe-Ton-Forschung und ihr erster Kongress (Hamburg, 2–5 März 1927)', *Zeitschrift für Musikwissenschaft*, IX (October 1926–September 1927), pp. 576–84

—, 'Das Farbenklavier', *Das Auftakt*, VII/4 (1928), pp. 85–8

—, 'Das Doppelempfinden in der Geistesgeschichte', *Zeitschrift für Ästhetik*, XXIII (1929), pp. 32–3

—, 'Beiträge zum Synästhesie-Problem', *Archiv für die gesamte Psychologie*, LXXVI (1930), pp. 193–201

—, 'Das homophone und kontrapunktierende Farbengehör und Farbenklavier', *Zeitschrift für Musik*, no. 4 (1930), pp. 257–62

—, 'Zur Geschichte und Kritik der Synästhesie-Forschung', *Archiv für die gesamte Psychologie*, LXXIX (1931), pp. 325–84

—, 'Renaissance- und Barock-Synästhesie', *DVfLG*, IX (1931), pp. 534–84

—, 'Farbenharmonie und Farbenklavier. Ihre Entstehungsgeschichte im 18. Jh.', *Archiv für die gesamte Psychologie*, XCIV (1935), pp. 347–75

—, 'Das Doppelempfinden im 18. Jh.', *DVfLG*, XIV (1936), pp. 75–102

—, 'Farbenhören' et 'Farbenmusik', in *Musik in Geschichte und Gegenwart*, III (Basel, 1954), pp. 1803–22

—, *Musikpsychologie und Musikaesthetik. Grundriss der systematischen Musikwissenschaft* (Frankfurt, 1963)

Werner-Jensen, Arnold, 'Malerischer und musikalischer Impressionismus. Gegenüberstellung von Monet und Debussy', *Musik und Bildung. Zeitschrift für Theorie und Praxis der Musikerziehung*, IX/7–8 (July/August 1977), pp. 402–7

Wham, Quincie Matalie, *Schoenberg / Kandinsky: The Genesis of a Tonality / Abstraction* (Ann Arbor, MI, 1990)

Will-Levaillant, Françoise, 'Klee et la musique', *Revue de l'art*, no. 66 (1985), pp. 75–88

Willsdon, Clare A. P., 'Klimt's Beethoven Frieze: *Tempelkunst* and the Fulfilment of Wishes', *Art History*, XIX/1 (March 1996), pp. 44–73

Winternitz, Emmanuel, *Gaudenzio Ferrari and the Early History of the Violin* (Varallo Sesia, 1967)

—, *Leonardo da Vinci as a Musician* (New Haven, CT, 1982)

Wittkower, Rudolf, *Architectural Principles in the Age of Humanism* (London, 1967)

Wolff, Hellmuth Christian, 'Das Musikalische in der modernen Malerei', *Jahrbuch für Aesthetik und allgemeine Kunstwissenschaft*, VII (1962), pp. 48–66

—, 'Max Klingers Verhältnis zur Musik', in *Max Klinger. Wege zum Gesamtkunstwerk* (Mainz, 1984), pp. 81–90

Wooster, Ann-Sargent, 'Art Sounds', *Art in America*, LXX/2 (February 1982), pp. 116–25

Wunberg, Gottart, *Die Wiener Moderne. Literatur, Kunst und Musik zwischen 1890 und 1910* (Stuttgart, 1981)

Würtenberger, Franzsepp, *Malerei und Musik. Die Geschichte des Verhaltens zweier Künste* (Bern, 1979)

Youngblood, Gene, *Expanded Cinema* (London, 1970)

Zeuch, Ulrike, 'Ton und Farbe. Auge und Ohr, wer kann sie commensurieren? Zur Stellung des Ohrs innerhalb der Sinneshierarchie bei J. G. Herder und zu ihrer Bedeutung für die Wertschätzung der Kunst', *Zeitschrift für Ästhetik und allg. Kunstwiss.*, XLI (1996), pp. 233–57

Zilczer, Judith, 'Synaesthesia and Popular Culture: Arthur Dove, George Gershwin and the *Rhapsody in Blue*', *Art Journal*, XLIV/4 (1984), pp. 361–6

—, '"Color Music": Synaesthesia in XIXth Cent. Sources for Abstract Art', *Artibus et Historiae*, no. 16 (1987), pp. 101–26

—, 'Music for the Eyes: Abstract Painting and Light Art', in Brougher (2005), pp. 25–82

Zimmermann, Gerd, 'Architektur ist gefrorene Musik', in Ingeborg Stein et al., *Raum und Zeit. Beiträge zur Analyse von Musikprozessen* (Iena, 1988), pp. 124–32

Collective Works

Musica e arti figurative, Quaderni della Rassegna musicale, no. 4 (Turin, 1968)

Plastik und Musik: Werke der Brüder Baschet (Cologne, 1977)

L'oeil et l'oreille: du conçu au perçu dans l'art contemporain, Critique, XXXVI/408 (May 1981)

Bildende Kunst und Musik, Bildende Kunst, no. 6 (1984), pp. 241–67

Imago Musicae, Annuaire international d'iconographie musicale (Bâle, 1984)

La sintesi delle arti, Ricerche di Storia dell'arte, no. 25 (1985)

D'un art à l'autre. Les zones de défi, Harmoniques, no. 5 (June 1989)

Mots, Images, Sons. Colloque du Collège international de philosophie – Centre international de recherche en esthétique musicale (Rouen, 1989)

Musik und Bild, Neue bildende Kunst, no. 5 (1993)

Espaces, Cahiers de l'IRCAM, I/5 (1994)

'Musica delle sfere', in *Enciclopedia della musica* (Milan, 1996), pp. 579–80

De la différence des arts (Paris, 1997)

Synesthésies / Fusion des arts, Cahiers du Musée national d'art moderne, no. 74 (Winter 2000/2001)

ACKNOWLEDGEMENTS

I would like to thank André Evrard, Colombier, Neuchâtel; the Musée historique de l'ancien évêché, Lausanne; Fondation Vallotton, Lausanne; Martial Leiter, Lausanne; Jack Ox, Albuquerque, New Mexico; Jean-Marie Jaccottet, Aigle, Vaud; Jean-Paul and Sylvie Robert, Thierrens, Vaud; the Institut Suisse pour l'Etude de l'Art, Lausanne; the Fogg Museum, Harvard University, Cambridge, Massachusetts; and Fondation Oscar Wiggli, Muriaux, Jura.

PHOTO ACKNOWLEDGEMENTS

The author and publishers wish to express their thanks to the below sources of illustrative material and/or permission to reproduce it.

© Archives de la construction moderne, EPFL, Lausanne: p. 174; photos author: pp. 14, 21, 61, 71, 102, 143, 169; from Jakob Balde, *Sylvae* (Italy, 1643): p. 10; © Charles Blanc-Gatti: p. 78 (top); from François Blondel, *Cours d'architecture* (Paris, 1657–83): p. 153; from Ferrucio Busoni, *Fantasia Contrappuntista* (Leipzig, 1910): p. 149; © André Évrard: p. 11; © Fondation Félix Vallotton, Lausanne: p. 17; from Franchinus Gafurius, *Practica musicae* (Bologna, 1496): p. 126; from Franchinus Gafurius, *Theorica musicae* (Milan, 1492): p. 31; Imaging Department © President and Fellows of Harvard College: p. 147; © Institut Suisse pour l'Etude de l'Art, Lausanne: pp. 105, 106; from Michel de Marolles, *Le Temple des muses* (Paris, 1655): p. 143; © Martial Leiter: p. 38; photos Metropolitan Museum of Art: pp. 131, 162; photo Musée de l'œuvre Notre-Dame, Strasbourg: p. 133; © Musée historique de l'ancien évêché, Lausanne: p. 8; © Jack Ox: pp. 65, 78 (bottom), 114; private collection: pp. 86, 98, 109; © Albert Schilling: p. 175; from Robert Fludd, *Utriusque cosmi . . . historia* (Oppenheim, 1618): p. 154; © Victoria & Albert Museum, London: p. 170; from Juan Bautista Villapando, *Ezechielem Explanationes* (Rome, 1596–1604): p. 152.

INDEX

Page numbers for illustrations are in *italic*.